ELIZABETH MARKHAM is Professor of Historical (E of History, University of Arkansas. She holds a PhD Cambridge, where she studied early musical sources Picken and also began her long-term commitmen and its publication series *Music from the Tang Court* (C University Press, 1981–). She is the author of a two volume monograph *Saibara: Japanese Court Songs of the Heian Period* (Cambridge University Press, 1983/2009) and in her essays has addressed the interaction between early practical treatises and neumated sources for Sino-Japanese Buddhist chant. Her research continues to focus on musical thinking and the voice in early East Asian poetry, declamation, chant, and song, and she is currently working to complete a songbook and a collaborative musico-analytical monograph on the secular art-songs of Chinese poet and musician Jiang Kui (1127–1278).

NAOKO TERAUCHI is Professor of Japanese Studies in the Graduate School of Intercultural Studies, Kobe University. She received an MA from Tokyo National University of the Arts (1987) and a DL from Osaka University (1999). Her research interests focus on performing arts of Japan and Asia. Recent publications include *Gagaku no kindai to gendai* (The "Modern" and "Contemporary" in *Gagaku*) (Iwanami shoten, 2010) and *Japanese Traditional Music: Kokusai Bunka Shinkokai 1941* (CD annotation) (World Arbiter, 2008–2016). She has also contributed chapters to *Performing Japan: Contemporary Expressions of Cultural Identity* (Global Oriental, 2008), *Analytical and Cross-Cultural Studies in World Music* (Oxford University Press, 2011), and *A History of Japanese Theatre* (Cambridge University Press, 2016).

REMBRANDT WOLPERT is Professor of History and a George M. and Boyce W. Billingsley Endowed Chair in Fulbright College, University of Arkansas. He trained as a 'cellist at the conservatory in München, then studied Sinology at the universities of München (MA, 1972) and Cambridge (PhD, 1975), and Computer Science at the University of Otago (MSc, 2000). He held research and teaching positions at the universities of Cambridge, Würzburg and Queen's, Belfast, and he was *Ordinarius* for Systematic Musicology and Ethnomusicology in the University of Amsterdam. He spent visiting residencies at Kyoto University's Jinbun kagaku kenkyūsho (twice), at NIAS (The Netherlands), and several times at Peterhouse, Cambridge. His research interests include historical sources for musicology and music in context in East Asia (especially 7th- to 13th-century China), grammars (musical and "a-musical"), and functional programming. Among his publications are the collaborative volumes of *Music from the Tang Court*, the co-edited *Music and Tradition: Essays on Asian and other Musics Presented to Laurence Picken* (Cambridge University Press, 1981/2009), the CD *Immeasurable Light* with Wu Man (Crossroads, 2010), and a body of articles on Sino-Japanese tōgaku. Since the late 1990s he has been developing (and maintaining) analytical computer software for the *Tang Music Project* and other large Sino-Japanese music corpora.

What the Doctor Overheard

Dr. Leopold Müller's Account of
Music in Early Meiji Japan

What the Doctor Overheard

Dr. Leopold Müller's Account of Music in Early Meiji Japan

Einige Notizen über die japanische Musik
Some Notes on Japanese Music
日本音楽に関するノート
(1874–1876)

Translated, Edited, with Prefaces and a Postface by
Elizabeth Markham, Naoko Terauchi, and Rembrandt Wolpert

East Asia Program
Cornell University
Ithaca, New York 14853

The Cornell East Asia Series is published by the Cornell University East Asia Program (distinct from Cornell University Press). We publish books on a variety of scholarly topics relating to East Asia as a service to the academic community and the general public. Address submission inquiries to CEAS Editorial Board, East Asia Program, Cornell University, 140 Uris Hall, Ithaca, New York 14853-7601

Cover Illustration: Tafel X, "Einige Notizen über die japanische Musik (Fortsetzung aus Heft VI)", Mittheilungen der deutschen Gesellschaft für Natur- und Völkerkunde Ostasiens Band I, Heft VIII (September 1875).

Set in 11/13 Trinité, Kozuka Mincho and Lilyboulez

Number 185 in the Cornell East Asia Series
Copyright ©2017 Elizabeth Markham, Naoko Terauchi, and Rembrandt Wolpert. All rights reserved.
ISSN: 1050-2955
ISBN: 978-1-939161-65-9 hardcover
ISBN: 978-1-939161 85 7 paperback
ISBN: 978-1-942242-85-7 e-book
Printed in the United States of America

∞ The paper in this book meets the requirements for permanence of ISO 9706:1994.

Contents

Acknowledgments

All three of us involved in this book have needed to work in bursts and short archival visits over a very long stretch of time. And we have needed to work with secondary sources that are rare or in foreign languages not readily available from our respective home universities. It goes without saying that it is to librarians and their libraries, at home and away, that our greatest debts of thanks are due. At the University of Arkansas, Robin Roggio of Interlibrary Loan in Mullins Library has been quite simply a lifeline. Nothing was ever too great or too small for her undertaking its search; without her dedication and determination our (EJM/RFW) parts of the book would still be unfinished. Tess Gibson, Micah Hampton, Lisa Dunigan-Little, Denise Rohr and Kareen Turner, also of Interlibrary Loan, have been likewise stalwart in their support of our many out of the ordinary requests. Beth Juhl, of Mullins Library too, has traced and unlocked web resources for us time and time again. And Lee Holt has generously helped us with essential digital services.

I (NT) wish to express my particular gratitude to Tokumaru Yoshihiko who first informed me of the existence of Müller's "Notes". Also, my sincere gratitude goes to the librarians of the *Ostasiatische Gesellschaft*'s library, OAG Haus, Tokyo, for their invaluable assistance with materials held there. And we (EJM/RFW) are equally indebted (again long term) to the music librarians in the Anderson Room, University Library, Cambridge, especially Anna Pensaert, Margaret Jones, Justin Burrows, and Sarah Chapman who have such patience with our repeat visits to the Chrysanthemum Pavilion, as the location of the *Kikutei-ke* collection of *gagaku* manuscripts is known there. Equally, on the other side of the glassed-in music partition in the Anderson Room, our gratitude goes to the librarians for the East Asian holdings in the Aoi Pavilion of the University Library. Help and advice from Koyama Noburo, recently retired as Head of the Japanese section, has been indispensable over the years, not only for us through his shared interests in the *Kikutei-ke* manuscripts and in pioneers of Japanese studies long resident in Japan, but before as well for Laurence Picken and the later Cambridge years of the *Tang Music Project*, the foundational premise of which is a major focus of this book. Robert Athol, college archivist at Jesus College, kindly allowed us to sift through the boxes of Laurence Picken's papers kept in the College. The libraries and librarians of Lucy Cavendish College and Peterhouse, Cambridge, were havens and helpers during our year as Visiting Fellows in 2014–2015; at Lucy Cavendish College, Celine Carty, Jo Harcus, Gill Saxon and the students who came to the weekly library coffee mornings were a continuous sustenance for me (EJM); and at the Ward Library of Peterhouse, Jodie Walker and Emily Grayton provided for me (RFW) that unique support and peaceful environment essential to sustained, uninterrupted work.

It was that full academic year 2014–2015 in Cambridge that enabled us to complete most of the German and English parts of the project. We wish to thank the President and Fellows of Lucy Cavendish College and the Master and Fellows of Peterhouse for their wonderful hospitality. The Porters of Lucy Cavendish College, as all students there know, are just exceptional, as too everyone who helped with our College accommodation and catering. As well, we thank Fulbright College and the *Center for the Study of Early Asian and Middle Eastern Musics*, University of Arkansas, for making that vital stay in Cambridge possible. We must specially thank Joe and Hiroko McDermott for the marvellous dinners and conversations about shared interests, in that year and others, in their beautiful Cambridge house and garden; in the *Faculty of Asian and Middle Eastern Studies*, Laura Moretti's generous welcome at the *East Asian Studies Seminar Series* and Brigitte Steger's workshop on "Timing Day and Night: Timescapes in Premodern Japan" were important; as were also meetings with our colleague Yang Yuanzheng, then Visiting Fellow at Hughes Hall, with Richard and Margaret Widdess, and with Michael Good and Patricia McGuire, all connected in some way or other with the *Tang Music Project*. Nicholas Cook and Martin Ennis of the *Faculty of Music* were especially helpful and welcoming; and to Ian Cross and Sarah Hawkins of the *Centre for Music & Science* we extend our thanks for generously having us at *Centre* seminars and guest talks, and for inviting us to share our own work with their excellent graduate students.

In Germany, Birgit Scheps-Bretschneider, Kerstin Fuhrmann, and Christiane Klaucke at the GRASSI *Museum für Völkerkunde zu Leipzig* helped trace the saga of the gift of the holdings of the Museum of the *Deutsche Gesellschaft für Natur- und Völkerkunde Ostasiens* and its transfer in 1878 from Tokyo to Leipzig; Ulrike Möhlenbeck of the *Historical Archive of the Academy of Arts*, Berlin, provided a vital clue about the success of Müller's exhibition and talks in Berlin after his return from Japan; and Lydia Kiesling of the *Landesarchiv Berlin* patiently supported our searches through Müller's literary estate, then kept at the *Landesarchiv*. The librarians in the Lesesaal Musik, Karten und Bilder of the *Bayerische Staatsbibliothek*, München, were always ready to fetch (or suggest) another resource. It is with great gratitude that we thank the descendants of Leopold Müller and his daughter Garimène Bloch for their permission, facilitated by Anette Frischmuth, to reproduce material from the *Bloch Archiv* in Berlin.

Over the years students have asked the sorts of questions that have helped, and colleagues have kindly answered many more of our own. Our debts are considerable on both counts. In particular, we (EJM/RFW) would like to thank the generations of graduate students in our regular seminar "Texts and Transmission: Cross-Cultural Perspectives" and the colleagues who have provided that special insight from reacting on the spot to our conference papers. Hermann Gottschewski offered valuable comments after our shared session "German Advisors in Meiji Japan" at the 2nd Bi-

ennial Conference of the East Asian Regional Association of the International Musicological Society (IMS), held in Taipei in 2013; the session was graciously chaired by Higuchi Ryuichi, whose input to the discussion likewise greatly enhanced the direction of the project at that stage. We also thank Henry Johnson, Justin Hunter, Kobayashi Hikari, Itoh Tatsuhiko, and Yang Yuanzheng for answering specific questions related to their respective specializations in the historiography of intercultural musical reception in nineteenth-century Japan and Europe.

To Yokoyama Toshio two of us (EJM/RFW) owe a debt of gratitude that is as longstanding as our interest in Leopold Müller. Our first serious encounter with Müller's essays on Japanese music was in the Library of Kyoto University during our year in Kyoto in 1984–1985, living under his benevolent jurisdiction in Kyoto University's international guest house in Shugakuin; in fact, our draft translation of the essays was made using the copies provided to us then by Kyoto University Library. His invitation to the Institute for Research in the Humanities, Kyoto University, as longer term guests in 2001, was when we actually decided to translate the essays, should opportunity and time become available. And when it came to thinking about how best to publish our study, it was his advice, as himself a distinguished scholar of nineteenth-century Japan in the Western imagination, that led us to broach the idea of a full Japanese translation to our colleague Naoko.

Financial support for the project has been generously provided by the Asian Studies Program under its director Zeng Ka, and by the Center for the Study of Early Asian and Middle Eastern Musics, both of Fulbright College, University of Arkansas. Awards from the Harvard-Yenching Library Travel Grant Program (EJM/RFW) and a Department of History Faculty Research Stipend at the University of Arkansas (EJM) are gratefully acknowledged. The support in our home Department of History, and in Fulbright College more widely, has been all-important to us. Our historian colleagues have humored our music interests and have made a research and teaching environment that must be second-to-none for its welcome and friendliness. A series of Chairs of History from Lynda Coon, Kathy Sloan, to Calvin White has provided understanding support and protected time; and a set of Deans of Fulbright College, Donald Bobbit, Bill Schwab, and Todd Shields, has made sure that the Center for the Study of Early Asian and Middle Eastern Musics has been able to function in its research and its student-outreach.

Finally, it is with greatest pleasure that we individually and collectively thank our editor at the Cornell East Asia Series Mai Shaikhanuar-Cota for making the venture such a thoroughly delightful one from start to finish; we are almost sorry the project has come to an end. Chris Ahn, our copy-editor, was rigorous but kind, even about our mixed-up British and American spellings and Germanic commas; and our anonymous readers for the Cornell East Asia Series gave us such good advice, most of

which we could include to the enrichment of the book, we think, and some of which sent us back to the archives. Two very much non-anonymous people fit in here as the last in this book, and with our (EJM/RFW) very particular thanks – Daniel Wolpert, for archival advice in Berlin, and Friederike Wolpert, for reading both the German and the German-to-English translations for us.

Elizabeth Markham

Naoko Terauchi

Rembrandt Wolpert

Conventions / 日本語訳凡例

Cross references between chapters, and between chapters and translation sections, are given with a "p." preceeding the page number; citations of external sources follow the Chicago manual's convention, that is, no "p." preceeding the page number.

Simple printer's errors are silently corrected. Editorial corrections are marked by square brackets. Editorial footnotes are distinguished from Müller's own footnotes by "– Ed.".

Müller's distinction by gender of "(das) Gagakku" for the office and "(die) Gagakku" for the music is expressed in the translation by roman and capitalized "Gagaku" for the former and italic *gagaku* for the latter.

Edition used

We have used the original versions of Müller's "Einige Notizen über die japanische Musik" published in 1874, 1875, and 1876; the 1890 reprint of the first installment has been consulted.

Orthographic adaptations of Müller's German

ae → ä (Pythagoraeer → Pythagoräer; but Archaeologe)

oe → ö (geoeffnet → geöffnet; but Phoenix)

ue → ü (ausgeuebten → ausgeübten; but quer or Feuer)

ss → ß (dass → daß; grüssen → grüßen; beissen → beißen; but wissen and compounds such as dasselbe)

Obvious or confusing orthographic inconsistencies in the German are emended silently.

Transliteration

Müller's transliterations are left unchanged in the German text. Occasional clarification is drawn from the 1890 reprint.

For our transliteration of Chinese and Japanese we follow the Guidelines of the Library of Congress (http://www.loc.gov/catdir/pinyin/romcover.html and https://www.loc.gov/catdir/cpso/romanization/japanese.pdf, respectively.)

Plates, tables, figures

Müller's system of numbering and ordering his plates and illustrations is complicated. To alleviate the problem we have left his system unchanged in the

German original; but in the parallel English text we have added page numbers. Müller's order of plates and figures is explained in "Organization of Plates and Figures" (pp. 323ff) and visually represented in a table (pp. 328f). This is followed by a list of where the plates and figures are referred to in his essays (pp. 331ff).

Naming of notes

Note names without octave designation are translated as lower-case italics; Müller is inconsistent in his usage. Otherwise, in our translations, we use the standard traditional system. (See https://en.wikipedia.org/wiki/Helmholtz_pitch_notation).

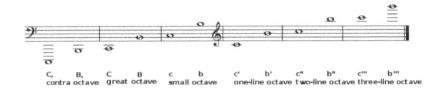

| C, | B, | C | B | c | b | c' | b' | c" | b" | c''' | b''' |
| contra octave | | great octave | | small octave | | one-line octave | | two-line octave | | three-line octave | |

Naming of strings

In standard Western-musicians' terminology, strings for instruments of the lute-family are named by numerals, starting with 1 for the string tuned to the highest pitch. Expressed differently, musicians start with the string closest to the purlicue (the space between forefinger and thumb); this thinnest string is therefore the first string. The next string up, the second thinnest string, is the second string, and so on from there. See https://www.guitarlessons.com/guitar-lessons/beginner-guitar-quick-start-series/fingers-frets-and-strings/. For the violoncello (a four-stringed bowed lute), for example, Wikipedia (http://de.wikipedia.org/wiki/Violoncello; accessed on Sep 2, 2013) gives:

Saite	Note	Wissenschaftsnotation
1 (Höchste Saite)	a	A_3
2	d	D_3
3	G	G_2
4 (Tiefste Saite)	C	C_2

String-numbers are traditionally given in Roman numerals IV, III, II, I (from lowest to highest). Open strings are designated with the Arabic numeral 0; the fingers on the fingerboard (or fret) as 1 (index finger), 2 (middle finger), 3 (ring finger) and 4 (little finger). Müller uses Arabic numerals for both, however.

Possible terminological confusion in Müller's "Notes" between European and East Asian conventions are addressed on pages 296ff below.

Prussian Measurements

1 (Prussian) inch	=	12 lines	=	2.6cm
		1 line	=	2.17mm

日本語訳凡例

- 人名
  原則として明治時代の記録の表記に従う。たとえば、Müller はミュルレル、Wagener はワグネル、等々。

- 音名
  原則としてドイツ語表記で行う。

- 文中の図表番号
  ミュルレルのノートの原文の図表と対照させるため、ドイツ語の原文の番号を表記する。たとえば、Taf. XX, Fig. 3 など。

- 文中の ( ) と [ ]
  文中で ( ) 内に補われている単語、文章などはミュルレルによるもの、[ ] 内は日本語訳者によるもの。

- 注について
  注には、1. ミュルレルの原文にある注、2. 英訳者 (Wolpert/Markham) による補注、3. 日本語訳者 (寺内) による補注の 3 種類があるが、日本語版ではすべてまとめて通し番号をつけた。そのため、ミュルレルのドイツ語原文、英語版、日本語版では注の番号、内容がずれたり異なったりする。2. と 3. については、日本語版では、それぞれ (英訳者補注)(日本語訳者補注) とことわりを入れて表記する。

- 日本語、中国語の原語表記
  日本語、中国語の元の単語、特殊な音楽用語等が特定できる場合は、原則としてその単語の初出時に、まずドイツ語表記をカタカナにし、次に [ ] 内に該当する漢字、ひらがなを入れて補う。たとえば、ガガク [雅楽]、ゴショウラク [五常楽] など。

Preface

Elizabeth J. Markham & Rembrandt F. Wolpert

"There can hardly be a more unusual and appeal-
ing field of observation in the intellectual domain
than what Japan since the year 1869 offers."[1]

Dr. Leopold Müller's (1824–1893)[2] illustrated essays on music and musical instruments in Japan of the early to mid-1870s have, with time, gone curiously under-
appreciated. Yet, published in Yokohama as "Einige Notizen über die japanische
Musik" ("Some Notes on Japanese Music"), in three installments, in 1874, 1875, and
1876, in the *Mittheilungen der deutschen Gesellschaft für Natur- und Völkerkunde Ostasiens*
("Transactions of the German Society for Natural History and Ethnology of East
Asia"),[3] they are at once a medical doctor and surgeon's matter-of-fact but discerning
testimony to the traditional in a cross-cultural musical encounter just as Japan was
embarking on a route of Western music acquisition and, at the same time, consti-
tute the pioneering systematic study of Japanese music in a Western language.[4] In

---

[1] "Ein seltsameres und anziehenderes Feld der Beobachtungen kann es auf geistigem Gebiete schwerlich geben, als es Japan seit dem Jahre 1869 bietet." Müller, "Tokio-Igaku (Nov.
1888)," 312.

[2] The commonly given birthdate of 1822 is questionable. Scheer, "Dr. med. Leopold Müller
– Biographie," 285, fn. 1, argues convincingly for the later birthdate of 1824, as it is given
in legal documents and by Müller himself.

[3] Müller, "Einige Notizen (1)"; idem, "Einige Notizen (2)"; idem, "Einige Notizen (3)."

[4] The "Christian Century" of Portuguese Jesuit residency in Japan (1549–1650) (Boxer, *The
Christian Century in Japan 1549–1650*) bequeathed valuable documentation about Japanese
musical traditions (Harich-Schneider, *A History of Japanese Music*, 445–486), and sporadic
smaller notices exist (for instance in Kämpfer, *Engelbert Kämpfers Geschichte und Beschreibung
von Japan*; Charlevoix, *Histoire de l'établissement, des progrès et de la décadence du christianisme dans
l'empire du Japon : ou l'on voit les différentes révolutions qui ont agité cette monarchie pendant plus d'un siècle*;
Mizler von Kolof, "Abbildung und kurze Erklärung der musikalischen Instrumenten der
Japoneser"; Siebold, *Nippon: Archiv zur Beschreibung von Japan und dessen Neben- und Schutzländern
Jezo mit den südlichen Kurilen, Krafto, Kooraï und den Liukiu-Inseln: nach japanischen und europäischen
Schriften und eigenen Beobachtungen*). However, as a directed larger-scale musicological investi-
gation, Müller's study stands as the first.

a musicological world now operating mainly in English and currently calling for an embrace of the cognitive-scientific and empirical along with the historical and ethnomusicological, Müller's firsthand observations of a foreign music which he made from a practical, body-orientated approach and with the ethnographic pen of a medical scientist, ought to find new resonance. Moreover, their content and early reception put them forward now, we suggest, as candidates for reconsideration, on the one hand, as forerunners to the Vergleichende Musikwissenschaft ("Comparative Musicology") associated with Carl Stumpf (1848–1936) and his "Berlin School," [5] and for which foundational publications are pin-pointed to the decade following Müller; [6] and, on the other, as hitherto unregistered precursors to Laurence Picken's (1909–2007) ground-breaking review [7] in the mid-1950s of historical structure and structuring in Japanese court music gagaku. [8]

---

[5] Comparative Musicology, as the "science of foreign music" (Wissenschaft von fremder Musik) (Sachs, Vergleichende Musikwissenschaft, 7) was first named, emerged in late nineteenth-century Germany among psychologists and psycho-acousticians interested in music and newly confronted by musical systems of "other" cultures. Based first at the Psychological Institute of Berlin, then at the Berlin Phonogram Archiv, it is linked there, in Berlin, with Stumpf, Erich M. von Hornbostel (1877–1935), Curt Sachs (1881–1959), and others (http://www.compmus.org/). See further, viewed from its younger sibling Ethnomusicology, Nettl, Nettl's Elephant; idem, Following the Elephant.

[6] Stumpf himself, in his germinal book of 1911, Die Anfänge der Musik ("The Beginnings of Music"), outlines this early research and lists publications precursive to his own study. However, he chooses to place Alexander Ellis right at the outset, as the founding father of the field: "The founder of Comparative Musicology based on precise natural-scientific methods is Alexander Ellis who, in his tract "On the Musical Scales of Various Nations", Journ. of the Society of Arts, Vol. xxxiii, 1885, first published extensive measurements on exotic musical instruments, which were played by indigenous performers and described as well tuned, and, for comparison of the results, introduced calculation in cents (in one-hundredths of the tempered half-tone)." ("Der Begründer der vergleichenden Musikwissenschaft nach exact-naturwissenschaftlicher Methode ist Alexander Ellis, der in seiner Abhandlung 'On the Musical Scales of Various Nations', Journ. of the Society of Arts, Vol. xxxiii, 1885 zuerst umfangreiche Messungen an exotischen Musikinstrumenten, die von Eingeborenen gespielt and als gut gestimmt bezeichnet wurden, veröffentlichte und zur Vergleichung der Ergebnisse die Cents-Berechnung (nach Hundertstel der temperierten Halbtonstufe) eingeführt hat." Stumpf, Die Anfänge der Musik, 62–74). For a recent translation of Die Anfänge der Musik see David Tripett: idem, The Origins of Music.

[7] For a biography that includes an account of this review see Widdess, "Laurence Ernest Rowland Picken 1909–2007," 226–255.

[8] "Refined" or "proper music." Although in China originally referring to Confucian ritual music (yayue), the term gagaku nowadays in Japan stands collectively for the instrumental and accompanied vocal and dance repertories associated with the Imperial household (although performed more widely) and of both indigenous and mainland Asian origin. The larger part of the latter comprises borrowed courtly entertainment music of Tang China (608–917) imported to Japan during the 7th to 9th centuries or even earlier, and known there as tōgaku (for details, see Nelson, "Court and Religious Music (1)," 36). Evidence for routes to the relatively late association of Japanese courtly musics with Chinese yayue and their influence on the casting of gagaku as sacred by the time of the Meiji period

In the wake of their initial publication – republications followed[9] – the installments of "Some Notes on Japanese Music" (henceforth "Notes") sparked curiosity and enjoyed further dissemination among Europeans in Japan, as well as among readers at home who were interested in Asia, especially in Germany itself. They also aroused considerable scholarly interest among an international readership of musicologists, particularly for their contributions on theory and tone system, and on instrumental tuning and intonation; central concerns of the day that would become central also for the early comparative musicologists. Specifically with respect to their focal attention to *gagaku*, "Notes" were to feature fundamentally, in fact, for Stumpf himself in his formative categorization of ways of ensemble music-making, which was made known among other places in Die Anfänge der Musik ("The Beginnings of Music"[10]) of 1911. Not surprisingly, although less traceable, Stumpf's sometime mentoree Curt Sachs (1881–1959) is also indebted to "Notes" for his brief coverage of *gagaku* in his own influential monograph on the evolution of music published in America in 1943, entitled The Rise of Music in the Ancient World, East and West.[11] But perhaps most significant, and once again for *gagaku*, is the reclaim of Müller's "Notes" by Eta Harich-Schneider (1894–1986) in "The Present Condition of Japanese Court Music," published in 1953.[12] Harich-Schneider's article was to be the catalyst for Picken's now well-known and far-reaching hypothesis in 1957 about ancient melodies of Tang China (608–917) preserved in writing as "genuine relics" in modern partbooks for the tōgaku[13] repertory of Japanese *gagaku* and demonstrably embedded in tōgaku as played today. They are hidden there, Picken showed, functioning now – unrecognizably to the ear – as underlying structures in an orally transmitted and considerably transformed performance idiom.[14]

This hypothesis, by calling into question the traditionalist view at the time of a sacrosanct Imperial Japanese *gagaku* "unchanged for a thousand years," was to become in its turn one of the most controversial and vehemently contested musicological issues of the mid- to late twentieth century.[15] Consideration now of Picken's hypothesis for the historical development of *gagaku* transmission and performance

---

(1868–1912) rests at present on the major, as yet unpublished study of Yang, "Japonifying the Qin."

[9] On printing and reprinting and the respective printers, see the sale-information of George C. Baxley, Alamogordo, NM, for Mittheilungen der Deutschen Gesellschaft für Natur- und Völkerkunde Ostasiens in Tokio Part 6, December 1874, Reprinted April 1890, http://www.baxleystamps.com/litho/meiji/mittheilungen_p6_1890.shtml; accessed 2015-07-26.

[10] See note 6.

[11] Sachs, The Rise of Music, 147–148.

[12] The Musical Quarterly 39, no. 1 (January 1953): 49–74.

[13] See note 8.

[14] Picken, "The New Oxford History of Music: Ancient and Oriental Music," 147.

[15] For Picken's own lucid account of the evolution of the ideas that informed his controversial approach to tōgaku and its earliest musical documentation, see the introduction to Picken

practices, however, should surely implicate Müller. That hypothesis builds, after all, upon both Stumpf's categorization of ways of music-making and what Eta Harich-Schneider's article, with its recognition of Müller, had brought to Picken's attention about present-day practices of the tōgaku tradition. Moreover, there is firm evidence that, post Harich-Schneider's article of 1953 but before formal publication of his observations and hypothesis in 1957, Picken engaged seriously with the *gagaku* notations that the "Notes" offer in facsimile.[16]

In addition, the premiere volume in the *Classic European Music Science Monographs*, a new series from the European Society for the Cognitive Sciences of Music (ESCOM), is built around Stumpf's *The Beginnings of Music*;[17] and Keith Howard returns with "Contested Contextualization: The Historical Constructions of East Asian Music,"[18] published as the ink on our pages here is barely dry, to problematize the intellectual basis of the Picken hypothesis. Both further reinforce the need, we suggest, to reach back beyond Picken in the 1950s, and to also gather up Müller and his "Notes" from the 1870s in order to reinstate and open for discussion work that may have been more basal for some of the disputed issues than previously recognized. For despite resurgence now and then on the hook of a selective scholarly angler,[19] the "Notes" have remained quietly in the backwaters throughout these specifically *gagaku*-related turbulences, right up to the most recent.

Furthermore, growing interest now among music theorists and music psychologists in the case of Japan – where traditional musics were running parallel to a program of Western musical modernization – and the convergence of turn-of-the-century discourses on musical intonation with the emerging discipline of Comparative Musicology[20] might well turn back to Müller's essays from thirty years earlier. The "Notes" situate themselves in a scientific musicological milieu between Hermann Helmholtz's *Lehre von den Tonempfindungen* of 1863[21] and the emergence of

---

et al., *Music from the Tang Court* 1; for further assessment of Picken's methodology, see Widdess, "Review of 'Laurence Picken et al.: *Music from the Tang Court. Fascs. 1–3*'," 176–177.

[16] Picken et al., *Music from the Tang Court* 1, 5–6.

[17] Carl Stumpf, *The Origins of Music*, edited and translated by David Trippet; Markham, "Review of Carl Stumpf, *The Origins of Music*, transl. by David Trippett."

[18] Chapter 10 in McCollum and Hebert, *Theory and Method in Historical Ethnomusicology*.

[19] Sachs, *The Rise of Music* of 1943 is an instance (see later, p. 52). But even Harich-Schneider's valiant appraisal of "Notes" in 1953, in her "The Present Condition of Japanese Court Music," failed to gain for them appreciation where it would have been most influential (see later p. 6).

[20] See a set of abstracts on a panel "Comparing Notes: Just Intonation, Japan, and the Origins of Musical Disciplines" at the joint meeting of the *American Musicological Society* and the *Society for Music Theory* in Vancouver in 2016. (Stone and Wheeldon, *AMS/SMT 2016 Annual Meeting*, 280–283); see also Hiebert, *The Helmholtz Legacy in Physiological Acoustics*.

[21] Helmholtz, *Die Lehre von den Tonempfindungen*; translated and annotated later by Alexander J. Ellis in 1873: idem, *On the Sensations of Tone*.

Vergleichende Musikwissenschaft in the mid-1880s. Although written before the musicological inquiry had become armed with Thomas Edison's invention of the phonograph in 1877 and before Alexander Ellis's scientific advances, in measuring pitch and musical intervals in "cents," published in 1885,[22] their particular engagement with the material culture of construction and measurements of classical and popular Japanese musical instruments may be useful nonetheless. Müller's inquiry involves comparative acoustic testing of tunings (conducted with European tuning-forks and Japanese "tuning-pipes"), detailed real-time accounts for several instruments of the tuning procedures and playing techniques of performers (rarely available for the acoustic experiments of that time back in Europe), and integration of his tuning- and acoustic-measurements with Sino-Japanese written tonal theory (along with noting discrepancies between theory and practice, and between Japanese and European intonation).

The oversight of "Notes" by modern (ethno)musicologists no longer needing extensive training in European languages as research tools may have been helped along by an unwieldy note-format and somewhat idiosyncratic nineteenth-century language and orthography. Müller's cumulative approach to the information he gives over the three installments – an approach standard for the natural (and medical) sciences, of course – including his not infrequent lengthy corrections of earlier statements in later places, may disturb the reader now, a hundred and forty years on, despite his explanation for this serial ethnographic strategy right at the outset of his opening installment of "Notes":

> ... in the following lines I want to record the result of my explorations, without thereby laying claim in any way to completeness. Should I succeed, as I hope, in gradually learning more, then I shall publish the result of my investigations in later issues. (p. 79)

And his medical Krankengeschichte ("patient history") perspective on the condition of the musical object, particularly perhaps in the minute detail of his dissections of parts of musical instruments that are now well known, or in his examination and then diagnosis as a strategy for description, may at first also bother the modern reader.[23] Reading him now requires reading the medical scientist for what his musical contributions got done and whom they addressed in their time. Although, to be fair, here as well Müller goes to great lengths in the final essay (Aufsatz is the term

---

22 Ellis, "On the Musical Scales of Various Nations."
23 Tsuge Gen'ichi, Japanese Music: An Annotated Bibliography, 100 (Entry 586). Tsuge wrongly attributes "Notes" to Friedrich W. K. Müller (1863–1930), author of the two articles that follow (as entries 587 and 588). Endō Hirosi's earlier bibliography also lists "Notes," in this case following the original attributions simply to Dr. Müller (without any initials); see Endō, Bibliography of Oriental and Primitive Music, 34 (Entry 388).

he uses for an installment of "Notes") to ensure that the reader knows he is (and has been) aware of his precarious yet potentially path-breaking position as a physician and surgeon – a non-musicologist – entrusted with such an invaluable opportunity for firsthand musical experience and long-term observation, untold up until then for the Western "outsider":

> I am certainly no musician by profession and have written this series of essays merely to motivate the study of this so-far totally unknown field, and to open paths, not, however, with the pretension of delivering something complete and finished. (P. 189)

The strong focus of "Notes" on courtly *gagaku*, an elite music[24] all but unknown in Europe at the time and for many a year to follow, and, as Müller put it, "difficult to access for the foreigner" (p. 79) in Japan itself in the early Meiji period (1868–1912), may have taken some of the edge off the significance of their content, at least early on. They address in detail, unsurpassed since in many respects, a music that only a few could have experienced, a music with an "other" notation (a foreign "script for notes" [Notenschrift]). Even among later scholars of *gagaku* working on its long history of written traditions, and notwithstanding Eta Harich-Schneider's post–World War II championing of Müller in her own seminal firsthand account of music at the Japanese Court,[25] reaffirmed twenty years later in her *magnum opus* of 1973, *A History of Japanese Music*,[26] Müller's "Notes" have not been been accorded the place they deserve.[27] Indeed, for two of us (EJM and RFW), it was our own astonishment,

---

24 For a discussion of the "elite" of Japanese *gagaku*, see Harrison, "*Gagaku* in Place and Practice."

25 Harich-Schneider, "The Present Condition of Japanese Court Music"; Harich-Schneider, like Müller over seventy years earlier, was a longtime resident in Japan able to study *gagaku* directly with the court musicians (*gakunin*) themselves by dint of employment in the Palace (see p. 143), in her case as their tutor for Western music. For autobiographical music-focused sketches of her time in Japan, see idem, *Musikalische Impressionen aus Japan 1941–1957.*

26 "We are lucky to have the notes of an unprejudiced Western observer of the *gagaku* remoulding during the years 1873–1876, Dr. Leopold Müller, the physician to the Emperor Meiji. His three consecutive papers are almost unknown, but are by far the best early reports on Japanese music which we possess. ... In the Imperial *gakubu* he personally took the measurements of all the instruments and informed himself about their techniques. He heard *gagaku* frequently and analysed it with admirable precision. ... Using an exemplary empirical method he interviewed the *gakunin* frequently and – from one installment to another – he apologises for their repeated contradictions and rectifications of earlier statements." idem, *A History of Japanese Music*, 550.

27 Although in many a publication "Notes" may be dutifully cited, if only on account of their early date, they have tended then to be relegated to the bibliography with little trace of their content in the body of the study. They have been completely obliterated in the most recent coverage of Japanese music in Sadie, *The New Grove Dictionary of Music and Musicians*,

in revisiting the initial stages in our Cambridge-based Tang Music Project,[28] at exactly what Müller had observed, discussed with Japanese musicians and colleagues, empirically tested, analyzed, and made available eighty years earlier than the mid-1950s start-up date assigned to the Project by the Picken hypothesis – and that Müller had accomplished this with such precision and at times unabashed candor – that finally drove our decision to re-present "Notes."[29] For one of us (NT), the impetus to translate "Notes" into Japanese came likewise from concern about their being overlooked in Japan as well. While the presence of documents on Japanese music written by foreigners who visited in the Meiji period has been recognized to some extent in Japan, and while some of these, such as the writings of Edward Morse[30] or Francis Piggott,[31] have been translated into Japanese and published there, they have not aroused the serious attention of Japanese musicologists. This is partly because these early writings are not necessarily academic and often include incorrect descriptions or misunderstandings. Still, they may comprise valuable information for exploring the practices of the time. Müller's "Notes" are especially important as one of the earliest documents on Japanese music in the Meiji period.[32] Their translation allows their sharing among present-day Japanese scholars.

Our approach (EJM & RFW) to Müller's own approach to his "Notes" and our choice of a full text-cum-translation layout in parallel columns (for German and

---

and are not included in *The Garland Encyclopedia of World Music / East Asia: China, Japan, and Korea*. Most tellingly, they are also not in the impressively comprehensive bibliographical coverage offered in Alison Tokita and David W. Hughes, eds., *The Ashgate Research Companion to Japanese Music*; Robert Garfias, on the other hand, includes Müller's contributions in his own excellent *Music of a Thousand Autumns: The Tōgaku Style of Japanese Court Music*; and Ingrid Fritsch in "Japan Ahead in Music? Zur Wertschätzung japanischer Musik im Westen" also recognizes Müller's pioneering role.

[28] Picken et al., *Music from the Tang Court*. Our review was mandated by our work for the Ancient Asian Musics Preservation Project of the Library of Congress, Washington, DC, a major commitment to which includes two documentary films on Laurence Picken, the Cambridge Group, and the early stages of the Tang Music Project. See Knott, Markham, and Wolpert, *On the Road to Tang*; idem, *On the Road to Tang through Cambridge*.

[29] A first step towards incorporating Müller's contribution into contemporary *gagaku* research is Wolpert, "Metronomes, Matrices, and Other Musical Monsters"; see also Markham, "Extrapolating Intent in Leopold Müller's Empirical Study of *Gagaku* in Early Meiji Japan"; Wolpert, "'Einige Notizen über die japanische Musik': Dr. Leopold Müller's Account of Music in Early Meiji Japan." Another study, not of *gagaku per se*, but of exoticism, "orientalism," and the early European reception of East Asian musics, mainly concentrating on Germany between 1870 and the end of the Weimar Republic, briefly portrays Müller himself (albeit somewhat less sympathetically than we can from what our reading of "Notes" affords us) and follows a surprising early twentieth-century reception as parlor music of Müller's full-score in his final essay (pp. 242–244 in this volume) for the *gagaku* item *Goshōraku no kyū* (see Revers, *Das Fremde und das Vertraute*, 49–51; 104–106; 256–258).

[30] Morse, *Japan Day by Day*.

[31] Piggott, *The Music and Musical Instruments of Japan*.

[32] Terauchi, "A Study on 'Einige Notizen über japanische Musik'."

English) for their re-presentation were both conditioned by recognizing their potential value as a primary ethnographic source for other scholars, who, like us, may have passed them by. The column-width organization of the text and translation achieves for both the German or the English, we think, something of the experience of reading notes, perhaps originally jotted-down on a handheld pad or on sheets of paper folded lengthwise, but likely crafted anyway in column-width as was Müller's usual practice (see facsimile, p. 13). The publication format of the *Mittheilungen der deutschen Gesellschaft für Natur- und Völkerkunde Ostasiens* was, in any case, in columns. Bearing in mind that the orthography of the earlier German texts may be tiresome to read for some, it seemed valuable to offer "Notizen" already adapted in terms of substituting the *Umlaut* for the collated form (*geöffnet* for *geoeffnet*), the consonant letter "ß" for "ss" after long vowels and diphthongs (*grüßen, beißen,* but *küssen*), but otherwise preserving Müller's late nineteenth-century spelling, rather than as sets of facsimiles from the difficult-to-read, two-column, close-leaded layout of the *Mittheilungen*.[33] Our English translation preserves Müller's note-format as far as we found it possible and, at the expense of attempting elegance, adheres as closely as we could manage to the ordering in his German sentence structuring. This option seemed to us worthwhile for our aim of producing a tight, neutral translation as a resource for research, which has been set out to facilitate reading in parallel with its minimally "prepared" original.[34] Japanese has a quite different language structure. Müller's sentences are generally long, and for the facility of Japanese readers, my (NT) approach to re-presenting them in Japanese has been first to cut his long sentences into multiple short phrases and then to translate these sequentially as shorter sentences in Japanese.

[33] One of us (EJM) wishes to thank specially two scholars who work on the early introduction of Western music to Japan, Itoh Tatsuhiko and Kobayashi Hikari, for discussing Müller and German orthography with me following our session "Asian Perspectives," chaired by Professor Itoh at the 19th *Congress of the International Musicological Society: Musics–Cultures–Identities,* Rome 2012. Ms. Kobayashi kindly answered my further questions in our correspondence afterwards.

[34] A guide to details of our conventions and layout is provided on pp. xi*ff*; a tabular guide to the organization of plates and figures in "Notes" is given on pp. 328*ff*.

Leopold Müller (1824–1893),[35] German physician in Tokyo (1871–1875)

In 1870, the Japanese government requested that two German physicians come to Tokyo to teach medicine and establish a German-style medical and surgical institution. The request was relayed via Maximilian August Scipio von Brandt (1835–1920), a Prussian diplomat in Yokohama, and in August of 1871 senior military surgeon Benjamin Karl Leopold Müller (1824–1893)[36] (as chief physician) aided by the younger Theodor Eduard Hoffmann (1837–1894), a naval doctor (as second physician), were dispatched from Berlin to Tokyo by the Prussian government. They set out for what would extend to a stay of almost four and a half years in a rapidly modernizing Japan. Von Brandt had advised that high-ranking military medical doctors would be seen as belonging to the warrior class, and thus likely to be well respected from the start; they would be drawn into aristocratic circles and might even become personal physicians to the emperor.[37] Müller's training had been in medicine (in Bonn and Berlin), then surgery at the famous Charité hospital (also in Berlin). Following his commission to the elite Gardes du Corps in Potsdam, in which Herrmann Helmholtz had also served before him, he had taught at the Pépinière, the distinguished establishment for training surgeons for the military. Most compellingly in his own eyes,[38] his recent successes during twelve years in charge of military medical science and hospital management in Haïti[39] had recommended his appointment to lead a German medical assignment in Tokyo.

The culturally engaged doctor not only attended to his mission in medical science in Japan. Early in 1873[40] Müller also cofounded with (by then Resident Minister)

---

[35] Regarding the common attribution of 1822 as birthdate, see fn. 2, p. 1.

[36] An excellent, extensive German-language biography of Müller's life before, during, and after his Japanese assignment is Christian Scheer, "Dr. med. Leopold Muller (1824–1893): Chef des Militarsanitatswesens der Republik Haiti, Leibarzt des Kaisers von Japan, Leitender Arzt des koniglich preußischen Garnisonlazaretts in Berlin – Eine nichtalltagliche Biographie aus der Geschichte des Invalidenfriedhofes." Shorter biographical accounts in English are in Bowers, *When the Twain Meet*, 65–81 and in Kim, *Doctors of Empire*, 23–25; 31–43.

[37] Müller, "Tokio-Igaku (Nov. 1888)," 316.

[38] Ibid.

[39] Müller's official titles in Haïti were: "Chef du service de santé de l'armée haïtienne; Inspecteur général des hôpitaux militaires et des écoles de médecine de la Republique; Président du jury médecinal du département du Sud."

Shortly after his arrival in Haïti, Müller married the Jewish-Haïtian Creole Anne Denise Geneviève Bonne Castel, whom he describes as a good musician, and with whom he had three children, one of whom, Olga, died in 1863. Their other daughter Garimène later studied singing in Paris, and became a successful teacher and singer both in Paris and in Berlin; their son Edgar played 'cello. One year after his wife's early death in 1866, he married her sister Amaïde Castel, who was also to accompany him to Japan.

[40] On the 22nd of March.

von Brandt, and later presided over, the Deutsche Gesellschaft für Natur- und Völkerkunde Ostasiens ("German Society for Natural History and Ethnology of East Asia"[41] [henceforth Gesellschaft]).[42] The Gesellschaft would function, von Brandt anticipated at its inception, as "an intellectual gathering place"[43] for the considerably sized German enclave resident in Tokyo and Yokohama. But its main goal was scholarly, specifically – given the high number of medical professionals and scientists among its founding members – scientific. In fact, the scientific membership and emphasis are seen as distinguishing the Gesellschaft from the outset from other associations founded in Japan around that time, in particular, from the oldest such learned society, the Asiatic Society of Japan (henceforth Asiatic Society), founded by British and American residents in merchant Yokohama the year before, in 1872. In contrast, the early membership of this Anglophone society "... consisted mainly of British and American diplomats, businessmen, and missionaries living in Japan – a significant number of whom were not specialists in any field of medical or natural sciences."[44] The intellectual climate back in Germany, where interest in science in general had widened beyond the specialist,[45] is held as a further contributing circumstance for the foundation of the Gesellschaft. The Berliner Anthropologische Gesellschaft ("Berlin Anthropological Society"), for instance, had been established shortly before, in 1869, also on the initiative of prominent physicians.[46]

In respect of the Gesellschaft's formal mission, stated in the third article of the charter approved on 26 April 1873, the date of its first general assembly:

> Mission of the Gesellschaft is to provide members with opportunity and motive to exchange their opinions and experiences with regard to the countries of East Asia, to support research on these countries, and, in the Mittheilungen to be published by the Gesellschaft, to create an archive for increasing our knowledge of East Asia.[47]

---

[41] Known in the English-language world as the German East Asiatic Society, in Japan as the Ostasiatische Gesellschaft (OAG).

[42] Accounts of Müller's functions in Japan are available in an historical overview of the Gesellschaft celebrating, in 1961, its eighty-fifth year of existence (Weegmann, "85 Jahre OAG"), and in a recent intercultural study of German and Japanese medics and medical science during the Meiji period (Kim, Doctors of Empire). For an earlier report, see Bowers, "The Adoption of German Medicine in Japan"; see also Spang, "Frühe OAG-Geschichte."

[43] Kim, Doctors of Empire, 105.

[44] Ibid., 106.

[45] Steege, "Music Theory in the Public Sphere."

[46] Kim, Doctors of Empire, 106.

[47] "Zweck der Gesellschaft ist, den Mitgliedern Gelegenheit und Veranlassung zum Austausch ihrer Ansichten und Erfahrungen in Betreff der Länder Ostasien's zu gewähren, die Erforschung dieser Ländern zu fördern, und in den von der Gesellschaft herauszugebenden 'Mittheilungen' ein Archiv für die Vermehrung unserer Kentniss Ostasien's zu schaffen." Mittheilungen, 1,1 (1873): 1, § 3.

The mission was to be fulfilled through monthly meetings with lectures and demonstrations, alternating between Tokyo and Yokohama, along with publication of the transactions of the meetings (the *Mittheilungen*). Meetings were held in those early days in rented rooms in the Tenkō-in of the temple Zōjōji, in Shiba Park, Tokyo, and in the by then ten-year-old German Club (*Klub Germania*) in Yokohama.[48] Exchange of journal publications with other scholarly societies and the establishment of a library and a museum were embraced as further tasks of the *Gesellschaft*. The founding seventy-one man membership comprised mainly Tokyo-based scientists in the employ of the Japanese government and Yokohama-based merchants and missionaries, but it included a further small representation from Hyōgo and Nagasaki in Japan, as well as from Shanghai, Peking, and Fuzhou in China, and from Singapore.[49]

Müller's enthusiasm for the *Gesellschaft* is captured in his own words in an account of his time in Japan drawn from his three final reports to the Prussian government, written on his way home late in 1875.[50] Circumspect then about the future fortunes of the medical institution he had established (the "medical and surgical" Academy in Tokyo, henceforth Academy), and about possible effects any criticism might have on his former Japanese hosts, he resolved to wait for quite some time before publishing what he would entitle "Tokio-Igaku: Skizzen und Erinnerungen aus der Zeit des geistigen Umschwungs in Japan, 1871–1876" ("Tokio-Igaku:[51] Sketches and Memories from the Time of Intellectual Change in Japan, 1871–1876"). Thirteen years later, in 1888, the account appeared in the influential and widely read *Deutsche Rundschau*:[52]

> When, in the year 1875, I stepped down from the directorate of the medical and surgical Academy in Tokyo (Edo), which I had founded, and soon afterwards left Japan after more than four-years stay there, I made up my mind to wait for at least ten years before I published something about the establishment of the first German Academy in East Asia.[53]

[48] Spang, "Frühe OAG-Geschichte," 67.

[49] *Mittheilungen*, 1,1: 2–3; ibid., 1,2: 1.

[50] The reports, evidently after undergoing some revision (from mid 1876, see facsimile p. 13), were filed with the Ministry of Foreign Affairs of Germany in November 1876. See Kim, *Doctors of Empire*, 16, fn. 2.

[51] "Tokyo – Medical Science."

[52] A conservative literary and scientific monthly periodical founded in 1874 and published until its politically enforced closing in 1942.

[53] "Als ich im Jahre 1875 die Direction der von mir gegründeten medicinisch-chirurgischen Akademie in Tokio (Yedo) niederlegte und bald darauf Japan nach mehr als vierjährigem Aufenthalte dasselbst verliess, nahm ich mir vor, mindestens zehn Jahre zu warten, bevor ich etwas über die Gründung der ersten deutschen Akademie in Ostasien veröffentlichte." Müller, "Tokio-Igaku (Nov. 1888)," 315.

Notwithstanding this deliberate delay, Müller insists in 1888 on the validity of an account drawn almost exactly from his official reports written promptly on leaving Japan, rather than, it is implied, on more fragile recollection from afar:

> ... the following description is taken, with only insignificant deviations, from three reports which I wrote in 1875 on the return journey from Yokohama to San Francisco, so under direct, fresh impression.[54]

Unlike "Notes," this contribution is well known in more recent times. Studied both in Japan and elsewhere,[55] it has been mined especially, and as might be expected, for what it holds about the medical activities of the early German physicians in Tokyo.[56] From its closing pages, however, we are able to offer here, in translation, Müller's own short but informative account of the function and activities of the internationally networked Gesellschaft he had evidently committed to and valued, and in whose proceedings he published "Some Notes on Japanese Music," with equally evident commitment and with conviction of their path-breaking potential.

Müller on the *Deutsche Gesellschaft für Natur- und Völkerkunde Ostasiens*

> Finally I must make mention here of another institution that likewise endures until today, even though perhaps no longer quite in its original splendor, and whose foundation and flourishing were connected, essentially, with the combination of capable people from all branches of the sciences brought about by the Academy: I mean the German *Gesellschaft für Natur- und Völkerkunde Ostasiens*,

---

[54] "... die folgende Darstellung ist, mit nur ganz unwesentlichen Abweichungen, drei Berichten entnommen, die ich auf der Rückfahrt von Yokohama nach San Francisco im Jahre 1875, also unter dem unmittelbaren, frischen Eindrucke schrieb." Müller, "Tokio-Igaku (Nov. 1888)," 315. The published account differs from Müller's personal, handwritten reports only in suppressing some of his more critical remarks. See Scheer, "Dr. med. Leopold Müller – Biographie," 316; the original manuscripts were held in the Landesarchiv Berlin in the collection E Rep. 200-35; they are now housed in the Bloch Archiv, Berlin.

[55] For instance Koseki, "Notes on Leopold Müller and Theodor Hoffmann"; for a translation into Japanese, see Müller, *Tōkyō-Igaku*; Bowers, "The Adoption of German Medicine in Japan."

[56] See especially Kim, *Doctors of Empire*.

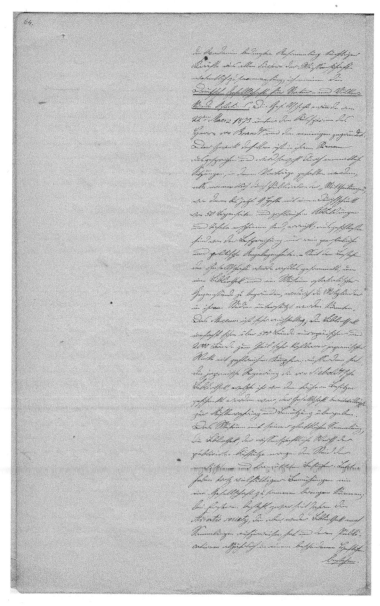

Example 1 – From a draft for Müller's report to the Ministry of Foreign Affairs submitted in 1876 (Landesarchiv Berlin, E Rep. 200-35 Nr. 47, p. 64)

which was inaugurated ceremoniously on the 22nd of March 1873 under the auspices of Herr von Brandt and myself, and whose mission

is pronounced in the name. This mission is achieved both through monthly meetings with lectures and demonstrations, as well as specifically also through publication of the Mittheilungen. By 1875 nine handsome issues with an average of fifty sheets of paper, numerous essays in various languages, many plates, illustrations, and musical attachments had come out, and fifty-four scholarly societies of all nations were exchanging their publications for ours. The library at that time already held over five hundred volumes of European and two thousand volumes of in part very valuable Japanese and Chinese works, valuable especially for their illustrations. Furthermore, the Japanese government, in the most commendable way, had turned over to the Gesellschaft for use and administration the von Siebold Library, which had been given it by the previous owner. Nonetheless there still remained enough to do for the generosity of the Germans residing in Japan, a generosity that is my duty to highlight with praise at this opportunity. Against high revenues – each of the around 130 members had to pay a yearly subscription of 100 Marks – stood not less considerable expenditures: 4,000 Marks for the production of the Mittheilungen, 2,400 Marks for the yearly rent etc. This situation, as well as concern about the ever threatening danger of fire in Japan, lead thereto that the museum, brought together with unending costs and labor – probably the most complete of its kind and, just like the library, frequently visited even by Japanese researchers and scholars – had been later donated to the Völkerkundemuseum, in Leipzig, where, however, until now it seems, unfortunately, no place has been found for installation. – My successor as president of the Gesellschaft was the German Minister Resident in Tokyo, Herr von Eisendecher.[57]

[57] "Endlich muß ich hier noch einer Institution gedenken, die gleichfalls bis heute weiter besteht, wenn auch vielleicht nicht ganz mehr in dem ursprünglichen Glanze, und deren Gründung und Gedeihen mit der durch die Akademie bedingten Vereinigung tüchtiger Kräfte aus allen Fächern der Wissenschaft wesentlich zusammenhing; ich meine die deutsche Gesellschaft für Natur- und Völkerkunde Ostasiens, die am 22. März 1873 unter den Auspicien des Herrn von Brandt und den meinigen feierlich eröffnet wurde, und deren Zweck in dem Namen ausgesprochen ist. Dieser Zweck wird sowohl durch monatliche Sitzungen mit Vorträgen und Demonstrationen, als namentlich auch durch Publication der 'Mittheilungen' erreicht. Bis 1875 waren neun stattliche Hefte mit einem Durchschnitt von fünzig Bogenseiten, zahlreichen Aufsätzen in verschiedenen Sprachen, vielen Tafeln, Abbildungen und Musikbeilagen erschienen, und vierundfünfzig wissenschaftliche Gesellschaften aller Nationen tauschten ihre Publicationen mit der unsrigen aus. Die Bibliothek umfaßte damals schon über fünfhundert Bände europäischer und zweitausend Bände zum Theil sehr wertvoller japanischer und chinesischer Werke, werthvoll besonders durch ihre Abbildungen. Außerdem hatte die japanische Regierung

Noteworthy here, in respect of "Notes," and apart from the significant distribution their three installments would have enjoyed through the international publication exchange of the Mittheilungen with over fifty other societies, is Müller's estimation of the Chinese and Japanese holdings of the Gesellschaft's library as "valuable especially by virtue of their illustrations,"[58] for he depends heavily himself on illustrations for his musical reports in "Notes."[59] Not unrelatedly, perhaps, for Müller's approach to his object of research and to the value he evidently placed on the illustration for its written description in general, is that German medical knowledge had been invited to Japan as "a sophisticated form of science that one should teach by 'showing (or displaying)' at hospital beds, operation tables, and laboratories."[60] In other words, the German physicians in Tokyo were there to "illustrate" their science, to "show German Medicine,"[61] just as Müller would "show" Japanese music to his European readers.

With respect to the von Siebold library entrusted to the Gesellschaft, this appears to be distinct from the library stewarded by the British legation translator and interpeter Alexander von Siebold (1846–1911).[62] Alexander was a son of Philipp Franz Balthasar von Siebold (1796–1866), the most renowned of the Franconian lineage of Würzburg physicians and medical professors. As twice longtime resident (1823–1829 and 1859–1862), first as physician to the Dutch settlement on Deshima, Nagasaki, he conducted pioneering medical, botanical, and zoological research of Japan and was also the first European to teach Western medicine in Japan. The family had handed over von Siebold's (earlier?) library to the Japanese government; the Gesellschaft re-

---

die von Sieboldt'sche Bibliothek, welche ihr von dem früheren Besitzer geschenkt worden war, in höchst dankenswerther Weise der Gesellschaft zur Benützung und Verwaltung übergeben. Nichtsdestoweniger blieb der Opferwilligkeit der in Japan residirenden Deutschen, welche bei dieser Gelegenheit rühmend hervorzuheben meine Pflicht ist, noch genung zu thun übrig. Den hohen Einnahmen – jedes der etwa 130 Mitglieder hatte einen Jahresbeitrag von 100 Mark zu zahlen – standen nicht minder beträchtliche Ausgaben gegenüber: für Herstellung der 'Mittheilungen' 4000 Mark, für Jahresmiethe 2400 Mark, u. s. w. Dieser Umstand, sowie die Besorgnis vor der in Japan immer drohenden Feuergefahr führte dazu, daß das mit unendlichen Kosten und Mühen zusammengebrachte Museum – wohl das vollständigste seiner Art, und ebenso wie die Bibliothek sogar von japanischen Forschern und Gelehrten häufig aufgesucht – nachmals dem Völkerkundemuseum in Leipzig geschenkt worden ist, wo sich aber bis jetzt für dasselbe leider noch kein Platz zur Ausstellung gefunden zu haben scheint. – Mein Nachfolger als Präsident der Gesellschaft wurde der deutsche Ministerresident in Tokio, Herr von Eisendecher." Müller, "Tokio-Igaku (Dec. 1888)," 458.

[58] To be noted is that the Mittheilungen published detailed records of gifts and acquisitions, for both the library and the museum.

[59] Pp. 21f.

[60] Kim, Doctors of Empire, 36.

[61] "Deutsche Medicin zeigen," see Wernich, "Über die Fortschritte der modernen Medicin in Japan," 447; Kim, Doctors of Empire, 35–36.

[62] Brown, "The Von Siebold Collection from Tokugawa Japan," 163.

ceived this gift in early 1875. That one part of Philipp von Siebold's monumental *Flora Japonica*, published in collaboration with German botanist Joseph Gerhard Zuccarini (1797–1848) in thirty volumes between 1835 and 1870, was apparently included in the gift to the *Gesellschaft* would alone have guaranteed the quality of the collection.[63]

The museum of the *Gesellschaft* was moved, as Müller relates, to safekeeping in the *Völkerkundemuseum*, Leipzig. However, the real reason for the move of the holdings of the museum from Tokyo to Leipzig may have had more to do with financial concerns than with considerations for preservation. After Müller's departure from Tokyo, the *Gesellschaft* had rapidly lost membership (from one hundred and twenty-one members in 1875, the year Müller left Japan, to fifty-eight members in 1877).[64] This resulted in a decisive shortcoming of revenue needed to keep all the *Gesellschaft's* ambitious projects alive, especially the maintenance of the museum. After politically and financially delicate deliberations among Tokyo, Leipzig and Berlin, the meteorologist Erwin Knipping, as curator in Tokyo, finally oversaw the packaging and shipping of the collection to Leipzig – paid for by the *Völkerkundemuseum*. The delight in receiving such a grand gift is recorded in the minutes of the Annual General Assembly of the Leipzig museum held on 29 March 1878:

> Furthermore we have to pay tribute to an important event, which, although it caused our budget a significant expense for packaging and shipping charges, furnished our institute with an enrichment of the most rare and comprehensive kind. This refers to the transfer of the rich and valuable collection of the "Deutsche Gesellschaft für Natur- und Völkerkunde Ost-Asiens" in Tokyo.[65]

The euphoria in Leipzig over this generosity of the expatriate Germans was dampened in the following year by a complete halt to acquisitions in order to recover from the cost of both importing the gift and cataloguing the greatly expanded museum holdings.[66]

---

[63] Bowers, *When the Twain Meet*, 78–79.
[64] Spang, "Frühe OAG-Geschichte," 69.
[65] "Sodann haben wir eines bedeutungsvollen Ereignisses zu gedenken, welches dem Budget zwar an Verpackungs- und Frachtspesen einen sehr bedeutenden Aufwand verursachte, aber unserm Institut eine Bereicherung seltenster und umfassendster Art zuführte. Es ist dies die Überweisung der reichhaltigen und kostbaren Sammlung der 'Deutschen Gesellschaft für Natur- und Völkerkunde Ost-Asiens' in Tokio." GRASSI, *Sechster Bericht des Museums für Völkerkunde Leipzig 1878*, 1. We are grateful to Dr. Birgit Scheps-Bretschneider for drawing our attention to this and the succeeding report when we visited the GRASSI Museum für Völkerkunde zu Leipzig in summer 2012.
[66] Idem, *Siebter Bericht des Museums für Völkerkunde Leipzig 1879*, 1.

Notes on "Notes"

> "... further, through my position as personal physician to His Majesty the Mikado, I have managed to study closely his private ensemble along with its instruments and performances; ..."[67]

As well as fulfilling his post at the Medical Academy in Tokyo, and significantly for his (and our) musical interests and for his academic contributions to the meetings of the newly founded *Gesellschaft* – each of the essay-installments of "Notes" was first delivered as a lecture to members at one of its monthly meetings – Müller served during the latter part of his four-and-a-half-year stay in Japan as personal physician to the Meiji Emperor and the Imperial family.[68] His privileged access to the Palace enabled his equally privileged access to its courtly "Mikado Musik," as he often refers to *gagaku* in the essays. For the scientific physician-ethnographer disposed by training to empirical testing, this meant access to the music theory and musical instruments of *gagaku*, their constructions, tunings, and their courtly players, as well as to their notations and their oral-aural methods of teaching and memory support. Moreover, the depth of his *gagaku* studies can surely be explained by the fact that, for at least eight of the fifteen months of his court appointment, he was relieved of all duties at the Academy. From Easter of 1875, his German medical successors took over his full teaching load[69] and he was left with only his medical obligation to the Emperor to fulfill until shortly before leaving Japan at the end of that year. This would apply especially to his *gagaku* coverage in the final installment of "Notes," published in March the following year, 1876, when he had already returned to Berlin. That "Notes" concentrate so heavily on *gagaku* might well be viewed as an outcome of what ethnomusicologist Justin Hunter has characterized as a "chance encounter";[70] for court appointments[71] for both Müller and second physician Hoffmann had been offered

---

[67] "... ferner habe ich durch meine Stellung als Leibarzt S. M. des Micado es erreicht, die Privatcapelle desselben nebst ihren Instrumenten und Aufführungen genau zu studiren, ..." p. 143, below.

[68] Müller, "Tokio-Igaku (Dec. 1888)," 455.

[69] *Ibid.*, 455–456.

[70] "Though as ethnomusicologists we actively seek new possibilities for research and academic endeavors, chance encounters or unsolicited musical experiences often prove to be the most impressive and exciting." Hunter, "Redefining Western Military Drumming," 67.

[71] Dated 8 July, 1874 (7th year of Meiji); Landesarchiv Berlin, E Rep. 200-35, 39; Landesarchiv Berlin, E Rep. 200-35, 46 (51–57, r° and v°).

as a way to secure a further fifteen-month "extension" of their initial three-year contracts at the Academy.[72]

> On the expiry of our first contract, besides other very valuable gifts, each of us was awarded by the Tennō his private war sword as sabre of honour, permission for whose acceptance and wearing with uni-form during our stay in Japan His Majesty the German Emperor most graciously deigned to grant us. – Without mention being made of it, it was nevertheless implicitly assumed by all concerned that the real purpose for our investiture was to retain our service to the Academy in an honourable manner for us until the arrival of our prospective successors. Therefore, when after our commissioning, a request to that end was put to us, we felt we should agree to this without further ado. We very well understood and appreciated the intent of the Japanese authorities that the transition of the Academy and the pupils out of our hands into those of our successors ought not be a sudden, unprepared one, but that the new teachers ought first work together with us and then begin their independent instruction while we would be still present. Our successors arrived at the end of the year 1874 in the persons of Herren Doctors Wernich (now in Köslin [Koszalin]) and Schultze (now in Stettin), took over the tuition at first in part and from Easter 1875 completely, while the directorship transitioned into Japanese hands. From Easter until November we remained only in our positions as personal physicians.[73]

---

72 Scheer, "Dr. med. Leopold Müller – Biographie," 315.

73 "Bei Ablauf unseres ersten Contracts wurde Jedem von uns, außer anderen sehr werthvollen Geschenken, vom Tenno sein Privatkriegsschwert als Ehrensäbel verliehen, zu dessen Annahme und Anlegung zur Uniform während unseres Aufenthalts in Japan Se. Majestät der deutsche Kaiser uns Allergnädigst die Erlaubnis zu ertheilen geruhte. — Ohne daß dessen Erwähnung geschah, ward doch von allen Betheiligten stillschweigend angenommen, daß der eigentliche Zweck unserer Ernennung war, der Akademie in einer für uns ehrenvollen Weise unsere Thätigkeit bis zur Ankunft unserer in Aussicht genommenen Nachfolger zu erhalten. Als daher nach unserer Installation ein darauf gerichtetes Gesuch uns vorgetragen wurde glaubten wir ohne Weiteres einwilligen zu sollen. Wir begriffen und würdigten auch ganz gut die Absicht der japanischen Behörden, daß der Übergang der Akademie und der Schüler aus unserer Hand in die unserer Nach-folger nicht ein plötzlicher, unvorbereiteter sein möge, sondern daß die neuen Lehrer erst gemeinschaftlich mit uns wirken und dann ihren selbstständigen Unterricht noch während unserer Anwesenheit beginnen möchten. Unsere Nachfolger langten Ende des Jahres 1874 in den Personen der Herren Doctoren Wernich (jetzt in Köslin) und Schultze (jetzt in Stettin) an, übernahmen den Unterricht erst zum Theil und von Ostern 1875 an gänzlich, während die Direktion in japanische Hände überging. Von Ostern bis November verblieben wir nur in unserer Stellung als Leibärzte." Müller, "Tokio-Igaku (Dec. 1888)," 455–456.

But music theory and the musical traditions of "sacred" (*heilige/geistliche*) music
– as *gagaku* was characterized, having been newly revived and restored, "sanitized
and sanctified,"[74] to bolster the prestige of the recently re-instated Meiji Emperor –
are not all that Muller experienced and reported on in "Notes." "Secular" (*weltliche*)
traditions of popular music (*zokugaku*), their instruments, tunings, and their performers and playing techniques are also addressed. Indeed, right when Müller began
to deliver the series of lectures that became "Notes," so before his Palace appointment,
he introduced at least two musicians as guest-performers following his academic
address to a *Gesellschaft* meeting, namely, at the meeting held in Tokyo on 13 June,
1874 (p. 41). Both musicians were bearers of secular traditions and both feature again
in "Notes": a *koto* player (p. 82) and a blind performer of the Japanese fiddle *kokyū* (pp.
102–105). He also includes in "Notes" details (of varying specificity) on the system of
guilds and ranks for musicians (pp. 80–82), on the classification of music as "sacred"
and "secular" and the association therewith of instruments as "pure" and "not-pure"
(pp. 80–86); on *nō* as the ceremonial music of the daimyōs (p. 81); on constructions,
tunings, and playing of the popular instruments *koto*, *shamisen*, and *kokyū*, as well as
of the elite Chinese *qin* (Jpn. *kin*) (pp. 93–105); on instruments used in the Buddhist
temple (pp. 220–224) and on the battlefield (p. 219); as well as on folk traditions and
folk and ancient instruments he had observed or been told about: an instrument
for chasing out snakes before tilling a field (p. 86), a pilgrim's instrument laid over
the genitals and beaten (p. 222), flutes played by jugglers and shepherds (p. 168), an
antiquarian stone flute (p. 191), and so on. And at the end of the third essay he covers
a substantial collection of Chinese musical instruments (pp. 224–229), at least part
of which he appears to have acquired personally on a short trip to China (p. 143), or
otherwise seems to have examined elsewhere, including possibly in the *Gesellschaft*'s
own museum.[75] A transcription of a Chinese piece, *Manban liushui*, collated from
two different performances is also given (p. 245).[76] Müller amplifies this Chinese
section with a lengthy set of historical "notes," translations from translations of
earlier Chinese sources. Unfortunately these extra notes on Chinese texts leave much
to be desired, even for their time, and could easily distract the modern reader from
appreciating the overall quality of Müller's "Notes." A final section on Chinese music
was submitted by fellow *Gesellschaft* member Herr Stein (p. 230).

---

[74] Nelson, "Court and Religious Music (2)," 48.
[75] A collection of nineteen Chinese instruments had been donated to the museum early in
1875; see p. 42.
[76] For summary discussion of the terms "transcription" and "transnotation" see Herzog,
"Transcription and Transnotation in Ethnomusicology," 100.

Approach and method

Significant for understanding Müller's manner of working and for any evaluation now of the essays as a whole are his express statements that he set out "to acquire notes" (*sich Notizen zu verschaffen*, p. 79), elsewhere to "collect notes" (*Notizen sammeln*, p. 193), on Japanese music from musicians and scholars from within Japanese culture – as opposed to merely observing and making notes himself, that is. To be borne in mind as well, is his recording, several times, the difficulty he had as a European in achieving his goal in the face of the culture of tacit knowledge held by the Japanese musicians who were willing to work with him. His recognition, expressly for *gagaku*, that an art of transmission and performance that relied on implicit knowledge embodied through rote oral-aural learning supported by sung memory aids,[77] mechanical drill, and memorization would not readily lend itself to explication may have been aided – if only as a sort of mirror-image – by his earlier surprise and experience with the Japanese medical students he first encountered at the Academy. At that stage they were studying medical texts in European languages by chanting them aloud as an aid to memorizing them,[78] albeit evidently, in this culturally transposed context, with little comprehension linguistically and, presumably, equally little practical outcome. In any case, this chanting-to-memory was being done without expectation of needing to explicate content.[79]

Specifically concerning the musical transmission of *gagaku* – whose, by contrast, efficient technology Müller clearly admires, for instance, for the precision in performance it achieves even though a "bandmaster or conductor is non-existent" (p. 200) – he says:

> Instruction takes place in the way that the pupils must learn the notes and the contour of the melody by heart at home from the *katakana* symbols ... ; only after that do they get the instruments in hand and learn their manipulation for the individual pieces, which are always played from memory. Already from this teaching method one will easily grasp that it is just a matter of mechanical drill, and that even in *gagaku* the fewest musicians are in a position to give any sort of information about their art. (P. 194)

---

[77] Known as *shōga*, "singing songs," although Müller refers to them according to their written-down form as "the *katakana* symbols."

[78] Müller, "Tokio-Igaku (Nov. 1888)," 318–320.

[79] Kim addresses at length this approach to knowledge acquisition as well as the cultural difference and epistemological gap between German physician and Japanese student in envisioning the medical science and knowledge represented by this approach. (Kim, *Doctors of Empire*, 34–36).

On setting out on his essay series and describing this difficulty in gaining formulated explanations in general, he characteristically draws a parallel from his own culture, namely, with fairground and tavern folk-musicians:

> One more or less lands in a situation as if wanting to know something more of our *Bierfiedler* or *Harfenistinnen*. (P. 79)

While making no "claim in any way to completeness" (p. 79), Müller is systematic and concerned with accuracy in how he deals with what he is able to address over the three cumulative essays. Remarkable is the number of precise, finely crafted illustrations he offers as engraved or woodblock prints, some hand-tinted, some apparently copied or even cut from his own line drawings (see Example 2 on the following page),[80] others possibly taken over from publications elsewhere. Twenty-four plates of figures containing musicians, musical instruments and parts of musical instruments (drawn to scale), and (Sino-)Japanese musical notations (with red color included) are provided. These are accompanied by a further ten pages or so of transcriptions and transnotations[81] of musical pieces into Western staff-notation and a song text for the court-song *Ise no umi* ("By the sea at Ise") (printed twice), each given *in toto*, as are all original notations on the plates. Together, plates, musical notations, transcriptions, and transnotations offer over two hundred and fifty individual items. The illustrations are tied tightly to the essays and are presented by and large in the order Müller takes for his textual notes; although space-saving concerns evidently necessitated squeezing a good number of figures onto plates out of order. (See the tabular description of the organization of plates and figures in "Notes," pp. 328*f*.)

The notes themselves would be scarcely understandable without following the author's precise cross-referencing to their appropriate illustrations. In many places, the text is in effect a set of directions for "reading" an illustration. For instance, Müller explains early in his first essay (pp. 89–91) how his facsimile of a standard circular Sino-Japanese pitch-diagram (his *Tonrose* ["tone-rose"], our "circle of notes", Fig. 21, p. 123) functions as a dynamic template for the generation of twelve fundamental chromatic notes in a tone-system linked calendrically with the twelve months of the year. While requiring emendations later in his essays (p. 146), the tone-rose serves him from there on in his evident wish to try to remain within Sino-Japanese music-theoretical thinking (as presumably explained to him) whenever he deals with matters of pitch, scale, mode, key, and tuning. Most accounts – informed ultimately by ancient Chinese pitch-calculation theory for twelve pitches in an octave

---

[80] In his second essay, Müller, correcting himself from the first essay, states about one of his illustrations that "... in my original drawing, December is to be found at the bottom, whereas on the woodblock it came to be at the top." (P. 146)

[81] Herzog, "Transcription and Transnotation in Ethnomusicology," 100, footnote.

Example 2 – Structural pencil copies of illustrations, see Plate VI, Figures 10–14 and
Figure 16 (p. 122). (Landesarchiv Berlin, E Rep. 200-35 Nr 52: 2)

derived by alternately adding and subtracting one-third of the length of a string or a
tuning-pipe – describe this generation process as a quasi-Pythagorean one, involving
an "up-and-down-principle" of fifths and fourths to give these twelve chromatic
pitches. Sino-Japanese templates (like the one Müller reproduces) typically link the
specific fourths and fifths involved by using lines that traverse the diameter of the
"circle-of-twelve." However, Müller takes up another option seemingly conveyed by
his Japanese informants; he operates around the circle's perimeter, asking his reader
to count with him (in semitones that make up the fifths and fourths) backwards and
forwards through the names of the months – rather than through the names of the
notes – to grasp the principle of generation.[82] For the remainder of his three-part
study, he will rely on the reader's comprehension to follow him repeatedly back to
the tone-rose when reading explanations and contemplating further illustrations
expressed in terms of months-linked-ṭo-pitches.

For another instance of Müller's built-in illustrations, the lengthy description
of the construction of the shō, the seventeen-piped mouth-organ used in gagaku (pp.
158–166), demands constant contact with precisely scaled sets of illustrations of the
instrument and its parts (on Plates IV (p. 120), V (p. 121), VI (p. 122), and X (p. 173)), as does

---

[82] The Chinese circular principle relevant to gagaku is discussed in Wolpert, "Tang Music
Theory of Ritual Calendrical Transposition Applied."

his laying-out of how the tablature system of notation for *shō* works (pp. 216–217, and Plate XIX, p. 255). His explanation of each of the individual instrumental notations for *gagaku* likewise refers to complete specimens for a single, sample piece from the Tang Chinese repertory of *tōgaku*, *Dshioh-raku* (= *Goshōraku [no kyū]*), namely, the "Quick" movement of the suite "Five Virtues Music," as well as to what Harich-Schneider describes as a transcription "done analytically"[83] of a full version of this same piece. Harich-Schneider stresses that this is a Western-style full-score, in staff-notation, that is the first such to be made for *gagaku*,[84] by any scholar, Japanese or Western. It is a score that attempts to represent for the Western reader the written notations Müller explains; it includes for certain instrumental parts how that written notation is then realized in performance. Historians of *gagaku* will recognize that this approach, when in a sense reversed by Picken eighty years later, led to the recognition for the *tōgaku* subsection of *gagaku* that the tune inherent in the written notation and embedded in the version performed today is a genuine relic of the ancient music borrowed from Tang China.[85] As pleaded earlier, it surely now deserves accounting for in the tracing of the intellectual steps behind advances in the field of historical study of *gagaku* in general.

That said about the integral role of illustrations, Müller's "Notes" are richly cast from the outset with the musicians, musicologists and other scholars, colleagues, and various "cultured persons" from whom he gathered information, whom he observed and interviewed, and who, in turn, helped in his experiments: whether by facilitating the enterprise in general (Herr Miyake, p. 103); by lending him their ears in attempting to determine the actually audible make-up of cluster-chords on the *shō* ("two musically knowledgeable gentlemen," p. 203); by measuring pitch frequencies in determining tone system and tunings of instruments (Herr Westphal, p. 102); by transcribing a musical piece for four-stringed fiddle (*kokyū*) into Western staff-notation then testing by playing it back to the performer on a Western violin (Herr Westphal and a blind musician, p. 102 and pp. 108–110); by identifying the maker of an old pitch-regulator (Herr Ōhata, p. 145); by providing historical information on musical instruments (Herr Ninagawa, p. 190); or by providing his own sets of notes on specific aspects of the project (Herr Stein, p. 230). Indeed, one repeatedly gleans the impression of collaboration and exchange, along with a mutual Japanese-European curiosity and, it must be said of Müller himself, colored, in the main, by a degree of non-biased evaluation and balancing that was unusual, to say the least, for early

---

[83] Harich-Schneider, *A History of Japanese Music*, 551.
[84] Also pointed out in Hirschfeld, *Beethoven in Japan*, 64.
[85] Picken, "The New Oxford History of Music: Ancient and Oriental Music," 147.

Westerners in Japan observing and listening to Japanese musical traditions for the first time.[86]

Discomfort with each other's unfamiliar music is candidly acknowledged in several places. In the second paragraph of the first essay we read:

> As means of finding out about something, I made use, in the main, of the curiosity of those concerned to see and hear something of our music and our musical instruments. However, should I have to say what impression European music makes on the Japanese, then I believe I am correct in stating that the Japanese find our music even more abhorrent than we theirs. A refined Japanese remarked, of course not to me, for that they are too polite, but he remarked: "Children, servants, and women find pleasure in European music, but a cultured Japanese cannot stand it." (P. 80)

Müller's own difficulty with the Japanese singing voice, while strongly and negatively expressed in "Notes" (p. 195), is nevertheless weighed to some extent (albeit only in a footnote) against his experiencing for himself that Italian coloratura singing apparently made little inroad with a "cultured" Japanese listener among a recital audience in Edo:

> Highly unpleasant is the constantly dominating, strangulated gurgling-sound, the out-of-tune trilling (I would prefer to call it a bleating). In short, it is torture for us to listen to this singing which the Japanese, however, find very beautiful. (P. 195)

The somewhat tempering footnote Müller adds to this outburst reads:

> Only recently I had the opportunity to see for myself how much our music displeases the Japanese; there were, in Edo, a couple of very competent Italian coloratura singers, and, after the concert, when I asked a very cultured Japanese his opinion, he held beautiful, solemn Japanese singing to be much more agreeable after all. (Ibid.)

And although he seems to have been unable to warm at all to the reed-pipe (hichiriki) in gagaku – its "screeching and out-of-tune tone," he maintains, "for our taste, spoils the otherwise most beautiful pieces" (p. 196) – his liking for the mouth-organ (p.

---

[86] Still to this day, the scathing remarks of Basil Hall Chamberlain ring hollow and disturbingly. Entry "Music," Chamberlain, Things Japanese, 339–344; Fritsch, "Japan Ahead in Music? Zur Wertschätzung japanischer Musik im Westen," 249–271.

158), the biwa and the koto (p. 197), and the large drum (p. 197), as well as his admiration for the art of gagaku performance and for the musicality of the court musicians (p. 200) are evident.

Doctor and surgeon, as we have noted, Müller is particularly aware of the hand, breathing, and, in general, of the human body functioning in its music, especially in respect of its capacities and the execution of instrumental playing-techniques. For the doctor, the minutely detailed description – written in the present tense as if observing in real time and inviting the reader to do the same – of how the mouth-organ (shō) is held in the hands and how its pipes are fingered demonstrates, on anatomical grounds, the "fully rationally motivated" (rationell ganz motivirt) ordering of pitches to pipes in the instrument's construction (pp. 165–166 and correction on p. 192). Meter as marked in notation for gagaku needs the integration of the oral-aural dimension and the hand; for, when singing the mnemonics, the hands mark the beats, clapped together vertically "with the beginning of the measure," drawn "close to each other rhythmically" for other beats (p. 213). When, in large-ensemble gagaku performance in the Palace, musicians deployed in horseshoe-formation sat so that players of the same instrument could see each other, they "paid precise heed to one another" (p. 200). This reading from body to body in the absence of a "bandmaster or conductor" (p. 200) explains for Müller how players know exactly on which note to enter by following the main instrument and why the "interplay between same-type instruments" is "extraordinarily exact" (p. 200). Priceless for us now are his empirical tests of gagaku performance tempos and his sets of metronome measurements (pp. 212–213).[87] Valuable also is his noting, in respect of breathing-capability, that tempo in gagaku performance may be altered for children and old people:

> I wanted to try to ascertain the tempo with the metronome; but that is completely impossible. When I had haya counted out for me, I got 92 crotchets per minute; when I then had the individual instruments play, the tempo fluctuated between 60 and 80; and when, later, the instruments played all together, I found for the same piece always only 40–60 per minute. So, an exact tempo is not held; rather, since the long holding-out of the notes on the wind-instruments is considered as especially beautiful, the tempo depends mainly on the greater or lesser long-windedness of the wind-players; also connected to this is that the same piece is played slower at the beginning, quicker later. A second peculiarity stands likewise in connection herewith, namely, that for children and old people notation and tempo of the wind instruments incur small alterations. (Pp. 212–213)

---

[87] See Terauchi, "Nijuseiki ni okeru gagaku no tempo to fure–zingu no henyū"; Wolpert, "Metronomes, Matrices, and Other Musical Monsters."

Müller's interest in pitch, tuning, and relationships between pitches reflects the growing interest in scientific exploration of sound and intonation in the second half of the nineteenth century generated by Hermann Helmholtz's *Lehre von den Tonempfindungen* of 1863.[88] Müller would have been aware of these latest developments, and they certainly may not only have influenced his scientific approach to Japanese musical theory and Japanese music in general, but perhaps also sparked his very interest in a scientific ethnographic musical study at the outset of his explorations. His appointment to the Japanese position came only shortly after he had served successfully for almost twelve years (1856–1867) as – among other positions – « Inspecteur général de l'armée et des Hôpitaux militaires » ("Inspector General of the Army and Military Hospitals") in Haïti.[89] He left with his Haïtian wife and his two children,[90] having lost his considerable belongings in Haïti during the chaotic times following the overthrow of President Fabre Geffrard in 1867.[91] The time between then and his departure with his wife to Japan saw him first put in charge of an outbreak of a typhoid epidemic in Eastern Prussia, on which he published an extensive report,[92] before opening a general practice in Berlin, a time which allowed him space to absorb the newest German scientific developments.[93]

The use of tuning-forks and pitch-pipes for acoustic measurements had been common in Europe,[94] but it was only around Müller's time that a supra-national European pitch standard was envisaged, when in 1858 the French Academy revised an earlier French standard pitch of 409 cycles per second and established a new standard frequency of 435 cycles per second.[95] This spread fairly quickly amongst European orchestras.[96] Müller was confronted in Japan with a Sinified musical culture which had long been seeking and preserving precise measurements for acoustic purposes. His extensive descriptions of the Sino-Japanese tonal system, of the cycle of twelve

---

[88] Helmholtz, *Die Lehre von den Tonempfindungen*; idem, *On the Sensations of Tone*; on the rapid reception and acceptance of music as science in the latter half of the 19th century in German society in general, see Rieger, *Helmholtz Musicus*, 158, and also Steege, *Helmholtz and the Modern Listener*.

[89] See note 39, p. 9.

[90] His third child had died in 1863. See fn. 39, p. 9.

[91] Scheer, "Dr. med. Leopold Müller – Biographie," 288–300.

[92] Müller, *Die Typhus-Epidemie des Jahres 1868 im Kreise Lötzen, Regierungs-Bezirk Gumbinnen, besonders vom ätiologischen und sanitäts-polizeilichen Standpunkte aus dargestellt*.

[93] "... to make myself familiar with the advances medical science had made during my absence." "... mich mit den Fortschritten, welche die ärztliche Wissenschaft während meiner Abwesenheit gemacht hatte, bekanntzumachen." From Müller's handwritten *curriculum vitae* of ca. 1869, Landesarchiv Berlin, E Rep. 200–35, 44: 29f. See Scheer, "Dr. med. Leopold Müller – Biographie," 299–300.

[94] Jackson, "From Scientific Instrument to Musical Instruments."

[95] Nowadays commonly abbreviated as Hz; Heinrich Hertz, after whom the measurement of cycles per second is named, was a student of Helmholtz.

[96] Weinstein, "Musical Pitch and International Agreement."

months related to twelve pitches (and pitch-pipes), of the various kinds of what he calls tuning-forks, which were in fact small tuning pitch-pipes, as well as both technical-mathematical and practical descriptions of tuning procedures for various instruments illustrate the impression made by the Japanese interest in pitch on his scientifically oriented mind. The "new Parisian tuning-fork" which Müller had acquired and adopted by the time of completing his second essay of 1875,[97] and to which he then re-adjusts his measurements from the earlier installment of "Notes,"[98] shows that he was aware and made use of the most recent developments in the musical sciences in Europe, applying comparatively the standards and calculations of the Western tonal system to those he found in Japan. From the second installment in the *Mittheilungen* he then adopts the new, scientifically up-to-date Helmholtz convention for pitch-notation.[99]

A focus on the written in *gagaku*

Already in the opening to his first essay, Müller announces his preoccupation with written notation in Japan and, hand in glove, his awareness of its oral-aural surround-culture of absorbed knowledge:

> It is very difficult to acquire notes on Japanese music, not merely on account of the innate reserve of the Japanese but also, mainly, because most musicians here know nothing about theory themselves, indeed quite likely have no idea at all that a notation and the like exist. (P. 79)

While a focus on musical notation (and its associated written pitch-theory) is not surprising in itself from a European of the later nineteenth century, what is startling for us now is that its outome in "Notes" would be neglected by comparative musicologists (and later, ethnomusicologists) seemingly hesitant to take on an unfamiliar script as evidence for conceptualization and performance. And this happened even though for his *gagaku* full-score, the crowning piece in his third essay, Müller would go on to set the written musical script (in transnotation) and explain it (verbally) in relief against the (orally transmitted) performance tradition such scholars presumably would have needed to take in in order to assuage these presumed concerns. Müller's first essay introduces Sino-Japanese pitch-theory. And this essay also includes a set of brief, loosely connected observations on notation (pp. 105*ff*), ranging

---

[97] See p. 145.

[98] The "new Parisian" standard pitch, *diapason normal*, became the accepted standard at the Berlin opera around 1867 (Meyer, *Meyer's Neues Konversations-Lexikon*, 14: 949).

[99] Compare Müller's pitch listing for the tuning of the 13-stringed *koto*, in Issue 1, p. 98, with his listings for the *koto/gaku-sō* used in *gagaku*, in Issue 2, p. 146*f*.

from primary pitch-related symbols used for *koto* and flute to secondary symbols for pitch alteration, octave placement, note-duration, and articulation; on written-down oral mnemonics; and on overall *mis en page* for traditional notations. But it is in his final essay that he provides the result of what is an exceptional endeavor for its time: there he lays out the integrated working of a full set of Sino-Japanese musical notations for an item of *gagaku*, Dshioh-raku/Goshōraku [*no kyū*], linking each to the mechanics of its instrument and its tuning, and providing, for reference and study, a Western-style full-score for his test-piece. This full-score is built out of his own transnotations of the individual notations, amplified in most cases by elements of actual performance practice. Even if his full-score is faulty in places, there had been no one before him; and many a *gagaku* full-score in Western format since, when likewise intended as study score and accompanied by original notations and verbal explantions, even up until the most recent, is not all that different in approach or in amount of essential information made available – although likely more detailed as a musical transcription, or fuller in its amplification if also based on transnotation.[100]

Müller nowhere uses musicology's technical term "tablature" (in German, *Griff-schrift*, literally a "script for the grasp," and from there a "fingering script," according to Curt Sachs[101]) to describe "linking the fingers of the player directly with his instrument, namely the strings and frets, fingerholes ..."[102] demanded by the *gagaku* notations. Nevertheless, he is constantly aware of the physicality of the system of music writing he is dealing with. He is also concerned, throughout his attention to the written, that his reader not lose sight of the centrality of the imitative oral-aural in face-to-face teaching-learning processes in the transmission of repertory: the musicians "always play from memory" (p. 200), indeed they need not even "know the proper notations" because "they first learn their part mechanically by ear and simple phonetic symbols, and only then do they learn to play it." (Ibid.) Voice and instruments, all introduced in the preceding essays, are presented once again, but now we are told how they are to be used in *gagaku* (pp. 195–200), how they are combined for specific court-repertories (pp. 199–200), and how their players are seated for performance (p. 200). From the outset, they are keyed-in, where appropriate, to the representation of their roles in his attached full-score (pp. 242–244). Indeed, his innovative full-score is truly interactive, requiring the reader to work to and fro with it and its supporting originals and verbal explanations to be able to understand what it is intended to show.

---

[100] Such a supported study score (with accompanying recording) of the repeat of the opening section of *Goshōraku no kyū*, the very piece Müller had chosen, is now available in Nelson, "Court and Religious Music (2)," 52–59.

[101] Sachs, *A Short History of World Music*, 24.

[102] Wolpert, "Lute Music and Tablatures of the Tang Period," 1.

It seems, however, that with his departure from Japan – which was before the printing of the last installment of "Notes" – Müller no longer had input into the editorial process of the *Mittheilungen*.[103] His plates of illustrations are not supplemented by a figure-by-figure guide as are those for the first installment, for instance. Beset by a number of printing errors, even in the Sino-Japanese notations themselves, Müller's explanations, as well as his transnotations for the full-score, need careful and indulgent reading to come through as he had planned them.[104] No doubt a fourth installment of "Notes," had it been forthcoming, would have started off with a lengthy section of corrections.

Building a full-score: "Symbols for notes"

The eight-part full-score[105] follows the traditional layout of a Western orchestral score in which wind-parts (above) tend to be separated from string-parts (below) by a percussion section (middle). Müller approaches one after the other, and as if moving down a score, here and there interleaving a description for an instrument not used for his particular test-piece, *Goshōraku no kyū*: three wind instruments, mouth-organ *shō*, double-reed-pipe *hichiriki*, and the transvers-flute *ōteki* (also *ryū-teki*); four percussion instruments, double-headed barrel drum *kakko*, big drum *taiko*, wooden clappers *shakubyōshi* (not used in the piece), and small bronze-gong *shōko*; three stringed instruments, lute [*gaku-*]*biwa*, thirteen-stringed long zither *gaku-sō* (which he calls by the common name *koto*),[106] and six-stringed long zither *wagon* (also not used in the piece); the last is followed by a short mention of a further flute, *kagurabue* (not used). His verbal descriptions are – as usual – closely linked to his illustrations, and the two depend on each other for understanding and verification.

Winds

Weaving into his notational explanations the physical structures and mechanical requirements of the instruments along with Sino-Japanese music-theoretical pitch assignments, he first establishes "the symbols for the individual notes on the different instruments" (p. 201). He begins with the mouth-organ *shō* (*ibid.* and Plate XVIII, Figures 1 and 2, p. 253), which he has already dealt with in detail and identified as

---

[103] Indeed, from his statement in *Tokio-Igaku*, p. 458, it would appear that he had voluntarily or involuntarily lost touch with the *Gesellschaft*, and felt rather disappointed with its development after relinquishing his leadership. (For translation of the passage, see p. 12*ff*; the German text is in footnote 57.)
[104] These issues are addressed further in the Postface (pp. 291*ff*).
[105] Pp. 242–244.
[106] Johnson, "A *Koto* By Any Other Name."

"really carrying the melody,"[107] relating the pitches he had given earlier (Plate X, Figure 39, p. 173) for the single pipes – whose names comprise the set of its notational symbols – with the Western equivalents he finds on his new Parisian tuning-fork (p. 202, correcting previous errors on p. 162 and pp. 192ff). An explanation (pp. 165–166) of the positioning and movement of the fingers of both hands on the sounding-holes of the instrument (with a practical, finger-movement based argument for the order of pipes, as we have seen, p. 25) is illustrated on Plate X, Figure 39 (p. 173).[108] The standard assignment of notational symbols to the pipes is shown in his Figure 1 on Plate XVIII (p. 253); there, pipe-names are linked to finger-names written around the outside or on the inside of the circle-of-pipes according to position of finger-hole; symbols for mute pipes are written in red. To match the Japanese notational symbols to the fingering map on Plate X, Figure 39, however, it is necessary to mentally rotate the circle in the latter so that the pipe numbered as 1 (ges/g♭) points due east.[109] Cluster-chords of notes "taken with the principal note" (p. 203) in performance idiom "for Chinese" items (tōgaku) are shown in Figure 2 (on Plate XVIII), translated as modified Helmholtz pitch notation (p. 202).[110] The odd sequence of chords here is the result of Müller's reading the Japanese chart as two parallel sets of symbols for chords (each chord marked with a red dot) running in blocks from right to left, rather than as one set of divided columns, each column to be read from top to bottom and carrying two blocks for chords (as marked by two dots per column). The cluster-chords are not represented in the full-score as performance-amplification of the transnotation; only the actual notation, of single pipe-names, is represented there.

For the two other winds, ōteki and hichiriki, Müller again links illustrations of the instruments with their associated notational symbols (Plate XVIII, Figures 3 and 4, p. 253) and ties these in turn to pitch: in the illustrations, the symbols for notes are written next to the finger-holes (really fingerings) they reference, supplemented for the hichiriki by a separate matching of holes with Japanese note names. In the text itself, tables for each (pp. 204–205) align holes and symbol names with pitches. The pitches equate with those known at present from pre-Meiji times, however. Massive deceleration, modal re-theorization, and changes in performance idiom of tōgaku over time since its importation from Tang China effected the transformation of orig-inally Chinese (diatonic) modal structures in the parts for these two flexible melodic

---

[107] "Die Shō, welche eigentlich die Melodie führt ..." p. 195; see also Wolpert, "Metronomes, Matrices, and Other Musical Monsters," 63. A correction to Figure 13 (p. 75) in this article is in order here: in the cluster-chords systematically erected on b′ and ♯″ the note d‴ should each time be d″.

[108] With corrections to the fingerings in the Figure given on p. 192.

[109] That is, matching the notational symbol 千 in Figure 1 on Plate XVIII.

[110] There are three printer's mistakes: the h′/b′ in the first chord (on a′) should be an e‴; d″ in the fourth chord (on g″) should be d‴; an e‴, also in the fourth chord (on g″), has been omitted.

instruments "in accordance with modal preference of musicians of later ages,"[111] so that they are now played in acculturated (non-diatonic) Japanese modality.[112] That these apparently conservative pitch-sets for ōteki and hichiriki were available to Müller and accordingly inform his transnotations in his full-score must be kept in mind when reading – and assessing those who earlier read – that full-score.[113] Further symbols are listed (p. 205): one for finger-flicking on the flute, and two used globally in the gagaku notations for durational indications for lengthening and shortening the basic time-unit, that is, for showing that "the note should be long held," and that "a quick change-over to the next note" should happen, respectively.

Percussion

The discussion of notations and representations for percussion (pp. 206–207), written mid-way down the Western-format full-score, follows the inspection of "the symbols for the individual notes" (p. 201) on the different wind-instruments in the upper part of that score. Müller works again with their physicality – coming to the hand, from graphic metric-dot, via named technique or pattern. For each of the three, kakko, taiko, and shōko (and, in a brief nod to outside the score, the shakubyōshi), the reader is shown how hand-with-beater is linked to the set of symbols for standardized and named playing techniques placed in time as events in (eventually combinatory) ostinati, as marked in graphic notation by sequences of red dots. These dots, shared by the notations for all parts in gagaku, melodic and percussive – visually staking out thereby a metric-grid for the whole – are written as a central column for the percussion-parts; symbols for playing techniques are aligned right and left of the columns of dots. Müller goes through the notation for kakko (Plate XIX, Fig. 2, p. 255) "dot by dot" for his reader:

> For the kakko ... the red dots usual for notating are written in the center. The seven upper symbols mean roll (rai), and, indeed, the signs to the right of the dots (from the reader's viewpoint) are beaten with the right hand, those to the left of the dots with the left hand.
> For the first three dots, therefore, both hands beat a roll; after the third

---

[111] Nelson, "Court and Religious Music (2)," 60.

[112] Picken et al., *Music from the Tang Court 5*, 107–123; especially 121; Marett, "Modal Practice in Hakuga no fue-fu," 1; idem, "Mode: Japanese chōshi," 854b; Ng, "Historical Development of Double-Reed Pipe Melodies."

[113] For discussion of the related fact that Müller exceptionally provides two facsimile versions of *Goshōraku no kyū* for ōteki and hichiriki, employing two different notational systems, one in tablature (honpu "original score") the other centered on the sung mnemonics (kanafu "syllable score"), see p. 71.

dot, and likewise after the 5th and 7th, the left hand rolls alone, that is, it begins slowly and carries on *accelerando*. (P. 206)

Strings

Stringed instruments, *biwa* and *koto*, round off Müller's first stage in describing the *gagaku* notations – his documenting of symbols for notes. The apparent loss of editorial control by the third installment seems to have allowed quite a few, for him atypical, mistakes or inconsistencies to creep in here, especially when it comes to his treatment of the notation for *biwa*. (See further, pp. 291*ff*.) The five Japanese figures with *biwa* tunings (Plate XVIII, Figure 5 (p. 253), Plate XVIIIa, Figures 6–9 (p. 254)) are inconsistent with his own correct (Western) diagrams in the body of his essay (pp. 207–211), and indeed inconsistent within themselves. Figure 5 – an equivalent for *biwa* of Plate XVIII, Figure 1 for *shō*, Figure 3 for oteki, Figure 4 for *hichiriki*, and of Plate XIX, Figure 1 (p. 255) for *koto* – is a correct representation of the strings and fretting of the *biwa*, along with their fingerings and associated notational symbols. Simply moving the column of Japanese pitch names for the open-strings from the far left side of the diagram and placing it, as here, to relate to the tablature-signs in the column labelled "a" to the far right (the column with the symbols for the open strings) results in the tuning for *hyōjō*, the tuning then required for the *biwa* part in the full-score transnotation of the piece *Dshio Raku/Goshōraku [no kyū]*.

e		d		c		b		a			
—	斗	—	フ	—	几	—	工	—	一	平 乙	(1)
—	ユ	—	乙	—	十	—	下	—	L	盤	(2)
—	之	—	ミ	—	ヒ	—	七	—	ク	平	(3)
—	也	—	ム	—	╎	—	八	—	上	黃	(4)

But the printed Japanese diagrams on Plate XVIIIa for four further tunings and pitches for all fret positions (including in red those not used) – for *ichikotsu* (Figure 6), *sōjō* (Figure 7), *ōshiki* (Figure 8), and *banshiki* (Figure 9) – do not match up with the string- and fret-position explanations from Figure 5 (Plate XVIII): compared with Figure 5 and with the set of Western tuning-diagrams on pp. 207–211, they are listed upside down, and back-to-front. To make the Japanese tuning-diagrams fit, fret-positions (indicated in the table as blocks) must be rotated by 180°, and the tuning of the open strings rotated and moved from the ("unblocked") last position to the first position (on the right), so that a revised Figure 6 (for *ichikotsu*), matching Müller's correct text-diagram on p. 208, would be:

		e		d		c		b		a		
壱	–	壱	–	上	–	神	–	盤	–	黄	‖	(A)(1)
越	–	双	–	下	–	勝	–	平	–	—114	‖	(d)(2)
調	–	黄	–	鳧	–	双	–	下	–	平	‖	(e)(3)
	–	壱	–	上	–	神	–	盤	–	黄	‖	(a)(4)

The remaining Japanese figures (Figures 7 to 9) on Plate XVIIIa require corresponding rearrangements to arrive at the tunings given in the set of text-diagrams on pp. 207–211. Having given the correct tunings in his Western diagrams – correct bar for being pitched an octave too high – Müller was obviously referencing these, not the Japanese figures as they were eventually presented in the published version of "Notes."[115]

True to his system of uniting note-symbol with finger and playing technique, Müller then attempts to describe (p. 211) the left-hand fret-stoppings and right-hand performance practice of striking chordal drones, "always played *arpeggio*," with

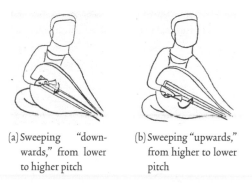

(a) Sweeping "down-wards," from lower to higher pitch

(b) Sweeping "upwards," from higher to lower pitch

Example 3 – Performance practice of "drones" for the *biwa*.

melody-notes, the latter alone indicated by the notation. In Meiji (and modern) technique, the *gaku-biwa* is played with a plectrum (*bachi*). Although sometimes "single

---

114 Another alternative for 壱/壹, the former used in the same diagram for the pitch of strings (1) and (4), fret (e).

115 The estate of Müller's written work at the Landesarchiv Berlin (now at the Bloch Archiv, Berlin) also shows that a few extant examples of designs for the Plates in his possession in Berlin were not yet labelled, and not yet assembled (Landesarchiv Berlin, E Rep. 200-35 Nr 52); Müller may well have always worked from not-yet arranged Japanese versions which were then placed by the printer according to his text. In this context, Müller notes mis-arrangements of illustrations in the printing process for earlier issues. He notes, for example, that the turning and labelling of one of his diagrams in the published version was done in such a way that it then gave wrong information (p. 146).

strings alone are struck" (p. 196), normally, whenever a melody-note is generated by the plectrum, any string tuned below that on which the notated note is generated is added. These "additional" strings are usually struck, "swept over with the *bachi*" (p. 211), starting from the lowest tuned and striking physically downwards, which is pitch-wise upwards (Example 3a on the previous page). But in certain circumstances indicated by a "small red hook" (p. 212) in the notation, the *arpeggio*-chord may be "swept over" from the melody-note upwards to the string tuned lowest (Example 3b on the preceding page). Notes not produced with the plectrum – and notated as smaller signs – are usually finger-plucked by the left hand alone "without the string being plucked anew" (p. 211). They are barely audible (although the player's actions are visible) in performance. To be noted already here is that, among other problems possibly stemming from miscommunication during the printing process, the transnotation of the *biwa*-part (like his Western tuning-diagrams) is in a wrong register.[116]

Symbols for notes on the thirteen-stringed *koto* for *gagaku* (more usually known as *gaku-sō* or *sō-no-koto*) are dealt with cursorily: "each string is just simply numbered" (p. 212), with ordinal numbers one to ten, "only the last three have symbols other than the usual numbers" (pp. 212). Actual pitches are tuning specific, and in the matching illustration (Plate XIX, Fig 1 [p. 255]), Müller sets out "bridged" strings and note-symbols with (in red) their corresponding pitches in Japanese nomenclature for the tuning required for his test-piece, namely *hyōjō*. Only later on (p. 217) does he explain performance idiom (see below, p. 36). *Wagon* and then *kagurabue* are but mentioned (p. 212).

"Further specifications": tempo, meter, sectioning

Stage two in unravelling the workings of *gagaku* notations for the reader moves on from "the bare notes" (p. 212) to "further specifications ... necessary for a musical piece" (p. 212). Specifications are for "tempo," both as assigned (*haya* "fast," *nobe* "slow") and as fluctuating in performance (pp. 212–213); for "meter" (pp. 213–214); for sectioning and repeats (p. 214); and for staggered entries, *ad libitum* endings, and intensification of percussive events in last repeats (pp. 214–215). Responsibility for sounding the metric-grid of red dots (p. 31), so to speak, draws the percussion instruments and their specific notations back again when Müller deals with indicating meter in *gagaku* notation in general. Of marking meter graphically and the cooperation of voice and expansional hand in the learning and internalization process, he observes (pp. 213–215):

---

[116] These issues are further discussed in the "Postface," pp. 291ff.

The meter is indicated in double fashion; the small red dots mark each time a beginning of a measure, and each measure is split into four equal parts which are not further notated, but of course, when studying, singing out loud and the like, are marked with the hand, and, namely, with the singer clapping both hands vertically with the beginning of the measure, for the three other quarters, merely drawing them close to each other rhythmically (p. 213).

He recognizes the mensural system of small intra-columnary black circles ("circles standing between the notes"), segmenting the strings of symbols for notes into units of two measures, as building "a support for the eye only" (p. 214). Moving up still further in size of notated mensural unit, he identifies the demarcation of the ostinato by a system of "big dots" that "recur in regular intervals," and (when red) "stand for the striking of the taiko" (with one stroke of the "male beater" (obachi) per ostinato), or (when black) "the hitting together of the shakubyōshi" (p. 213). And a yet larger unit is formed by "partitioning into sections" of so-and-so many ostinati, the sections themselves repeatable, as indicated in notation by a special repeat sign. Müller refers the reader to how he marks the staggered entries and gradual stoppings of the instruments into his full-score (with "E" for Eintritt "entrance," and the [Western] pause sign, respectively), noting that these are not marked in the Japanese notation but stipulated "in a special commentary for each piece" (p. 215). Percussion-intensification over the second repeat of the piece, over the final two ostinati (pp. 243–244), is stipulated (as a direction "add [beats]" kuwae(ru) [hyōshi]), effected by insertion of beats on the taiko and strokes on the shōko, and marked in the full-score: for taiko, as a set of lower notes on the stave shared by the regular pattern in the upper notes (Die unteren Noten bei der Wiederholung "The lower notes during the repeat"); for shōko, simply as more activity.

Scoring and transnotation

Finally, Müller's explanation of actual Sino-Japanese notation for his test-piece is unassumedly announced mid-paragraph (p. 215) with "The piece is now notated in the following manner: ..." Since for all parts, which are written separately for each instrument, "title and red dots (big and small) are the same" (p. 215), Müller indicates that this shared metric-grid facilitates coordination among the notes of those parts. The parts themselves, reproduced on the plates in full in each instance (Plates XIX to XXI), include one for each melodic and percussion instrument together with, for both hichiriki and flute, a part in tablature and a second part (in the style used today)

with the *katakana* symbols for its mnemonic singing-tradition (*shōga*).[117] They are all considerably reduced in size, but "otherwise reproduced exactly," he states.

Taking the notation for mouth-organ *shō* (Plate XIX, Fig. 5 [p. 255]) as his example, Müller first deals precisely with the prefatory matter that precedes the actual notation and stipulates for the piece to follow – in a set of shorthand labels which he tracks alphabetically – much of what he has already introduced in detail: (a) name of the instrument (*shō*); (b) mode (with final by default), which Müller misreads and expands to include fixed-pitch according to the calendrical pitch-circle, so that mode *hyōjō* as given is effectively glossed as "on *taizoku* [*taisō*], February [*e*];" (c) name of the piece; (d) movement-type in context in the suite-form (*Goshōraku no kyū* "Five Virtues Music"; the final "short" [Quick] movement, the two other movements in a typical suite being unmeasured *jo* "in which no tempo is specified," and *ha* "a fairly long piece"); (e) size of the piece (*shōkyoku* "little piece"); (f) tempo (*haya[byōshi]* "fast tempo"); and (g) number of measures in a section [ostinato] (*hyōshi hachi*, "eight measures"). Müller confuses the last two stipulations, (f) and (g); (f) should also indicate the number of measures in an ostinato (namely, eight), (g) the number of ostinati in the piece (also eight). That "beats" on the percussion are "added" over the repeat of the last two ostinati (h), Müller does not detail here beyond noting that the direction addresses the percussion instruments; but he had noted this earlier (p. 35) and marks these additions in his full-score. Prefatory matter is shared by all notations.

In a single sentence, Müller then drops the notes themselves into the metric-grid-units he has so carefully prepared for the reader: "Now come the notes as they belong to the individual measures" (p. 216). He directs the reader to which Sino-Japanese notation (on which plate and which figure) is for which instrument, and from there leaves it up to self-help via his full-score "to now decipher the individual parts and to rectify possible small errors." (P. 217)

Now fleshing out his earlier scanty coverage of the koto-notation for *gagaku*, he carefully describes the notational complex of two symbols (for two strings) linked by a red slur and the (typically) unwritten formulaic chordal structures that it too delivers in performance. He notes, though, the possibility of glossing the main notation with the symbols (written small and linked by a red line) for the strings involved in these chordal structures. His transnotation accordingly amplified in the full-score is accurate but an octave too high.

Müller closes this treatise on musical notation for *gagaku*, situated within the larger essay, as he had opened it by stressing that pupils learn by heart (p. 194), not according to the instrumental notations he has just introduced, but according to the tradition of sung mnemonics (*shōga*). Referring to full reproductions for the test-

---

[117] See p. 71.

piece (Plate XXI, Figures 2 and 3, p. 257) and again tying *shōga* to fingerings and the common graphic metric-grid, he addresses the oral mnemonics written down in the *katakana* script by which *hichiriki* and *ōteki* parts are actually transmitted, in a face-to-face, ear, eye, and body interaction of "singing-and-keeping-time":[118]

> The *katakana* signs for the *hichiriki* (Fig. 2) read from top until, but excluding, the *taiko* symbol: *Te e rū, rē ē, ta ā, re e*, whereby the comma indicates each time the red dot [marking the first beat in a measure]. These sounds are sung to the pupil, while giving the beat with the hand in the manner described above, and he must practice them at home until he knows them by heart. (P. 218)

An interactive hybrid study score?

Müller's *gagaku* full-score, then, can hardly be called a transcription, nor even somewhat more satisfactorily a transcription "done analytically," as Harich-Schneider offered (see above p. 23). Rather, we suggest that because it is (1) so heavily based on transnotation of written parts for the individual instruments (almost directly so for the *shō*, *hichiriki*, and *ōteki*), but with amplification from performance idiom (and/or from *shōga*-singing?) – namely, with fleshed-out patterns for percussion, chordal and figurated patterns for *biwa* (faultily) and *koto*, and minimal articulatory aspects for *hichiriki* and *ōteki*, (2) so reliant for its communication on Müller's verbal explanations, and (3) so clearly intended to be integrated with both original notation and explanation, it might be described more properly, if clumsily, along the lines of an "interactive hybrid study score built on transnotation-*cum*-amplification-from-performance-practice." Providing a printed version of the indigenous notation, verbal description, and transnotation makes, as he intends, his transnotational process directly "replicable" (and his errors easily correctable).[119] His process thereby requires interaction with his material, and thus offers a scholarly procedure we nowadays require in our scientific method.

In the Imperial Palace, Müller was able to work directly with those musicians, practices, and artifacts responsible for transmission and performance of what he knew was a "so remarkable music" (p. 194) – that of *gagaku*, or *gaku*, as, he points out, imported repertory was also known by (p. 81). At the Academy, Müller and his German associate Hoffmann worked in English or German with translators, at least in the earlier days of instruction before a pre-medical program that included language studies in German and Latin was in place for their beginning medical students.

---

[118] Markham, "The Concept of a 'Basic Melody'," 67.
[119] "… with the help of Plates XVIII to XXI and the explanations just given, it will not be very difficult to now decipher the individual parts and to rectify possible small errors," p. 217.

Müller studied Japanese language privately, setting aside an hour and a half each day at the outset of his stay,[120] and later still managing as many as three slots a week.[121] It seems, however, linguist as he was,[122] his professional medical work, conducted daily over long hours in German and English (with simultaneous translation into Japanese), may have been too demanding for him to make the progress he (and presumably his tutor) had planned for the necessarily formal spoken language that would befit his station in Japan.[123] In the Palace, at the end of his time in Tokyo, he evidently had help from many people, including from colleagues who knew European languages (see below pp. 63–75), and we can probably assume much transpired through translation there too. At the same time, however, Müller's experience with script and formal written Japanese during his efforts at spoken language acquisition[124] ought be kept in mind for his confident approach to the written in *gagaku* and all that this approach to – and perhaps fascination for – a foreign script expressly for music eventually enabled for his essay.

While in the Palace, Müller provided the observant, practical, firsthand detail of a doctor faced with the "totally unknown field" (p. 189) of *gagaku*, yet able to empirically test and measure its instruments as tuned and used by their players, and to take the pulse of its music as notated, and as learned, rehearsed, and performed by these same musicians, who were in any case also his main informants. It is perhaps here that his particular contribution, both to early Comparative Musicology and to the Historical Musicology of East Asia, could have lain and where, with the recent surge of interest in both these fields of Musicology, it may still achieve retrospective recognition and impact.

---

[120] Müller, "Tokio-Igaku (Dec. 1888)," 457.

[121] Ibid., 444.

[122] His doctoral dissertation was written in Latin, as was required at that time; he was fluent in English and French and had spent twelve years in multilingual Haïti prior to his appointment in Japan.

[123] All the while, his Haïtian wife was running their household in less formal Japanese. In fact, Müller acknowledges his dependency upon his wife's conversational Japanese for his own interactions with their Japanese home-helpers (ibid.).

[124] A vocabulary notebook among his papers in Berlin shows he was studying Japanese in the original script rather than only in some sort of transliteration. However, more telling for our interest in his fearless approach to notations for *gagaku* is his own later admission that he had developed unwittingly a curious spoken "book-language" by basing his studies on Johann J. Hoffmann's recently published *A Japanese Grammar* (1867): "Specifically, I had made a really wrong choice in the otherwise so famous Hoffmann's grammar; I indeed learned a language, but one that nobody understood, because it was the written language only used in scholarly tracts." "Namentlich hatte ich mich in der sonst so berühmten Hoffman'schen Grammatik arg vergriffen; ich lernte wohl eine Sprache, aber eine, die kein Mensch verstand, denn es war die nur bei gelehrten Abhandlungen übliche Schriftsprache." Ibid.

Traces of Early Reception

> "Dr. Müller says – and he has studied the
> Japanese and their music intelligently ..."[125]

Almost immediately on the heels of the December 1874 appearance in the *Mittheilungen* of the first of Müller's essays, the widely read English-language newspaper *The Japan Weekly Mail*[126] (or as it was best known, *The Japan Mail*, or even simply as *Japan Mail*) gave out, on February 20, 1875, an English translation. This happened again with the second essay of September 1875, which was soon available in *The Japan Mail* in translation on Christmas Day of that same year. A note in the Christmas Day issue anticipated a third installment from Müller, who by then had already departed on his return to Europe. Müller's final, longest essay was indeed published in the *Mittheilungen* in March 1876. It too appeared just as promptly as the other two in the translation series in *The Japan Mail*, only this time in two parts, on May 6, and a week later on May 13, 1876.[127]

These English translations continued to receive attention from a generally musically interested lay audience, as we shall see, but they seem to have slipped through the net in the English-language scholarly world. They are not included in *Japanese Music: An Annotated Bibliography*, Tsuge Gen'ichi's comprehensive 1986 coverage of Western writings on Japanese music up until the early 1980s, although the original German essays are included and commented upon, as noted earlier (p. 5); neither the English translations nor, as also noted earlier (p. 7), the original German versions appear in the extensive bibliography provided for the most recent of authorative accounts of Japanese music in English, *The Ashgate Research Companion to Japanese Music*, published in 2008.[128] In fact, it was only by stumbling ourselves via *Googlebooks* on the facsimile reprint series of *The Japan Weekly Mail*, made available in 2006 by the Yokohama Archives of History[129] that we learned of the translations' existence. Unfortunately for the modern English-language reader interested in early musical ethnography, the translations are marred by inaccuracies in a significant number of vital places. Most seriously for their time, though, the non-inclusion of the essential illustrations from the originals would have rendered them in any case exceedingly difficult to comprehend without firsthand experience of what they address, even

---

[125] Bird, *Unbeaten Tracks*, 2: 208.
[126] *The Japan Weekly Mail. A Political, Commercial, and Literary Journal* was published in Yokohama from 1870–1917.
[127] The translations have been available since 2006 in the reprint series of the complete newspaper for the years 1870–1899 (Yokohama Archives of History, *The Japan Weekly Mail*).
[128] Tokita and Hughes, *The Ashgate Research Companion to Japanese Music*.
[129] Yokohama Archives of History, *The Japan Weekly Mail*.

for a persistent scholarly reader.[130] In addition, the understandably compensatory, "explanatory" approach to translation further diminishes their usefulness now as the sort of neutral companion to the original we deem necessary to re-present Müller adequately for modern scholars with varied scholarly interests.

Translation and publication issues notwithstanding, however, the English versions were clearly read in Japan in their time, and for some time afterwards, as authorities, as well as, one might imagine, for the sensational newness of their subject matter alone. Isabella Lucy Bird (1831–1907), intrepid traveller in Japan in 1878, acknowledges in the preface to her travel narrative *Unbeaten Tracks in Japan* of 1880 the "valuable help" afforded her by the *Transactions* of both the "English and the German Asiatic Societies of Japan."[131] In the fiftieth letter-entry to her sister (dated October 11 [1878]) – her complete narrative is in this letter format[132] – she writes of reading during bad weather while staying in Edo (Tokyo) in the residence of Sir Harry Parkes (1828–1885), the British Consul-General, and his wife Lady Parkes:

> I have been utilising the bad weather by studying several volumes of the *Japan Weekly Mail*, and files of the *Tōkiyō Times*, and the "Transactions" of the Asiatic Society for several years, the three combined being better than all the books of travels put together for steeping one in a Japanese atmosphere.[133]

Further on in the letter she tells of attending two musical events. The first was a juggling and balancing diversion accompanied by drumming to entertain "the diplomatic body"[134] at the Shiba Pavilion, "one of the Mikado's smaller palaces."[135] The other was an after-dinner concert of traditional Japanese music organized by Ernest Satow, British diplomat, Japanologist, and founding member of the *Asiatic Society of Japan*, and played in his evidently beautiful house. This second occasion featured, among other solo and vocal items, ensemble music and music-with-dance

---

[130] Regret over this unavoidable omission is expressed in the "Notes of the Week" that open this issue of the newspaper itself: "We have given elsewhere a translation of a paper which will excite a lively curiosity in a large class of readers on the other side of the world. We refer to 'Dr. Müller's Notes upon Japanese Music,' published in the last number of the German Asiatic Society's Journal. The readers of our translation will labour under the grave disadvantage of not being able to follow the paper with the assistance of the ample and admirable diagrams which accompany it in the Society's journal. This could not be avoided; but the loss is severe, for Dr. Müller's researches disclose some extremely complex and fanciful ideas relating to music among the Japanese." Yokohama Archives of History, *The Japan Weekly Mail*, Vol. 6, No. 8; Saturday February 20, 1875, 153.

[131] Bird, *Unbeaten Tracks*, 1: ix.

[132] It "places the reader in the position of the traveller." *Ibid.*, 1: viii.

[133] *Ibid.*, 2: 202.

[134] *Ibid.*

[135] *Ibid.*, 2: 202–203.

of *gagaku*, it seems, for which "There were five *kotos*, two *sho*, a Corean *fuyé* or flute, and eventually a Japanese *fuyé*."[136] Miss Bird found this difficult to appreciate, she relates (several times), but she is motivated to give her sister a lengthy account of Japanese music and acknowledge Müller as her source. The account starts out by embedding a direct quotation,[137] which reveals that she is actually reading from the English version(s) of "Notes" in *The Japan Mail*[138] (in the Consul's library?). Nevertheless, here we may have an instance of the sort of currency Müller's essays, whether as "Notizen" or as "Notes," enjoyed among foreigners in Japan at the time.

During his stay in Japan, Müller was not the only lecturer on Japanese music from among members of the *Gesellschaft*. Papers were read by others at *Gesellschaft* meetings on musical topics ranging from Japanese song to comparison of Japanese and Chinese musics.[139] Furthermore, an added dimension of practical demonstration accompanied at least one of Müller's lectures that became "Notes," for the one that turned into their very first installment, in fact. At the meeting in Tokyo on the 13th of June, 1874, when Müller introduced to the *Gesellschaft* traditional musicians, a *koto* player and a blind performer of the *kokyū* (see p. 19), this was evidently after explaining the Japanese instruments with the aid of models. The transactions for that meeting read:

> Herr Dr. Müller then spoke, along with presentation of models, about the musical instruments of the Japanese, and at the end of his lecture

---

[136] Ibid., 2: 208.

[137] "Dr. Müller says – and he has studied the Japanese and their music intelligently – 'If I am asked what impression our music makes upon the Japanese, I am sure I shall not be far wrong in saying that they find it far more detestable than we do theirs. A prominent Japanese said, not to me, indeed, for their politeness would forbid it, "Children, coolies, and women may find pleasure in European music; but an educated Japanese can never tolerate it!"'." *Ibid.*

[138] Compare Yokohama Archives of History, *The Japan Weekly Mail*, Vol. 6, No. 8; Saturday February 20, 1875, 156.

[139] The very first musical contributions to be actually published in the *Mittheilungen* were two short articles by V. Holtz that appeared in September 1873 and January 1875, respectively, in Issues 3 (*Mittheilungen*, 1, 3: 13–14) and 4 (ibid., 1, 4: 45–47) of the first volume. Both addressed Japanese songs and both included transcriptions into Western staff-notation and translations into German of their texts, the former entitled "Zwei japanische Lieder" ("Two Japanese Songs"), the latter, conveying three more songs in transcription and with translation, called simply "Japanische Lieder" ("Japanese Songs"). Following Müller's essays in Issues 6, 8, and 9 (of December 1874, September 1875, and March 1876), this first volume went on to offer in its 9th issue (March 1876), an article entitled *Zur Vergleichung japanischer und chinesischer Musik* ("On Comparison of Japanese and Chinese Music") by F. Stein (60–62), who had contributed notes on Chinese music for Müller's final essay. Stein's essay was also published in translation in *The Japan Weekly Mail* as "A Comparison between Chinese and Japanese Music" on May 13, 1876 (424–425), immediately following the final portion of the translation series of Müller's "Notes," but, once again, without its original musical transcriptions.

had some Japanese musical pieces performed by Japanese artists on
stringed instruments (see essay).[140]

For the following meeting in Yokohama, on the 4th of July, 1874,[141] it is recorded
that Frau Dr. Hoffman had made a gift of a *koto* to the *Gesellschaft*'s museum, and
for the meeting of the 24th of April, 1875,[142] that Frau Heyden had presented the
museum with nineteen Chinese musical instruments. Later that same year, for an
extraordinary meeting in Tokyo on 23rd October, 1875, celebrating the reopening of
the *Gesellschaft*'s newly reorganized museum, and presided over by Müller himself,
Muller was able to present, as one of three presentations of a more "festive" and
generally accessible nature and to an audience much wider than usual because of its
inclusion of women,[143] a lecture that was incorporated in the third of his installments of "Notes":

> On the occasion of the re-opening of the newly organized museum of
> the *Gesellschaft* a more social meeting was held at which women also
> took part.
>
> Herr Dr. Funk held a lecture on Japanese *games*, Herr Westphal spoke
> about *fortune-telling*, Herr Dr. Müller on East Asian *music*.[144]

Interest in Japanese music among resident foreigners – as evidenced by such
formal lectures and presentations both to the *Gesellschaft* and to its English-language
counterpart, the *Asiatic Society*, and backed-up by peer-reviewed publication in the
Mittheilungen and the *Transactions of the Asiatic Society of Japan*, respectively – continued
after Müller had returned to Europe.[145] Some of these papers acknowledge, draw on,

---

[140] "Herr Dr. Müller sprach darauf unter Vorlegung von Modellen über die Music-
Instrumente der Japaner und liess am Schlusse seines Vortrages von japanischen Künstlern einige Musikstücke auf Saiteninstrumenten aufführen. (Siehe Aufsatz)" *Mittheilungen*,
1, 5: 7.

[141] Ibid.

[142] Ibid., 1, 7: 4.

[143] In the first decades of its existence, women were admitted at such special occasions. Spang,
"Frühe OAG-Geschichte," 76.

[144] "Bei Gelegenheit der Wiedereroeffnung des neugeordneten Museums der Gesellschaft
wurde eine mehr gesellige Sitzung abgehalten, an welcher auch Damen theil nahmen
... Herr Dr. Funk hielt einen Vortrag über japanische *Spiele*, Herr Westphal sprach über
Wahrsagen, Herr Dr. Müller über Ost-asiatische *Musik*" *Mittheilungen*, 1, 9: 5.

[145] Musical interest did not abate after the inaugural volume of the *Mittheilungen*. Wagener's
(referred to by Müller as Dr. Wagner) "Bemerkungen über die Theorie der chinesischen
Musik und ihren Zusammenhang mit der Philosophie" ("Remarks on Chinese Music Theory and its Interrelationship with Philosophy"), announced already in Müller's
"Notes," appeared in the 12th issue of the second volume, 42–61; Franz Eckert contributed
two articles in Volumes 2 (423–428) and 3 (131) respectively, entitled "Japanische Lieder"

and even correct aspects of Müller's introductory coverage of Japanese music,[146] but none seriously takes up his main focus, his study of *gagaku*.

Shortly after arriving back in Germany – April 8, 1876, is the date Müller and his wife reached Berlin itself[147] – Müller was offering lectures based largely on Japan-related materials he had presented there and then published, primarily in the *Mittheilungen*. In early 1877, for instance, in connection with an exhibition of Japanese artifacts he had brought back from Japan at the Academy of Art (*Kunst-Akademie*) in Berlin,[148] he delivered, as the final lecture in a series on Japan shared with his colleague Dr. Funk, formerly also of the *Gesellschaft* in Tokyo (p. 42), one entitled "On Sino-Japanese Music." The catalogue for the Exhibition lists the lecture series as taking place in the exhibition venue itself:[149]

First lecture: Friday, 19 January: Pictures from Japanese Life.

Second lecture: Friday, 26 January: Japan and her Inhabitants.

Third lecture: Friday, 2 February: On Fengshui. Outline of the Sino-Japanese View of the World and Nature.

Fourth lecture: Friday, 9 February: On Sino-Japanese Music.

Lecture 2 will be held by Dr. Funk, the others by Dr. Müller.[150]

("Japanese Songs") and "Die japanische Nationalhymne" ("The Japanese National Anthem"); in Volume 4 (107; 129–145), Freiherr von Zedtwitz published "Japanische Musikstücke" ("Japanese Musical Pieces"), and in Volume 6 (376–391), R. Dittrich, his "Beiträge zur Kentniss der japanischen Musik" ("Contributions to Knowledge of Japanese Music"). Meanwhile, in the publication series of the English-language *Asiatic Society of Japan* over this same period – up until about 1890 – music was likewise frequently addressed. The Reverend Dr. Syle's "On Primitive Music, Especially that of Japan," was published in Volume 5, part 1 (170–179); Volume 7 (76–86) contained the Reverend P. V. Veeder's "Some Japanese Musical Intervals," and Volume 19 offered three articles on music, the first by the still well-known writer on Japanese music F. T. Piggott, "The Music of the Japanese, with Plates and Specimens of Melodies" (271–367), another by F. Du Bois, "The Gekkin Musical Scale with Specimen Melodies" (369–371), and a third by C. G. Knott, "Remarks on Japanese Musical Scales" (373–391).

[146] *The Japan Weekly News* for April 29, 1876, for instance, in its report for the *Asiatic Society of Japan*, lists a paper entitled "On the Musical Notation of the Chinese with its Counterpart in Japan," delivered by the Reverend E. W. Syle at a general meeting on April 19. But even more interestingly, it records at some length a Professor Ayrton's reporting at the same meeting – evidently with at least one instrument at hand – on experiments with instrumental tunings for the *shamisen*, *koto*, and *gekkin* that were carried out in his laboratory by a Mr. Takamine, compared against Müller's findings, and found partly to corroborate them, partly to disagree.

[147] Müller, "Tokio-Igaku (Dec. 1888)," 459.

[148] Scheer, "Dr. med. Leopold Müller – Biographie," 317–318.

[149] A copy is held among Müller's papers in the Landesarchiv Berlin, E Rep. 200–35, Nr. 51 (7).

[150] "Vorträge, welche im Ausstellungslokale gehalten werden. / 1. Vortrag: Freitag, den 19. Januar: Bilder aus dem japanischen Leben. / 2. Vortrag: Freitag, den 26. Januar: Japan und seine Bewohner. / 3. Vortrag: Freitag, den 2. Februar: Über den Feng-shui. Grundzüge

The exhibition was clearly a success and was even extended.[151] Not surprisingly, the catalogue records a considerably sized musical exhibit.[152] A complete section, "Section 7: Items relating to music," comprises: thirty-seven Chinese and Japanese items, of which, in all, thirty-one are musical instruments, including three different tuning-regulators, three types of *koto*, several drums, and both a Chinese and a Japanese mouth-organ; two sets of models of instruments; woodblock prints of musical entertainers; a music tutor, "Musikschule"; booklets with notations; and his eight-part full-score of *Goshōraku no kyū*. On request, the booklets, the score, and his "Notes" could be made available by a supervisor.[153] This collection was apparently a personal one, since the Tokyo museum's collection had not yet been relocated to Leipzig.

The impact of Müller's published "Notes" on the wider music scene and in the academic musicological domain of a Europe with expanding interest in Asia was likewise almost immediate. The internationally distributed weekly magazine for contemporary trends in music, the *Neue Zeitschrift für Musik* ("New Journal for Music"), founded in the early 1830s[154] and published in Leipzig, ran a whole series based on Müller's "Notes" over 1875–1876. These were written, "re-worked" (*bearbeitet*), by B. M. Kapri under the rubric "Ueber japanische Musik" ("On Japanese Music") and are indeed paraphrases, or digests – truncated, re-ordered, but otherwise scarcely altered versions – of the original essays, with brief introductions, and, this time, with some selected illustrations included.[155] Notable is a reproduction of the transcription of *Fudjiyu/Fujiue-ryū* for Japanese fiddle *kokyū*, made by Herr Westphal[156] from the performance by an unnamed blind musician and contained in the first of Müller's published essays (pp. 108–110). With its wide distribution, the *Neue Zeitschrift für Musik*

---

der chinesisch-japanischen Welt- und Naturanschauung. / 4. Vortrag: Freitag, den 9. Februar: Über die chinesisch-japanische Musik. / Den 2. Vortrag wird Herr Dr. Funk, die übrigen Herr Dr. Müller halten." Müller, *Katalog*, 2.

151 Neither exhibition catalogue nor further information about the exhibits is preserved in the Academy; the Archiv der Preußischen Akademie der Künste has only a short reference dealing with this extension of the Japanese exhibition of 1877: PrAdK 310, *Privatausstellungen und Veranstaltungen in der Akademie.- Enth. u.a.: Gesuch um Verlängerung der japanischen Ausstellung, 1877* (Bl. 35). We are indebted to Dr. Ulrike Möhlenbeck, Head of the Historical Archive of the Academy of Arts, Berlin, for searching this information out for us. The only copy of the catalogue known to us is preserved in the Landesarchiv Berlin (see note 149).

152 None of the actual exhibits seem to be preserved in an official collection in Berlin.

153 Items 432–469; ibid., 33–36.

154 By Robert Schumann, Friedrich Wieck, and Ludwig Schuncke.

155 Kapri, "Ueber japanische Musik"; *idem*, "Ueber japanische Musik"; Müller's circular pitch-diagram (his *Tonrose*, illustrations of "tuning forks" (pitch-regulators) and of a movable bridge for the *koto* are reproduced in the last installment, *idem*, "Ueber japanische Musik," Illustrations as "Extra-Beilage".

156 For a short Japanese appraisal of Alfred Westphal's contributions to Japanese science, see Ozawa, "Tōkyō Kaisei Gakkō: Alfred Westphal."

must be viewed as a player in the early dissemination of the gist of Müller's musical accounts, and particularly, perhaps, for the remarkable dissemination through various avenues of this fiddle-piece, Fudjiyu/Fujiue-ryū.

In 1878, the Florentine pianist, independent scholar of non-Western musical cultures, and collector of non-Western musical instruments Baron Alessandro Kraus *figlio* (1853–1931) – whom Daniele Sestili has (re-)introduced to the ethnomusicological world as a "pioneer ethnomusicologist"[157] – published in Italy what Sestili calls a "pamphlet," written in French and entitled La Musique au Japon.[158] Alessandro Kraus refers to Müller prominently at the outset of the opening chapter in the pamphlet and, for some of his coverage, clearly draws on information Müller had provided in "Notes." With real photographic prints of over eighty instruments from his own collection included, Kraus understandably seems to have had little cause to reproduce any of Müller's illustrations, although he does import, in an appendix, the transcription of the fiddle-piece Fudjiyu/Fujiue-ryū, correctly attributed to the ear and transcriptional skill of Alfred Westphal.

Sestili documents that, as an active participant in the intellectual life of Florence, Kraus was associated with many Florentine academic societies, including Oriental studies circles. Japanese instruments from his collection were shown as part of an "Oriental Exposition" held in tandem with the Fourth International Oriental Congress in Florence in September 1878. Moreover, on the opening evening of the Congress, a "Soirée de musique orientale," hosted by the Kraus family in their villa and performed by Italian musicians and singers using Western instruments, included in its twenty-five-item program a Japanese solo piece for violin. Although not attributed to its correct origin for the concert, it turns out to be a rendering of the transcription of Fudjiyu/Fujiue-ryū. Now, Westphal's original transcription, incorporated and separately signed[159] in Müller's "Notes," was reproduced, we recall, among the digest series on "Notes" run by the Neue Zeitschrift für Musik in 1875–1876, so two years or more earlier than Kraus's La Musique au Japon. It is also reproduced in an appendix to La Musique au Japon itself and duly acknowledged there to Westphal. The concert program, however, attributes it to the author, Kraus himself, announcing the item (and its performer) as follows:

---

[157] Sestili, "A Pioneer Work on Japanese Music."
[158] Kraus, La musique au Japon.
[159] Westphal, "Fudjiyu auf der Kokiu."

7. E Japanese Foudjiyou [Fudjiyu/Fujiue-ryū] for kokiou [kokyū]. Fiddle-solo of the Japanese blind musicians, extracted from La Musique au Japon by A. Kraus the Younger. Mr. Giovacchini.[160]

The exhibition of Japanese instruments was a highlight of the Florence Congress, as Sestili documents, and the concert an event that "must have caused much sensation in Italy."[161] Earlier that same year, at the Paris World Exhibition that began on the first day of May 1878, Kraus had been prevented by a managerial decision from exhibiting his Japanese instruments – "modern artifacts of that country"[162] – among a collection dedicated to ancient European instruments; he displayed the catalogue and copies of the photographs in La Musique au Japon only. The book itself, however, with (of interest to us) its documented indebtedness to Müller, was awarded a gold medal in the Musical Exposition contest and achieved thereafter substantial recognition in France.[163]

Müller and Kraus nothwithstanding, however, the enduringly dominant position in the early Western-language historiography of the field is a full-length monograph on Japanese music by English consultant in law to the Meiji government from 1887 to 1891 and member of the Asiatic Society of Japan, Sir Francis T. Piggott (1852–1925), whose The Music and Musical Instruments of Japan was published in 1893. "[F]requently posited among Japanese and Western (ethno)musicologists [...] [as] the pioneer survey written by a Western writer,"[164] Piggott's book, which, as he states in his preface, "appeared in its earliest form as a Paper read before the Asiatic Society of Japan, in January, 1891," is nowadays the work most commonly given as the earliest reliable account we have.[165] While Piggott acknowledges in the preface having made use of Kraus's La Musique de [sic] Japon, and so, by default, would have absorbed in any case some of Müller's contribution that way, he himself nowhere even mentions Müller, despite Kraus's own prominent acknowledgment. This omission is made all

---

[160] 7. E. Foudjiyou japonais pour Kokiou. Solo de Violon des musiciens aveugles japonais, extrait de "La Musique au Japon" de A. Kraus fils. M.ʳ Giovacchini. (Program reproduced in Sestili, "A Pioneer Work on Japanese Music," 90–91.)

[161] Ibid., 87.

[162] Ibid.

[163] In the study of Kraus and his La musique au Japon, Sestili laments that his contribution to Japanese musicology has been neglected in later scholarship, as we lament the overlooking of Müller's "Notes." Ibid., 98.

[164] Ibid., 83.

[165] For instance, it heads the chronological general bibliography for "Japan" in the Grove Music Online article (Shigeo Kishibe et al., "Japan." Grove Music Online. Oxford Music Online. Oxford University Press, http://www.oxfordmusiconline.com/article/grove/music/43335pg1.), and it is elevated also in Tsuge Gen'ichi's authorative 1986 resource for Western writings on Japanese music (Tsuge Gen'ichi, Japanese Music: An Annotated Bibliography, 80–81; 113) as "the pioneer work on Japanese music by a Westerner."

the more curious in the light of what we now know of the English translation series of "Notes" having been published in 1875–1876 in Yokohama by *The Japan Weekly Mail*, a newspaper closely connected to the *Asiatic Society of Japan*. Be that as it may, as a full-length monograph written almost twenty years on from Müller's "Notes," Piggott's study is, as to be expected, far more comprehensive and able to avail itself of scholarly advances since the mid 1870s. It lays particularly heavy emphasis on tone system and tunings for the *koto*, an interest taken up by Müller, too (pp. 94–97). As was the trend, it treats *gagaku* lightly, especially in comparison with Müller's essays.

To end with, the distinguished French scholar of East Asian cultures Maurice Courant (1865–1925) brings balance to evaluating those who had written before him in his brief historical coverage of the music of Japan, "Japon. Notice Historique," written in 1912 for the *Encyclopédie de la musique et dictionnaire du conservatoire* ("Encyclopedia of Music and Dictionary of the Conservatory").[166] This is the same publication that includes his well-known, book-length essay on the musics of China and Korea.[167] He remarks at the outset of his note that Japanese music had been the object of conscientious studies in German and English and that, not having had time himself in Japan to consult original works, he leans on these studies. His prefatory list of principal works consulted for his "Note" on Japan then comprises: all musical contributions to the German *Mittheilungen*, in other words all German articles cited above[168] along with Müller's "Notes" themselves; most of the English contributions to *Transactions* including the first paper by Piggott;[169] and Piggott's book *The Music and Musical Instruments of Japan*. Courant expresses his admiration for Piggott's "superb volume" then states in the same breath his reliance on the "indispensable basis" provided him by both pioneers, Piggott and Müller: "... this work, with that of Dr. Müller, forms the indispensible basis of our knowledge in Japanese Music."[170]

---

[166] Courant, "Japon."
[167] Idem, "Chine et Corée."
[168] See footnote 139, p. 41 and footnote 145, p. 42.
[169] See footnote 145, p. 42.
[170] "... cet ouvrage avec celui du Dr Müller forme la base indispensable de nos connaissances en musique japonaise." Idem, "Japon," 242.

"Notes" and the Berlin School of Comparative Musicology

> "Script [Notation] is always the strongest means to intellectualize music, to force a theoretical engagement."[171]

We now leave this sketch, roughly for the years covered by the Meiji period (1868–1912), of the early reception of "Notes" among Müller's target German-language readership of Europeans, in Japan and back in Europe – and that is all we offer, more is beyond the scope of our intent. Timewise, we turn back to our initial positioning of Müller's in situ perspectives on Japanese music and musical instruments as intended path-opening contributions to the early scholarly discourse on "other" musics. And we again place Müller's essays possibly as a foreshadow to Vergleichende Musikwissenschaft ("Comparative Musicology") that faded too quickly (p. 2). Not suprisingly we find that his work was in fact known among the early Berlin comparative musicologists. Indeed, "Notes" were expressly acknowledged for their "great thoroughness" (p. 51). Yet it seems that their full potential could not be accommodated in the direction these scholars were taking from the mid-1880s on. Scientific advances measuring pitch and musical interval had been brought to the field in 1885 by John Ellis's formative measuring in "cents";[172] and even earlier, in 1877, Edison had invented the phonograph. Müller's own concern with, and empirical investigations of, pitch, tonal system, instrumental tunings, and tuning-procedures using tuning-forks and frequency-relationships would have been of limited interest, perhaps, in this new "scientific" milieu. But, as we shall propose, their incomplete appreciation of the indigenous written notation as bearer of indigenous musical conceptualization was a missed opportunity, one to be perpetuated for the next eighty years at least.

Müller's "Notes" made tempered inroads, then, to the young discipline of Comparative Musicology, with one significant exception: for having provided tangible support for Carl Stumpf's taking up from the ancient Greek world the term "heterophony" and introducing it to this new field of musicology. Stumpf chose to reintroduce the term for the particular sort of musical behaviour he had observed personally in Berlin in a visiting Siamese tradition[173] and "read" in the full-score "analytic transcription"[174] of Dshioh-raku/Goshōraku [no kyū], the test-piece of in-

---

171 "Immer ist die Schrift das stärkste Mittel, die Musik zu intellektualisieren, eine theoretische Einstellung zu erzwingen." Hornbostel, "Melodie und Skala," 14.

172 Ellis, "On the Musical Scales of Various Nations"; Stock, "Alexander J. Ellis and His Place in the History of Ethnomusicology," see also; Steege, Helmholtz and the Modern Listener.

173 Stumpf, "Tonsystem und Musik der Siamesen," 127–32.

174 "It is done analytically," Harich-Schneider, A History of Japanese Music, 551.

strumental ensemble *gagaku* in Müller's final installment (pp. 242–244). If Alfred Westphal's transcription of the solo-fiddle piece Fudjiyu/Fujiue-ryū became a hit, and then spread among a lay audience in Europe (pp. 44–46), Müller's *gagaku* full-score, as in a mirror, became an obligatory scholarly reference point for Stumpf's heterophony.

Let us take up, briefly, Stumpf's reliance on Müller for what was one of his own major musical concerns, namely, his wide-ranging interest in simultaneity in musical processing in multipart musical traditions (*Vielstimmigkeit*, also *Mehrstimmigkeit* in his usage), a concern shared by his disciple then colleague Erich von Hornbostel (1877–1935),[175] and addressed by a number of other early scholars of "world musics."[176] In Die Anfänge der Musik ("The Beginnings of Music") of 1911, Stumpf explains his rationale for borrowing the ancient Greek term heterophony for the ensemble practice of playing a melody "as if several variations of a theme were played at the same time instead of one after another,"[177] and for his drawing on what was known of Asian ensemble traditions to substantiate his choice:

It seemed to me that Plato had meant with "heterophony" the simultaneous playing about a melody with variants, as happens with oriental peoples today, and therefore I suggested the name heterophony for this type of musical practice.[178]

In China, Japan, Indo-China, and the Sunda Islands there are complete orchestras that perform a melody somewhat as if several variations of a theme were played at the same time instead of one after another. The one instrument performs the theme unvaried, the other gives more or less free digressions. But overall the basic melody sounds through nevertheless.[179]

---

175 Hornbostel, "Über Mehrstimmigkeit in der außereuropäischen Musik."
176 Adler, "Über Heterophonie"; Lachmann, Musik des Orients, 84–91; Sachs, The Rise of Music, 145–148.
177 "... als wenn mehrere Variationen eines Themas zu gleicher Zeit statt nacheinander gespielt würden." Stumpf, Die Anfänge der Musik, 58–59.
178 "Es schien mir, das Plato mit 'Heterophonie' das gleichzeitige Umspielen einer Melodie durch Varianten gemeint habe, wie es bei orientalischen Völkern heute vorkommt, und darum schlug ich für diese Art der Musikübung den Namen Heterophonie vor." Ibid., 96.
179 "Es gibt in China, Japan, Hinterindien und den Sundainseln ganze Orchester, die eine Melodie ungefähr so vortragen, als wenn mehrere Variationen eines Themas zu gleicher Zeit statt nacheinander gespielt würden. Das eine Instrument trägt das Thema unverändert vor, das andere gibt mehr oder weniger freie Umschreibungen. Aber im Ganzen klingt doch die Grundmelodie durch." Ibid., 58–59.

He refers directly to Müller, alongside some others, including pioneer scholars of Javanese *gamelan*,[180] and he also references one of the earlier places in his own writings[181] where he had already drawn attention to Müller's full-score:

> Long before, Dr. Müller and von Zedtwitz had published Chinese and Japanese full-scores, Land and Groneman, Javanese [scores], from which this condition was to be inferred – as I mentioned also already in *Tonpsychologie.* II (1891), p. 402, by the way. Daniël de Lange, who is cited by Land-Groneman and by me ("Siamesen," p. 131), had also already quite correctly described this type of music-making.[182]

Volume two of Stumpf's *Tonpsychologie* was published in 1891, a full twenty years before *Die Anfänge der Musik*, and he makes an even earlier reference to Müller in 1886, in his review of Ellis's influential "On the Musical Scales of Various Nations."[183] But his own seminal article, "Tonsystem und Musik der Siamesen" ("Tonal system and Music of the Siamese"),[184] published in between, in 1901, is where he makes his fullest assessment of "Notes." There he estimates Müller's essays highly in general, noting that their thoroughness lends credulity to the *gagaku* full-score; he observes that this pioneering full-score is based on original Japanese notation ("deciphered according to the Japanese notation" [*nach der japanischen Notirung entziffert*] is what he actually writes):

> Until now, as far as I know, no exotic full-scores have been published except for one Japanese and two Javanese. The former, comprising 8 instruments, was deciphered according to the Japanese notation by Dr. Müller, personal physician to the Mikado. It belongs to the ancient "Gagaku-Music," only used still at court and stemming from Korea. A Japanese bandmaster studying at the Berlin Hochschule für Musik, whom I questioned about this score, didn't trust himself to give a more confident opinion about it, since he was not acquainted with this old

---

[180] Groneman, *De gamelan te Jogjakarta, uitgegeven, met eene voorrede over onze kennis der Javaansche muziek*; see also Terwen, "De Lange en de gamelan: een negentiende-eeuwse ontmoeting tussen Oost en West."

[181] Stumpf, *Tonpsychologie.*

[182] "Lange vorher hatten Dr. Müller und v. Zedtwitz chinesische und japanische, Land und Groneman javanische Partituren veröffentlicht, aus denen der Sachverhalt zu entnehmen war, die ich übrigens auch bereits Tonpsychol. II (1891) S. 402 erwähnte. Daniel de Lange, der von Land-Groneman und von mir (Siamesen S. 131) zitiert wird, hatte diese Art des Musizierens auch schon ganz richtig beschrieben."

[183] *Idem*, Review of Alexander J. Ellis, *On the Musical Scales of Various Nations.*

[184] *Idem*, "Tonsystem und Musik der Siamesen."

style of music, yet the rendition seemed to him likely trustworthy. The great thoroughness which shows itself in Dr. Müller's tract in general also inspires confidence.[185]

Yet even Müller's unique provision for this item of ensemble *gagaku* of the full set of instrumental parts in indigenous notations (from an "other" musical culture) upon which he had built the hybrid analytical transnotation-*cum*-amplification, which Stumpf leans on for his proposed heterophony, did not make the fuller impact it might have had at this time. What it harbors of indigenous musical thinking went unnoticed. These early scholars were concerned with capturing and fixing in Western staff-notation their newly made possible sound recordings – of musics often from "scriptless peoples" (*schriftlose Völker*), or in any case of musics transmitted without written support. So concerned were they with this task, for their own analyses and for the scholarly world of print, that an "other" analytical notation passed them by. This overlooking is perhaps all the more surprising given that Stumpf himself, having postulated in his "Siamese" study that securing reliable (trans-)notations was one of the main tasks for research of exotic music, embraced precisely how Müller had proceeded. Stumpf's recommendations read:

> In the main, however, to gain reliable notations two paths are followed: the one is made up of musicians in the country concerned training themselves in our music writing or also of transcription from an indigenous notation into ours taking place. The other is in phonographic recording. Wherever possible, of course, both methods are to be combined.[186]

Müller had certainly transnotated Dʃhioh raku/Goʃhōraku [no kyū] from indigenous notations into Western staff-notation; and, furthermore, for his final, Western-style

---

[185] "Bisher sind, soviel ich weiss, keine exotischen Partituren ausser einer japanischen und zwei javanischen veröffentlicht worden. Die erstere, aus 8 Instrumenten bestehend, ist von Dr. Müller, Leibarzt des Mikado, nach der japanischen Notirung entziffert. Sie gehört der uralten, nur am Hofe noch gebräuchlichen, aus Korea stammenden "Gagakku-Musik" an. Ein auf der Berliner Hochschule für Musik studierender japanischer Capellmeister, den ich über diese Partitur befragte, getraute sich nicht ein genaueres Urtheil darüber abzugeben, da ihm diese alte Musikweise nicht geläufig sei, doch schien ihm die Wiedergabe wohl glaubwürdig zu sein. Auch die grosse Gründlichkeit, die sich in der Abhandlung Dr. Müller's überhaupt kundgiebt, erweckt Zutrauen." Ibid., 127–128.
[186] "Hauptsächlich aber sind zur Gewinnung sicherer Notationen zwei Wege beschritten: der eine besteht darin, dass Musiker des betreffenden Landes sich auf unsere Notenschrift einüben oder auch dass Transscription aus einer einheimischen Notirung in unsere stattfindet. Der andere besteht in der phonographischen Aufnahme. Wo immer möglich sind natürlich beide Methoden zu verbinden." Ibid., 135.

full-score, he had partially amplified his transnotations, even if faultily in certain places, according to performance practice he had personally observed and heard.

Of epistemological and methodological relevance at this point in our discussion is an article by one of us (NT) on the Western impact on traditional music during the Meiji (1868–1912) and Taishō (1912–1926) periods. The article gives an account of a Japanese government-assigned transcription project (NT's term of description for the process) in Western notation that ran from 1907 on into the late 1920s[187] and that included, from early 1916 on, rendering ensemble *gagaku* into Western full-score format. It addresses not only cultural policy on music for this time, but – especially relevant for our interest in the earlier transnotational-*cum*-amplificatory activities of Müller at the Japanese court and then of the approach to transcription and to musical notations among the Berlin School of comparative musicologists – it describes the actual transferral process into Western staff-notation by the Japanese musicologists. The article casts the process as the "unification of [indigenous] notational systems into one that was regarded as 'scientific' and 'universal'."[188] In particular, the deliberate terminological choice of "scientific" and "universal" (with their implications of "more reliable" and "more relevant"?) may be worth keeping in mind for our approach to the attitudes to transcription, and by extension to notation, among the early comparative musicologists. (We note, in passing, that as article and bibliography indicate, Müller had been forgotten in Japan, too, by this time: his "Notes" play no part, his full-score for Dshioh-raku/Goshōraku [no kyū] likewise.)

It would take until the 1950s for it to gradually dawn on the Western scholarly imagination just how significant for world music history in general, and for *gagaku* in particular, the enduring practice and function of music writing in East Asia could be. For that was when Picken, faced with a single piece of Sino-Japanese *gagaku* notation, for the first time, it appears – and as he himself has told it – went on to recognize the fundamental melodic construct in present-day performance of a *tōgaku* item of *gagaku* as an ancient relic of Tang melody. This melody is inherent in the modern written parts for certain instruments in the ensemble[189] and functions structurally in the extremely slow and complex texture of modern performance practice in a manner akin to the working of the structural *cantus firmus* in fifteenth-century Europe. Yet the Picken discovery was also in a sense "delayed" until then. He also seems not to have known of Müller's contribution, or at least not to have perceived its potential significance, despite the coverage published in the various outlets we have mentioned, and even despite Curt Sachs's including part of Müller's

187 Terauchi, "Western Impact," 27–28.
188 As she elegantly puts it, "[the government] encouraged traditional genres to explain themselves using Western vocabulary." *Ibid.*, 14
189 Picken, "The New Oxford History of Music: Ancient and Oriental Music," 147.

full-score only ten years earlier, in *The Rise of Music in the Ancient World, East and West* of 1943. There, daunted by the prospect of transcribing a recording of *gagaku* himself, Sachs reproduced, untitled but acknowledged, an excerpt from Müller's full-score for *Goshōraku no kyū*.[190]

But without an accompanying sample of *notation*, the excerpt apparently made no mark on Picken at this stage. The vital facet of Picken's ultimate recognition of the ancient melodic structure intrinsic to the modern written notation was to be that the sample he did encounter, on a plate in Harich-Schneider's essay, "The Present Condition of Japanese Court Music" of 1953,[191] writes out, side by side, versions of a shared melody for two instruments, mouth-organ *shō* and four-stringed lute *gaku-biwa*, rather than the patterned chordal accompaniments of their modern performance idioms. Like Sachs, Picken could have accessed *gagaku* recordings by then, even if he had missed Müller's verbal explanations of what is added to the written in actual performance practice. He could have listened to the texture of performance where nowadays both these instruments execute "chords, not tunes," as he has since put it, their original melodies no longer sounding through as tunes. Harich-Schneider herself had in any case provided a full-score transcription of the piece in question, chordal structures included. Although overlooked in many an account of his scholarly work, Picken himself has stressed[192] that his first shock for the historiography of East Asian melody was seeing in Harich-Schneider's plate of notation the principle of heterophony preserved in writing for the *tōgaku* repertory of *gagaku* in the parts for two instruments, mouth-organ and lute, whose executions in performance are now chordal, not melodic.[193] The lively, ancient tune recoverable from their written heterophony, he proffers as a second shock for the discovery.

Stumpf, of course, if he had been working from Müller's full-score with less attention to its verbal explanations, would have seen only the transnotation in long note-values of the single notes of the written part for mouth-organ, not a representation of the series of complex cluster-chords erected on those notes in actual performance; in the full-score, Müller attempts representations for the chordal activities of lute and *koto* only. However, he explicitly states in "Notes" that the mouth-organ "really carries the melody" (p. 195), and elsewhere that "the principal note [in a mouth-organ cluster-chord] is further supported by the other instruments" (p. 203). Taking these statements together with the minimally amplified transnotations of the written reed-pipe- and flute-parts in the full-score (transnotations from written

---

[190] Sachs, *The Rise of Music*, 147.

[191] Harich-Schneider, "The Present Condition of Japanese Court Music," sixth plate inserted between pages 60 and 61.

[192] Knott, Markham, and Wolpert, *On the Road to Tang*.

[193] He refers to Müller's full-score precisely for its first revelation of the principle in *tōgaku* (Picken, "The New Oxford History of Music: Ancient and Oriental Music," 147).

parts based on conservative pitch-sets, we recall, not transcriptions from actual performance), it is not difficult to imagine that – in the absence back then of an available
sound example – Stumpf "saw" his idea of heterophony reconfirmed there, in the
three winds: with the mouth-organ as the instrument that "performs the theme
unvaried," the flute (and/or reed-pipe) as the other that "gives more or less free digressions," but overall with the basic melody "sounding through nevertheless" (p.
49, and note 179). After all, even Sachs, advantaged by sound in 1943 and preferring
to describe "the orchestra of the Mikado" as performing "in a very elaborate form of
polyphony," nevertheless states of the winds: "All three of these wind-instruments
play heterophonically."[194] Of the strings, moreover, and their (from Picken's viewpoint) obscuring patterned chordal additions, he writes: "Below this strident clamor,
the lute follows the same trend, in fourths or other chords, and the zither koto joins
in with a short, dry ostinato motive."[195] His accepting both Müller's mistaken register for the strings and his wrong representation of lute-drones, however, betrays that
he, too, like Stumpf, is relying heavily on "reading" the full-score at face-value, rather
than following his ears from a "listening." Nevertheless his observations underscore
the shock Picken experienced on realizing that chordal accretions to the written parts
for mouth-organ and lute conceal a deeper and slowly moving structural foundation,
one originally shared through the whole ensemble as a lively, coherent melody, as it
would eventually emerge from the earliest surviving documentation for tōgaku.

To return to the wider group of early comparative musicologists shows Stumpf's
positive evaluation of "Notes" echoed, and Müller's contribution on gagaku especially
noted, in studies of Stumpf's own sometime students, Otto Abraham and Erich von
Hornbostel. For instance, in the opening to their "Studien über das Tonsystem und
die Musik der Japaner" of 1903, a study that emanated from working directly with
a Japanese theatre group playing in Berlin in 1901, and that draws for its title and
approach on Stumpf's "Tonsystem und Musik der Siamesen" published that same
year, in 1901,[196] they write:

> There already exists a rather substantial literature on Japanese music.
> The oldest communications come from the missionaries Dr. Syle[197]
> and Dr. Veeder;[198] the latter also made some measurements on very
> old Japanese flutes with the help of a siren. We are indebted to a more

---

[194] Müller's access to – and perhaps reliance on – conservative pitch-sets for flute and reed-
pipe must be kept in mind, however, when evaluating his transnotations of these two
parts (see p. 30).

[195] Sachs, The Rise of Music, 147.

[196] Abraham had worked together with Stumpf on the recordings addressed in this earlier
paper when a Thai theatre group with their musicians were in Berlin in September 1900.

[197] Syle, "On Primitive Music: Especially that of Japan," 170–179.

[198] Veeder, "Some Japanese Musical Intervals," 76–85.

detailed work by Dr. Müller[199] for, among other things, the only communications on the court music (Gagaku), which became accessible to him as personal physician to the Mikado. F. T. Piggott[200] has given a very extensive account; the discussions on Japanese scales of F. Du Bois[201] and C. G. Knott[202] follow up on this.[203]

Specifically in respect of the study of musical instruments, the authors go on to list A. Kraus *figlio* and others; they document also a contribution on creation-myths for music and musical instruments in Japan;[204] and with regard to musical transcription, among other of the contributing members of the *Gesellschaft* and the *Asiatic Society* now familiar to us, Müller features once again for his *gagaku* full-score. To be noted is that now Müller's score is listed as having been "notated by ear." His reliance on indigenous *gagaku* notations for his full-score is entirely overlooked.

> Among others, V. Holtz, Fr. Eckert, v. Zedtwitz, Westphal and, in already mentioned works, Müller (orchestral score), Piggott, and Kraus have published Japanese musical pieces and songs notated by ear.[205]

In the body of the essay, Abraham and von Hornbostel quote Müller in various places, for instance, in connection with their consideration of concert-pitch,[206] which Müller had tested comparatively for *gagaku* with various European tuning-forks and Japanese pitch-regulators (p. 145). When communicating the system of ranks for musicians and the division of music into classical and popular,[207] their text is clearly

---

[199] Müller, "Einige Notizen (1)," 13–31; *idem*, "Einige Notizen (2)," 41–48; *idem*, "Einige Notizen (3)," 19–35.

[200] Piggott, *The Music and Musical Instruments of Japan*; *idem*, "The Music of the Japanese, with Plates and Specimens of the Melody," 271–368; *idem*, "The Music of Japan," 103–120; *idem*, "Principal Tunings of the Modern Japanese Koto"; *idem*, "The Japanese Musical Scale."

[201] Du Bois, "The Gekkin Musical Scale," 369–371.

[202] Knott, "Remarks on Japanese Musical Scales," 373–391.

[203] "Es existiert über japanische Musik schon eine ziemlich umfangreiche Literatur. Die ältesten Mitteilungen stammen von den Missionaren Dr. Syle[197] und Dr. Veeder[198]; letzterer machte auch einige Messungen an sehr alten japanischen Flöten mit Hilfe einer Sirene. Einer eingehenderen Arbeit von Dr. Müller[199] verdanken wir u.a. die einzigen Mitteilungen über die Hofmusik (Gagaku), die ihm als Leibarzt des Mikado zugänglich wurde. Eine sehr ausführliche Darstellung hat F. T. Piggott[200] gegeben; an diese schliessen sich die Diskussionen über die japanischen Tonleitern von F. Du Bois[201] und C. G. Knott[202] an." Abraham and Hornbostel, "Studien über das Tonsystem und die Musik der Japaner," 303.

[204] *Ibid.*, 182.

[205] "Nach dem Gehör notierte japanische Musikstücke und Lieder haben u.a. V. Holtz, Fr. Eckert, v. Zedtwitz, Westphal und in bereits erwähnten Arbeiten Müller (Orchesterpartitur), Piggott und Kraus publiciert." *Ibid.*

[206] *Ibid.*, 308, footnote 1.

[207] *Ibid.*, 210.

close to Müller, even if this is the result of having worked with one or another of the digests we have mentioned, be it in Kraus's *La Musique au Japon*, or from elsewhere. But with Abraham and von Hornbostel, as with Stumpf, it is again *gagaku* as heterophony[208] which is singled out from Müller's essays via that important and evidently eye-catching ensemble full-score for *Goshōraku no kyū*. Much later, in 1909, but nevertheless two years before Stumpf's *Die Anfänge der Musik*, von Hornbostel would present to the *Congress of the International Musicological Society* in Vienna, the Berlin School's views on multivoiced musical practices (*Mehrstimmigkeit*), including on heterophony, where he would once again bring up Müller's full-score.[209]

Of course, the one thing Müller could not have done in Japan in the early to mid-1870s was document his music studies in sound – had these studies been his empirical testings of tuning procedures, of performance tempos, of cluster-chord make-up for the *shō*, or of ensemble performance of his test-piece for *gagaku*. As we have noted, *gagaku* remained a music unfamiliar in Europe for long after Müller. Conversely, after Edison and the phonograph in 1877, the early comparative musicologists or their colleagues in the field could do just this. In "Über die Bedeutung des Phonographen für vergleichende Musikwissenschaft" ("On the Significance of the Phonograph for Comparative Musicology"), published in 1904 but based on a presentation in June the year before, Abraham and von Hornbostel, in a sense reinforcing Stumpf's 1901 recommendations for securing reliable transcriptions from the field (see p. 51), once more mention Müller's *gagaku* studies. This is in connection with what they deem the "noteworthiness" of "... the records of intelligent indigenous people or of people who had resided for a long time in the country."[210] But it is Stumpf's own comments on his former students' study and evaluation of the value of the phonograph, recorded from the discussion of the original presentation in 1903, that are the most valuable for us now for what they reveal about the Berlin School's attitude towards transcriptions provided in travel reports in the days before the phonograph, and for preserving his further recommendation that these notations only be drawn upon when they have been compared with reliable transcriptions obtained via the phonograph:[211]

> For when there were still no phonographs one was limited to notations made by ear [transcriptions] contained in travel reports, and

---

208 Or to be precise a sub-category that these authors liken to *Discantus* and for whose melodic behavior around a base melody they introduce the word *umranken* "to entwine around [someone or something]."

209 Hornbostel, "Über Mehrstimmigkeit in der außereuropäischen Musik."

210 "... die Aufzeichnungen von intelligenten Eingeborenen oder Leute, die sich lange Zeit im Lande aufgehalten haben." Abraham and Hornbostel, "Bedeutung des Phonographen," 226.

211 Ibid., 234–235.

these suffer from many maladies. Even for a very practiced ear it is
often impossible to securely grasp such unfamiliar tunes and to bring
them into notes [notation], so much more so then for an acoustically
not particularly pre-trained traveler. It is because of this that also the
many [field-]notes which I have collected in the course of the years
with the help of ethnographers and geographers have become pretty
much wastepaper for the moment – I say: for the moment; because
only once we have made exact studies with help of phonographs and
our acoustic machines will we also consult the earlier notations, and
so will be able to isolate the reliable from the unreliable. Some, hope-
fully many, will then turn out to be still useful.[212]

Stumpf, although accepting of Müller's full-score as support for his suggested
heterophony and well aware that Müller had "deciphered" Japanese notations for
this score, is wary overall, it seems in 1903, of the earlier, non-professional field transcription (and, by extension, of the non-professional field transnotation?) untested
by science, unmatched to the acid-tested version of the phonograph. There was no
recording of Müller's piece. In the gaping absence of the sound of gagaku, it is perhaps
this attitude – an attitude favoring a "scientific" and perceived "neutral" transcription from a recording, and not unrelated to that held about the only slightly later
Japanese transcription-assignment that encouraged traditional genres to "explain
themselves by using Western vocabulary" (p. 52) – that may help explain why Müller's
musical studies, reported by Stumpf as "likely trustworthy" (wohl glaubwürdig [p. 51]),
were ultimately not to be followed up as they might have been. In addition, and in
the light of Stumpf's stance vis-à-vis pre-phonograph transcriptions from travelers
in the field, it is of interest that in 1910, it was on the expressed wish of von Hornbostel
himself, by then head of the Berlin Phonogram Archive, that Heinrich Werkmeister,[213] resident music teacher in Japan, with the "relevant connections,"[214] was to

---

[212] "Denn als es noch keine Phonographen gab, war man auf die in Reiseberichten ent-
haltenen, nach dem Gehör aufgenommenen Notierungen beschränkt, und diese leiden
an vielen Übelständen. Es ist selbst für ein sehr geübtes Ohr oft unmöglich, solche fremd-
artigen Weisen sicher aufzufassen und in Noten zu bringen, umsomehr für einen akus-
tisch nicht besonders vorgebildeten Reisenden. Deshalb sind auch die vielen Notizen,
die ich mir im Laufe der Jahre aus solchen Reiseberichten mit Hilfe von Ethnologen und
Geographen gesammelt habe, augenblicklich ziemlich Makulatur geworden – ich sage:
augenblicklich; denn wenn wir erst einmal die genauen Studien mit Hilfe der Phonographen und unserer Akustischen Apparate gemacht haben, dann werden wir ja auch
die früheren Notationen heranziehen, und so das Zuverlässige von den Unzuverlässi-
gen sondern können. Manches, hoffentlich Vieles, wird sich dann noch als brauchbar
erweisen." Ibid., 234–235.
[213] 1883–1936; a cellist, Werkmeister was a professor at the Tōkyō Kunitachi Conservatory.
[214] Fritsch, "Walzenaufnahmen japanischer Musik (1901–1913)," 27.

make for him phonograph recordings of *gagaku*, performed by a small ensemble of three wind instruments;[215] von Hornbostel received the wax-cylinders with the recordings in October 1911.[216]

In the final count, though, Müller's pioneering *gagaku* full-score in Western staff-notation along with its supporting Sino-Japanese notations and their explanations were to be viewed selectively, then left hanging in the air, by these early comparative musicologists and their successors – both before, and for a considerable time after, gaining access to *gagaku* recordings (right up into the 1950s with the attention of Eta Harich-Schneider and Laurence Picken). The reason may hinge less on a Stumpfian distrust of Müller's non-professional transcriptional accuracy, for the supposed performance idiom some came to assume stood as the source of that full-score,[217] than on an attitude to a vastly unfamiliar musical script and what it might have meant to its Japanese users in transmission and performance. And this transpired despite Müller's detailed introductions to the Sino-Japanese notations that stood behind his full-score, despite his part-by-part guide to their individual readings and/or to their representations (and eventual performance-amplifications) in that full-score – itself a sort of mandatory "study score" offered as a reader's key to unlocking those indigenous notations, as we have proposed (p. 37). They chose to read, and to draw their conclusions from, the full-score for *gagaku* as they might have for a Western orchestral full-score.

In the conclusion to an article in 2006, "Comparative and Systematic Musicology in Relation to Ethnomusicology: A Historical and Methodological Survey," Albrecht Schneider may have formulated something that links us back to a fundamental interest of Comparative Musicology that is relevant to why neither the potentially significant principles that ground Müller's hybrid (transnotation-*cum*-transcription) full-score for *Goshōraku no kyū*, nor his contributions on *gagaku* in general, made it through any further in the early approaches and scholarship of Comparative Musicology other than – albeit importantly – as support for the dynamic process of heterophony. For, charged there with summarizing the philosophies and achievements of Comparative Musicology, Schneider isolates a primary interest in the analysis of musical structure: "Comparative studies in many cases have been, and continue to

---

215 The performance Isabella Bird attended at the home of Ernest Satow in 1878, likely also of *gagaku*, was also for a small ensemble. See p. 40.

216 Fritsch, "Walzenaufnahmen japanischer Musik (1901–1913)"; idem, "Some Reflections on the Early Wax Cylinder Recordings of Japanese Music in the Berlin Phonogramm Archive (Germany)."

217 Abraham and Hornbostel, for instance, list Müller's full-score "notated by ear" (*nach dem Gehör notiert.*) See p. 55.

be, first of all analytical studies of musical structures which are regarded as intrinsic order that can be detected, and described in a rational way."[218]

And back in 1912, although in an overall context of concern for limiting effects of notation, von Hornbostel had already laid out, in his "Melodie und Skala" ("Melody and Scale"), that the materiality of music writing (Notenschrift, literally, "script for notes," we recall) in its abstraction from the dynamic – in its simplifying and schematicizing – encourages and facilitates analysis:

> It [notation] detaches the work of art from maker and from performer and makes it into a thing that one gives and takes like any other. It abstracts from the living, momentary nuance, which it cannot at all reproduce, or only from afar through tedious circumlocution. In that way it shifts the focus to that which is accessible to analysis and conceptualization, to the physically given, the notes and their acoustic and durational relations which, in the spirit of theory, it simplifies and schematicizes. What lies far apart temporally, it brings together before the eye, [an eye] that demands regular order, even also in detail where the ear alone had never missed it. ... Script is always the strongest means to intellectualize music, to force a theoretical engagement.[219]

Unintentionally in the light of his thesis of concern, von Hornbostel nevertheless exposes for us thereby, we suggest, that, although Müller's full-score in Western staff-notation encouraged the "theoretical engagement" that yielded support for the concept of heterophony, what we would like to identify as a fear of the foreign notation, of the indigenous "script for notes," prevented grounding this intellectualization from "outside" with evidence for conceptualization from "inside." This fear may have been what was in the way of early Comparative Musicology's recognizing, despite Müller's verbal explanations, that it is, in a sense, abstraction of Schneider's musical structure that certain indigenous gagaku notations provide, and so what Müller in that transnotated full-score and its explanations had offered. What the

---

[218] Schneider, "Comparative / Systematic Musicology and Ethnomusicology," 254.

[219] "Sie [die Notenschrift] löst das Kunstwerk vom Schaffenden und vom Ausführenden und macht es zu einem Ding, das man gibt und nimmt, wie ein anderes. Sie abstrahiert von der lebendigen augenblicklichen Nuance, die sie gar nicht oder doch nur von ferne durch mühsame Umschreibung wiedergeben kann. So verlegt sie den Schwerpunkt auf das, was der Analyse und begrifflicher Fassung zugänglich ist, auf das physikalisch Gegebene, die Töne und ihre akustischen und zeitlichen Relationen, die sie im Sinne der Theorie vereinfacht und schematisiert. Das zeitlich Auseinanderliegende bringt sie zusammen vor das Auge, das regelmäßige Ordnung auch noch im Detail verlangt, wo sie das Ohr allein nie vermißt hätte. ... Immer ist die Schrift das stärkste Mittel, die Musik zu intellektualisieren, eine theoretische Einstellung zu erzwingen." Hornbostel, "Melodie und Skala," 13–14.

comparative musicologists did not realize they had there in transnotation was, so
to speak, a (pre-)analysis of the intrinsic order of an eventual sounding edifice.[220]
Admittedly, it would take until the 1950s and Picken's restriction to that very "script
for notes" – to the written parts for the tōgaku repertory of gagaku, with deliberate
exclusion, for their reading, of the contemporary idioms of dynamic performance
practice – for this recognition to be made and its consequences followed up. But the
raw materials for Picken's far-seeing proposal had lain expressed but dormant in
Müller's illustrations, explanations, and full-score in "Notes" for a long, long time
beforehand.

By making "Notes" available in Japanese, and to the English language world
now dominant in scholarly discourse in our field, it is our hope that Leopold Müller's
later nineteenth-century German essays on Japanese music and musical instruments
might be accorded a place hitherto denied to them for their having been forgotten.
What Bruno Nettl has gathered together as effects of war – the associated dissolution
of Comparative Musicology, and, specifically, as a post-World War II wish, during the
1950s especially, a desire to create distance from earlier German-language scholarship,
– may be partly to blame for the neglect among English-language readers.[221] But
on either side of that mid-twentieth-century hiatus, in a certain musical notation
we detect another split-barrier to Müller's focal study of gagaku: a "script for notes"
that was too unfamiliar to reach the analytical interests of the one (of the early comparative musicologist), and so familiar for the other (for the traditionalist [post-war]
Japanese performer or performance-influenced scholar) as to function tacitly and
long "non-intellectualized." This recalls, too, Müller's own realization that practices
of gagaku transmission would not easily lend themselves to explication. Although
Müller took great pains to elucidate this "script" (in its various manisfestations as
"script for the grasp") and to "show" its working principles, it was skirted unrecog-
nized for its indigenous structural "analysis" by the comparative musicologists of
the Berlin School. Picked up by Picken in the 1950s for the fundamental and archaic
melodic structure it conveys, and further substantiated by his Cambridge Group in
the 1970s and '80s as preserving an ancient melody shared heterophonically through
the early tōgaku ensemble and still there as "deep structure" in performance practice today,[222] it is only of late earning acceptance as such among gagaku scholars in
Japan itself.[223] Although some are now combing through the gagaku scholarship
for earlier traces of such recognition for this fundamental structure from within
Japanese musicology, perhaps wishing to distance themselves, in turn, from yet

[220] Widdess, "Historical Ethnomusicology," 225–226.
[221] Nettl, Nettl's Elephant, 82–83; see also Savage and Brown, "Toward a New Comparative
      Musicology," 185.
[222] Terauchi, "Surface and Deep Structure in Tōgaku."
[223] Ibid., 20.

another conflict set in flames by the initially highly controversial work of the Cambridge Group,[224] these scholars and closer colleagues have still, to our knowledge, no more seriously entertained Müller's "Notes" published in Japan than we had, until lately, for the *Tang Music Project* (EJM/RFW)[225] and for a first Müller essay published in Japan (NT).[226] And so, having decided that leaving Müller the last word in our Preface to re-presenting his "Notes" might be the best we can do for those notes, we translate for him herewith the optimistic closing sentence to his account of his time in Japan in "Tokio-Igaku": "Still often I think with pleasure of the time of bracing work, cheerful accomplishment, and eventful living in Japan. Would that I am also warmly remembered there!"[227]

[224] David Hughes, in a recent summary of the early Cambridge-based work of what he calls the "Picken School," includes an account of recent reaction in Japan to its findings: "Over time, however, it seems that the Picken approach has been absorbed and largely accepted, even if without acknowledging that it derived from Cambridge rather from Japanese scholars in Japan. In 2000, when I asked one respected Japanese musicologist (not a *tōgaku* researcher) for his opinion of the Picken School findings he said: 'Oh we (*wareware*, "we Japanese") already knew all that.'" Hughes, "The Picken School," 235.

[225] Starting with Wolpert, "Metronomes, Matrices, and Other Musical Monsters"; see also *idem*, "'Einige Notizen über die japanische Musik': Dr. Leopold Müller's Account of Music in Early Meiji Japan"; Markham, "Extrapolating Intent in Leopold Müller's Empirical Study of *Gagaku* in Early Meiji Japan."

[226] Terauchi, "A Study on 'Einige Notizen über japanische Musik'."

[227] "Noch oft denke ich mit Freuden an die Zeit frischer Arbeit, frohen Schaffens und bewegten Lebens in Japan. Möge man auch meiner sich dort freundlich erinnern!" Müller, "Tokio-Igaku (Dec. 1888)," 459.

Dr. Leopold Müller's Collaborators and Meiji Japan (1868–1912)

Naoko Terauchi

Dr. Leopold Müller (1824–1893)[228] needed various people's help to conduct his musicological research in early Meiji Japan (1868–1912) and write "Einige Notizen über die japanische Musik" ("Some Notes on Japanese Music"), published serially in the *Mittheilungen der deutschen Gesellschaft für Natur- und Völkerkunde Ostasiens* (henceforth *Mittheilungen*) as three essays, in 1874, 1875, and 1876 (referred to from now on collectively as "Notes"). Indeed, scattered through his essays are several persons' names, both foreign and Japanese. If we take the background of that time in Japan into consideration, it is quite understandable that these encounters were inevitable. This essay tracks in "Notes" persons who assisted Müller's research in Japan or directly gave him information on Japanese music, outlines briefly how these personages related to the new social movements in the early Meiji period, and evaluates the special position in this social and cultural context of Müller's focal interest: the instruments, music, and systems of transmission for *gagaku* (Japanese Imperial court music).

When Müller came to Japan in late August 1871, he had been hired by the Japanese government as an *oyatoi gaikokujin* (foreign advisor).[229] He taught medicine at the Daigaku Tōkō (Eastern College, the Medical Academy) until 1874. After his contract expired, he stayed on in Tokyo as a physician to the Emperor, until he finally left on October 25, 1875.[230] Japan, right after the Meiji Restoration (1868), had just begun to work on the construction of "modern Japan," accepting various branches of Western knowledge and adopting all manner of Western technologies. It was also in the midst of reforming traditional cultures and systems. The "Notes" show that the people

---

[228] Scheer, "Dr. med. Leopold Müller – Biographie," 285, fn. 1.

[229] Up until the middle of the Meiji period, more than 2,500 foreigners were invited as advisors, mostly by the Japanese government, to bring Western scholarship and technologies into Japan. Their fields of expertise included education, arts, law, diplomacy, science, technology, and military affairs.

[230] Müller, *Tōkyō-Igaku*, 81 (Japanese translation).

whom Müller met were largely from among those who promoted the construction of "modern Japan."

Müller enthusiastically conducted research on Japanese traditional music, in addition to teaching at the Medical Academy, research for which he needed many coordinators or informants. It seems he made the most of his privileged status as a governmental foreign advisor and then as Imperial physician, and asked officials as well as scholars to introduce him to musicians. In his own words, he reveals that "through my status as a medical doctor, I successfully got permission from various noble officials and scholars to conduct detailed research on musical instruments." (For the original German, see p. 79.)[231] In his first installment of "Notes," published in 1874, we find, for instance, the names of several persons associated with an episode about hearing a Japanese traditional piece for kokyū (Japanese fiddle) that was then transcribed into Western staff-notation and played back by violin. We encounter a "Mr. Westphal," a "Mr. Holtz," a "Dr. Funk," and a "Mr. Miyake," as well as an unnamed "blind musician":

> I owe this transcription as well as the calculation of frequencies to a mathematics teacher Mr. Westphal. (To me, he is a great supporter with unlimited kindness, like Mr. Holtz and Dr. Funk. Finally, I would express my warmest thanks to Mr. Miyake, whose efforts enabled me to carry out my research.) After he [Westphal] transcribed the piece into staff-notation, he played it on violin and let the blind musician hear it. The musician felt happy and evaluated the performance highly. (For the original German, see p. 102ff.)

Müller presumably asked Westphal to calculate frequencies (of pitches) and transcribe some Japanese tunes into Western staff-notation. But it is not clear from the description above how Mr. Holtz and Dr. Funk may have helped him. Mr. Miyake looks like the only Japanese here who might have introduced Japanese musicians to Müller, or served as an interpreter.

"Mr. Westphal" can be identified as Alfred Julius Westphal (1850–1924)[232] who was also one of the foreign advisors and taught mathematics from 1874 to 1875 at the Tōkyō Kaisei Gakkō (College of Law, Chemistry, and Technology).[233] Westphal

---

[231] All English translations in this essay are my own (NT); accordingly, they differ slightly here and there from the parallel German-English translation-section in our volume.

[232] Ozawa, "Tōkyō Kaisei Gakkō: Alfred Westphal."

[233] The Bureau of Personnel of the University of Tokyo has kept documents related to foreign advisors. These are available as microfilm at the General Library of the University. The records until 1889 are published in Higashi Ajia Bunka Kenkyū Senta, *Shiryō oyatoi gaikokujin*. Westphal is on p. 158 in the *List of foreign advisors*.

published several articles on Japanese and Chinese calculators and the history of Japanese mathematics in the Mittheilungen.[234] The kokyū piece he transcribed for Müller is titled in "Notes" as Fudjiyu (or, for the transcription itself, Fudjiyu auf der Kokiu), although Fudjiyu is actually not the title of a piece but indicates the Fujiue-ryū, a school of kokyū-playing. The Fujiue-ryū was established in Edo in the middle of the eighteenth century by a master Fujiue Kengyō, who developed the four-stringed kokyū out of the ordinary three-stringed type. The school had been preserved by keeping close connection to the Yamada-ryū, a school of koto (zither) music. According to Müller's description, foreign visitors rarely had the chance to hear such music at that time, and they invited musicians on 13 June 1874[235] to play at a regular meeting of the Deutsche Gesellschaft für Natur- und Völkerkunde Ostasiens ("German Society for Natural History and Ethnology of East Asia" (henceforth Gesellschaft)). Of the "blind musician" himself, Müller states that he is the only kokyū player in Edo (see p. 102). At the beginning of the Meiji period, there was indeed a well-known kokyū player named Yamamuro Yasuyoshi (1839–1907). Though Müller does not refer to this name, it is highly possible that the "blind musician" was Yamamuro. Evidently the musician also played another piece on that occasion, one given as Shohoyu in "Notes." This too seems to refer to the name of another school of kokyū-playing, the Shōō-ryū, established in the late Edo period (1603–1868), with its origins in Nagoya.

"Victor Holtz" (1846–1919), whose speciality was pedagogy, was also a foreign advisor from 1871 to 1874. He taught at both the Daigaku Nankō (Southern College) and the Tōkyō Igakkō (Tokyo Medical Academy, which had changed its name in the course of its existence from the earlier Daigaku Tōkō).[236] Holtz reported on Japanese popular songs and Japanese chess in the Mittheilungen.[237] In the former article, three songs were introduced in Western staff-notation with lyrics; the first was a widely spread children's song, a kazoe-uta ("counting song"), the second and third were popular songs accompanied by shamisen (three-stringed lute), usually sung by geisha.

[234] Westphal, "Über die chinesisch-japanische Rechenmaschine"; idem, "Über das Wahrsagen auf der Rechenmaschine"; idem, "Über die chinesische Swan-Pan"; idem, "Beitrag zur Geschichte der Mathematik in Japan."

[235] See p. 19.

[236] Higashi Ajia Bunka Kenkyū Senta, Shiryō oyatoi gaikokujin, 417. Holtz's letters describing his stay in Tokyo are held in the Landeshauptarchiv Koblenz – Bestand 405, Nr. 4363; a transcription is available at http://ome-boppard.de/bericht-des-lehrers-viktor-holtz/ (Last accessed 2015-07-17).

[237] Holtz, "Zwei japanische Lieder"; idem, "Das japanische Schachspiel"; idem, "Japanische Lieder."

"Dr. Funk" can be identified as Hermann Funk (1844?–?),[238] who taught German and Latin from 1873 to 1876, likewise as a foreign advisor, at the Tokyo Medical Academy. He was also a member of the *Gesellschaft* and wrote several articles on Japanese tea ceremony, fortune telling using tortoise shells, and exorcism.[239] Funk seems to have been interested in traditional Japanese religion or belief systems.

According to Müller's own account of his time in Japan, published after he went back to Europe as "Tokio-Igaku" ("Tokio-Igaku: Skizzen und Erinnerungen aus der Zeit des geistigen Umschwungs in Japan, 1871–1876"),[240] "Mr. Miyake" was Miyake Hiizu (1848–1938), who was evidently fluent in both German and English, and who served as a translator at the Academy during the period of Müller's stay. Miyake also published in the *Mittheilungen* – in fact, among his several articles on midwifery, one is in collaboration with Müller.[241] He was a son of Miyake Gonsai (1817–1867), a scholar of Dutch medicine in the late Edo period. In 1863, he was sent to Europe as part of a mission for the Tokugawa Shogunate, and later undertook British studies with James C. Hepburn[242] and medical studies with Alexander Weddle[243] in Yokohama. He was hired to the Academy in 1870, and in 1874 became Deputy Principal of what was by then called the Tokyo Medical Academy. The Museum of the University of Tokyo has preserved among its special collections a substantial holding of medical items donated by the Miyake family.[244]

We find more names of intellectuals and musicians in Müller's second installment of "Notes" in 1875. The following is a report of a meeting with *gagaku* musicians when he visited the Gagaku Kyoku (Bureau of Gagaku), just established in 1870:[245]

> I made a comparison with the tuning-pipe of the Bureau and one of
> my own property, which is 160 years old. When I took my tuning-pipe
> out, one of the musicians suddenly declared with joy that he was an

---

[238] Higashi Ajia Bunka Kenkyū Senta, *Shiryō oyatoi gaikokujin*, 417. The dates of his birth and death are unknown. However, *Shiryō oyatoi gaikokujin*, 416, says Funk came to Japan in 1873 at the age of 28.

[239] Funk, "Über die japanischen Theegesellschaften Cha no ju"; *idem*, "Über japanische Gebete"; *idem*, "Über Wahrsagung aus dem Panzer der Schildkroete."

[240] Müller, "Tokio-Igaku (Nov. 1888)"; *idem*, "Tokio-Igaku (Dec. 1888)."

[241] Miyake and Müller, "Ueber die japanische Geburtshuelfe (1)"; *idem*, "Ueber die japanische Geburtshuelfe (2)"; *idem*, "Ueber die japanische Geburtshuelfe (3)."

[242] James C. Hepburn (1815–1911) was resident in Japan from September 1859 to October 1892. He conducted medical activity, propagated Christianity, edited a Japanese-English dictionary, and established the Meiji Gakuin mission school.

[243] Alexander Weddle, a former naval surgeon on the battleship *Stonewall*, opened a business at Yokohama (Takazawa Hiroshi, "ANEXCDOTA 32").

[244] Fujio, "Miyake korekushon no sekai."

[245] Established under the Grand Council of State; the forerunner of today's Kunaichō Gakubu (Bureau of Gagaku of the Imperial Household Agency).

eighth-generation descendant of the musician Ōhata Hirotame. They
still call themselves Ōhata. The tuning-pipe clearly matched with the
standard tuning. The lowest pitch of the new tuning-pipe in Paris
is d and therefore the 8th note is a. This coincides with the standard
tuning of the Mikado-music. Other tuning-forks for secular purposes
differ from it by up to nearly a whole tone. (For the original German,
see p. 145f.)

Here we come into contact with a musician who is stated to be an eighth-
generation descendant from Ōhata Hirotame. Ōhata, also known as Uzumasa or
Hata, is a clan of *gagaku* musicians that belonged to Shitennōji temple in Osaka.
There are four branch families under the Ōhata clan: Sono, Hayashi, Tōgi, and Oka.
According to *Jige kaden*,[246] a collection of genealogies of hereditary bureaucrats, there
indeed existed a musician Hayashi Hirotame (1638–1717), and his eighth-generation
descendant was Hayashi Hiromori (1831–1896), one of the composers of the present-
day national anthem *Kimigayo*. Hiromori was born a son of Hayashi Hirotomo but
was adopted by Hayashi Hironaru. Here Müller adds a footnote on the Ōhata family
in order to introduce the Japanese adoption system and its purpose of maintaining
family lineage:

To understand Japanese generations, we should always consider the
adoption system. This system contributes to keeping hereditary family professions. For example, if a son of a musician is adopted into a
medical family, the musician's family will accept another musician
to succeed in their profession. (For the original German, see p. 145.)

Müller gives accounts of several actual performances of *gagaku* he attended; at
least four kinds of performance are reported on in "Notes." In his final installment,
published in 1876, he tells how, one day, he was able to participate in a rehearsal
of singing. A man and a woman, both unnamed, were involved. Their song was
accompanied by *kagurabue* flute and *shakubyōshi* clappers. Müller says there was no
wagon (the indigenous six-stringed zither of Japan), but that it should have been
included. Müller's description is as follows:

The man and woman sang a monotonous song in unison in a slow
tempo. The man beat clappers on the first beat of every two measures.
At the end of the measure, always a loud and sharp note was beaten.

---

[246] Thirty-three volumes of genealogies of various hereditary professions compiled by
Mikami Kagefumi around 1844. It was printed in 1938 in *Nihon koten zenshū*. Volumes
10 to 13 are dedicated to families of *gagaku* musicians.

The kagurabue sounds impure and was almost in unison with the vocal melody. (For the original German, see, p. 198.)

Here, a woman is included in the singing. Müller seems to be observing a rehearsal of kagura-uta, a genre of sacred ritual song performed in the circle of higher-ranked nobles, not in that of hereditary court musicians. The song sounded monotonous to Müller, the kagurabue impure.

On another occasion Müller heard three pieces. For the first piece, he described the performance as follows:

> There are two singers. A leader beat shakubyōshi clappers, and in unison came one hichiriki [reed pipe] and one ryūteki [flute]. On the beat of the shakubyōshi, two biwa [lute] joined in. Two koto [zither] marked beats and made ornamentation. (For the original German, see p. 199.)

The song here seems to be one of the saibara.[247]

The second piece was played with shō (mouth-organ), ōteki (flute), and hichiriki (3 each), biwa, koto, taiko (big drum), kakko (small drum), and shōko (gong) (1 each). This seems to be a small sized tōgaku ensemble.[248]

For the third piece, the ensemble consisted of 6 players each for shō, ōteki, and hichiriki, 3 players each for biwa and koto, 1 each player for taiko, kakko, and shōko, giving a total of 27 musicians. This is larger than the standard present-day ensemble, which is composed of 16 musicians. Müller writes that only hichiriki, biwa, and koto remain until the end of the piece. The piece must have been in nokorigaku, a special performance style which repeats a melody three times and gradually reduces percussion and winds until finally biwa and koto close the music.

Müller also makes mention of the ending pattern in gagaku performance:

> "In these pieces, after the interval of the fifth, the fundamental tone comes as the ending. Same instruments are thoroughly in unison. In former times, it is said that they sometimes did it in a different way, but not now." (For the original German, see p. 200.)

---

[247] Saibara is one of the vocal genres of gagaku, accompanied by shō, hichiriki, ryūteki (ōteki), biwa, koto, and shakubyōshi. Usually sung in a small concert of aristocrats.

[248] Tōgaku is an instrumental ensemble of gagaku brought from China. There are two ways of performance of the ensemble: kangen (literally meaning "pipes and strings," that is, an instrumental ensemble) and bugaku (literally "dance and music"). Present-day standard kangen consists of shō, ōteki, and hichiriki (3 each), biwa, koto (2 each), taiko, kakko, and shōko (1 each), while bugaku consists of shō, ōteki, and hichiriki (4 or more each), and taiko, kakko, and shōko (1 each).

The explanation that "after the interval of the fifth, the fundamental tone comes as the ending" suggests the ending pattern called *tomede* today. For example, in a piece in *hyōjō* mode (fundamental note = E), the *shō* (mouth-organ) plays e''-e'''-b', followed by a long E note on *hichiriki* and *ryūteki*.

Returning to our interest in the people Müller's "Notes" show he worked with for his musicological research, we find a "Mr. Machida" in installment two where Müller mentions the *kin* (*qin* in Chinese). The *kin/qin*, a seven-stringed Chinese zither, was brought into Japan as early as the Nara period (710–794). A beautiful example from the eighth century has been preserved until today in the Shōsōin storage of Tōdaiji temple in Nara. The music of the *kin* flourished until Heian times (794–1192), but was forgotten afterwards. It was revived again in the Edo period (1603–1868) and was enjoyed mainly among *bunjin* literati who adored Chinese culture. Müller explains that this music was not popular (in the early Meiji period) and that only higher-ranked people or well-educated intellectuals knew the tradition. It is in this context that he mentions Mr. Machida as someone who gave him information about how to use (play) this instrument (p. 153). Mr. Machida can be identified as Machida Hisanari (1838–1897) who was hired as an official of the Southern College and later inaugurated as the first director of the Tokyo Imperial Museum.[249] (Further discussion of Machida's position is deferred until later.)

In the final installment of "Notes," we find yet another erudite personage, a "Mr. Ninagawa." Müller describes him as a well-known scholar and archaeologist (p. 190). This person is most likely Ninagawa Noritane (1835–1882) who acquired enormous knowledge on antiques and was hired by the government in the section for establishing a museum.[250] (Ninagawa is also discussed further, later.)

In a footnote in installment two, a "Dr. Wagner" appears.[251] Müller mentions that Wagner will write on the division of measurements of the Chinese and Japanese in the next issue of the *Mittheilungen*. He can be indentified as Dr. Gottfried Wagener (1831–1892), another of the foreign advisors, who three issues later actually published the essay that Müller anticipated.[252] Wagener came to Japan in 1871 and stayed there until his death in 1892. As his speciality was the manufacturing of porcelain and glassware, he taught in the College of Law, Chemistry, and Technology at Tokyo University and other institutions, and also was involved in a project to participate in the Vienna World Exposition.[253]

---

[249] Seki Hideo, *Hakubutsukan no tanjō: Machida Hisanari to Tōkyō Teishitsu Hakubutsukan.*
[250] Yonezaki Kiyomi, *Ninagawa Noritane Nara no sujimichi*; Tokyo National Museum, "140th Anniversary Thematic Exhibitions."
[251] See below, p. 144.
[252] Wagener, "Bemerkungen ueber die Theorie der chinesischen Musik und ihren Zusammenhang mit der Philosophie."
[253] Higashi Ajia Bunka Kenkyū Senta, *Shiryō oyatoi gaikokujin*, 473–474.

Then, there is "Mr. Stein" who provided Müller with knowledge of ancient Chinese musical thought along with some examples of Chinese music in Western staff-notation, and whose contribution to the Chinese section at very the end of the final essay Müller expressly acknowledges (p. 230). The history of this person is not clear. However, he registered in the Shanghai branch of the *Gesellschaft* and published an article in the *Mittheilungen* titled "Zur Vergleichung japanischer und chinesischer Musik" ("On Comparison of Chinese and Japanese Music"). In this article, three Chinese tunes are given: two, *Lieu-ye-ain* and *Tsi-Tschong*, are borrowed from a book by John Barrow, who was associated with the British Embassy in China in the late eighteenth century;[254] the third, for which a title is not provided, is his own transcription of a piece. There are some other musicians of *koto* or of Chinese music who helped Müller, but who they were is not clear.

Thus, we can identify a number of figures who supported Müller in writing his "Notes." Several were important not only to Müller for his musicological interests, but also to the nation. They were key persons of the period when social structure and cultural context were drastically changing. Let us take a brief look at this social and cultural context and then at the specific situation of *gagaku*, the musical tradition to which Müller dedicated such a large portion of his musicological description.

At the beginning of the Meiji period, the Japanese government tried to establish an Emperor-centered social system, and therefore Imperial rituals had to be reorganized, urgently. After a second visit to Tokyo in late March 1869,[255] the Emperor never returned to Kyoto, and Tokyo became a new capital in 1869. *Gagaku* musicians, traditionally based in Kyoto, Nara, and Osaka, were gradually called to Tokyo, where a new bureau of Gagaku, Gagaku Kyoku,[256] was established in 1870. Under the Bureau's supervision, various systematic reorganizations were carried out, among which were included the selection of a standard repertoire and the compilation of unified scores. The present-day Kunaichō Gakubu ("Bureau of Gagaku of the Imperial Household Agency") chooses *gagaku* pieces to play from the repertoire written in the *Meiji sentei-fu* ("Meiji Selection Score").[257] Though the first selection was formally completed in

---

[254] John Barrow (1764–1848) worked in the British Embassy to China during 1792–1794 as a private secretary to Sir Staunton (Barrow, *Travels in China*; Reed and Demattè, *China on Paper*).

[255] A first visit had been made from October to December, 1868.

[256] The Gagaku Kyoku changed its name to Shikiburyō Gagakuka (Department of Ceremonies, Bureau of Gagaku) in August 1871. Thereafter it changed its name several more times, finally fixing on Kunaishō Shikibushoku Gakubu (Ministry of Imperial Affairs, Department of Ceremonies, Bureau of Gagaku) in 1907. This name lasted until 1945. Nowadays the name used is Kunaichō Shikibushoku Gakubu (Agency of Imperial Affairs, Department of Ceremonies, Bureau of Gagaku).

[257] Three kinds of copies (hand-written manuscripts) have been preserved in the Kunaichō Gakubu. Each copy consists of more than 40 volumes, and each volume is labeled with a

1876, followed by an additional selection in 1888, compilation had been in progress already from 1870 on. A draft score, *Meiji san-nen gosentei gagaku zenpu* ("Complete Gagaku Score of the 3rd Year of Meiji") (hereafter *Gagaku zenpu*), has been preserved in the Kokuritsu Kōbunshokan (National Archives of Japan).[258] The "3rd year of Meiji" (1870) is actually not the finishing but the beginning year of compilation, as some parts of the surviving score were written in 1874.[259]

The *Gagaku zenpu* exhibits a characteristic that the *Meiji sentei-fu* does not. That characteristic is, namely, the provision of two versions employing two different notational systems, *honpu* ("original notation") and *kanafu* ("syllable notation"), for notating the *hichiriki* and *ryūteki* melodies.[260] *Honpu* writes down tablature-signs; while *kanafu* notates syllables of *shōga* (mnemonic sounds), which musicians sing to remember melodies, in a central column with small tablature-signs down the left side of the *shōga*. Historically, *honpu* is far older.[261] *Kanafu* appeared recently, in the Edo period. The fact that the two systems were employed in the draft *Gagaku zenpu* suggests the compilation was still in process until *Meiji sentei-fu* finally chose *kanafu* as the official version in 1876.

Among the illustrations Müller displays at the end of his final essay, Tafel/Plate XX, Fig. 1 and Fig. 2 (p. 256) are *honpu* for *ryūteki* and *hichiriki*, respectively, for *Goshōraku no kyū*; while Tafel/Plate XXI, Fig. 2 and Fig. 3 (p. 257) are the respective *kanafu* for the two instruments for that same piece. The period of Müller's stay in Japan (1871–1875) overlapped with the period of the work of compiling standard scores. Thus, the illustrations in "Notes" reflect this transitional situation, namely, parallel employment of *honpu* and *kanafu* in score-compilation. When Müller visited the Bureau, he must have observed tuning-pipes, instruments, and been given explanations about them. But he must have also been permitted to copy examples from the *Gagaku zenpu* while still in the process of compilation.

As mentioned before, Müller visited the Bureau of Gagaku and met Hayashi Hiromori and other musicians. According to the research of Tsukahara Yasuko,[262]

---

different name such as *Ryūteki chūsho-kyoku-fu* ("Middle and small pieces for *ryūteki* [flute]"), *Kagura-uta-fu* "Kagura songs," and so on. See Gamō Mitsuko, "Meiji sentei-fu," 205–238.

[258] Manuscripts in 18 volumes.

[259] For several parts, year and month of compilation are precisely indicated as December 1874.

[260] Scores of *hichiriki* (reed-pipe) in volumes 8 and 9 and scores of *ryūteki* (flute) in volumes 10 and 11, consist of two parts; the first part is that given in *honpu* tablature and the second part is the one in *kanafu* syllables.

[261] For example, the flute score *Shinsen gakufu* (also known as *Hakuga no fue-fu*) completed in 966 is given only in tablature. For more information see Hayashi, "Hakuga no fue-fu kō"; Marett, "Tunes Notated in Flute Tablature from a Japanese Source of the Tenth Century"; idem, "Tōgaku: Where Have the Tang Melodies Gone, and Where Have the New Melodies Come From?"

[262] Tsukahara Yasuko, *Kindai gagaku seido no kenkyū*, 47–50.

the highest rank of musicians in the Bureau between 1870 and 1877 was titled *dai-reijin* ("great musician"). The list of *dai-reijin* in the early Meiji is as follows:

1870 December: Tōgi Fuminari, Ono Tadanobu, Tsuji Chikatsura, Ue Sanetake, Tōgi Suenaga, Hayashi Hiromori

1871 August: Tōgi Fuminari, Ue Sanetake, Tōgi Suenaga, Hayashi Hiromori, Yamanoi Kageaya

1874 June: Ayanokōji Arikazu, Yotsutsuji Kinmasu, Ogimachi Saneatsu, Ue Sanetake, Tōgi Suenaga, Hayashi Hiromori, Yamanoi Kageaya[263]

1875 June: Ayanokōji Arikazu, Yotsutsuji Kinmasu, Ogimachi Saneatsu, Ue Sanetake, Tōgi Suenaga, Hayashi Hiromori, Yamanoi Kageaya

Since Hayashi Hiromori was ranked as *dai-reijin* from the beginning days of the Bureau, it is quite understandable that he attended to foreign guests like Müller on behalf of Bureau members.

Early in the Meiji period, reorganization of the transmission system and musical tradition was ongoing inside the Bureau. At the same time, the external dispatch of *gagaku* as a representative genre of Japanese traditional music was also an important task allotted to the Bureau. In the very early period, a "dispatch" was simply an attendance or explanation to the foreign visitors who occasionally came to the Bureau. However, when a "dispatch" was led by the government on a full scale, it developed into a real dispatch of musical instruments to World Expositions. In 1873, Japan participated in the Vienna World Exposition for the first time after the Meiji Restoration. A large number of art objects, including musical instruments, were sent out. Traditional musical instruments are often beautifully ornamented with painting, lacquer, inlay, or wrought metals. They are almost like art objects. However, the instruments dispatched to Vienna were not the Bureau's property. Individual musicians, instrument makers, or owners provided instruments, as is documented in a list of the articles sent:[264]

- *dadaiko* (big drum for outdoors) = Nikkō Rinnōji temple
- *taiko* (big drum), *kakko* (small drum), *shōko* (gong) = Uenoya Zenzō (instrument maker)
- *shō* (mouth-organ), *ōteki* (flute), *hichiriki* (reed-pipe), *komabue* (flute), *utabue* (*kagurabue*) (flute), *shakubyōshi* (clappers), *chōshibue* (tuning-pipes), *koto* (zither), *biwa* (lute) = Kanda Shigesuke (instrument maker)

---

[263] Ayanokōji, Yotsutsuji, and Ogimachi were of the higher-ranked nobles who had transmitted vocal genres until the end of Edo period and served here, in the Bureau, to teach songs to *gagaku* musicians.

[264] Tōkyō kokuritsu bunkazai kenkyūjo, *Meijiki bankoku hakurankai bijutsuhin shuppin mokuroku*.

· *wagon* (zither) = Yamanoi Kageaya (*gagaku* musician)

According to Tsukahara, the Bureau's overall commitment was realized for the Paris World Exposition of 1878.[265] For this the Bureau seriously and deliberately prepared a "music exhibition." In addition to instruments, the Bureau sent to Paris notations, illustrations of *bugaku* dance and an explanatory book. By using figures, illustrations, and verbal explanations, the Bureau tried to explain what kind of music was produced with the instruments displayed and what kind of dance was performed accompanied by that music, in order that the audience could not just "see" instruments but could also "understand" the music. *Gagaku* musicians, Ue Sanetake, Tōgi Suenaga, Hayashi Hiromori, and six other members of the Bureau, were in charge of selecting items or writing explanations.[266]

For Meiji Japan, participation in World Expositions and construction of a museum were among the symbolic projects for modernizing the nation. Inside Japan, a number of industrial promotion exhibitions were also held, as domestic versions of World Expositions and the construction of a permanent space for display or storage was needed. Machida Hisanari and Ninagawa Noritane, who appear in Müller's "Notes," were key persons in the materialization of Japan's participation in the Vienna World Exposition (preceded by a preliminary domestic exhibition at Yushima Sacred Hall in 1872), and they claimed the necessity of a museum. If the Bureau of Gagaku was involved in the movement for expositions or a museum, then Machida, Ninagawa, and *gagaku* musicians should quite naturally have been acquainted with one another.

Now that we have cursorily introduced the movement for expositions and a museum, we can look more closely at these two important men, Machida and Ninagawa, both of whom were among those who helped Müller in his musicological study. Machida was born in the Satsuma region. As he was delegated by the Fief of Satsuma to go to Britain in 1865 to study Western technology and culture, he was evidently good at English. He experienced the Paris World Exposition in 1867 and was familiar with Western expositions and museum systems. He was one of the chief persons involved in preparing for the Vienna World Exposition in 1873. He was inaugurated as the first director of the Tokyo Imperial Museum, the first national museum of Japan, in 1882. According to *Machida Hisanari Ryakuden* ("A Concise History of Machida Hisanari")[267] written by his brother, Machida was good at painting and playing the *ryūteki* flute of *gagaku*, which he had learned from the Imperial musician Yamanoi. Machida organized a *gagaku* concert on board a boat twice a year, in spring and autumn, inviting Imperial musicians to participate. Thus, he had

---

[265] Tsukahara, *Meiji kokka to gagaku.*
[266] Ibid., 143–150.
[267] Kadota Akira, "Machida Hisanari ryakuden."

established a close friendship with *gagaku* musicians, not only through a formal professional acquaintance when preparing the Exposition, but also through a private artistic mentor/protégé relationship.

Ninagawa Noritane was born to a family of half-sacred/half-secular priests who had served the Tōji-temple in Kyoto for generations. From his early years, he studied antiques and old customs and was hired by the Japanese government in 1869 for his vast knowledge. For the preparation of the Vienna Exposition of 1873, he conducted the year before, in 1872, a national investigation of treasures preserved mainly in shrines and temples of the Nagoya, Ise, and Kansai regions. The itinerary and articles investigated are reported in detail in his diary *Nara no sujimichi* ("A Way to Nara").[268] Though it is unclear whether Ninagawa formally learned *gagaku* or not, it seems that he had many opportunities to see and handle antique musical instruments in shrines and temples. In actuality, as a result of the investigation in 1872, he reported on various instruments in the Shōsōin treasure house of Tōdaiji and other places. Interestingly, Ninagawa left *kagurabue* (the flute used for *kagura*, the sacred music for the gods)[269] as offerings to shrines such as Atsuta, Ise, Kasuga, Tamukeyama, Isonokami, Tōnomine, and Yoshino, which he visited during the investigation of 1872. In *Nara no sujimichi* he introduces an episode relating that, during his investigation in Nara he himself one day played a flute and Machida a grass reed on the way down from Mount Wakakusa to the Torii gate of Kasuga shrine. This suggests that Ninagawa could indeed play flutes. The flutes he offered to the shrines might even have been of his own hand-making.

Ninagawa had close relationships with such foreign advisors as Alexander von Siebold (1846–1911)[270] and Edward S. Morse (1838–1925),[271] who placed their full confidence in him for his deep knowledge of antiques. Morse, in particular, purchased many ceramic wares based on the advice of Ninagawa.[272] Siebold was a member of the *Gesellschaft*. Registration is recorded (as of 27 February 1875) for both a "Freiherr von Siebold" and "Heinrich von Siebold." Freiherr von Siebold is Alexander von Siebold who was ennobled with the title of Freiherr in February 1870 by Emperor

---

[268] Reprinted in Yonezaki Kiyomi, *Ninagawa Noritane Nara no sujimichi*.

[269] He left a memorial note with each flute, which says, "I was ordered (by the government) to investigate treasures of shrines and temples in June 1872. Here I offer this flute and wish it would serve in *kagura* performance for a long time in the future." Ibid., 21.

[270] Son of Philipp Franz von Siebold (1796–1866), a physician and botanist. Alexander served as a translator in the British Consulate before he was hired as a foreign advisor by the Japanese government in 1870. He prepared for Japan's participation in the Vienna Exposition in 1873.

[271] A zoologist who found the Omori shell mound during the first scientific archaeological excavation in Japan. He stayed in Japan in 1877, 1878–1879, 1882–1883 and taught at Tokyo Imperial University.

[272] Morse, *Japan Day by Day*; Yonezaki Kiyomi, *Ninagawa Noritane Nara no sujimichi*, 438–453. Morse's porcelain collection is now in the Boston Museum.

Franz Joseph I of Austria-Hungary for his contribution in concluding a commercial treaty between Japan and Austria in 1869.[273] Heinrich (1852–1908) was his younger brother.

Almost all the people who helped Müller write "Notes" were important figures for constructing the culture and system of "modern Japan." Moreover, these people did not have a relationship solely with Müller but established multilateral connections with each other. Müller's "Notes" can be read not only as an invaluable documentation of the musical circumstances of early Meiji Japan, but also as a brilliant witness of cross-cultural communications between people who encountered each other coincidentally but with historical inevitability in early Meiji Japan.

---

[273] Imamiya, "Alexander von Siebold."

Leopold Müller

Einige Notizen über die japanische Musik

Some Notes on Japanese Music

日本音楽に関するノート

(1874–1876)

1874

Es ist sehr schwer, sich über die japanische Musik Notizen zu verschaffen, nicht blos wegen der angebornen Zurückhaltung der Japaner, sondern auch hauptsächlich, weil die meisten Musiker hier selbst nichts von der Theorie wissen, ja wohl gar nicht einmal ahnen, daß es eine Notirung und dergleichen giebt. Man kommt ungefähr in die Lage, als ob man von unseren Bierfiedlern oder Harfenistinnen irgend etwas genaueres erfahren wollte. Die theoretisch gebildeten Musiker sind sehr selten und sehr über das Land zerstreut; die heilige Musik ist dem Fremden überhaupt schwer zugänglich und nur durch ganz besonders günstige Conjuncturen kann man einmal dazu kommen, die Instrumente etwas näher zu studieren. Durch meine Stellung als Arzt ist es mir gelungen, daß verschiedene hohe Herren und Gelehrte mir gestatteten, die Instrumente etwas eingehender zu studieren; ich kam so auch in Berührung mit einigen gebildeten Musikern und will in den folgenden Zeilen das Resultat meiner Forschungen niederlegen, ohne dabei irgend wie auf Vollständigkeit Anspruch zu machen. Sollte, wie ich hoffe, es mir gelingen,

It is very difficult to acquire notes on Japanese music, not merely on account of the innate reserve of the Japanese but also, mainly, because most musicians here know nothing about theory themselves, indeed quite likely have no idea at all that a notation and the like exist. One more or less lands in a situation as if wanting to know something more precise of our Bierfiedler or Harfenistinnen.[1] Musicians knowledgeable in theory are very rare and widely dispersed over the land; sacred music is in general difficult to access for the foreigner, and only through particularly advantageous interconnections can one get to examine the instruments in some detail. Via my position as medical doctor, I have managed that various high-ranking personages and scholars allowed me to study the instruments somewhat more closely; in this way I also came into contact with some educated musicians, and in the following lines I want to record the results of my explorations, without thereby laying claim in any way to com-

[1] "Beer-fiddlers or harpists," fairground, tavern, or salon musicians, so to speak. – Ed.

79

nach und nach mehr zu erfahren, so werde ich das Resultat meiner Nachforschungen in spätern Heften publiciren.

Als Mittel, etwas zu erfahren, benutzte ich hauptsächlich die Neugier der Betreffenden, von unserer Musik und unsern musicalischen Instrumenten etwas zu sehen und zu hören. Wenn ich aber sagen soll, welchen Eindruck europäische Musik auf die Japaner macht, so glaube ich mit der Behauptung das Richtige zu treffen, daß die Japaner unsere Musik noch viel abscheulicher finden als wir die ihrige. Ein vornehmer Japaner äußerte, allerdings nicht gegen mich, dazu sind sie zu höflich, aber er äußerte: "Kinder, Koolis und Frauen finden Gefallen an der europäischen Musik, aber ein gebildeter Japaner mag sie nicht leiden".

Hinsichtlich der Musik gilt nun ganz dasselbe, was wir überhaupt bei allen Äußerungen geistiger Thätigkeit in Japan wiederfinden, nämlich wenig in Japan Urwüchsiges, sondern auch auf diesem Gebiete ist das Meiste fertig von China und Korea nach Japan gekommen, und hier erst lange Zeit mit gewissenhaftester Sorgfalt bewahrt, später mannigfach geändert, verbessert und auch wohl großentheils verschlechtert worden.

Die Musiker bilden gewisse Zünfte, die sich zu bestimmten Zeiten und zum ganz bestimmt vorgeschriebenen Zweck geistlicher und weltlicher Aufführungen zusammen finden, außerdem halten und hielten sich namentlich in früherer Zeit der Taikun, der Micado und die

pleteness. Should I succeed, as I hope, in gradually learning more, then I shall publish the result of my investigations in later issues.

As means of finding out about something, I made use, in the main, of the curiosity of those concerned to see and hear something of our music and our musical instruments. However, should I have to say what impression European music makes on the Japanese, then I believe I am correct in stating that the Japanese find our music even more abhorrent than we find theirs. A refined Japanese remarked, of course not to me, for that they are too polite, but he remarked: "Children, servants, and women find pleasure in European music, but a cultured Japanese cannot stand it."

With regard to music, quite the same holds true as what we find generally for all expressions of intellectual activity in Japan, namely, little that originated in Japan. Rather, in this field too, most came to Japan ready-made from China and Korea and here was at first long preserved with most scrupulous care, later altered in many respects, bettered, but probably also to a great deal changed for the worse.

Musicians form certain guilds that come together at set times and for the exactly prescribed purpose of sacred and secular performances. Furthermore, the Taikun, the Mikado, and the daimyōs maintain – and maintained especially in earlier times –

Daimios Privatkapellen,[2] endlich giebt es ganze Klassen von Musikern, die gegen Entgelt auch bei Privatpersonen spielen.

Im Allgemeinen werden die Musiker in folgende Klassen eingetheilt:

1. Solche, die nur *geistliche Musik* spielen, theoretisch gebildet sind, Kenntnis der Noten besitzen (gakkunin). Sie gehören zu der Klasse der hochgeachteten Leute und durfte von je her diese Art der Musik auch von den Daimios gelernt werden. In China ist diese Musik verschwunden, dagegen wird sie noch heute in Japan aufgeführt; namentlich auch von der Privat-Kapelle des Mikado, doch ist zu den meisten Stücken der Text verloren gegangen, so daß nur die Musik übrig bleibt und die Spielenden die Bedeutung ihrer Tonstücke selbst nicht mehr kennen.

2. Solche, die nur *weltliche Musik* spielen, aber nicht theoretisch gebildet sind, auch keine Noten kennen (gehnin); nur der Kôto Spieler kennt die Lehre von den Tonarten und die Notirung der weltlichen Musik. Sie stehen in einer Rangstufe mit Kaufleuten u. dgl., gehören also zu den wenig geachteten Klassen.

private ensembles.[2] And, finally, there are complete categories of musicians who can be hired to perform for private persons.

In general, musicians are grouped into the following categories:

1. Those who play only *sacred music*, are educated in theory, and possess a knowledge of notation (*gakunin*). They belong to the class of highly respected people. Traditionally this type of music could also be learned by the daimyōs. In China this music has disappeared, whereas it is still performed today in Japan, in particular by the private ensemble of the Mikado. For most pieces, though, the text is lost, so that only the music remains, and the performers themselves no longer know the meaning of their musical pieces.

2. Those who play only *secular music* but are not educated in theory and also know no notation (*geinin*); only the koto-player knows the learning of the modes and the notation of secular music. In rank they stand alongside merchants and the like, so belong to the less respected classes.

---

[2] Die weltliche Musik des Taikun heißt No, die geistliche des Micado *gagakku* oder *gaku*; diese letztere spielte früher nur in Nara, Tenodji und Kioto und zwar spielte sie nur von Alters her vererbte Musikstücke.

[2] The secular music of the Taikun is called nō, the sacred music of the Mikado, *gagaku* or *gaku*; this latter formerly played only in Nara, Tennōji and Kyoto and, what is more, from of old played only inherited musical pieces.

3. Musik der Blinden, hat zwei Rangstufen Kenggiò und Kôto, von denen die Erstere die Höhere ist; diese Benennungen werden mit Geld erkauft. Sie spielen nur gewöhnliche Musik.

4. Die sehr zahlreiche Klasse der weiblichen Musiker lasse ich hier ganz außer Acht, da sie in der Musik nur eine ganz untergeordnete Rolle spielen. Nur sehr selten ist der Fall vorgekommen, daß eine Frau sich zu einer höheren Stufe aufschwang. Selbst die Frauen und Mädchen aus den höheren Ständen pflegten von jeher nur die niedere weltliche Musik zu lernen.

Früher hatten alle diese Musiker noch in derselben allgemeinen Rangklasse unter sich wieder verschiedene Ränge; dies besteht zwar jetzt nicht mehr, doch steht an der Spitze der Associationen noch immer der Lehrer, der auch gewisse Belohnungen und Auszeichnungen austheilt; so z.B. hatte der eine der von mir in der Sitzung von 13ten Juni d. J. vorgeführten Musiker das Recht erhalten, auf der Koto die erste Saite eine Octav tiefer gestimmt zu haben als gewöhnlich. Solche Auszeichnungen können entweder als Belohnung für wirkliche Verdienste oder gegen Bezahlung verliehen werden. Die bessern Musikstücke sind Eigenthum einer bestimmten Zunft und dürfen von andren nicht gespielt werden; außerdem giebt es aber auch eine reiche Volksmusik.

3. Music-of-the-blind has two ranks, kengyō and kōtō, of which the former is the higher; these titles are bought with money. They play only common music.

4. I leave the large category of female musicians completely out of consideration here, since they play but a very subordinate role in music. Only very rarely has it happened that a woman rose up to a higher level. Even women and girls of the higher classes were always used to learning lowly, secular music only.

Formerly, even within the same general category, all these musicians had yet again various ranks amongst themselves. This exists no longer though. Yet, at the head of associations still stands the teacher, who also distributes certain awards and distinctions. In this way, for example, one of the musicians I introduced at the meeting of 13 June of this year had received the privilege of tuning the first string on the koto an octave lower than usual. Such honors can be conferred either as reward for actual merit or against payment. The better musical pieces are the property of a particular guild and may not be played by others. In addition, however, there is also a flourishing folk music.

Die in Japan gebräuchlichen Instrumente zerfallen in

The instruments in use in Japan break down into:

1. Schlaginstrumente, sowohl von Metall und Holz als aus Fellbezügen gemacht.
2. Blaseinstrumente aus Holz und Muscheln; Metall wird nur zur Anfertigung von Zungen in Blaseinstrumenten gebraucht.
3. Saiteninstrumente, die entweder mit verschiedenartigen spitzen Instrumenten (batschi) oder mit einem Bogen (Kiu)[3] gespielt werden.

1. Percussion instruments made both of metal and of wood as well as out of animal hides.
2. Wind instruments out of wood and seashells; metal is used only for the manufacture of tongues in wind instruments.
3. Stringed instruments which are played either with various types of pointed implements (bachi) or with a bow (kyū).[3]

Complicirtere Instrumente mit Ventilen, Klappen oder Klaviaturen giebt es nicht in Japan.

More complicated instruments with vents, keys, or keyboards do not exist in Japan.

Alle Instrumente werden eingetheilt in:

All instruments are grouped as:

I. — Reine (gakkuki) d.h. solche die bei geistlichen Musikaufführungen ausschließlich gebraucht werden.

I. Pure (gakugi), that is to say, those which are used exclusively in sacred musical performances.

A. Instrumente, welche bei Aufführung Chinesischer oder Koreanischer Musikstücke benutzt werden:

A. Instruments which are used for the performance of Chinese or Korean musical pieces:

1. SAITENINSTRUMENTE:

1. STRINGED INSTRUMENTS:

a. siebensaitige Koto, Fig. N° 5.
b. Biwa, eine Art Guitarre, Fig. N° 2.

a. Seven-stringed koto, Fig. 5 (p. 120).
b. Biwa, a type of guitar, Fig. 2 (p. 118).

2. TROMMELN:

2. DRUMS:

a. Taikô, die große Trommel, Fig. N° 15, wird mit zwei dicken Paukenklöppeln geschlagen.

a. Taiko, the big drum, Fig. 15 (p. 121), struck with two large beaters.

---

[3] Kiu bedeutet auch den Bogen als Waffe.

[3] Kyū also stands for the bow as a weapon.

b. Kakko, die schiefstehende, kleine Trommel, welche mit zwei Stäbchen geschlagen wird, Fig. N° 16.

c. Yôko oder Sanno tsudsumi, Fig. 17, steht zwischen beiden, wird wie b geschlagen.

d. Shôko, Schlaginstrument aus Metall, Fig. N° 18.

3. BLASINSTRUMENTE:

a. Shô, aus Holz und Metallzungen, Fig. N° 10.

b. Hidschiriki, aus Bambus und Metallzungen, Fig. N° 11.

c. Ohteki, die chinesische Flöte, Fig. N° 12.

d. Komafuye, die koreanische Flöte, Fig. N° 13.

B. Instrumente, welche bei Aufführungen rein alt japanischer Musik gebraucht werden:

1. Wanggong oder Yamato Koto, die 6 saitige Kôto, Fig. N° 6.
2. Kangura Fuye, die japanische Flöte, Fig. N° 14.
3. Shaku Bioshi, Holzklapper, Fig. N° 20.

II.— Nicht reine Instrumente, welche nur zu profanen Zwecken benutzt werden. Ihre Zahl ist sehr groß und werden zu profanen Zwecken häufig auch die reinen Instrumente benutzt, dann aber in etwas modificirter Form oder mit einem andern Saitenbezug und dgl.

b. Kakko, the small sideways drum, which is struck with two sticks, Fig. 16 (p. 122).

c. Yōko or san-no-tsuzumi, Fig. 17 (p. 122), comes between the two, is struck like b.

d. Shōko, percussion instrument out of metal, Fig. 18 (p. 121).

3. WIND INSTRUMENTS:

a. Shō, out of wood and metal tongues, Fig. 10 (p. 122).

b. Hichiriki, out of bamboo and metal tongues,[4] Fig. 11 (p. 122).

c. Ōteki, the Chinese flute, Fig. 12 (p. 122).

d. Komabue, the Korean flute, Fig. 13 (p. 122).

B. Instruments which are employed for performances of pure old Japanese music:

1. Wagon or yamato-goto, the 6-stringed koto, Fig. 6 (p 120).
2. Kagurabue, the Japanese flute, Fig. 14 (p. 122).
3. Shakubyōshi, wooden clapper, Fig. 20 (p. 121).

II. Non-pure instruments, which are only used for secular purposes. Their number is very great. While pure instruments are frequently used also for secular purposes, they are then in a somewhat modified form or are strung differently, and so on.

---

[4] Printer's error in original: description taken over from previous entry. – Ed.

Besonders vorzuheben sind unter ihnen:

A. Die Instrumente, welche zu den Nô Tänzen benutzt werden; diese Nô Musiker und Tänzer hielten sich der Taikun und die Daimios, welche wegen ihres Ranges öffentliche Theater nicht besuchen durften.

Es sind:

1. Die große Trommel Taiko, Fig. N° 15.
2. Tsudsumi, zwei Trommeln, von denen die eine auf der linken Schulter, die andere auf dem Schoße liegt und die mit den Fingern der rechten Hand geschlagen werden, Fig. N° 19.

B. Außerdem werden für gewöhnliche Zwecke benutzt:

1. Die Samiseng, Fig. N° 3.
2. Die Dreizehnsaitige Kôto, Fig. N° 1.
3. Die Kokiu, eine Violine, Fig. N° 4. Die Combination dieser drei Instrumente heißt Sankioku.
4. Verschiedene Flöten und Metallklappern.

III. — In der Mitte zwischen der heiligen und profanen Musik stehen verschiedene Monochorde, Pfeifen, Klappern, u.s.w. die nur als Spielzeuge benutzt werden; da dies aber auch in vornehmen Familien geschieht, so sind diese Instrumente geachtet.

To be particularly mentioned among them are:

A. The instruments which are used for nō dances; the Taikun and the daimyōs, who because of their status could not go to public theaters, maintained these nō musicians and dancers for themselves.

They are:

1. The big drum, taiko, Fig. 15 (p. 121).
2. Tsuzumi, two drums, of which one rests on the left shoulder, the other in the lap, and which are struck by the fingers of the right hand, Fig. 19 (p. 121).

B. In addition, for ordinary purposes are used:

1. The shamisen, Fig. 3 (p. 118).
2. The thirteen-stringed koto, Fig. 1 (p. 117).
3. The kokyū, a violin, Fig. 4 (p. 119). The combination of these three instruments is called sankyoku.
4. Various flutes and metal clappers.

III. Midway between sacred and secular music stand various monochords, pipes, clappers, and so on, which are used only as toys; however, as this happens also in genteel families, these instruments are accordingly respected.

Ich sah außerdem einige Instrumente, die von Alters her benutzt werden, um vor Bebauung eines Ackers aus demselben Schlangen und andere giftige Thiere zu vertreiben. Es waren dies Klingeln nach Art unserer Schlittengeläute, von denen drei bis vier entweder um einen an drei Kettchen aufgehängten Metallring oder an irgend einem Griff befestigt waren. Nach dem Gebrauche werden diese Instrumente mit einem Spiegel, dem Bilde der Reinheit, den Göttern verehrt und in dem Tempel aufgehängt.

Wenn wir nun die *Theorie der Musik* etwas näher ins Auge fassen, so finden wir auch hier die gewöhnliche chinesische mystische Speculation.

Das Reich der Töne wird mit anderen Naturkräften, mit den Himmelszeichen und den Monaten in Verbindung gebracht und daraus folgende Theorie entwickelt.

Alle Kräfte und Verrichtungen der Natur sind durch die Zahl *fünf* characterisirt; so giebt es:

5 functionirende Eingeweide:

Magen
Lungen
Leber
Herz
Nieren.

Ich bemerke hierzu, daß in dieser, wie in allen folgenden Reihen die Rangordnung von oben anfängt, so daß jedes höher stehende Wort einen wichtigern und dem nächstfolgenden übergeordneten Gegenstand bezeichnet.

I saw, besides, some instruments which from olden times have been used to chase out snakes and other poisonous animals before tilling a field. These were bells like our sleighbells, three to four of which were attached either around a metal ring suspended on three chains or to some kind of handle. After use, these instruments, along with a mirror, the image of purity, were dedicated to the gods and hung up in the temple.

If we now take a closer look at the *theory of music*, then here too we find the usual Chinese mystical speculation.

The realm of notes is linked up with other natural forces, with the signs of the zodiac and the months [of the year], and out of this the following theory is developed.

All forces and acts of nature are characterized by the number *five*; accordingly there are:

5 functioning organs:

stomach
lungs
liver
heart
kidneys

I note here that in this, as in all following series, the hierarchy begins from the top, so that each higher-placed word indicates a more important and privileged object than the following.

5 Farben:	5 colors:
Gelb	yellow
Weiß	white
Grün	green
Roth	red
Schwarz.	black

5 Arten des Geschmacks:	5 kinds of taste:
Süß	sweet
Herb	tart
Sauer	sour
Bitter	bitter
Salzig.	salty

5 Elemente:	5 elements:
Erde	earth
Metall	metal
Holz	wood
Feuer	fire
Wasser.	water

5 Planeten:	5 planets:
Saturn	Saturn
Venus	Venus
Jupiter	Jupiter
Mars	Mars
Mercur.	Mercury

5 Himmelsgegenden:	5 directions:
Centrum	center
West	west
Ost	east
Süd	south
Nord.	north

u.s.w. Da nun die Töne zu den Äußerungen der Natur gehören, so *muss* es ihrer ebenfalls fünf geben.

Das System der 5 Töne heißt gôïn; ihre Reihenfolge ist:

And so on. Now, since notes belong to the expressions of nature, there *must* be five of them as well.

The system of five notes is called *goin*; their order is:

1ter Ton	Kiu—Tempel—Herr.	1st note	kyū – temple – master.
2ter Ton	Shô—Handel—Diener.	2nd note	shō – trade – servant.
3ter Ton	Kaku—Horn—Bauer.	3rd note	kaku – horn – farmer.
4ter Ton	Tshi—Zeichen—ein materieller Gegenstand.	4th note	chi — sign – a material object.
5ter Ton	U—Feder—ein abstracter Gegenstand.	5th note	u – feather – an abstract object.

Auch bei den Tönen gilt das allgemeine Gesetz, daß der vorausstehende höher gilt, als der folgende; so wird in der Musikschule Kiu als sehr groß, U als sehr klein bezeichnet.

Nun sind aber diese Ton-Namen nicht so aufzufassen, daß sie bestimmten Tönen unserer Tonleiter entsprechen, sondern sie entsprechen unsern Begriffen der Secunde, Terz, Quinte u.s.w., die dann in den verschiedenen Tonarten in einem constanten Verhältnis zum Grundtone Kiu stehen; es ist also etwas Ähnliches, wie in unsern verschiedenen Tonleitern.

Obgleich nun blos diese fünf Töne als officielle Töne anerkannt werden, so dürfte man doch nicht glauben, daß bei den Japanern nur fünf Töne in einer Tonart bekannt sind, vielmehr wenden sie bei Saiteninstrumenten auch die Zwischentöne an, die sie durch einen auf die Saite je nach der Natur des Instruments ausgeübten Druck oder Zug (jenseits des Stegs zur Erschlaffung der Saite) erzeugen.

For notes, too, the general rule applies that the preceding is considered superior to the following; hence, in the music tutor, kyū is marked as very big, u as very small.

These note-names, however, are not to be understood as corresponding to fixed notes of our scales. They correspond, rather, to our terms of second, third, fifth, and so on, which in the various keys then stand in turn in constant relation to the ground-note, kyū. It is therefore something like in our different scales.

Even though only these five notes are recognized as official notes, one should not think that the Japanese only know of five notes in a mode; rather, on stringed instruments they also use the semitones, which they produce executed on the string, depending on the nature of the instrument by pressure or dragging (on the other side of the bridge so as to slacken the string).

Die Grundtöne selbst stehen nun in einem bestimmten Connex zu den Monaten und zwar äußert sich dieser Connex so, daß in jedem der zwölf Monate der Wind nur Geräusche in einer bestimmten Tonart hervorbringt, so daß in jedem Monat eine verschiedene, aber für diesen Monat ganz bestimmte Tonart dominirt.

The ground-notes themselves stand in a certain connection to the months. In fact, this connection manifests itself in that in each of the twelve months the wind brings forth only sounds in a certain key. In each month, then, a different key dominates, but [one] exactly destined for this month.

So dominirt	im	December	Kôshô.
″	″	Januar	Tairiô.
″	″	Februar	Taisoku.
″	″	März	Kiôshô.
″	″	April	Kossen.
″	″	Mai	Tschurio.
″	″	Juni	Suischin.
″	″	Juli	Ringsho.
″	″	August	Isoku.
″	″	September	Nanrio.
″	″	October	Buëki.
″	″	November	Oshô.

- -

Thus	in	December	kōshō	dominates.
″		January	tairyo	″
″		February	taizoku [taisō]	″
″		March	kyōshō	″
″		April	kosen	″
″		May	chūryo	″
″		June	suihin	″
″		July	rinshō	″
″		August	isoku	″
″		September	nanryo	″
″		October	bueki	″
″		November	ōshō	″

Die Reihenfolge der Töne wird nun auf folgende Weise bestimmt:

The order of the notes is determined in the following way:

Die Namen der Monate und der in ihnen herrschenden Töne werden symmetrisch um einen Kreis geschrieben (Fig. N° 21) und zwar von December ausgehend links herum.

Will man nun die fünf Töne bestimmen, welche zu einer Tonart gehören, so verfährt man folgender Maßen.

Nimmt man Kôshô, den December Ton als Grundton und zählt von December als 1 gerechnet vorwärts (nach japanischer Art von rechts nach links herum) acht Monate, so kommt man auf Juli als 2ten Ton, Shô; nun zählt man 6 rückwärts von Juli als eins, und kommt auf Februar als Kaku, nun 8 vorwärts, September als Tshi, 6 rückwärts April als U.

So sind nun die fünf Haupttöne bestimmt. Indem man nun wieder 6 zurückzählt, erhält man November als Hülfston für December, 8 vorwärts Juni als Hülfston für Juli, 6 zurück Januar als Hülfston für Februar, 8 vor August als Hülfston für September, 6 zurück März als Hülfston für April. Mai und October gehören in die December Tonart nicht hinein. Der Hülfston ist einen halben Ton tiefer als der Hauptton. Ganz in derselben Weise werden die zu jeder Tonart gehörigen 5 Haupt- und 5 Hülfstöne bestimmt.

Eine *zweite Art*, die zu dem Hauptton gehörenden Töne zu bestimmen, ist die *mathematische*. Man setzt den Grundton Kiu als Einheit 9, dividirt diese Ziffer durch 3 und zieht dieses Drittel von dem Grundton ab, also $9 - 3 = 6$. Jetzt nimmt man diese 6 als Einheit, dividirt sie durch 3 und addirt dieses Drittel zu

The names of the months and the notes that govern within each are written symmetrically around a circle (Fig. 21, p. 123), anti-clockwise starting out from December.[5]

If one now wants to determine the five notes that belong to a key, one proceeds in the following manner.

One takes *kōshō*, the December note, as ground-note and counts from December as 1 forwards (according to Japanese custom around from right to left) eight months, arriving thus on July as the 2nd note, *shō*; now one counts 6 backwards from July as 1 and comes to February as *kaku*, now 8 forwards [to] September as *chi*, 6 backwards [to] April as *u*.

In this way the five main notes are determined. By back-counting again 6, one obtains November as auxiliary note for December, 8 forwards, June as auxiliary note for July, 6 back, January as auxiliary note for February, 8 forwards, August as auxiliary note for September, 6 back, March as auxiliary note for April. May and October do not belong in the December key. The auxiliary note is a half tone lower than the main note. In exactly the same way the 5 main and 5 auxiliary notes belonging to each key are determined.

A *second way* to determine the notes belonging to the main note is *mathematical*. One sets the ground-note *kyū* as entity 9, divides this figure by 3, and subtracts this third from the ground-

---

5 Müller takes great pains to correct this account in the succeeding instalment (see p. 146). – Ed.

der neuen Einheit, als $6 + 2 = 8$. Nun verfährt man noch dreimal ebenso, abwechselnd ein Drittel subtrahirend und addirend und das Ergebnis stets als neue Grundzahl nehmend, und erhält:

note, thus $9-3=6$. Now one takes this 6 as entity, divides it by 3, and adds this third to the new entity, as $6 + 2 = 8$. One proceeds three more times like this, alternately subtracting and adding and taking the result each time as new base-number, and obtains:

$$\frac{24}{3} - \frac{8}{3} = \frac{16}{3}$$

$$\frac{48}{9} + \frac{16}{9} = \frac{64}{9}$$

$$\frac{192}{27} - \frac{64}{27} = \frac{128}{27}$$

Nach diesen Verhältnissen bestimmt man nun die Länge der Saiten, welche zu den Tönen einer Tonart gehören, also z.B. daß wenn die Saite des Grundtons 9 Maaßtheile lang ist, der zweite Ton eine Saite von 6 Maaßtheilen Länge braucht u. s. w. Die Octave wird bestimmt indem man die halbe Saitenlänge nimmt und für die folgenden Saiten die Verhältnisse wie oben bestimmt.

According to these ratios one now determines the length of the strings that belong to the notes of a key. Let us say, for example, that if the string of the ground-note is 9 units of measurement long, the second note needs a string of 6 units length, and so on. The octave is determined by taking half the string length, and for the following strings the ratios are determined as above.

Um einfacher zu rechnen, setzen Manche als Einheit für Kiu 81 statt 9 und erhalten so die Zahlen 81, 54, 72, 48, 64.

To calculate more simply, some set the entity for kyū at 81 instead of 9 and so obtain the numbers 81, 54, 72, 48, 64.

Die Töne der Monate werden nun auf Stimmgabeln übertragen und zwar ist December unser Es je nach der Größe der Stimmgabel in der zwei- oder eingestrichenen Octave. Von December auf der Figur 21 links herumgehend folgen die Töne unserer chromatischen Tonleiter scharf, nicht temperirt, gestimmt auf einander, so daß November d bekommt.

The notes of the months are now transferred on tuning-forks, and, in fact, December is our eb, depending on the size of the tuning-fork, in the two- or the one-line octave.[6] From December, in Fig. 21 (p. 123), moving around to the left, the notes follow our chromatic scale, tuned sharp to one another, not tempered, so that November ends up with d.

---

[6] Following Müller's use here of the "German method" of pitch notation. – Ed.

Solche Stimmgabeln habe ich drei verschiedene Arten gesehen:

1. Ein *kleiner Cylinder aus Bambus oder Elfenbein* (Fig. N° 22) der auf einem Ende offen, auf dem andern geschlossen ist. Derselbe ist auf beiden Seiten, wie eine Flöte mit Öffnungen versehen und wird der Ton erzeugt, indem man mit dem Nagel des Mittelfingers gegen das geschlossene Ende knippst. Die Figur zeigt die genaue Form und Größe der Stimmgabel, das daneben stehende Schema (Fig. N° 23), giebt die Löcher an, welche zur Erzeugung der verschiedenen Töne geschlossen werden müssen.

2. Eine andere Art Stimmgabeln besteht aus 12 Metallzungen, die entweder in einem Windkasten kreisförmig eingesetzt sind (Fig. N° 24) oder in neben einander drehbar befestigten Bambusstäbchen stecken (Fig. N° 25). Um das Instrument zu vereinfachen und zugänglicher zu machen, hat man ein billigeres, das nur die sechs ersten als Grundton gebräuchlichsten Töne, also 3 Haupt- und 3 Nebentöne enthält (Fig. N° 26).

3. Die dritte Art besteht aus 12 oben und unten offnen und aneinander gereihten Bambuscylindern (Fig. N° 27); der gewünschte Ton wird erzeugt, indem man mit dem Finger den betreffen-

I have seen three different types of such tuning-forks:

1. *A small cylinder made out of bamboo or ivory* (Fig. 22 [p. 123]) which is open at one end, closed at the other. This is provided with holes on both sides like a flute, and the note is produced by flicking with the nail of the middle finger against the closed end. The figure shows the exact form and size of the tuning-fork; the diagram beside it (Fig. 23 [p. 123]) indicates the holes which must be closed to produce the different notes.

2. Another type of tuning-fork consists of 12 metal tongues which are either assembled in a circle in a wind chamber (Fig. 24 [p. 124]) or are inserted into bamboo sticks rotatably fixed next to each other (Fig. 25 [p. 125]). To simplify the instrument and to make it more accessible, there is a cheaper one that embraces only the first six notes most commonly used as ground-notes, that is, 3 main notes and 3 auxiliary notes (Fig. 26 [p. 125]).

3. The third type consists of 12 bamboo pipes, open top and bottom and lined up one next to the other (Fig. 27 [p. 124]); the desired note is produced by closing the relevant pipe at one end and then using it

den Cylinder auf einem Ende
schließt, und ihn dann wie eine
Papageno-Flöte benutzt.

like a pan-pipe.

Gehen wir nun zur Betrachtung der
einzelnen Instrumente über, so ist es
der größern Deutlichkeit wegen nöthig,
nicht einer strengen Trennung nach heiligen und nicht heiligen Instrumenten
zu folgen, sondern ich werde zum Theil
davon vollständig abweichen.

If we move now to consideration of the
individual instruments, then for the
sake of greater clarity it is necessary not
to follow a strict separation according
to sacred and non-sacred instruments.
Rather, in part, I shall deviate from this
completely.

Unter den *Saiteninstrumenten* tritt
uns als wichtigstes und als Basis des
Orchesters für die Erklärung zunächst
die Kôtô entgegen.

Amongst the *stringed instruments* we
encounter the *koto* first for explanation
as the most important and as basis of the
orchestra.

Kôto heißt die ganze Klasse der langen, viereckigen auf die Erde zu legenden
und mit Saiten bespannten Instrumente.
Es giebt davon folgende Hauptarten:

Koto is the name for the complete
class of long quadrangular instruments
placed on the ground and strung with
strings. There are of them the following
main types:

1. Die Kin Koto zu 25 und 50 Saiten,
   ist veraltet.

2. Die dreizehnsaitige Sōno Koto (Fig.
   N° 1). Ich bemerke hierbei ausdrücklich, daß dies die richtige
   Benennung dieser Art von Koto
   ist, welche von Sieboldt fälschlich
   als Kin Koto bezeichnet.

3. Die sechssaitige Yamato-no-Koto
   oder Wanggong (Fig. N° 6). Sie gehört wie die vorige zur heiligen
   Musik, siehe oben.

4. Die zweisaitige Idsumo Koto und
   die einsaitige Summa Koto sind
   fast nur Spielzeug (Fig. 8 u. 9).

1. The *kin-no-koto* with 25 and 50
   strings, which is obsolete.

2. The 13-stringed *sō-no-koto* (Fig. 1
   [p. 117]). I emphatically note herewith that this is the correct term
   for this type of *koto*, which von
   Siebold incorrectly identified as
   kin-no-koto.

3. The six-stringed *yamato-goto* or
   wagon (Fig. 6 [p. 120]). Like the
   preceding, this belongs to sacred
   music, see above.

4. The two-stringed *izumo-goto* and
   the one-stringed *suma-koto* are all
   but toys (Figs. 8 [p. 120] and 9 [p.
   122]).

Von der Summa Koto geht die Sage, daß sie von einem Kuge (Edelmann) erfunden sei, der nach der Provinz Summa (daher der Name) verbannt gewesen sei und sich aus langer Weile ein Monochord geschaffen habe, indem er eine Saite über seinen Hut spannte. Unter der Saite befinden sich niedrige Stege, auf welche die Saite zur Erzeugung der verschiedenen Töne mittelst eines am Finger befestigten Bambus gedrückt wird.

Die wichtigste ist also die *Sono Koto* (Fig. N° 1). Sie ist mit 13 gleich dicken, gleich langen und gleich gespannten Saiten bezogen die durch 2 feste Stege gehalten werden. Durch den einen Steg gehen sämmtliche Saiten durch, um das untere Ende der Koto herum und durch ein im Resonnanzboden befindliches Loch zurück nach dem Stege, wo sie befestigt werden; gespannt werden die Saiten vermittelst eines durch dieselben gezogenen Holzes.

Für die Dimensionen der Koto existiren bestimmte Regeln, von denen aber vielfältig abgewichen wird. Ein mir zu Gebote stehendes Normalexemplar war 72 Zoll lang, die Entfernung der beiden großen Stege von einander betrug 53 Zoll, die größte Breite 10½ Zoll, die kleinste 9 Zoll, die größte Höhe 3½ Zoll in der Mitte, die kleinste Höhe 1½ Zoll auf beiden Seiten.

Der Resonnanzboden besteht aus dem sehr festen Kiriholz und hat auf der Unterseite zwei Öffnungen. Das Instru-

Legend has it of the *suma-koto* that it was invented by a *kuge* (nobleman) who had been banished to the Province of Suma (hence the name) and out of boredom made himself a monochord by stretching a string over his hat. Under the string are arranged low bridges, onto which for production of the different notes the string is pressed by means of a [piece of] bamboo attached to the finger.

The most important, then, is the *sō-no-koto* (Fig. 1 [p. 117]). It is strung with 13 strings of equal thickness, equal length, and equal tension, which are held by 2 fixed bridges. All of the strings pass through one bridge, around the lower end of the *koto*, and, through a hole found in the sounding board, back to the bridge, where they are fastened; the strings are stretched by means of a [piece of] wood with which they are pulled.

There exist precise rules for the measurements of the *koto*, although they are departed from in many cases. One standard exemplar at my disposal was 72 inches long, the distance of the two large bridges from one another amounted to 53 inches, the maximum width, 10½ inches, the minimum, 9 inches; the maximum height, 3½ inches in the middle, the minimum height, 1½ inches on both sides.

The sounding board is made of very hard *kiri* wood and has two openings on the underside. The instrument stands

ment steht auf vier niedrigen Füßen.

Die Stimmung der einzelnen Saiten geschieht nun durch untergeschobene bewegliche Stege (Figur N° 28 in natürlicher Größe). Der Spieler, der ja zugleich Sänger ist, bestimmt die Tonart nach seiner Stimme; *gute Stimme* wird dabei als gleichbedeutend mit *hoher Stimme* betrachtet.

Hat nun der Spieler auf diese Weise den Grundton festgesetzt, so überträgt er diesen Ton durch Unterschieben eines Steges auf die zweite ihm zunächst liegende Saite, die erste bleibt vorläufig ungestimmt.

Nun berechnet er die folgenden Töne in der früher angegebenen Weise. Den zweiten Ton überträgt er auf die fünfte Saite, den dritten Ton auf die dritte, den vierten Ton auf die sechste, den fünften Ton auf die vierte Saite. Die Töne folgen also nun aufeinander von der zweiten Saite an gerechnet: 1, 3, 5, 2, 4. Wenn wir nun diese Töne nach der astronomischen Methode aufsuchen und in unsere Töne der Stimmgabel entsprechend umsetzten, dabei aber der Einfachheit wegen *c* als Grundton nehmen, so erhalten wir, acht Töne links herum gehend, als zweiten Ton *g*, als dritten, *6* rechts herum gehend, *d*, als vierten *a* und als fünften *e*; beim vierten und fünften Ton wird aber statt des Haupttons der Hülfston gebraucht, also *as* und *es*. Wenn wir nun die Töne wie oben gesagt ordnen, so erhalten wir die Folge:

on four low feet.

The tuning of the individual strings is done through moveable bridges, pushed under [the strings] (Figure 28 in actual size [p. 125]). The performer, who is actually at the same time singer, determines the key according to his voice; *good voice* is considered to mean the same as *high voice*.

Once the performer has thus fixed the ground-note, he transfers this note to the second string nearest him by pushing under a bridge; the first remains untuned for the time being.

Now he calculates the next notes according to the method described earlier. The second note he transfers to the fifth string, the third note to the third, the fourth note to the sixth, the fifth note to the fourth string. The notes thus follow one another, counting from the second string on: 1, 3, 5, 2, 4. If we now locate these notes following the astronomical method and convert them into our notes according to the tuning-fork, taking *c* as ground-note for simplicity's sake, then, going eight notes around to the left, we obtain as second note *g*, as third, *6* around to the right, *d*, as fourth *a* and as fifth *e*; for the fourth and the fifth note, however, instead of the main note the auxiliary is used, so *ab* and *eb*. If we now arrange the pitches as stated above, we get the order:

1te Saite noch ungestimmt
2te ” -1ter Ton $-c$.
3te ” -3ter Ton $-d$.
4te ” -5ter Ton $-es$.
5te ” -2ter Ton $-g$.
6te ” -4ter Ton $-as$.

Hätten wir noch um zwei fortgefahren, so würden wir als 6ten Ton, der hinter dem vierten kommen müsste, h erhalten und als 7ten *ges*, das zwischen den 5ten und 2ten eingeschoben aber um einen halben Ton vertieft werden würde (da *ges* als Hülfston zu unbedeutend ist, um selbstständig zu zählen) f.

Es ist demnach einleuchtend, daß *die Stimmung der Koto mit unserer harmonischen Molltonleiter übereinstimmt*, wobei nur die Quart und Septime weggelassen sind, weil durch sie die für alle Naturkräfte als Norm geltende Zahl fünf überschritten werden würde.

Hätten wir aber statt der astronomischen Berechnungsweise die oben erwähnte *mathematische* genommen, so würden sich folgende Resultate ergeben: Die Schwingungsverhältnisse der eben aufgeführten Töne sind:

$$c \quad = \quad \frac{81}{81} \quad = \quad 1 \quad = \quad 1{,}00000.$$

$$d \quad = \quad \frac{81}{72} \quad = \quad {}^9/_8 \quad = \quad 1{,}12500.$$

$$es/e\flat \quad = \quad \frac{81}{64} \quad = \quad \quad = \quad 1{,}26562.$$

$$g \quad = \quad \frac{81}{54} \quad = \quad {}^3/_2 \quad = \quad 1{,}50000.$$

$$as/a\flat \quad = \quad \frac{81}{43} \quad = \quad {}^{27}/_{16} \quad = \quad 1{,}68750.$$

Eine Vergleichung mit den durch unsere Physik festgesetzten Schwingungsverhältnissen ergiebt, daß die

---

1st string still untuned
2nd ” 1st note c.
3rd ” 3rd note d.
4th ” 5th note $e\flat$.
5th ” 2nd note g.
6th ” 4th note $a\flat$.

Had we continued on for two, then as 6th note, which has to come after the fourth, we would have obtained b, and as 7th, $g\flat$, which, inserted between the 5th and the 2nd, however, would be lowered by a semitone to f (since $g\flat$ as auxiliary is too unimportant to stand on its own).

It is thus obvious that *the tuning of the* koto *agrees with our harmonic minor scale*, except that the fourth and the seventh are left out because through them the number five, held as norm for all forces of nature, would be exceeded.

However, had we taken in place of the astronomical method of reckoning, the *mathematical* referred to above, then the following results would have ensued. The frequency-ratios of the notes just presented are:

A comparison with the frequency-ratios fixed by our physics reveals that the ratios of the whole notes to one another

Verhältnisse der ganzen Töne zu einander vollständig übereinstimmen; die Verhältnisse von c : es und c : as differiren aber. Unsere Schwingungsverhältnisse sind:

correspond fully; the ratios of c : eb and c : ab differ, however. Our frequency-ratios are:

$$c \quad : \quad es/eb \quad = \quad 1 \quad : \quad 1{,}20000$$
$$c \quad : \quad as/ab \quad = \quad 1 \quad : \quad 1{,}60000$$

Im erstern Verhältnis haben wir also eine Differenz von 0,06562, im letzteren eine Differenz von 0,08750. Bedenkt man aber, daß nach der Theorie e und a statt es und as genommen werden müssen, so würde sich die Differenz noch geringer herausstellen, nämlich:

In the first ratio, therefore, we have a difference of 0.06562, in the latter, a difference of 0.08750. If one considers, however, that according to theory e and a are to be taken instead of eb and ab, then the difference would turn out slighter still, namely:

Ton / Note	Japanische Schwingungszahl / Japanese frequency	Physicalische Schwingungszahl / physical frequency	Differenz / Difference
es/eb	1,26562	1,25000	0,01562
as/ab	1,68750	1,66666	0,02084

Nachdem man nun die 2te bis 6te Saite so gestimmt, stimmt man die 1te gleich mit der 5ten, also man überträgt auf sie den 2ten Ton g; ich erwähnte schon früher, daß der eine Kotospieler als Belohnung die Erlaubnis erhalten hatte, diese erste Saite eine Octav tiefer zu stimmen. Hierauf werden die 7te bis 11te Saite gestimmt, indem man die halben Längen der 2ten bis 6ten nimmt, die 12te und 13te, indem man die halben Längen der 7ten und 8ten nimmt. Bei dem Grundton c ist also die Reihenfolge der 13 Saiten:

After one has tuned the 2nd to the 6th string in this way, one tunes the 1st the same as the 5th; that is, one transfers the 2nd note g to it. I mentioned earlier already that a koto-player had received as an award the permission to tune this string an octave lower. After that the 7th to 11th strings are tuned by taking half the lengths of the 2nd to the 6th, the 12th and 13th, by taking half the lengths of the 7th and 8th. With c as ground-note, then, the sequence of the 13 strings is:

1te	Saite / String	...	g.	
2te	"	...	c.	
3te	"	...	d.	_ Eingestrichene Octav.
4te	"	...	es / eb.	One-line octave
5te	"	...	g.	
6te	"	...	as / ab.	

7te	Saite / String	...	c.	
8te	"	...	d.	
9te	"	...	es / eb.	_ Zweigestrichene Octav.
10te	"	...	g.	Two-line octave
11te	"	...	as / ab.	

12te	Saite / String	...	c.	_ Dreigestrichene Octav.
13te	"	...	d.	Three-line octave

Der gewöhnliche Kotospieler macht nun selbstredend alle diese Berechnungen nicht, sondern stimmt einfach nach dem Gehör.

Die *Saiten* sind für alle Saiteninstrumente aus Seide gemacht und mit Wachs durchzogen. Die Saiten für die reine Koto werden nur in Kioto gemacht. Sie sind sehr theuer (der Bezug kostet 5 Dollar), weil sie so selten gebraucht und nur auf besondere Bestellung angefertigt werden. Die Saiten für die gewöhnliche Koto werden in Yedo gemacht und sind billig.

Die Samiseng und die Violine haben ähnliche Saiten, nur etwas dünner; die Saiten zur Geking, einer Art Guitarre (Fig N° 7), kommen aus China.[7]

The normal *koto*-player does not make all these calculations but, of course, tunes simply by ear.

The *strings* for all stringed instruments are made of silk and are waxed. The strings for the pure *koto* are made only in Kyoto. They are very expensive (the set costs 5 dollars) because they are so seldom needed and are made only on special order. The strings for the normal *koto* are made in Edo and are cheap.

The *shamisen* and the violin have similar strings, just somewhat thinner; the strings for the *gekkin*, a type of guitar (Fig. 7 [p. 120]), come from China.[7]

---

[7] Sämtliche Saiten sind in dem Museum der Gesellschaft vertreten, und würde die Gesellschaft sich ein Vergnügen daraus machen, Personen, die sich besonders dafür interessiren, Proben davon zu übermitteln.

[7] All strings are represented in the Museum of the *Gesellschaft*, and the *Gesellschaft* would be delighted to give samples of them to persons who are especially interested.

Für die verschiedenen Dicken der Saiten giebt es verschiedene Nummern u. zw. so, daß die höhern Nummern dickere Saiten bezeichnen. Zu vielen Bezügen gehören Saiten von verschiedener Dicke; dann wird der Bezug nach der Nummer der dicksten Saite benannt. Die Bezüge für die verschiedenen Tonarten tragen die Namen ihrer Erfinder.

Gespielt wird die Koto mit drei viertel Zoll langen Elfenbeinspitzen (Fig. N° 38) die vermittelst kleiner Lederinge auf der Beugeseite des Daumens, Zeige- und Mittelfingers der rechten Hand befestigt werden, während die linke flach auf die Saiten jenseits der beweglichen Stege aufgelegt wird, um die Saiten nöthigen Falls zur Erzeugung der Zwischentöne durch Druck zu spannen oder durch Zug zu entspannen. Vor dem Spielen reibt sich der Spieler die Hände mit Stärke ein.

Die *sechssaitige japanische Koto oder Wanggong* (Fig. N° 6) ist 6,33 Fuß lang, 0,5 Fuß am schmalen Ende breit, 0,78 am breiten Ende, die Höhe beträgt 0,4 Fuß ohne die Füße. Sie hat an der untern Seite außer der Öffnung zum Durchtritt der Saiten eine zweite für die Resonnanz.

Die genaue Stimmung derselben habe ich noch nicht erforschen können, doch differirt sie wesentlich von der der dreizehnsaitigen Koto, indem die erste die tiefste ist, dann folgt in einem kleinen Intervall, wahrscheinlich der Secunde, die vierte Saite, dann die zweite und fünfte gleich, wahrscheinlich in der Quart, dann die sechste in der Quint und endlich die dritte in der

For the various thicknesses of strings there are different numbers, such that the higher numbers designate thicker strings. To many sets belong strings of different thicknesses; then the set is named according to the number of the thickest string. The sets for the various keys bear the names of their inventors.

The *koto* is played with three-quarter-inch-long ivory picks (Fig. 38 [p. 119]) which are fastened with little leather rings to the inside of the thumb, index, and middle fingers of the right hand, while the left is laid flat on the strings on the far side of the moveable bridges, in order to tighten the strings by pressure or loosen by pulling if required for producing the semitones. Before playing the performer rubs his hands with starch.

The *six-stringed Japanese koto or wagon* (Fig. 6 [p. 120]) is 6.33 feet long, 0.5 feet wide at the narrow end, 0.78 at the wide end; the height amounts to 0.4 feet, without the feet. On the under-side, in addition to the opening for the passage of the strings, it has a second for resonance.

I have not yet been able to study the exact tuning of same, yet it differs substantially from that of the thirteen-stringed *koto* in that the first [string] is the lowest, then follows at a small interval, probably a second, the fourth string, then the second and fifth the same, probably at a fourth, then the sixth at a fifth and, finally, the third at a flattened sixth. But, as stated, I am in no

verminderten Sexte. Aber wie gesagt ich bin meiner Sache keineswegs sicher, weil ich noch keine richtig gestimmte Wanggong untersucht, sondern mir nur nach einer oberfächlich die Stellung der Stege angebenden Zeichnung die oben ausgesprochene Idee gebildet habe.

Die siebensaitige chinesische Koto habe ich noch gar nicht erforschen können (Fig. N° 5).

Die Biwa (Fig. N° 2) ist mit 4 Saiten, von denen je zwei gleich dick sind, bespannt. Der Körper is 33,5 Decimalzoll lang, wovon 7,5 auf das Griffbrett kommen, auf welchem sich 4 zum Greifen bestimmte Querleisten befinden. Die Biwa hat die Gestalt einer durchgeschnittenen Birne; sie verjüngt sich von unten nach oben. Die größte Breite beträgt in der Höhe von 11 Zoll = 12,2 Zoll, in der Höhe von 16,3 Zoll = 8,7 Zoll. Der Kopf, and dem sich die 4 Wirbel befinden ist 7,75 Zoll lang, wovon 2,75 Zoll auf eine das Ganze krönende Verzierung kommen.

Die Stimmung ist Prim, Quint, Octav, Terz, also genau die Folge, die das preußische Infanteriehorn-Signat "das Ganze" giebt.

Gespielt wird die Biwa mit einem aus Horn, Holz, Schildpatt oder Elfenbein gefertigten, 6,3 Zoll langen beilförmigen Schläger, dem Batsi, (Fig. N° 33).

Die Samiseng, das gewöhnlichste japanische Saiteninstrument, das auch von allen Gescha's (unseren Harfenistinnen entsprechenden Sängerinnen) gespielt wird, hat 3 Saiten, 3 Wirbel, einen

way confident because I have examined no properly tuned wagon yet, but have formed the ideas expressed above only according to a drawing superficially indicating the placing of the bridges.

The seven-stringed Chinese koto I have not been able to examine at all (Fig. 5 [p. 120]).

The biwa (Fig. 2 [p. 118]) is strung with 4 strings of which two apiece are of the same thickness. The body is 33.5 decimal inches[8] long, of which 7.5 account for the neck on which 4 horizontal ridges for stopping are located. The biwa has the shape of a sliced-through pear; it tapers from bottom upwards. The greatest width, at a height of 11 inches, is 12.2 inches, at a height of 16.3 inches, 8.7 inches. The head, on which the 4 pegs are located, is 7.75 inches long, of which 2.75 inches account for a decoration crowning the whole.

The tuning is prime, fifth, octave, third, so exactly the series which the Prussian infantryhorn-signal "The Whole" produces.

The biwa is played with a 6.3-inch-long hatchet-formed plectrum, the bachi, made of horn, wood, tortoiseshell, or ivory (Fig. 33 [p. 125]).

The shamisen, the most common Japanese stringed instrument, which is also played by all geisha (singers corre-

---

8   decimal reckoning, i.e., 33.5 = 33½. – Ed.

glatten Steg, über welchen die Saiten in gleichen Distancen laufen. Die Größe und überhaupt alle Verhältnisse der Samiseng wechseln sehr nach der Stimme des Sängers oder der Sängerin; gute d.h. hohe Stimmen brauchen ein kleines Instrument. Ein von mir gemessenes Instrument für eine mittlere Stimme ist 37 Zoll lang, wovon 7½ auf den eigentlichen Körper kommen, der 6½ Zoll breit und 3 Zoll hoch ist und an seiner untern Seite einen Knopf als Saitenhalter hat. Die vier Seiten des Körpers sind aus Holz, die Ober- und Unterseite sind mit Fell bespannt, auf welches sich dann auch der Steg (Fig. N° 30) stützt. Dieses Fell soll aus dem Euter der Katze gearbeitet werden, und der Beweis, daß es echt ist, wird in kleinen schwarzen Flecken gesucht, die von Verdünnungen der Haut herrühren und von denen behauptet wird, daß sie nicht nachgemacht werden können. Die geschätztesten Instrumente haben je vier solche Flecken auf der Ober- und der Unterseite; ordinärere Instrumente haben nur zwei Flecken; die Instrumente ohne alle Flecken sind ganz billig. Der größern Bequemlichkeit wegen werden die Instrumente häufig so construirt, daß Körper und Griffbrett getrennt werden können, wodurch sie transportabler werden. Gespielt wird die Samiseng ebenfalls mit dem Batsi; der Batsi des obenerwähnten Instruments war 7 Zoll lang, die zugeschärfte Seite 3 Zoll breit, der Griff maß 1½ Zoll im Quadrat. (Fig N° 32). Abgesehen von der Höhe des Grundtons kann die Samiseng in fünf verschiedenen Weisen gestimmt

sponding to our Harfenistinnen[9] – Ed.), has 3 strings, 3 pegs, a flat bridge over which the strings pass at equal distance. The size and generally all measurements of the shamisen vary greatly according to the voice of the male or female singer; good, that is to say, high, voices need a small instrument. An instrument I measured for a middle-range voice is 37 inches long, out of which 7½ account for the actual body, which is 6½ inches wide and 3 inches high and has a knob as string-holder on its lower end. The four sides of the body are of wood; the upper and the lower surfaces are covered with skin, on which the bridge also rests (Fig. 30 [p. 125]). This skin should be worked from the udder of a cat, and the proof that it is genuine is sought in little black flecks that come from the thinning of the skin and concerning which it is maintained that they cannot be imitated. The most valued instruments have four such flecks on each of the upper and lower surfaces; more ordinary instruments have only two flecks; instruments without any flecks are very cheap. For greater convenience, the instruments are often constructed so that body and neck can be separated, whereby they become more transportable. The shamisen too is played with the bachi; the bachi of the instrument mentioned above was 7 inches long, the bevelled side, 3 inches wide, the size of the grip, 1½ square inches (Fig. 32 [p. 125]). Irrespective of the pitch of the ground-note, the shamisen can be tuned

---

9 see fn. 1, p. 79.

werden, die verschiedene Namen tragen: in five different ways that bear different
                                           names:

Hontziosi .	=	Prim, Quart, Octav.
Niagari ...	=	Prim, Quint, Octav.
Sansagarie .	=	Secunde, Quint, Octav.
Itsisagarie .	=	Prim, Quint, None.
Sansasagarie	=	Prim, Quart, Quint der tieferen Octav.

----

hon-chōshi .	=	prime, fourth, octave.
ni-agari ...	=	prime, fifth, octave.
san-sagari .	=	second, fifth, octave.
ichi-sagari .	=	prime, fifth, ninth.
sansa-sagari	=	prime, fourth, fifth of lower octave.

Die Kokiu, Violine, (Fig N° 4), ist in ihrer allgemeinen Construction der Samiseng sehr ähnlich, nur daß sie statt des Batsi mit dem Kiu, Bogen gespielt wird. Sie wird jetzt überhaupt nur sehr wenig gespielt und ist der Spieler, den ich in der Sitzung der Gesellschaft vorführte und der zur Blindenmusik gehört, der einzige Kokiu Spieler in Yedo. Er hat zweierlei Klassen Stücke, die er spielt, Fudjiyu, das von den Vorfahren überkommene Spiel, und Shohoyu, das gewöhnliche Spiel. Das diesem Aufsatze beigegebene Musikstück gehört der ersten Art zu, ist also ganz alt japanisch und wird abwechselnd mit Gesang unisono begleitet. Herr Westphal, Lehrer der Mathematik, dem ich die Notirung dieses Stückes, sowie die Berechnung der Schwingungsverhältnisse verdanke, (wofür ich ihm, sowie Herrn Holz und Herrn Dr. Funk, die mich bei meinen Nachforschungen vielfach freundlichst unterstützt, endlich Herrn Miyake,

The *kokyū*, violin (Fig. 4 [p. 119]), in its general construction is very similar to the *shamisen*, except that it is played with the *kyū*, bow, instead of the *bachi*. It is now really played very little, and the performer whom I introduced in the meeting of the *Gesellschaft*, and who belongs to music-of-the-blind, is the only *kokyū* player in Edo. He plays two types of pieces, *Fuji[ue-r]yū*, the playing transmitted from his forefathers, and *Shōō-[r]yū*, the standard playing. The musical piece attached to this essay belongs to the former sort, so it is very old Japanese, and is accompanied alternately by unison song. Herr Westphal, mathematics teacher, to whom I owe the notating of this piece as also the calculation of the frequencies, played the piece to the blind man on a violin after it was notated. (I express my warmest thanks to him [Herr Westphal] as well as to Herr Holz [Holtz] and Herr Dr. Funk, who most kindly supported me in many

durch dessen Bemühungen mir die Forschungen überhaupt ermöglicht worden sind, meinen wärmsten Dank sage) spielte dem Blinden das Stück, nachdem es notirt war, auf einer Violine vor, und der blinde Musiker sprach sich auf das freudigste und anerkennendste darüber aus. Kleine Nuancen differiren allerdings etwas, denn der Blinde variirte sie bei jedesmaligen Vorspielen etwas, aber bis auf diese kleinen Abweichungen ist das Stück ganz genau richtig, nur ist es der Einfachheit wegen eine Octav zu tief notirt.

Die ganze Länge des Instruments ist 25 Zoll, vom Steg bis zur Brücke 14 Zoll; der Körper, dessen Seiten etwas nach außen geschweift sind, ist 5 Zoll lang und ebenso breit, 2½ Zoll hoch, sonst ganz der Samiseng gleich, auch ebenso mit Fell bezogen. Statt des Saitenhalterknopfs hat die Kokiu einen 2½ Zoll, langen, runden Metallstab; der Saitenhalter wird durch eine seidene Schnur gebildet. Die vier Wirbel sind keilförmig, schief eingesetzt, auf beiden Seiten abwechselnd.

Der Steg (Fig. N° 27) ist lang, sehr niedrig, in der Mitte erhöht und gewölbt. Er zeigt vier Einschnitte zur Aufnahme der Saiten, von denen drei durch gleiche Intervalle von einander, der vierte vom dritten aber nur durch einen ganz geringen Zwischenraum getrennt ist.

Die Saiten waren F, B, Es gestimmt und zwar die beiden dicht neben einander verlaufenden unisono auf Es. Der 45 Zoll lange Bogen, besteht aus vier Stäbchen von rothem Sandelholz, die durch

ways in my investigations, and finally to Herr Miyake, through whose efforts the researches were made even possible for me.) The blind musician spoke out about it most elatedly and appreciatively. Small nuances differ somewhat, admittedly, because the blind man varied them slightly with each performance, but except for these small deviations the piece is exactly right, only that for ease it is notated an octave too low.

The full length of the instrument is 25 inches, from bridge to nut, 14 inches; the body, the sides of which are slightly bent outwards, is 5 inches long and equally wide, 2½ inches high, otherwise just the same as for the *shamisen*, also covered in the same way with skin. Instead of the tailpiece knob, the *kokyū* has a 2½-inch-long, round metal spike; the tailpiece is made with a silk cord. The four pegs are tapered, inserted askew alternately on both sides.

The bridge (Fig. 29,[10] [p. 125]) is long, very low, and in the middle raised and rounded. It displays four incisions for taking up the strings, of which three are separated by the same interval from one another, but the fourth from the third only by a very narrow space.

The strings were tuned *f*, *bb*, *eb*, the two lying close together actually in unison on *eb*. The 45-inch-long bow consists of four rods of red sandalwood which are

---

[10] Correction from Fig. 27. – Ed.

silberne Hülsen zusammengehalten werden und zum Transport auseinander genommen werden können. Sie sind auf dem Rücken flach, vorne oval. Der Körper des Bogens ist oben beinahe rechtwinklig gebogen, die Biegung 2½ Zoll lang. Der 9 Zoll lange Griff hat dieselbe Form, wie der Körper, nur ist er etwas dicker, der ganze Körper ist sehr elastisch.

Der 31 Zoll lange Bezug besteht aus weißen Pferdehaaren, die besonders zu diesem Zwecke importirt werden, da es so lange Pferdehaare hierorts nicht giebt. Ich hielt sie erst grade dieser Länge wegen für Pflanzenfasern; die microscopische Untersuchung ergab aber, daß es wirklich Haare sind. Der Bezug ist oben durch einen silbernen Halter, unten durch eine seidene Schnur befestigt.

Vor dem Spiele reibt sich nun der Spieler die Hände mit Stärke ein, was überhaupt alle Musiker thun.

Nun faßt er den Bogen mit Daumen, Mittelfinger und kleinem Finger, den Zeigefinger legt er auf den Rücken des Bogens, mit dem gerade ausgestreckten vierten Finger spannt er den bis dahin schlaffen Bezug, der dann zwischen viertem und kleinem Finger durchläuft. Darauf faßt er die Kokiu am Griffe, hält sie vertical vor sich hin, stemmt den Körper derselben auf seine Kniee, zwischen welche er den die Saiten haltenden Metallstab fixirt. Dann stützt er den Bezug des Bogens gegen den Rand des Resonnanzbogens und schiebt nun einfach den Bogen horizontal vor und rückwärts, wobei er nur das mittlere

held together with silver sleeves and can be taken apart for transport. They are flat at the back, oval in front. The body of the bow is bent almost at a right angle at the top, the bend 2½ inches long. The 9-inch-long grip has the same shape as the body, only it is somewhat thicker. The whole body is very elastic.

The 31-inch-long set of bow-hairs is made of white horsehairs which are specially imported for this purpose, since such long horsehairs do not exist here. In the beginning I took them for plant fibres because of that very length, but microscopic examination revealed that they are really hair. The set of hairs is fixed above with a silver fastener, below with a silk cord.

Before playing, the performer now rubs his hands with starch, which actually all musicians do.

Now he takes the bow with thumb, middle finger, and little finger; the index finger he lays on the back of the bow; with the fourth finger stretched straight out he tightens the hairs, loose up until that point, which then pass between fourth and little finger. After that he takes the kokyū by the neck, holds it vertically in front of himself, props the body of same on his knees, between which he fixes the metal rod holding the strings. Then he rests the hairs of the bow against the rim of the sounding board and simply slides the bow horizontally backwards and forwards, in doing so using only the middle third of the

Drittel des Bogens gebraucht; die zu benutzende Saiten werden durch Drehung der Kokiu um ihre Verticalaxe mit dem sich ruhig und gleichmäßig hin und her bewegenden Bogen in Berührung gebracht. Von den beiden Es Saiten spielt er bald nur eine, bald spielt er sie beide; ebenso streicht er bald nur eine der beiden andern Saiten, bald beide, Doppeltöne werden wie das Musikstück zeigt nur selten gebraucht. Der Klang des Instruments hat viel Ähnlichkeit mit dem der Leyer.[11]

Indem ich nun die nähere Betrachtung der Blase- und Schlag-Instrumente für das nächste Heft reservire, will ich noch Einiges über die Notirung sagen.

Eine wirklich richtige Notirung besteht nur für die reinen Instrumente, und zwar wird für die Koto einfach die Nummer der anzuschlagenden Saite, bei der Flöte die Nummer der zu stopfenden Löcher angegeben. Es kann aber auch die Nummer oder der Name des Tons in der Tonreihe angegeben werden. Sollen Zwischentöne erzeugt werden, so steht neben dem Tonzeichen ein zweites Zeichen, welches Drücken oder Nachlassen bedeutet. Die tiefere Octav wird durch Nebenstellung eines kleinen Kreises, die noch tiefere durch zwei concentrische

bow; the strings to be used are brought into contact with the bow, gently and regularly moving to-and-fro, by turning the *kokyū* on its vertical axis. Of the two *eb* strings, he plays now only one, now he plays them both; likewise he bows now only one of the other two strings, now both. Chords are – as the musical piece shows – only seldom used. The sound of the instrument is very like that of the hurdy-gurdy.[11]

Since I reserve the closer examination of the wind and percussion instruments for the next issue, I want to say something still about notation.

A really proper notation exists only for the pure instruments; in fact, for the *koto*, simply the number of the string to be struck, for the flute, the number of the holes to be covered is indicated. However, the number or name of the note in the note-series can be indicated. Should semitones be produced, then next to the sign for the note stands a second sign that means pressing or slackening. The lower octave is marked by placing a small circle to the side; that lower still, by two concentric double circles (Fig. 36 [p. 119]).

[11] Eine andere Art Violine habe ich einmal zufällig in einer chinesischen Musik gesehen; konnte sie aber nicht näher besichtigen; sie war der Kokiu sehr ähnlich, nur war der Steg keilförmig, wodurch die Mittelsaite einige Linien über den beiden andern stand; der Bezug des Bogens ging zwischen den Saiten durch, so daß deren Vorder-und-Rückseite abwechselnd benutzt wurden.

[11] I have once seen by chance another type of violin in Chinese music; couldn't view it more closely, however; it was very like the *kokyū*, only that the bridge was wedge-shaped, so that the middle string stood a few [fraction-]lines above the other two; the bow hairs went through between the strings, so that their front- and back-sides were used alternately.

Doppelkreise bezeichnet werden. (Fig.
N° 36)

Der Werth der Noten kann auf doppelte Weise angegeben werden: Entweder man macht neben der Note für die ganzen Noten einen Kreis, für die halben einen Halbkreis, für die Viertel einen Viertelskreis (Fig.N° 37), oder indem man die Noten, wie überhaupt, untereinander schreibt, lässt man zwischen den einzelnen Noten einen der Zeitdauer derselben entsprechenden Intervall.

Tact und Rhythmus werden nicht besonders angegeben, doch ist mir in der ganzen Musik, die ich bisher gehört, noch kein Stück vorgekommen, das nicht im 4/4 oder 2/4 Tact gespielt worden wäre. Eine Art Rhythmus wird zuweilen dadurch angegeben, daß man das namentlich in der alt japanischen Musik sehr beliebte Sforzando-Abstoßen eines langangehaltenen Tones, das dann durch ein Zusammenschlagen der beiden Hölzer der Shaku-Bioshi (Fig. N° 20) markirt wird, durch eine Art seitlich gestellten Komma's bezeichnet.

Für profane Zwecke werden ebenfalls die Nummern angewendet, es wird dann aber noch daneben der Klang durch Buchstaben nachgemacht, wie unser "dideldum, taterata, bumbum" und dergleichen; so schreiben die Japaner z.B. te te ten u.s.w.; das nin ten bedeutet die Dehnung des Tons. Für verschiedene Instrumente ist die Buchstabenbezeichnung verschieden, so z.B. für Blaseinstrumente ra u.s.w.

Die Notenzeichen werden wie gesagt van oben nach unten geschrieben,

The value of the notes can be specified in two ways: either one makes a circle next to the note for a whole note; for the half, a half-circle; for the quarter, a quarter-circle (Fig. 37 [p. 119]), or while one writes the notes, as in general, one beneath the other, one leaves between the individual notes a space appropriate to the duration of each.

Meter and rhythm are not specifically indicated, yet in all the music I have heard so far I have come across no piece that was not played in 4/4 or 2/4 meter. One type of rhythm is sometimes marked, in that the *sforzando*-articulation of a prolonged note, very much liked especially in the old Japanese music, and highlighted in turn by hitting together the two pieces of wood of the *shakubyōshi* (Fig. 20 [p. 121]), is signified by a sort of slanting comma.

For secular purposes, numbers are likewise used, but then, alongside, the sound is imitated in letters like our "dideldum, taterata, bumbum," and the like: so the Japanese write, for example, *te te ten*, and so on; *nin-ten* means the drawing-out of a note. For different instruments the marking by letters is different; so, for example, for wind-instruments, *ra*, etc.

The signs for the notes are written from top to bottom, as stated above; the

der Text links davon, die andern Zeichen bald rechts, bald links. Die einzelnen Linien, zwischen denen ein größerer Intervall bleibt, werden wie alle japanische Schrift von rechts nach links geschrieben.

Die meisten Stücke sind nun so geschrieben, daß sie mit und ohne Begleitung von andern Instrumenten oder Gesang aufgeführt werden können. Der Gesang ist immer unisono mit dem Hauptinstrument; die Begleitung anderer Instrumente kann unisono oder harmonisch sein; im letztern Falle gilt aber die strenge Regel, daß bei der heiligen Musik die Intervalle durch das ganze Stück gleich sein müssen, bei der profanen können sie wechseln. Der mir die Sache erklärende Musiker suchte mir die Regel graphisch so klar zu machen, daß er mir sagte, bei der heiligen Musik müßten Melodie und Begleitung gehen wie zwei parallele Schlangenlinien, bei der profanen Musik könnte die Begleitung aber gehen, wie eine ganz unregelmäßig gezackte Linie.

text to the left of them, the other signs, at times to the right, at others to the left. The individual columns, between which remains a larger space, are written from right to left, like all Japanese script.

Most pieces are written in such a way that they can be performed with and without accompaniment of other instruments or singing. The singing is always in unison with the main instrument; the accompaniment of other instruments can be in unison or harmonic; in the latter case, however, the strict rule applies that for sacred music the intervals must remain constant through the entire piece; for the secular, they may change. The musician explaining the matter to me tried to make the rules clear to me graphically, in that he told me: in sacred music, melody and accompaniment must move like two parallel snake-lines; in secular music, the accompaniment could move like a quite irregularly zigzagged line.

DR MÜLLER.

DR MÜLLER

FUJI[UE-R]YŪ ON THE KOKYŪ

PLAYED BY A MEMBER OF THE Music-of-the-blind IN THE MEETING OF THE EAST ASIAN SOCIETY ON 13 JUNE, IN EDO.

The complete piece an octave higher.

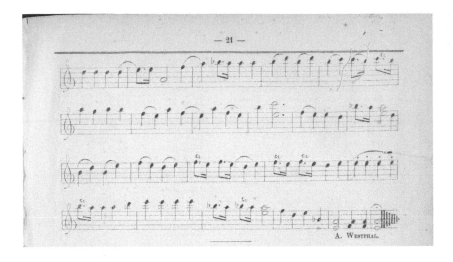

ERKLÄRUNG DER ABBIL-DUNGEN.[12]

Fig. 1.— *Gescha* (Sängerin) mit der drei-zehnseitigen Sono Koto; das ne-ben ihr stehende Kästchen dient zum Unterbringen der Stege und der auf die Finger zu steckenden Elfenbeinspitzen. Der erste Steg steht auf der tiefern Octav der Quinte, wie es dem einen Spieler erlaubt war, ihn zu stellen. Es ist dies der Deutlichkeit der Figur wegen so gemacht worden, ist aber nicht der gewöhnliche Fall, vielmehr müsste er in einer Höhe mit dem fünften Stege stehen. Die über die linke Wange herab-

[12] Die neben den Figuren befindlichen Bruchzahlen bedeuten das Verhältnis der Größe der Abbildung zu der natürlichen Größe des Gegenstands; 1/1 ist die natür-liche Größe.

GUIDE TO THE ILLUSTRA-TIONS[12]

Fig. 1. *Geisha* (female singer) with the thirteen-stringed *sō-no-koto*; the little box standing next to her is used for storing the bridges and the ivory plectra for putting on the fingers. The first bridge stands at the lower octave of the fifth, as it was permitted for that one player to place it [See p. 82]. This has been done like this to make the illustration clearer, but is not the usual case; rather, it should stand at the level of the fifth bridge. The strands of hair

[12] The fractions to be found next to the fig-ures indicate the proportion of the size of the illustration to the natural proportion of the object; 1/1 is the natural size.

fallenden Haarbüschel gehören
zu der feinen Kleidung.

hanging down over the left cheek
go with the elegant attire.

Fig. 2.— *Biwa Spieler* in der großen offici-
ellen Fest-Kleidung der Blindenmusik.

Fig. 2. *Biwa player* in the grand official
ceremonial-attire of the music-
of-the-blind.

Fig. 3.— *Samiseng Spieler* im Festgewand,
wozu namentlich die breiten Flü-
gel auf den Schultern gehören.

Fig. 3. *Shamisen* player in ceremonial
robe, to which belong notably
the broad wings on the shoul-
ders.

Fig. 4.— (Tafel III) *Kokiu Spieler* in der
gewöhnlichen Kleidung der Blin-
den, die sonst nur von Frauen
getragen wird.

Fig. 4 (Plate III). *Kokyū* player in the
usual attire of the blind, which is
otherwise only worn by women.

Taf. IV:

Plate IV:

Fig. 5.— *Siebensaitige* chinesische *Kino
Koto*, ohne daß die Stege aufge-
setzt sind.

Fig. 5. *Seven-stringed* Chinese *kin-
no-koto*, without the bridges
mounted.[13]

Fig. 6.— *Sechssaitige*, altjapanische
Yamato koto oder *Wanggong* mit
aufgesetzten Stegen, doch ist
die Stellung derselben nicht als
genau richtig anzusehen.

Fig. 6. *Six-stringed* old-Japanese *yamato-
goto* or *wagon* with bridges
mounted, although the positioning of the same is not to be
regarded as exactly right.

Fig. 7.— *Geking*, chinesisch.

Fig. 7. *Gekkin*, Chinese.

Fig. 8.— *Zweisaitige*, oder *Idsumo Koto*.

Fig. 8. *Two-stringed* or *izumo-goto*.

Fig. 9.— (Tafel VI). Einsaitige oder
Suma Koto. Sie ist ganz zerleg-
bar und können die sämmt-
lichen auseinander genom-
menen Stücke in den hohlen
Resonanzkasten gepackt werden.

Fig. 9 (Plate VI). *One-stringed* or *suma-
koto*. It can be completely disman-
tled and all the separated pieces
can be stored in the hollow res-
onating box.

[13] The author had not personally witnessed
the instrument being played, therefore
this inaccuracy. – Ed.

Fig. 10.— (Tafel VI). Shio. Die obere ist so wie sie gespielt wird; wenn sie nicht gebraucht wird, wird ein Kissen zwischen die Stabenden gesteckt, damit sie sich nicht verbiegen, dies ist in der untern Figure dargestellt. Die einzelnen Theile des Instruments sind auf der Tafel IV abgebildet, nämlich a, der Windkasten, b, der Ring, welcher die Stäbe zusammenhält, c, das Mundstück des Windkastens in der Vorderansicht. Das ganze Instrument ist kostbar lackirt, die Beschläge sind von Silber.

Fig. 10 (Plate VI). Shō. The upper [depiction] is as it is played; when it is not used, a pillow is inserted between the ends of the rods so that they do not bend. This is depicted in the lower figure. The individual parts of the instrument are pictured on Plate IV, namely, a. the wind-chest, b. the ring which holds the rods together, c. the mouth-piece of the wind-chest seen from the front. The complete instrument is sumptuously laquered, the fittings are of silver.

Fig. 11.— (Tafel VI). Hidschiriki, rechts Vorderansicht, links Hinteransicht, a, das herausgenommene Zungenmundstück, die Spitze durch einen kleinen Deckel geschützt, der beim Gebrauch abgenommen wird.

Fig. 11 (Plate VI). Hichiriki. Right, front view, left, rear view; a. the mouthpiece taken out, the top protected by a small cover which is taken off for use.

Fig. 12.— (Tafel VI). Ohteki.

Fig. 12 (Plate VI). Ōteki.

Fig. 13.— (Tafel VI). Koma fuye.

Fig. 13 (Plate VI). Komabue.

Fig. 14.— (Tafel VI). Kagura fuye.

Fig. 14 (Plate VI). Kagurabue.

Fig. 15.— (Tafel V). Taiko, a, Seitenansicht der Trommel ohne Ständer.

Fig. 15 (Plate V). Taiko; a. side-view of the drum without stand.

Fig. 16.— (Tafel VI). Kako.

Fig. 16 (Plate VI). Kakko.

Fig. 17.— (Tafel VI). Yoko.

Fig. 17 (Plate VI). Yōko.

Fig. 18.— (Tafel V). Shioko, a, Seitenansicht.

Fig. 18 (Plate V). Shōko; a. side-view.

Fig. 19.— (Tafel v). *Tsudsumi, a*, Vorderansicht, *b*, Durchschnitt des Fellbezugs.

Fig. 20.— (Tafel v). *Shaku Bioshi*, Holzklapper.

Fig. 21.— (Tafel vii). *Tonrose* berechnet für die Tonart des December.

Fig. 22.— (Tafel vii). *Stimmgabel* aus Bambus oder Elfenbein, *a*, obere Ansicht, *b*, untere Ansicht.

Fig. 23.— (Tafel vii). *Schema* dazu; die schwarz bezeichneten Öffnungen werden mit den Fingern geschlossen, um die einzelnen Töne zu erzeugen; die Fortsetzung des Schemas befindet sich auf Tafel VIII. Diese Stimmgabel beginnt, wenn alle Öffnungen geschlossen sind (*a*) mit dem Februarton F, während alle andern Stimmgabeln vom December anfangen. Die Reihenfolge der Töne ist: *a*, Februar (F), *b*, April (G), *c*, Juni (A), *d*, März (Ges), *e*, Mai (As), *f*, Juli (B), *g*, (Tafel VIII) August (H), *h*, October (Des); die folgenden Töne sind in der höhern Octav: *i*, December (Es), *j*, Februar (F), *k*, April (G). Die folgenden Töne sind wieder eine Octav tiefer, also wie Anfangs: *l*, September (C), *m*, November (D); die folgenden sind wieder eine Octav höher: *n*, Januar (E), *o*, März (Ges), *p*, Mai (As).

Fig. 19 (Plate V). *Tsuzumi; a*. front view, *b*. cross-section of the skin covering.

Fig. 20 (Plate V). *Shakubyōshi*, wooden clapper.

Fig. 21 (Plate VII). *Circle of notes* calculated for the key of December.

Fig. 22 (Plate VII). *Tuning-fork* made from bamboo or ivory; *a*. view from above, *b*. view from below.

Fig. 23 (Plate VII). *Corresponding diagram*; the holes marked black are closed with the fingers to produce the single notes. The continuation of the diagram is to be found on Plate VIII. This tuning-fork begins, when all holes are closed (*a*), with the note of February F, whilst all other tuning-forks begin from December. The order of the notes is: *a*. February (F); *b*. April (G); *c*. June (A); *d*. March (Gb); *e*. May (Ab); *f*. July (Bb); *g*. (Plate VIII), August (B); *h*. October (Db). The following notes are in the higher octave: *i*. December (Eb); *j*. February (F); *k*. April (G). The next notes are once more an octave lower, that is, as at the start: *l*. September (C); *m*. November (D). The following are again an octave higher: *n*. January (E); *o*. March (Gb); *p*. May (Ab).

Fig. 24.— (Tafel VIII). Kreisförmige Stimmgabel mit 12 Zungen, Seitenansicht, a, obere Ansicht.

Fig. 24 (Plate VIII). Circular tuning-fork with 12 tongues, side-view; a. view from above.

Fig. 25.— (Tafel IX). Stimmgabel mit neben einander gestellten Zungenpfeifen, Ikada (floßförmige Stimmgabel). Die Pfeifen sind in der Mitte durch einen Stift verbunden, um welchen sie sich drehen, sie können von beiden Enden durch Aspiration in Schwingungen versetzt werden, erzeugen aber auf jedem Ende einen verschiedenen Ton von December anfangend und dann links herum streng nach der Tonrose Fig. 21; a obere und untere Ansicht.

Fig. 25 (Plate IX). Tuning-fork with tongued-pipes set one beside the other; ikada (raft-shaped tuning-fork). The pipes are connected in the middle with a pin around which they turn; they can be set in oscillation from both ends through aspiration, but produce a different note at each end, beginning with December and then round to the left strictly according to the circle of notes (Fig. 21 [p. 123]); a. view from above and below.

Fig. 26.- (Tafel IX). Halbe Stimmgabel für die sechs gebräuchlichsten Töne.

Fig. 26 (Plate IX). Half tuning-fork for the six most used notes.

Fig. 26A.- (Tafel XI). b, obere, c, seitliche Ansicht.

Fig. 26a (Plate IX). b. view from above, c. side-view.

Fig. 27.— (Tafel VIII). Stimmgabel mit Pfeifen, nach Art der Papageno Flöte, gestimmt wie Figur 25.

Fig. 27 (Plate VIII). Tuning-fork with pipes, in the style of the pan-pipe, tuned as Fig. 25.

Fig. 28.— (Tafel IX). Steg der Koto aus Holz oder Elfenbein, rechts Seitenansicht, links Vorderansicht.

Fig. 28 (Plate IX). Bridge of the koto, of wood or ivory; right, side-view; left, front view.

Fig. 28A.- Steg der Wanggong, es werden hierzu passend geformte Ahornzweig-Gabeln genommen und dann geschnitzt; die kleinen Kreise geben die Durchschnittsfläche.

Fig. 28a [Plate IX]. Bridge of the wagon; for the purpose, appropriately shaped maple branch forks are taken and then carved; the small circles give the area of the cross-section.

Fig. 29.— (Tafel IX). Steg der Kokiu.

Fig. 29 (Plate IX). Bridge of the kokyū.

Fig. 30.— (Tafel IX). Steg der Samiseng; rechts, obere Ansicht, links oben, vordere Ansicht, links unten, Durchschnitt. Da bei Todesfällen, Landestrauer u. dgl. jeder Lärm und namentlich auch Musiciren allgemein verboten ist, so bedienen sich in solchen Fällen diejenigen, welche trotz des Verbotes die Samiseng spielen wollen, eines ganz schweren Bleistegs, um den Ton zu dämpfen.

Fig. 30 (Plate IX). Bridge of the shamisen; right, view from above; left above, front view; left below, cross-section. Since for deaths, national mourning, and the like, all noise is in general forbidden, and especially music-making, those who wish to play the shamisen despite the ban make use in such cases of a very heavy bridge made of lead to dampen the sound.

Fig. 31.— (Tafel IX). Steg der einsaitigen Koto; die obere Figur stellt den Querschnitt dar, die mittlere die Seitenansicht, die untere den Längsdurchschnitt.

Fig. 31 (Plate IX). Bridge of the one-stringed koto; the upper figure shows the cross-section; the middle, the side-view; the lower, the lengthwise cross-section.

Fig. 32.— (Tafel IX). Batsi der Samiseng, Vorder- und Seitenansicht.

Fig. 32 (Plate IX). Bachi of the shamisen, front- and side-view.

Fig. 33.— (Tafel IX). Batsi für die Biwa, Vorder- und Seitenansicht.

Fig. 33 (Plate IX). Bachi for the biwa, front- and side-view.

Fig. 34.— (Tafel III). Batsi für Geking aus Schildpatt, Vorder- und Seitenansicht.

Fig. 34 (Plate III [p. 119]). Bachi for the gekkin [wagon], of tortoiseshell, front- and side-view.

Fig. 35.— (Tafel III). Batsi für die einsaitige Koto, aus Bambus oder Holz, a, Längsdurchschnitt, b, untere Ansicht.

Fig. 35 (Plate III). Bachi for the one-stringed koto, of bamboo or wood; a. lengthwise cross-section; b. view from below.

Fig. 36.— (Tafel III). Zeichen für die tiefern Octaven, a, nächsttiefere, b, zweittiefere.

Fig. 36 (Plate III). Signs for the lower octaves: a. the next lower, b. two lower.

Fig. 37.— (Tafel III). Aus Versehen auf der Tafel mit 38 bezeichnet: Zeichen für a, halbe, b, Viertelnoten.

Fig. 37 (Plate III). Mistakenly indicated as Fig. 38 on the plate. Signs for a. the half-note, and b. the quarter-note.

Fig. 38.— (Tafel   III). Elfenbeinspitzen
zum Spielen der Koto, a, hin-
tere Ansicht, b, Seitenansicht, c,
Durchschnitt.

Fig. 38 (Plate III). Ivory picks for playing
the koto; a. view from behind, b.
side-view, c. cross-section.

Fig. 1.

– (Plate I) –

– (Tafel)/Plate II –

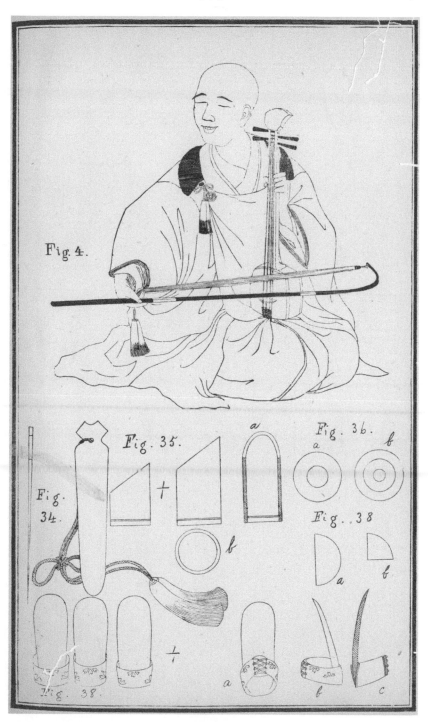

Fig. 4.

Fig. 35.

Fig. 36.

Fig. 34.

Fig. 38

Fig. 38.

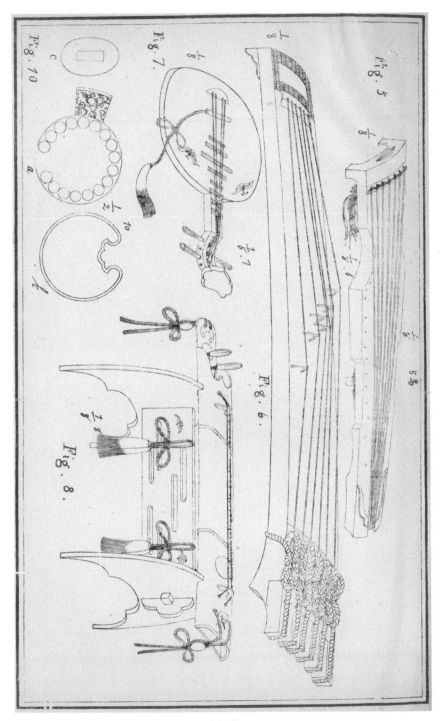

Fig. 5

Fig. 6

Fig. 7

Fig. 8

Fig. 10

– Tafel/Plate IV –

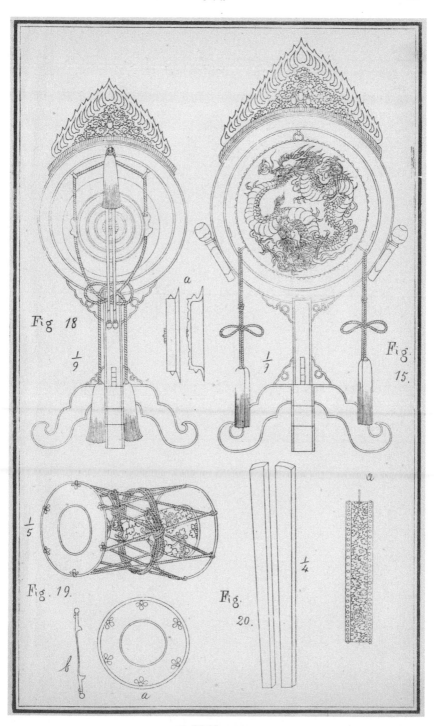

Fig. 18
$\frac{1}{9}$
a

Fig. 15.
$\frac{1}{7}$

Fig. 19.
$\frac{1}{5}$
a
b

Fig. 20.
$\frac{1}{4}$
a

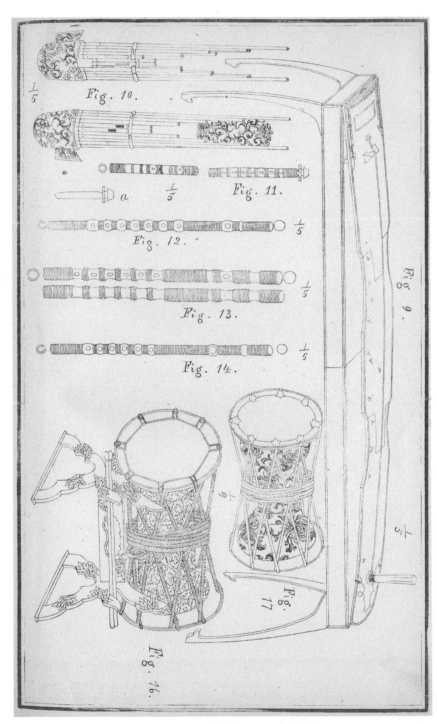

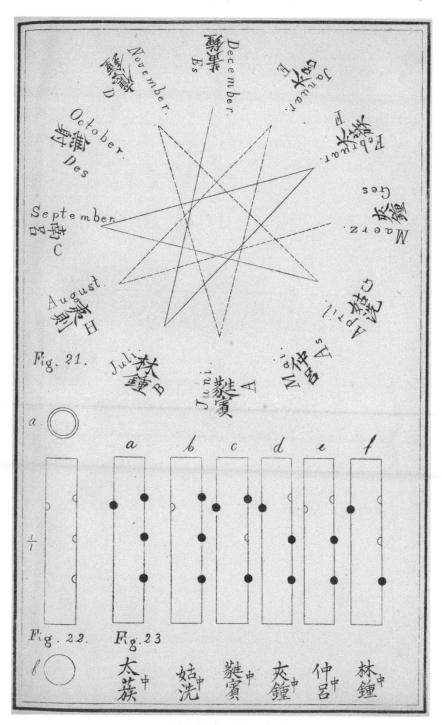

Fig. 21.

Fig. 22.   Fig. 23

– Tafel/Plate VII –

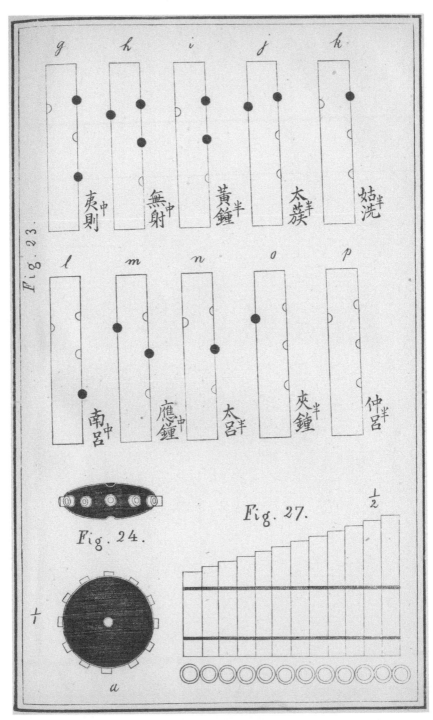

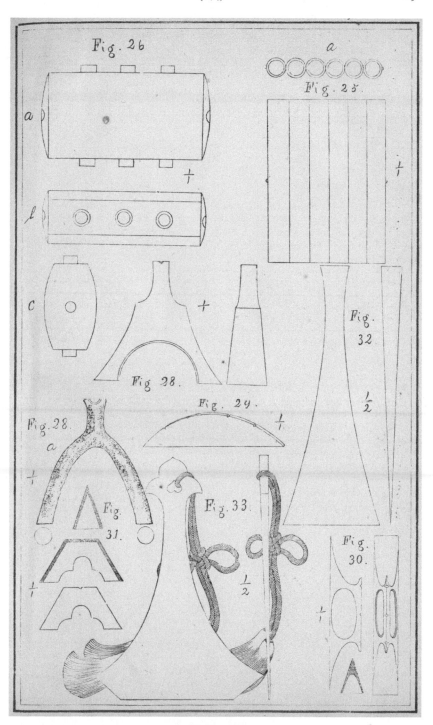

Fig. 26

a

Fig. 25

Fig. 28.

Fig. 28. a

Fig. 29.

Fig. 31.

Fig. 33.

Fig. 32.

Fig. 30.

1874

日本音楽に関する記述を入手することは本当に難しい。それは、日本人の生来の控えめさによるだけでなく、主に、ここではほとんどの音楽家自身が理論を知らないことによる。楽譜やそれに類するものがありそうにはまったく思えない。まるで我々のヴァイオリン弾き Bierfiedler やハープ奏者 Harfenistinnen¹³ について、もっと正確に知りたいと望む状況にいるようなものである。理論に詳しい音楽家は非常に稀で、国の中に散在している。神聖な音楽は概して外国人にとっては近づきがたくまったく特別にうまく連携が成立した時だけに、ある程度詳しく楽器を調べることができる。医者としての立場によって私は、さまざまな高官や学者に詳しい楽器の研究を許してもらうという状況になんとかこぎ着けた。このようにして、私はまた、教養ある音楽家何人かに接触することができた。以下の文章で研究の結果を述べたいが、完璧を期すという要求はあまり持たないでおく。私は、自身でも望んでいるように、次第にもっと多くを知るようになるはずなので、研究結果は後の号で発表することにする。

　調査の方法として、私は主に、私たち [西洋] の音楽や楽器を見たり聞いたりしたいという思う人々の好奇心を利用した。ただし、もしヨーロッパ音楽が日本人に与える印象がどんなものかを言わねばならないとすれば、私たちが日本の音楽に嫌悪感を抱く以上に、日本人は私たちの音楽を不快に感じると主張するのは正しいと思う。ある上流の日本人は、もちろん彼らはあまりにも慇懃なので私に対してではないのだが、このように言った。「子供、下級労働者、女性はヨーロッパ音楽を気に入っているが、教養ある日本人は耐えられない」。

　音楽に関してもまた、日本のすべての知的活動表現について我々が発見したことがまったく当てはまる。すなわち、日本で自然に生まれたものはほとんどなく、むしろ、この分野では、多くのものは完成品として中国、朝鮮から日本にやってきた。そしてここで、まず長い年月、非常にまじめな几帳面さで保存され、後に様々な点で改変、改良されたが、改悪されたものもまた多いだろう。

　音楽家たちはある種の同業者団体を作っている。それは所定の日時に集まり、きっちり規定された神聖な演奏や世俗的な演奏をするためのものである。その他に、タイクン [大君 (将軍)]、ミカド [天皇]、ダイミョウ [大名] は、特に昔は私設楽団を持っていたが、これを現在も持っている。¹⁴ つきつめれば、報酬を得て演奏する音楽家は完全に分類されている。

　総じて、音楽家は以下のようなカテゴリーに分けられる。

1. 神聖な音楽だけを演奏する者。理論的に教育されていて、記譜の知識を持っている [ガクニン [楽人]]。彼らは非常に尊敬される階層の人々に属する。伝

---

¹³ (英訳者補注) いわゆる市場、酒場、サロンなどのヴァイオリン、ハープ弾き。
¹⁴ 大君の世俗的音楽はノウ [能] といい、ミカドの神聖な音楽はガガク [雅楽] またはガク [楽] という。後者は昔、奈良、天王寺、京都だけで演奏され、それらは古くからの、先祖から伝承されてきた作品を演奏している。

統的にこの音楽は大名も習うことができた。中国ではこの音楽は消滅し、そ
れに対して日本では今日まで、とりわけミカドの専用楽団で演奏されてい
る。ほとんどの作品では歌詞は失われたが、音楽だけは残っている。そし
て、演奏者自身も作品の意味についてもうわからない。

2. 世俗的な音楽だけを演奏する者。彼らは理論に疎く、楽譜も無い [ゲイニン
   [芸人]]。ただ箏の演奏家だけが調子に関する知識と世俗音楽の楽譜を知って
   いる。階層的に、彼らは商人などと同等で、より低い階層に属す。

3. 盲人音楽にはケンギョウ [検校] とコウトウ [勾当] という 2 つの階級があり、
   検校のほうが高位である。これらの位はお金で買う。彼らは庶民的な音楽の
   みを演奏する。

4. おびただしい数の女性音楽家の階層があるが、ここでは触れない。というの
   も、彼女らは音楽的には完全に従属的な役割しか持っていないからである。
   女性が階層を越えて上にあがることはめったにない。身分の高い階層の女性
   や娘たちも、ここでは低い世俗的な音楽を習うのが常である。

　昔は、1 つの大きな分類の中にさえ、さらに様々な音楽家の階層があった。こ
れは現在ではもうなくなったが、いまだに音楽家団体の頂点には教師が君臨してお
り、何らかの報償や名誉を分配している。たとえば、本年 6 月 13 日の [OAG の] 例
会で私が紹介した音楽家の 1 人は、第 1 絃を通常よりも 1 オクターヴ低く調絃する
権利を得ていた。このような名誉は、本当の [実力による] 報償として、もしくは金
銭の代価として授与される。より優れた作品は団体の所有物であり、外の人によっ
て演奏されることは許されない。この他、さらに、豊かな民俗音楽がある。
　日本で使われている楽器は以下のように分かれる。

1. 打楽器。金属製、木製、動物の革で作られたものなど。

2. 管楽器。木製、貝製。金属は舌 [簧、リード] の作成のみに使われている。

3. 絃楽器。様々なバチ、もしくは弓 (キュウ)[15] で演奏される。

ヴェント、キー、鍵盤のついた、より複雑な楽器は日本にはない。
すべての楽器は次のように分けられる。

I. 純粋な、すなわち神聖な音楽演奏だけに使われる楽器。

A. 中国もしくは朝鮮の楽曲演奏に使用される楽器

　1. 絃楽器

---

[15] 弓は武器の弓も意味する。

a. 7絃のコト [七絃琴]。(Fig. 5)

b. ビワ [琵琶]。ギターのような楽器。(Fig. 2)

2. 太鼓類

a. タイコ [太鼓]。大きな太鼓。(Fig. 15.) 2本の太いバチで打たれる。

b. カッコ [鞨鼓]。斜めに置く小さい太鼓。2本の細いバチで打たれる。(Fig. 16)

c. ヨウコ [腰鼓] あるいはサンノツヅミ [三鼓]。(Fig. 17) 両者の中間。b. [鞨鼓] のように打たれる。

d. ショウコ [鉦鼓]。金属製打楽器。(Fig. 18)

3. 管楽器

a. ショウ [笙]。木製。リードは金属製。(Fig. 10)

b. ヒチリキ [篳篥]。竹製。リードは金属製 (ママ)[16] (Fig. 11)

c. オウテキ [横笛]。中国の笛。(Fig. 12)

d. コマブエ [高麗笛]。朝鮮の笛。(Fig. 13)

B. 純粋古代日本音楽の演奏に使われる楽器

1. ワゴン [和琴] またはヤマトゴト [大和琴]。6絃のコト。(Fig. 6)

2. カグラブエ [神楽笛]。日本の笛。(Fig. 14)

3. シャクビョウシ [笏拍子]。木製の拍子木。(Fig. 20)

II. 非純粋楽器。世俗的な目的のみに使用されるもの。その数は膨大である。純粋楽器もまた世俗的な目的にしばしば使用されるが、その場合は、少し変えた形もしくは別の弾き方をするなどする。

その中で特に言及されるべきは、

A 能の舞踊に使用される楽器。

大君と大名は、その身分ゆえに一般大衆の劇場に行くことができず、お抱えの演奏家と舞踊家を持っていた。

　　それらは、

---

[16] (英訳者補注) オリジナル版における誤植。(日本語訳者補注) 篳篥のリードは葦から作る

1. 大きな太鼓「タイコ [太鼓]」。(Fig. 15)（ママ）

2. ツヅミ [鼓]。2 種の鼓。そのうち一方は左肩に乗せられ、他方は腿のあたりに置かれ、右手の指で打たれる。(Fig. 19)

B その他、日常的な目的で使われるもの。

1. シャミセン [三味線]。(Fig. 3)

2. 13 絃のコト [箏]。(Fig. 1)

3. コキュウ [胡弓]。ヴァイオリン。(Fig. 4) この3つの楽器の組み合わせはサンキョク [三曲] と呼ばれる。

4. いろいろな笛と金属製打楽器。

III. 神聖な音楽と世俗的な音楽の間に、さまざまな一絃琴、管楽器、拍子木等々があり、それらは玩具としてのみ使われる。しかし、これらはまた身分の高い家族でも使われており、したがって敬意を払われている。

私はさらに、田畑を刈りとる前に、蛇やその他の有害な動物を追い払う時に鳴らされる昔ながらの楽器を目にした。それは、私たちのソリのベルのようで、3、4 個のベルが、三本鎖に吊るされた金属の輪、もしくは取手のようなものにつながれている。使用の後は、これらの楽器は、清らかさの象徴である鏡とともに神に捧げられ、寺社に吊るされる。

　音楽理論を詳しく見ると、我々は、ここにもまた中国によくある神秘的な思索を目にする。

　音の領域は、星座や月などの他の自然の力と結びついており、そこから以下のような理論が発展した。

　すべての自然の力と営みは 5 という数によって特徴づけられる。よって、

　5 つの機能を持った内蔵であれば、胃、肺、肝臓、心臓、腎臓。

　ここで注意しておきたいのだが、以下においてもすべて同様に、ヒエラルキーは上から始まり、より上位の語の方が後続するものより重要で優位であることを意味する。

5 色:	黄、	白、	緑、	赤、	黒
5 味:	甘、	辛、	酸、	苦、	塩
5 元素:	土、	金、	木、	火、	水
5 星:	土星、	金星、	木星、	火星、	水星
5 方角:	中央、	西、	東、	南、	北

等々である。音も自然の表れであるので、同様に5でなければならない。
5つの音のシステムは「ゴイン [五音]」といい、以下の順番である。

第1音:	キュウ、	宮、	主
第2音:	ショウ、	商、	従
第3音:	カク、	角、	農
第4音:	チ、	徴、	物質
第5音:	ウ、	羽、	抽象

これらの音についてもまた、先行するものが後続するものより上位であるという一般法則が通用する。ゆえに、音楽の教則では、宮は非常に偉大、羽は非常に小さいと見なされる。

しかしながら、これらの音名は我々の音階の決まった音と対応するわけではなく、むしろ2度、3度、5度などの概念と一致する。すなわち、さまざまな調においてそれぞれ常に基音「宮」との関係性において成り立つのである。よって、我々の様々な音階 [における階名] と似たようなものなのである。

正式な音としてはこれらの五音しか認められていないにもかかわらず、日本人が旋法で五音しか知らないなどと思う人はいないだろう。むしろ、絃楽器で彼らは中間音も使用していて、それらは、絃楽器の特性を活かして行われる絃の「押し」や「引き (柱 (じ) の向こうで絃を緩める)」によって生み出される。

基音は [12の] 月と一定の結びつきがある。実際のところ、その結びつきは、12の月それぞれにおいて空気がその調の音だけを生じさせることによって表れる。すなわち、それぞれの月において異なる、しかし、その月にとっては決まった調が支配するのである。

12月は	コウショウ	[黄鐘] が	支配する。	
1月	タイリョ	[太呂]	〃	
2月	タイソウ	[太簇]	〃	
3月	キョウショウ	[夾鐘]	〃	
4月	コセン	[姑洗]	〃	
5月	チュウリョ	[仲呂]	〃	
6月	スイヒン	[蕤賓]	〃	
7月	リンショウ	[林鐘]	〃	
8月	イソク	[夷則]	〃	
9月	ナンリョ	[南呂]	〃	
10月	ブエキ	[無射]	〃	
11月	オウショウ	[応鐘]	〃	

この音の順番は、以下の様な手順で決まる。[17]

月の名前とその月を支配する音の名前は、円環の中で対称的な位置に記され、12月から反時計回りに回る (Fig. 21)。

ある調に属する五音を決めるには、以下の様な方法をとる。

黄鐘 = 12月の音を基音にとり、12月を1とし、そこから前へ8ケ月進む (日本のやり方では、右から左へ回る) と7月 = 2つ目の音/商へ到達する。今度は7月を1としてそこから6後退し、2月 = 角へ来る。今度は8前進し、9月 = 徴に至り、6後退して4月 = 羽に至る。

このようにして5つの主要音が決まる。再び、6引き返すと、12月の補助音として11月が得られる。8前進し、7月の補助音として6月が、6後退し、2月の補助音として1月が、8前進して9月の補助音として8月が、6後退して4月の補助音として3月が得られる。5月と10月は12月調の中には含まれない。補助音というのは、主要音より半音低い。このようにして、各調に属する主要5音と補助5音が決められる。

主要音に属する音を決める第二の方法は、数学である。基音「宮」を9とし、この数を3で割り、3分の1を引くと、9–3 = 6となる。ここで、この6を新しい単位としてこれを3で割り、3分の1を6に加えると、6 + 2 = 8となる。同様のことをあと3回、つまり、3分の1の引き算と足し算を、毎回得られる数字をあらたに基礎単位として交互に行うと、以下が得られる。

$$\frac{24}{3} - \frac{8}{3} = \frac{16}{3}$$

$$\frac{48}{9} + \frac{16}{9} = \frac{64}{9}$$

$$\frac{192}{27} - \frac{64}{27} = \frac{128}{27}$$

これらの比率によって、ある調に属する各音の絃の長さが決まる。たとえば、基音の長さが9という単位だとすると、第2音は6という長さの絃を必要とする、等々。オクターヴは半分の絃長にした時に得られる。また、それに続く絃は上記の比率で決まっていく。

もっと簡単に計算するために、9の代わりに81を宮の単位にして、81, 54, 72, 48, 64という数を得る人もいる。

月の音は音叉にもなっている。2または1オクターヴの音叉[18] の大きさにもよるが、12月は我々のEs(e♭)である。Fig. 21では、12月から左に回っていくと、我々の半音階となる。シャープのついた音になって行き、平均律ではない。11月が終わりで、dとなる。

音叉で、私は3つの異なる種類を目にした。

---

[17] (英訳者補注) ミュルレルは後続の号で、非常に苦労してこの記述を訂正している。

[18] (英訳者補注) ミュルレルが使っているヘルムホルツの音高表記による。

1. 竹もしくは象牙の小さな筒 (Fig. 22)。一方が開いていて、他方は閉じている。両側に笛のように穴があいており、中指の爪で閉じた端をパチンと弾いて音を出す。図は、音叉の正確な形と大きさである。その横の図表 (Fig. 23) は様々な音高を出すためにどの穴を閉じるかを示している。

2. もう1つのタイプは 12 枚の金属製リードから成る。空気腔のまわりに円形に配置されているか (Fig. 24)、ピン留めされ、回転するように並べられた竹管に埋め込まれている (Fig. 25)。簡略化し、より手に入れやすくするために、安いものも考案された。これは基本音として最もよく使われる最初の6つの音、すなわち3つの主要音と3つの補助音だけがついている (Fig. 26)。

3. 3つ目のタイプは、上も下も開いた、並んだ 12 本の竹筒からなる (Fig. 27)。該当する筒の端を指で閉じ、パパゲーノの笛 [パンパイプ] のように使うと、欲しい音が得られる。

　　ここで、個々の楽器の観察に進むとして、より明快にするためには、神聖な楽器とそうでない楽器の区別には従う必要はない。むしろ私は、部分的には完全にそこから逸脱しようと思う。

　　絃楽器の中で、最も重要かつ合奏の基本となるものとして、コトの説明から始めよう。

　　「コト」とは、長く四角い形で、床に置いて絃を弾く、すべての楽器を指す名称である。

1. キンコト [琴ノコト] は 25 絃と 50 絃があるが、廃れている。

2. 13 絃のソウノコト [箏ノコト] (Fig. 1)。ここではっきり述べておくが、これがこのタイプのコトの正しい名称である。フォン・シーボルトはこれを間違って「琴ノコト」と呼んだ。

3. 6絃のヤマトノコト [大和琴] あるいはワゴン [和琴] (Fig. 6)。前項と同様に、神聖な音楽に属する。上記参照。

4. 2絃のイズモコト [出雲琴] と1絃のスマコト [須磨琴] はほとんど玩具のようなものである (Figs. 8, 9)。

　　須磨琴については言い伝えがある。それによると、この楽器はあるクゲ [公家](貴族) によって発明された。彼は須磨地方に流され (楽器名の由来)、つれづれの暇に、烏帽子に絃を張って一絃琴にしたという。絃の下には低いコマが並んでおり、様々な音を作るためには、指に着けた竹片でそのコマの位置で絃を押さえる。

　　最も重要なのは箏ノコトである (Fig. 1)。同じ太さ、長さ、張力の 13 絃が張られていて、2つのコマ [龍角] に乗っている。すべての絃は一方の龍角を通って箏の

下の端にまわり、共鳴胴にある孔を通って龍角に戻り、そこでしっかりと固定される。絃は、自ら引っ張っている木によって引っ張られている。

　箏の寸法には厳格な規則があるが、多くの場合はそこから外れている。私が所有する標準規格のものは 72 インチ長である。2 つの大きな龍角の間隔は 53 インチで、幅は最大が 10 と ½ インチ、最小が 9 インチ、高さは真ん中が最大で 3 と ½ インチ、最小は両端で 1 と ½ である。

　共鳴胴は非常に固いキリ [桐] の木からできており、下側に 2 つの孔がある。楽器は 4 本の低い足で支えられている。

　調絃は可動式の柱 (じ) を [絃の] 下で動かして行う (Fig. 28、実物大)。演奏者は実際には同時に歌い手でもあり、自分の声 [の高さ] に合わせて調を決める。「よい声」は「高い声」と同義と思われる。

　演奏者はこのようにして基音を定めると、柱を押してこの音を第 2 絃に調絃する。第 1 絃はしばらく調律されないまま置かれる。

　前述の方法で、演奏者は以下の音を割り出して行く。2 番目の音を第 5 絃に、3 番目の音を第 3 絃に、4 番目の音を第 6 絃に、5 番目の音を第 4 絃に置く。音列はこのように相前後して割り出されていき、第 2 絃から 1, 3, 5, 2, 4 となる。もし、天文学的な方法でこれらの音をつきとめ、われわれの音叉の音に変換するとすれば、簡単にするために基音を c とすると、左まわりに 8 つ音を進めると 2 番目の音 g, 3 番目の音は右回りに 6 つ行って d、4 番目の音は a、5 番目の音は e になる。しかし、4 番目と 5 番目の音については、主要音の代わりに補助音が使われ、つまり a♭ と e♭ になる。上記の音を並べると、以下の様な順番になる。

第 1 絃	未調絃	
第 2 絃	第 1 の音	c
第 3 絃	第 3 の音	d
第 4 絃	第 5 の音	e♭
第 5 絃	第 2 の音	g
第 6 絃	第 4 の音	a♭

　我々は [さらに]2 つの音のために [作業を] 続け、6 番目の音として、それは 4 番目の音の次に来なければならないが、b を得る。そして、7 番目の音として g♭ を得る。それは 5 番目と 2 番目の音の間に挿入されるが、半音下げられる。つまり、f となる。(g♭ は補助音で、独立して数えられるほどの重要性は無いからである)。

　ゆえに、箏の調絃は、西洋和声の短調と一致することは明らかである。ただし、第 4 音と第 7 音は除かれている。なぜなら、それらがあると、すべての自然の力の規範として通用している 5 という数字が越えられてしまうからである。

　しかしながら、天文学的な計算の代わりに、前述の数学的な方法によって、我々は次のような結果を得た。さきほど示された音の振動数の比はこうなる。

$$c \quad = \quad \frac{81}{81} \quad = \quad 1 \quad = \quad 1,00000.$$

$$d \quad = \quad \frac{81}{72} \quad = \quad {}^9/_8 \quad = \quad 1,12500.$$

$$es/e\flat \quad = \quad \frac{81}{64} \quad = \quad \quad = \quad 1,26562.$$

$$g \quad = \quad \frac{81}{54} \quad = \quad {}^3/_2 \quad = \quad 1,50000.$$

$$as/a\flat \quad = \quad \frac{81}{43} \quad = \quad {}^{27}/_{16} \quad = \quad 1,68750.$$

　我々の物理学で確定している振動数比と比較したところ、全ての音の相互の比は完全に一致した。ただし、c 対 e♭、c 対 a♭ の比率は異なる。我々の振動数比は

$$c \quad : \quad es/e\flat \quad = \quad 1 \quad : \quad 1,20000$$
$$c \quad : \quad as/a\flat \quad = \quad 1 \quad : \quad 1,60000$$

　前者の比率は 0,06562 異なり、後者は 0,08750 異なっている。しかし、理論に従い e♭ と a♭ の代わりに e と a を考慮すべきだとすると、差異は少し減らされ、

音	日本の振動数	物理的振動数	差
es/e♭	1,26562	1,25000	0,01562
as/a♭	1,68750	1,66666	0,02084

となる。

　このようにして、第2絃を第6絃に対して調絃した後、第1絃を第5絃と同じに調絃する。つまり2番目の音 g と同じにするのである。すでに述べた通り、褒美として許可を得た箏奏者は、この第1絃を1オクターヴ低く調絃する。このあと、第7から第11絃までが調絃されるが、[それぞれ]第2から第6絃までの半分の長さをとって調絃される。第12と第13絃は、第7と第8絃の半分の長さとなる。甚音を c とすると、つまり13絃はこういうことになる。

第 1 絃	...	g.
第 2 絃	...	c.
第 3 絃	...	d.
第 4 絃	...	e♭.
第 5 絃	...	g.
第 6 絃	...	a♭.

— 第1オクターヴ

第 7 絃	...	c.
第 8 絃	...	d.
第 9 絃	...	e♭.
第 10 絃	...	g.
第 11 絃	...	a♭.

— 第2オクターヴ

$$\left.\begin{array}{llll}\text{第 12 絃} & \ldots & c. \\ \text{第 13 絃} & \ldots & d.\end{array}\right\} - \text{第3オクターヴ}.$$

ふつうの箏奏者は、もちろんこのような計算は行わず、単に耳で調絃する。

すべての絃楽器の絃は絹でできていてワックスが塗られている。純粋な箏[19] の絃は京都だけで作られていて、大変高価(1 セット 5 ドル)である。なぜならとても稀にしか必要とされず、特別注文によってしか作られないからである。普通の箏の糸は江戸で作られ、安価である。

三味線とヴァイオリン [胡弓] は似たような絃を使うが、少し細い。ゲッキン [月琴] はギターのような楽器だが(Fig. 7)、糸は中国から来る。[20]

様々な絃の太さには異なる番号が振られていて、より大きな番号はより太い絃を表す。異なる太さの絃が入っているセットもあるが、セットは一番太い絃の番号がつけられている。さまざまな調子のためのセットは、その発明者の名にちなんで付けられている。

箏は、象牙の 3/4 インチの爪 (Fig. 38) で弾かれる。爪は小さな革製の輪によって右手の親指、人差し指、中指の指の内側に固定される。一方、左手は可動式の柱の向こう側に平らに置かれるが、絃を押して張ったり、絃を引いて緩めたりして、必要な場合に中間音を作るためである。演奏する前に、演奏者はデンプンを手につけてこする。

6 絃の日本のコトもしくは和琴 (Fig. 6) は、長さ 6.33 フィート、細い方の端が幅 0.5 フィート、広い方の端は幅が 0.78 フィートである。高さは足を入れないで 0.4 フィートである。下側には、絃を通す開口部の他に、共鳴用の第 2 の開口部がある。

正確な調絃はまだ調べられていないが、13 絃のコトとは本質的に異なっている。第 1 絃が一番低く、それに続いて小さな音程、恐らく 2 度、が第 4 絃で、第 2 絃と第 5 絃が同じでおそらく 4 度、そして第 6 絃が 5 度となり、最終的に第 3 絃が半音下げられた 6 度となる。しかし、前述した通り、私の [この] 説に確信は全くない。というのも、正しく調絃された和琴を調べたことはなく、柱の位置が示す見た目の模様によって、こう考えただけだからである。

7 絃の中国のコト [七絃琴] については、まったく調査できていない (Fig. 5)。

琵琶 (Fig. 2) には 4 絃が張られていて、2 本ずつ同じ太さである。胴は 33.5 (10 進法) インチ長[21] で、そのうち 7.5 インチが頸であり、その上に絃を押さえるための 4 つの水平な柱 (じゅう) がある。琵琶は洋梨をスライスした形をしている。下から上に行くほど細くなっている。高さ 11 インチのところがもっとも幅が広く 12.2 インチ、高さ 16.3 インチのところは 8.7 インチだった。4 つの糸巻きがある頭部は 7.75 インチ長で、そのうち 2.75 インチは頭頂部を飾る装飾 [海老尾] である。

---

19 (日本語訳者補注) 俗箏に対して雅楽の箏の意味か。
20 絃はすべて協会の博物館で展示しており、特に興味のある人には喜んでサンプルを分けてくれる。
21 (英訳者補注) 十進法では、たとえば 33.5＝33½ となる。

調絃は、主音、5度、オクターヴ、3度で、まさにプロイセンの歩兵ラッパの合図 "Das Ganze" と同じである。

琵琶は 6.3 インチ長の斧のような形をしたバチによって弾かれる。バチは角、木、鼈甲、または象牙で作られる (Fig. 33)。

三味線は、もっとも一般的な日本の絃楽器で、芸者 (われわれのハープ弾き[22] に当る歌手) もまた皆これを弾じる。この楽器は 3 絃で、3 つの糸巻きがあり、平らなコマがあり、絃はその上に等間隔で乗っている。三味線の大きさと各部の寸法は、男性もしくは女性歌手の声によって大いに異なる。よい声、つまり高い声は小さい楽器を必要とする。私が計測した中音域の声に合う楽器は長さ 37 インチで、そのうち 7 と ½ インチが胴である。胴の幅は 6 と ½ インチで高さは 3 インチである。下部に絃をとめる突起がついている。胴体の 4 面は木でできていて、表面と裏面は革が張ってある。その革の上に駒が乗っている (Fig. 30)。これらの革は猫の胸の革から作られる。それが本物の革だという証拠は、[革の表面の] 小さな黒点にある。これは革を薄くのばすことから生じるもので、この黒点については偽造できないと言われている。もっとも高価な楽器は、4 つの点が上の革と下の革に付いている。並の楽器は点が 2 つしかない。点がまったく無いものはとても安い。利便性を高めるために、この楽器はしばしば、胴体と棹が分離できるよう作られている。それにより運搬がより容易になるのである。三味線もまたバチで弾かれる。前述の [三味線の] バチは長さ 7 インチで、細く尖っている側は 3 インチの幅、握る部分は 1 と ½ 平方インチである (Fig. 32)。基音の高さに関係なく、三味線は 5 種類に調絃され、それぞれ名前がついている。

本調子	1度、	4度、	オクターヴ
二上り	1度、	5度、	オクターヴ
三下り	2度、	5度、	オクターヴ
一下り	1度、	5度、	9度
さんさ (ママ) 下がり	1度、	4度、	1オクターヴ低い5度

胡弓、ヴァイオリン (Fig. 4) は、全般的な構造は三味線とよく似ている。ただし、バチの代わりにキウ、つまり弓を用いて弾かれる。胡弓は現在、とても稀にしか演奏されない。私が OAG 例会の席で紹介した演奏者は、盲人音楽団体 [当道] に所属し、江戸で唯一の胡弓奏者だった。彼が弾いたのは 2 つのタイプの作品だった。「フジユ [藤植流]」は昔から伝えられて来た伝統的な演奏、「ショホユ [松翁流]」は普通の演奏である。この論文に添えられた楽曲例 [五線譜] は前者に属し、したがって非常に古い日本のもので、斉唱の歌が交互に付いている。数学教師であるヴェストファル氏に、私は振動数比と同様これらの楽曲の採譜を負っているのだが (彼には、ホルツ氏やフンク博士と同様に、最大の謝辞を述べたい。彼は私の研究を限りなく親切に援助してくれた。そして最後に三宅氏だが、彼の骨折りによって研究が

---

[22] (英訳者補注) 79 頁、脚注 1 参照。

可能になったのである）、彼はこの曲を採譜して、その盲人に向かってヴァイオリンで演奏してみせた。盲人はとても嬉しそうに、[その演奏を] 褒めながらしゃべった。細かいニュアンスはもちろん異なっていた。というのも、盲人は演奏のたびごとに変奏したからだ。しかし、これらの小さなズレを除いて、楽譜は非常に正確で、ただ、見やすくするために、1 オクターヴ下に記されていた。

　この楽器の全長は 25 インチで、コマから上駒までは 14 インチである。胴体の脇は外側に少し曲がっていて、長さ、幅とも 5 インチ、高さは 2 と ½ インチである。それ以外は三味線とまったく同様で、革を張るのも同様である。[絃をひっかける] 突起の代わりに 2 と ½ インチの丸い金属棒がある。[絃をとめる] 部分は絹糸で作られている。4 つの糸巻きは先が細くなっており、2 絃ずつ交互に斜めにはめ込まれていている。

　駒は長く、たいへん低い (Fig. 29[23])。中央部が高くなりアーチ状になっている。絃を通すために 4 つの切り通しが見えるが、3 つは等間隔に配置され、第 4 溝のみ第 3 溝と非常に狭い間隔に配置されている。

　絃は f, b♭, e♭ に調弦され、接近している 2 絃は e♭ の同音で調弦される。長さ 45 インチの弓は、銀のさやで束ねられた紫檀の 4 本の細い棒から成り、持ち運びのために分解することが可能である。この弓は、背面は平らで、前面は楕円にカーブしている。弓の本体は、上部がほとんど直角に曲がっていて、湾曲部は 2 と ½ インチの長さである。9 インチの長さの握り手は、本体と同じ形だが、すこし太い。本体全体はたいへんしなやかである。

　長さ 31 インチの擦絃部は白馬の毛でできていて、この目的のために特別に輸入されている。ここにはそれほど長い馬の毛はないからである。最初、私はこれを、その長さゆえ植物繊維だと思ったが、顕微鏡で調べたところ本当に毛だとわかった。擦絃部は、上部は銀の固定金具で、下部は絹の紐で固定されている。

　演奏の前に、演奏者は手にデンプンをつけ、こする。これはすべての音楽家がしていることである。

　まず、親指、中指、小指で弓をつかみ、人差し指を弓の裏側に置く。まっすぐに伸ばした薬指で、それまでだらりとしていた弓をピンと張ると、弓は薬指と小指の間を通る。それから胡弓の棹を持ち、自分の前に垂直に構え、膝の上に胴を乗せ、膝の間に絃をとめる金属棒を固定するのである。そして、弓の毛の部分を共鳴胴の縁に置き、弓を単純に水平に行ったり来たりさせる。弓は真ん中の 3 分の 1 だけを使う。使用される絃は、胡弓 [本体] を垂直の心棒を軸に回転させることにより、静かに規則的に行ったり来たり動かされる弓と接触する。2 本の e♭ 音の絃については、彼は 1 絃だけ弾いたり、2 絃とも弾いたりする。同様にまた、他の 2 絃についても、

---

23 (英訳者補注)「Fig. 27」より編集者による訂正。

1絃だけ弾いたり、2絃一緒にこすることもある。二重音は譜例が示すように、稀に
しか使われない。音はハーディガーティ[24] のようである。

　管楽器と打楽器を詳しく見ることは次の号にとっておくことにして、記譜法に
ついてまだ少し述べたい。

　本当にきちんとした記譜法は純粋楽器にしかない。実際、箏の場合は単純に弾
く絃の番号、笛の場合は押さえる孔の番号が記されているだけである。しかしまた、
音列の中の音の番号あるいは音名を記してもよい。中間音を出す場合は、音の記号
のそばに第二の記号をつけ、「押し」か「引き」を表す。オクターヴ低い音は記号の
脇に小さい丸をつけ、さらに低いオクターヴは二重丸をつけて示される [Fig. 36]。

　音価は 2 つの方法で示される。全音には○を、二分音符には半円を、四分音符
には 1/4 円をつける [Fig. 37]。または、一般的に書かれているように、一方を他方
の下に書いたり、音価に相当する間隔を個々の音符の間に置く、などがある。

　拍子とリズムは特には示されない。が、今まで聞いた限りでは、4/4 拍子か 2/4
拍子で演奏されない作品はなかった。時折、特定のタイプのリズムが示されること
がある。長く延ばされる音を大きな音で突然区切るような場合である。これは、特
に日本の古い音楽で好まれ、2 枚の木片からなる笏拍子 [Fig. 20] という楽器を打ち
鳴らすことによって強調される。これは横向きコンマのような記号で示される。

　世俗 [音楽] 用には、数字も同様に用いられるが、さらに、我々の「ディデル
ドゥン」「タテラタ」「ブンブン」などのように、文字で音をまねることもある。日
本人は、たとえば「テテテン」などのように書く。「ニン・テン」というのは音を
延ばすことを意味している。楽器が異なると違う文字で表す。たとえば管楽器には
「ラ」の音などがある。

　楽譜記号は、すでに述べた通り、上から下へ書く。歌詞はその左側に書く。そ
の他の記号は右側の場合も、左側の場合もある。個々の行は間に大きな間隔を置き、
すべての日本の文章と同じく、右から左へ書かれる。

　たいていの楽曲は、他の楽器や歌と一緒にあるいはそれ無しで演奏できるよう
書かれている。歌は常に主要楽器とユニゾンである。その他の楽器の伴奏はユニゾ
ンでも和音でもいい。後者の場合はしかし厳格な規則があり、神聖な音楽では楽曲
全体を通して音程関係は一定でなければならい。世俗的な音楽では変えてもよい。
私にそのことを説明してくれた音楽家は、この規則を図で明らかにしようとしてく
れた。彼が言うには、神聖な音楽では、旋律と伴奏は平行して上下しなければなら
ないが、世俗音楽では、伴奏は不規則でギザギザの線で動いてもかまわない。

ミュルレル博士

---

[24] 別の種類のヴァイオリンを偶然に中国音楽の中で見たことがあるが、間近に観察することはでき
　　なかった。それは胡弓にとてもよく似ていたが、コマは三角形で、真ん中の絃が両側の絃より高く
　　置かれていた。弓の擦絃部は絃の間を通っていて、前面と背面が交互に使われる。

胡弓「藤植流」

[OAG ドイツ] 東洋文化研究協会 6 月 13 日例会 (江戸) における当道の会員による
演奏。

実音は 1 オクターヴ高い。

【楽譜】108–110 頁参照

図版解説[25]

Fig. 1　13 絃の箏のコトを弾く芸者 (女性歌手)。そばにある小箱は柱と指にはめる象
牙の爪を収めるためのもの。演奏者は、許可が出ると、第 1 柱を 5 度のオク
ターヴ下に調絃する。この図ではそうなっているが、通常は異なり、むしろ
[第 1 柱は] 第 5 柱と同じ位置に立てなければならない。左頬に垂れ下がって
いる髪飾りの房は優雅な装いの一部である。

Fig. 2　晴の場の盛装をした当道の琵琶奏者。

Fig. 3　衣装の肩が翼のように突き出した儀式的な着物 [裃 (かみしも)] の三味線奏者。

Fig. 4　(Taf. III) 盲人の通常の装束の胡弓奏者。それ以外は女性のみが着る。

Taf. IV

Fig. 5　柱を置かない中国の 7 絃のキンノコト [七絃琴]。[26]

Fig. 6　6 絃の古い日本のヤマトゴトまたは和琴。柱を置く。ただし、[この図の] 柱
の位置は正確とは言えない。

Fig. 7　中国のゲッキン [月琴]。

Fig. 8　二絃琴または出雲琴。

Fig. 9　(Taf. VI) 一絃琴もしくは須磨琴。これは完全に分解でき、分解されたすべて
の部品は、中空の共鳴胴内に収めることができる。

Fig. 10　(Taf. VI) 笙。上は、演奏される時の図。使われない時は、竹管が曲がらない
ように竹管の先に枕をはさむ。これは下の図で示している。個々の部品は
Taf. IV (Fig. 10) で示した。すなわち、a. 空気部屋 [頭 (かしら)]、b. 竹管を束
ねる輪、c. 頭の吹口を正面から見た図。楽器全体は高価な漆塗りで、金具は
銀である。

Fig. 11　(Taf. VI) 篳篥。右は正面図。左は背面図。a. は取り外した簧。先端は小さな
帽子で保護する。演奏の時は取り外す。

---

[25] 図の横にある分数は、本物に対する図の縮尺率である。1/1 は実物大。
[26] (英訳者補注) 著者は実際にこの楽器が演奏されているところを見ていないので、図は不正確である。

Fig. 12 (Taf. VI) 横笛。

Fig. 13 (Taf. VI) 高麗笛。

Fig. 14 (Taf. VI) 神楽笛

Fig. 15 (Taf. V) 太鼓。a. 枠なし側面図。

Fig. 16 (Taf. VI) 鞨鼓。

Fig. 17 (Taf. VI) 腰鼓 [三鼓]。

Fig. 18 (Taf. V) 鉦鼓。a. 側面図。

Fig. 19 (Taf. V) 鼓 [能]。a. 正面図 b. 革の断面。

Fig. 20 (Taf. V) 笏拍子。拍子木。

Fig. 21 (Taf. VII) 「音の輪」。12月の調子の場合。

Fig. 22 (Taf. VII) 竹または象牙の音叉 [調子笛] a. 上から見た図、b. 下から見た図。

Fig. 23 (Taf. VII) 音の対応表。黒い記号は音を出すために指で塞がれる指孔。この続きは Taf. VIII にある。この調子笛は、孔が全部閉じられたポジションから音が始まり (a)、それは2月の音=F である。一方、他の調子笛はすべて12月 [の音] から始まる。音の順番は、a. 2月 (F), b. 4月 (G), c. 6月 (A), d. 3月 (Gb), e. 5月 (Ab), f. 7月 (Bb), g. (Taf. VIII) 8月 (B), h. 10月 (Db) となる。それに続く音は、1オクターヴ高い。すなわち、i. 12月 (Eb), j. 2月 (F), k. 4月 (G) である。次の音は再びオクターヴ低くなり、始めと同じようになる。すなわち、l. 9月 (C), m. 11月 (D) となる。次の音はまたオクターヴ高くなり、n. 1月 (E), o. 3月 (Gb), p. 5月 (Ab) である。

Fig. 24 (Taf. VIII) 12のリードがついた円盤状調子笛。a. 上からの図。

Fig. 25 (Taf. IX) 並んだリード付き調子笛 [イカダ [筏] 型調子笛]。管は真ん中がピンで留められていて回転する。両端いずれも息を吹き込んで振動を作ることができるが、違う音高が出る。音は12月の音から始めて、「音の輪」(Fig. 21) に厳密に従って左廻りに行ったもの。a. は上から、b. は下からの図。

Fig. 26 (Taf. IX) 半分調子笛。最もよく使う6音のみ。

Fig. 26A (Taf. IX) b. 上からの図。c. 側面図。

Fig. 27 (Taf. VIII) パパゲーノの笛のようなパンパイプ型調子笛。Fig. 25 のように調律されている。

Fig. 28 (Taf. IX) 箏柱。木または象牙。右は側面図、左は正面図。

Fig. 28A (Taf. IX) 和琴の柱。ちょうどよい形の二股になった楓の枝を切って、削って作る。小さい丸は断面部分。

Fig. 29 (Taf. IX) 胡弓のコマ。

Fig. 30 (Taf. IX) 三味線のコマ。右は上からの図。左上は正面図。左下は断面図。人が死んだり国喪の場合などは、一般に音をたてること、なかんずく音楽を演奏することが禁止される。禁止にも関わらずそのような時に三味線を弾きたい場合は、非常に重い鉛のコマを用いて音が響かないようにする。

Fig. 31 (Taf. IX) 一絃琴のコマ。上の図は断面図。真ん中は側面図。下は縦に見た断面図。

Fig. 32 (Taf. IX) 三味線のバチ。正面と側面図。

Fig. 33 (Taf. IX) 琵琶のバチ。正面と側面図。

Fig. 34 (Taf. III) 月琴のバチ。鼈甲製。正面と側面図。

Fig. 35 (Taf. III) 一絃琴のバチ。竹または木製。a. 縦の断面図。b. 下からの図。

Fig. 36 (Taf. III) オクターヴ下の記号。a. 1 オクターヴ下、b. 2 オクターヴ下。

Fig. 37 (Taf. III) a. 二分音符の記号。b. 四分音符の記号。

Fig. 38 (Taf. III) 箏の象牙の爪。a. 後ろからの図。b. 側面図。c. 断面図。

1875

Fortsetzung aus Heft VI

Continuation from Issue VI

Die Hoffnung, die ich in meinem ersten Aufsatze aussprach, daß es mir gelingen würde, eine weitere Einsicht in die japanisch-chinesische Musik zu erlangen, hat sich realisirt, wenn ich auch noch immer weit entfernt davon bin, auf irgend welche Vollständigkeit Anspruch zu machen. Zunächst habe ich die Bekanntschaft einiger neuer japanischer und chinesischer, gelehrter und practischer Musiker gemacht; ferner habe ich durch meine Stellung als Leibarzt S. M. des Mikado es erreicht, die Privatcapelle desselben nebst ihren Instrumenten und Aufführungen genau zu studiren, endlich habe ich einen kurzen Aufenthalt in China dazu benutzt, um mir eine vollständige Sammlung der chinesischen Instrumente zu verschaffen.

Ich fange daher zuerst damit an, einige Mittheilungen aus meinem ersten Aufsatze zu berichtigen und zu ergänzen, bevor ich zu neuen Dingen übergehe.

Zunächst habe ich noch eine andere Form der Stimmgabel gesehen; sie glich äußerlich der Fig. 27 Taf. VIII, dagegen bestand sie aus Zungenpfeifen wie Fig. 25 Taf. IX. Sie stimmte mit dieser letztern im

The hope I expressed in my first essay that I would manage to attain a further insight into Japanese-Chinese music has been realized, even if I am still far removed from laying claim to any sort of completeness. First of all, I have made the acquaintance of some new learned and practicing Japanese and Chinese musicians; further, through my position as personal physician to His Majesty the Mikado, I have managed to study closely his private ensemble along with its instruments and performances; finally, I have used a short stay in China to procure a complete collection of Chinese instruments.

I begin, therefore, first with emending and supplementing some information from my first essay, before I go over to new things.

For a start, I have seen yet another form of the tuning-fork; outwardly it resembled Fig. 27, Plate VIII (p. 124), except it consisted of tongued-pipes like Fig. 25, Plate IX (p. 125). It agreed exactly

Tone genau überein, nur stand sie eine Octav tiefer.

Die ursprüngliche Form der Stimmgabel ist aber die in Fig. 27 abgebildete ohne Zungen und wird die Länge der Pfeifen mathematisch in Übereinstimmung mit den Längen- und Gewichtsmaßen bestimmt.[1] Sie heißt Ritsu kwan (Ton-Rohr); die auf Tafel VII, Fig. 22 abgebildete heißt Shi-kedzu (Vier Löcher) die auf Taf. VIII Fig. 24 und Taf. IX Fig. 25 & 26 abgebildeten heißen Choshifuye (Stimmungsflöte).

Die als Normalstimmgabel in Kioto seit 1000 Jahren deponirte Ritsu kwan ist im Tempel Dai-tsu-ji in Kioto gemacht und ist eine genaue Beschreibung derselben veröffentlicht.

Noch älter soll eine Ritzu kwan sein, welche im Besitz der Gagakku (Musik des MiKado, s. Heft VI, pag. 13 Anmerk.) ist; sie ist sorgfältig in Seide eingewickelt und in einem Kästchen verschlossen; sie wird nie in Gebrauch gezogen, sondern nur als Reliquie bewahrt und zuweilen zur Controle für andere Stimmgabeln benutzt; nur die seidenen Schnüre, welche die Pfeifen zusammenhalten, sind verblichen und zeigen an, daß sie wohl sehr alt ist; die Pfeifen selbst sind sehr gut erhalten; nur zwei sollen im Laufe der Zeit erneuert sein. Die gute Conservirung erklärt sich nur dadurch, daß sie

with this latter in pitch, only it stood an octave lower.

The original form of the tuning-fork, though, is that depicted without tongues in Fig. 27 (p. 124); the length of the pipes is mathematically calculated in accordance with the measurements for lengths and weights.[1] It is called ritsu-kan (pitch-pipe); that depicted on Plate VII, Fig. 22 (p. 123) is called shiketsu (four holes), those depicted on Plate VIII, Fig. 24 (p. 124) and Plate IX, Figs. 25 & 26 (p. 125) are called chōshibue (tuning-flute).

The ritsu-kan kept as the standardized tuning-fork in Kyoto for 1,000 years was made in the temple Daitsūji in Kyoto; an exact description of it has been published.

Even older is deemed to be a ritsu-kan which is in the possession of the gagaku (music of the Mikado, see Issue VI, page 81, footnote); it is carefully wrapped in silk and locked in a little box; it is never drawn into use, but kept only as a relic and sometimes used as a control for other tuning-forks; only the silk laces that hold the pipes together are faded and reveal that it is no doubt very old; the pipes themselves are very well preserved; only two are said to have been renewed over the course of time. The good conservation can only be explained through the fact that from the outset it was always

---

[1] Herr Dr. Wagner wird im 9ten Hefte einen längeren Aufsatz über Maß- und Gewichsteintheilung der Chinesen und Japaner publiciren und überlasse ich es seiner competenteren Feder, auch diese Verhältnisse dabei zu besprechen.

[1] Dr. Wagner (Wagener) will publish a longer essay in the 9th issue on the division of measurements and weights of the Chinese and Japanese, and I leave it to his more competent pen to also discuss these relationships there.

von Anfang an immer in den Händen der Gagakku-Musiker gewesen und von ihnen sorgsam gepflegt wurde. Mit dieser Stimmgabel habe ich nun eine verglichen, die in meinem Besitze ist und über 160 Jahre alt ist; als ich sie heraausnahm, erklärte mit einem Male einer der anwesenden Musiker ganz freudig, sie sei von Ohata Hirotame, seinem Ahnen vor 8 Generationen angefertigt, und er selbst heiße noch Ohata.[2] Es fand sich, daß sie mit der Normalstimmgabel genau übereinstimmte; mit einer neuen Pariser Normalstimmgabel verglichen stellte sich der tiefste Ton auf d, der Ton der achten Pfeife war also a, dies ist demnach die Normalstimmung der Mikado-Musik; andere Stimmgabeln für profane Zwecke differiren von ihr bis beinahe einen ganzen Ton. Nach dieser Stimmgabel sind auch die Töne an der Tonrose, Fig. 21, Taf. VII in der Weise zu berichtigen, wie es auf Tafel X geschehen ist. Die Monatsnamen stimmen nicht genau, da die japanische Zeitrechnung von der unsern wesentlich differirt.[3]

in the hands of the gagaku musicians and was carefully looked after by them. Now, I have compared this tuning-fork with one that is in my possession and over 160 years old; as I took it out, one of the musicians present all of a sudden announced, quite delightedly, that it was made by Ōhata Hirotame, his forebear of 8 generations, and that he himself was still named Ōhata.[2] It turned out that it agreed precisely with the standardized tuning-fork; when compared with a new Parisian standardized tuning-fork, the lowest note was found to be d, the note of the eighth pipe was therefore a; this is therefore the standard tuning of the Mikado-music. Other tuning-forks for secular purposes differ from it by up to nearly a whole tone. Following this tuning-fork, the notes of the circle, Fig. 21, Plate VII (see p. 123), should be emended as has been done on Plate X (p. 173). The names of the months do not agree exactly, because the Japanese calculation of time differs substantially from ours.[3]

[2] Man muß bei Beurtheilung der Generationen immer das japanische Kinder-Adoptions-System vor Augen haben, welches das Fortbestehen desselben Geschäfts in derselben Familie begünstigt. Ein Musiker z. B. erkennt vielleicht irgend einen Musiker als Sohn an, während vielleicht sein leiblicher Sohn von einem Arzte adoptirt ist und dessen Generation fortsetzt.

[3] Der feststehende Punkt ist das Winter Solstitium; mit dem Neumond vor demselben beginnt der [11te] Monat, den ich deshalb als December angesetzt habe; auf ihn wird der tiefste Ton der Stimmgabel bezogen. Jeder folgende Monds-

[2] When judging generations one always needs to keep in sight the Japanese children-adoption-system, which promotes the continuity of the same trade in the same family. A musician, for example, perhaps recognizes some musician or other as his son, while perhaps his birth son is adopted by a doctor and continues his [the doctor's] generation.

[3] The fixed point is the winter solstice; with the new moon before that begins the 11th month which I have therefore set as December; the lowest pitch of the tuning-fork corresponds to it. Each subsequent lunar month is counted as a month and so about every three years the

Auch bemerke ich noch, daß die genannte Figur der Tafel VII mit den Ausdrücken "rechts und links herum" im Text nicht stimmen; in meiner Originalzeichnung befand sich nämlich "Dezember" unten, während er auf der Holzplatte nach oben gekommen ist. Auch dies ist auf Taf. X rectificirt. Es ist also immer bei der Bezeichnung "rechts und links herum" der dem Leser zunächst liegende Punkt der Rose als Ausgangspunkt genommen.

Was die dreizehnsaitige *Koto* betrifft, so ist die in Heft VI, pag. 17 angegebene Stimmung nicht in der Gagakku gebräuchlich. Hier werden als Grundton angewandt: December (d), Februar (e), Mai (g), Juli (a), und September (h). Die gebräuchlichsten sind jedoch die beiden ersten und zwar kommt der Grundton immer auf die zweite Seite [Saite]. Um die Tonart zu bezeichnen, setzt man hinter den Grundton das Wort *choshi* (Stimmung.)

Die Reihenfolge der Töne ist.

I note also that the figure on Plate VII (p. 123) referred to in the text with the expressions "around right and left" is not correct: that is to say, in my original drawing, December is to be found at the bottom, whereas on the woodblock it came to be at the top. This too has been rectified on Plate X (p. 173). Always with the designation "around right and left," the point on the circle which is nearest the reader is taken as starting point.

Concerning the *thirteen-stringed koto*, the tuning given in Issue VI, p. 98, is not customary in *gagaku*. Employed as ground-notes here are: December (d), February (e), May (g), July (a) and September (b). The most common, however, are the first two and, in fact, the ground-note always comes on the second string. To indicate the key, one appends the word *chōshi* (tuning) to the ground-note.

		BEI KOSHO CHOSHI (December) d	BEI TAISOKU CHOSHI (Februar) e
1te	Saite	December, d′	September, h′
2te	″ ..	December, d′	Februar, e′
3te	″ ..	Juni, a (kleine Octav) . .	April, ges′
4te	″ ..	August, (kleine Octav) h	Juli, a′

---

monat wird nun als ein Monat gerechnet und so tritt etwa alle drei Jahre das Bedürfnis ein, den 10ten Monat als den letzten vor dem festen Ausgangspunkt doppelt zu nehmen.

necessity arises of taking the 10th month twice as the last before the fixed starting point.

5ᵗᵉ	" ...	December, d′	September, h′
6ᵗᵉ	" ...	Februar, e′	November, des″
7ᵗᵉ	" ...	April, ges′	Februar, e″
8ᵗᵉ	" ...	Juli, a′	April, ges″
9ᵗᵉ	" ...	October, c″	Juli, a″
10ᵗᵉ	" ...	December, d″	September, h″
11ᵗᵉ	" ...	Februar, e″	November, des‴
12ᵗᵉ	" ...	April, ges″	Februar, e‴
13ᵗᵉ	" ...	Juli, a″	April, ges‴

The order of the notes is:

		IN KŌSHŌ-CHŌSHI (December) d	IN TAIZOKU-CHŌSHI[4] (February) e
1st	string	December, d′	September, b′
2nd	" ...	December, d′	February, e′
3rd	" ...	June, a (small octave) ..	April, gb′
4th	" ...	August, b (small octave)	July, a′
5th	" ...	December, d′	September, b′
6th	" ...	February, e′	November, db″
7th	" ...	April, gb′	February, e″
8th	" ...	July, a′	April, gb″
9th	" ...	October, c″	July, a″
10th	" ...	December, d″	September, b″
11th	" ...	February, e″	November, db‴
12th	" ...	April, gb″	February, e‴
13th	" ...	July, a″	April, gb‴

Ich habe in der Tonleiter des und ges statt cis und fis beibehalten wegen der Vergleichung mit der Stimmrose.[5]

Die Wanggong oder sechsaitige japanische Koto hat in der Gagakku folgende Stimmung:

In the scale, I have retained db and gb instead of c♯ and f♯ for the sake of comparison with the tuning circle.

The wagon or six-stringed Japanese koto has the following tuning in gagaku:

---

[4] Taisō-chōshi. Tuning pitched an octave too high. – Ed.

[5] "Tuning-rose," hence "tuning circle" here; elsewhere Tonrose "tone-rose," our "circle of notes." – Ed.

Vom Spieler aus gerechnet:

1te Saite ==   d (2 gestrichen.)
2te "   ==   a (1 gestrichen.)
3te "   ==   d (1 gestrichen.) Dieser Ton wird
                        zuerst nach der Stimmgabel gestimmt
                        und von ihm aus alle andern.
4te "   ==   h (1 gestrichen.)
5te "   ==   g (1 gestrichen.)
6te "   ==   e (1 gestrichen.)

. . . .

Counting outwards from the player:

1st   string ==   d (2-line octave)
2nd   "   ==   a (1-line octave)
3rd   "   ==   d (1-line octave) This note is tuned
                        first, according to the tuning-fork,
                        and from it all the others.
4th   "   ==   b (1-line octave)
5th   "   ==   g (1-line octave)
6th   "   ==   e (1-line octave)

Sollte für die 3te Saite ein anderer Grundton genommen werden, so würden die übrigen Töne in den entsprechenden Intervallen gestimmt werden, und wird dann wie immer die Stimmung nach dem Grundton, der sich auf der dritten Saite befindet, benannt. Ursprünglich sind wie bei der *Sōno-Koto* alle Saiten gleich dick und gleich gespannt.

Andere Stimmungen, welche in alt-japanischer Musik gebräuchlich sind, aber in der Gagakku nicht benutzt werden, sind meist nur willkürliche Abänderungen; der Grundton wird immer auf die 3te Saite gelegt, die erste Saite wird immer in der tiefern Octav gestimmt, die

Should another ground-note be taken for the third string, then the remaining notes are tuned in the appropriate intervals; as always, the tuning is named according to the ground-note, which is located on the third string. As with the *sō-no-koto*, all strings are originally of equal thickness and equal tension.

Other tunings, customary for old-Japanese music but not used in *gagaku*, are for the most part only arbitrary modifications; the ground-note is always set on the third string, the first string is always tuned in the lower octave, the 2nd is the fifth [degree], the 6th the second,

2te ist die Quint, die 6te die Secunde, die 4te die Sexte oder Septime, die 5te ist die Terz oder Quart. Diese Stimmungen werden theils nach den Ländern, aus denen sie stammen, theils nach den Zwecken, zu denen sie dienen, z. B. zu geistlichen Tänzen (Kagura choshi) benannt.

Ein großer Werth wird auf das richtige Stimmen gelegt. Nachdem die einzelnen Saiten in bestimmt vorgeschriebener Reihenfolge, meist nach Octaven oder aufsteigend nach Quinten, absteigend nach Quarten gestimmt sind, wird die ganze Stimmung nochmals untersucht (Nētori, Ton abnehmen) und zwar durch zweierlei Manipulationen:

1. Mit der rechten Hand wird das Schildpathstäbchen benutzt und mit demselben rasch über die Saiten gefahren, welche zu jeder Operation besonders vorgeschrieben sind.

2. Unterdessen werden mit der linken Hand entweder a, mit Daumen und einem der andern Finger zwei Saiten geknipst; dies heißt Tsunne oder b, mit dem Nagelrücken eines Fingers der Ton schnell angeschlagen (Oru).

Die Vorschriften zur Untersuchung selbst sind nun zwar sehr genau, aber ohne besondere innere Wichtigkeit. Gespielt wird sie auf zweierlei Art;

1. Man fährt mit dem Schildpathstab (Kotosangi), Fig. 34, Taf. III, über sämmtliche Saiten in der Nähe des Stegs und dämpft sofort mit den fünf Fin-

the 4th the sixth or seventh; the 5th is the third or the fourth. These tunings are sometimes named after the provinces from which they come, sometimes after the functions they serve, e.g., for religious dances (kagura-chōshi).

Great importance is attached to the correct tuning. After the individual strings are tuned in precisely decreed order, mostly in octaves or in rising fifths, falling fourths, the complete tuning is tested once again (netori, taking over the note) and, in fact, through two methods of manipulation:

1. With the right hand, the small tortoiseshell rod is used, rapidly run with that [hand] over those strings which are specially prescribed for each operation.

2. Meanwhile with the left hand, either a, two strings are plucked by thumb and one of the other fingers (this is called tsumi), or b, the note is quickly struck with the back of the nail of one of the fingers (oru).

The directions for testing are in themselves indeed very exact, but without particular importance otherwise. It [the wagon] is played in two ways:

1. With the tortoiseshell rod (kotosagi) (Fig. 34, Plate III [p. 119]), one runs close to the bridge over all strings and with the five fingers immediately dampens five of the

gern fünf der Töne, so daß nur einer nachklingt; die verschiedenen Handgriffe zum Dämpfen bestimmter Tongruppen tragen bestimmte Namen und sind als Notirung vorgeschrieben. Diese Art des Spiels wird nur benutzt, um die guten Tachtteile anzugeben (siehe unten).

2. Einzelne Töne werden mit einem freien Finger gegriffen, und zwar sowohl mit der Rück- als mit der Vorder-Seite des Nagels *aber nur mit der linken Hand*, was als eine Art Fioritur benutzt wird.

notes, so that only one lingers on; the various hand techniques for dampening specific groups of notes have specific names and are prescribed as notation. This type of playing is used only to mark the main beats (see below).

2. Single notes are plucked with a free finger, and in fact both with the back- and front-side of the nail, *although only with the left hand*; this [technique] is used as a kind of *fioritura*.

Ein besonderes Interesse bietet auch die Geschichte der Wanggong. Die Mythe der Entstehungsweise ist ganz dieselbe, wie die der Harfe bei den Griechen, wonach Appollo zuerst die Fülle und Schönheit des Tons bemerkte, welchen die Saite an dem Bogen seiner Schwester Diana beim Schwirren hören ließ, und dann absichtlich mehrere solcher Saiten neben einander spannte, um eine harmonische Wirkung durch ihre Vereinigung zu erzielen (Buch der Erfindungen, Bd. II, pag. 407). So soll lange vor Jinmu-tenno (665 v. Chr.) ein Krieger, *Kanatomono Mikoto* sechs Bogen neben einander aufgestellt und zum Spielen benutzt haben; wie? ist nicht bekannt. Die erste historische Angabe, die man über die Benutzung der sechs Bogen hat, stammt aus dem Jahre 205 n. Chr., wo ein Begleiter des berühmten Feldherrn *Takeno-Ujino-Sukune*, Namens *Jingu Kongu* mit seinem Chef über die Koto sprach und ihm zeigte, wie man

The history of the *wagon* also has special interest. The myth of how it originated is rather like that for the harp with the Greeks, according to which Apollo first of all perceived the fullness and beauty of the sound which the string on the bow of his sister Diana made audible when twanged, and then intentionally strung several such strings next to each other, to produce an harmonic effect through their combination (Buch der Erfindungen, Volume II, p. 407). Likewise, long before *Jimmu-tennō* (665 BCE), a warrior *Kanatomo-no-mikoto* is held to have set up six bows next to each other and used them for playing; how is not known. The first historical information one has about the use of the six bows is from the year 205 CE, when an attendant on the famous general *Takenouchi-no-sukune* by the name of *Jingū-kōgō*, talked about the *koto* with his leader and showed him how one can make music on 6 bows; he had set these up attractively, surrounded

auf 6 Bogen Musik machen kann; er hatte dieselben hübsch aufgestellt, mit Feldzeichen umgeben und erzielte durch sein Spiel einen großen Effect. Wie und wann daraus die Wanggong entstanden, weiß man nicht genau; wahrscheinlich kurz nach dem Tode des Kaisers Ing-Kio (453 n. Chr.), weil der Herzog von Korea damals zur Todtenfeier desselben 80 mit Geschenken beladene Schiffe schickte, auf denen sich auch 80 Musiker befanden. Sie fuhren von der Insel Chushima nach Tsukushi, (Chikuzen) gingen von da nach Osaka, Kio-to und machten die Japaner zuerst mit ausgebildeterer Musik bekannt. Wahrscheinlich übertrugen nun die Japaner ihre 6 Bogensaiten auf ein der herübergebrachten Koto (7 und 13 saitig) ähnliches Gestell und nannten diese sechssaitige die Wanggong oder Yamoto Koto.[6]

Die damaligen Kaiser begünstigten nun die Pflege der importirten Musik; besonders that dies der Kaiser Ankan (534), welcher in Japan Instrumente nach koreanischen Mustern anfertigen ließ. Unter der Kaiserin Tsuiko (611) kam dann der Koreaner Mimashité nach Japan und lehrte dort chinesische Musik, worauf das Studium der Musik anfing, in Japan ernster betrieben zu werden. Andere Kai-

by military emblems, and made a great impression with his playing. It is not known exactly how and when the *wagon* developed from this: probably shortly after the death of Emperor *Ingyō* (453 CE), because for the funeral, the Duke of Korea sent at the time 80 gift-laden ships, on which there were also 80 musicians. They travelled from the island of Tsushima to Tsukushi (Chikuzen), went from there to Osaka, [to] Kyoto, and were the first to introduce the Japanese to more developed music. Presumably the Japanese then transferred their 6 bow-strings onto a frame similar to the imported *koto* (7- and 13-stringed) and named this six-stringed [one] the *wagon* or *yamato-goto*.[6]

The Emperors at that time promoted the fostering of imported music; this was done, in particular, by Emperor *Ankan* (534) who had instruments made in Japan according to Korean models. Under Empress *Suiko* (611), the Korean Mimashi came to Japan and taught Chinese music there, whereupon the study of music began to be more seriously undertaken in Japan. Other emperors

---

[6] Eigentlich Wa-gong geschrieben aber Wanggong ausgesprochen. *Wa* und *Yamato* sind aber alte Namen für Japan, *gong* ist der chinesische Name für ein tönendes Instrument; beide Namen deuten also darauf hin, daß man es mit einem für Japan abgeänderten, aus der Fremde kommenden Instrument zu thun hat.

[6] Actually written *wa-gong* but pronounced *wanggong*. *Wa* and *Yamato* are old names for Japan, *gong* is the Chinese name for a sounding instrument. Both names indicate therefore that one is dealing with an instrument of foreign origin modified for Japan.

ser, welche dieses Studium begünstigten, waren *Temmu* (673), und *Mommu* (697), unter dem einige neue Flöten gemacht wurden; seitdem haben die Kaiser die Musik nicht mehr besonders gepflegt, sondern auf dem alten Standpunkte stehen lassen, so daß wenig Neues mehr entstanden ist.

In Nara befindet sich eine *Wanggong*, welche 738 n. Ch. angefertigt ist und im Übrigen genau der jetzt noch üblichen gleicht, nur daß sie schmäler ist. Eine 200 Jahr jüngere gleicht genau der jetzigen.

Die *Wanggong* wird heute im größern Orchester äußerst selten gebraucht, obgleich sie zuweilen für die *dreizehnsaitige Koto* eingesetzt werden kann. Für gewöhnlich wird sie nur bei den sehr seltenen Aufführungen rein alt japanischer Musik und dann in Verbindung mit der Kagura Fuye und der Shaku Bioshi (Heft VI, pag. 14). Für die Wanggong allein existirt nur eine einziges Stück, welches Niwa-bi-no-kioku (Gartenfeuer) heißt, aber doch auch mit Gesangbegleitung aufgeführt wird.

Die siebensaitige Kino-Kōto (Taf. IV fig. 5) wird in Japan fast gar nicht gespielt; nach dem, was mir ein sehr gelehrter Musiker sagte, giebt es in Yedo, Kioto und Osaka nur je einen Musiker, der dies Instrument wirklich zu spielen versteht. Auch in China wird es nur in ganz hohen Häusern gespielt und sagte mir ein vielwissender chinesischer Musiker der die meisten chinesischen Instrumente practisch und theoretisch kennt, der aber niedern Ranges war, über dieses mysteriöse Instrument wisse er

who patronized this study were *Temmu* (673) and *Mommu* (697), under whom several new flutes were made; since then the emperors have no longer specially cultivated the music, but have left it as it was, so that little new has come into being.

In Nara there is a *wagon* which was made in 738 CE and which, nevertheless, is precisely like that now still customary, only that it is narrower. One 200 years younger is exactly like that of today.

Today the *wagon* is used extremely rarely in the larger orchestra, although it can sometimes be substituted for the *thirteen-stringed koto*. Normally it is only used for the very rare performances of pure old-Japanese music, and then in combination with the *kagurabue* and the *shakubyōshi* (Issue VI, p. 84). For the *wagon* alone there exists only a single piece, which is called *Niwabi-no-kyoku* (garden-fire). But it too is performed with song accompaniment.

The seven-stringed *kin-no-koto* (Plate IV, Fig. 5 [p. 120]) is almost not played at all in Japan; according to what a very learned musician told me, in Edo, Kyoto, and Osaka each, there is only one musician who understands how to really play this instrument. In China, too, it is played only in very elevated households, and a knowledgeable Chinese musician who is acquainted in practice and theory with most of the Chinese instruments, but who was of low rank, said to me that about this mysterious instrument he

mir nur wenig zu sagen; es würde nur bei ganz besondern Gelegenheiten benutzt z. B. wenn trotz schönen Wetters ein sehr hoher Mann traurig sei, dann würde ein solches Instrument herbeigeholt und gespielt, um ihn zu erheitern, aber niedere Leute kennten es gar nicht.

Herr Machida, der oben erwähnte Gelehrte, erklärte mir nun die Gebrauchsweise des Instruments.

Die Kino Koto ist 118 cm. lang. Die Länge der Saiten ist 111 cm. Sie sind unter dem schmalern Ende des Instruments um zwei Füße desselben festgeschlungen und laufen durch 7 Rinnen, welche sich auf der Kante dieses Endes befinden. An dem breitern Kopfende befindet sich 6 cm. weit von demselben quer über das Instrument ein Steg, über welchen die Saiten laufen. Dicht oberhalb desselben befinden sich 7 Öffnungen, durch welche 7 Schlingen, aus starken Seidenschnüren oder starken Saiten gefertigt, hervorragen, in welchen dann die Saiten mit einem eigenthümlichen Knoten festgebunden werden.

Die beiden freien Enden der eben genannten Schlingen sind nun auf der Unterseite des Instruments an 7 senkrecht gegen dessen Boden gestellten Wirbeln in folgender Weise befestigt:

Der einzelne Wirbel ist 4 cm. lang und gleicht im Ganzen unsern Spielkegeln; 1 cm. oberhalb des flachen Fußes hat er rings herum einen tiefen Einschnitt, von diesem Einschnitt geht ein Kanal aus, der grade in der Mitte des flachen Fußes mündet.

had only little to tell me; it would be used only on quite special occasions, e.g., if, despite fine weather, a very high-ranking man was sad, then such an instrument would be fetched and played to gladden him, but lowly people knew it not at all.

Herr Machida, the scholar mentioned above, explained to me how the instrument is used.

The kin-no-koto is 118 cm long. The length of the strings is 111 cm. Under the narrower end of the instrument, they are tightly wound around two feet, and run through 7 grooves which are found on the rim of this end. On the wider top-end, at 6 cm distance away from same and crossways over the instrument is a bridge, over which the strings pass. Right above this are 7 openings through which protrude 7 slings made of strong silk laces or strong strings, into which the strings are then tied with a peculiar knot.

The two free ends of the slings just mentioned are now fastened on the underside of the instrument to 7 pegs placed perpendicular to its floor in the following way:

The individual peg is 4 cm long and, on the whole, resembles our ninepin; 1 cm above the flat foot it has, all round, a deep incision; from this incision emanates a canal that opens out exactly in the middle of the flat foot.

In diese Mündung werden dann die eben genannten Schlingenenden hineingesteckt durch den Kanal geführt und nachdem sie aus dem andern Ende der Kanals herausgezogen sind, um den Einschnitt des Wirbels so befestigt, daß der Fuß des Wirbels fest an den Boden des Instruments sich anlehnt und der eben erwähnte Kanal die Verlängerung der Öffnungen im Boden der Koto bildet. Wird nun der Wirbel um seine Längsaxe gedreht, so wickeln sich beide Theile der Schlinge um einander und die Saite wird mehr oder weniger gespannt, und zwar wird die Einrichtung so getroffen, daß die Saite beim Rechts-herumdrehen des Wirbels gespannt, beim Linksherumdrehen loser wird.

Die Kino-koto unterscheidet sich nun von den bisher erörterten Koto's sehr wesentlich dadurch, daß

1^{tens}, sie keine beweglichen Stege hat, sondern daß die Saiten durch Wirbel gestimmt werden.

2^{tens}, daß die Saiten ungleich dick sind; die 4 tiefern sind übersponnen, die 3 oberen nicht; die übersponnenen versteht man in Japan nicht anzufertigen.

In alten Zeiten hatte das Instrument nur 5 Saiten, welche die in Heft VI pag. 15 angegebenen fünf Namen "Kiu" u.s.w. trugen; als später noch 2 Saiten dazu kamen, welche in der höhern Octav waren, erhielten diese die Namen kleine Kiu oder Bung und kleine Shō oder Bu, aber diese Namen gelten nur für dies Instrument.

Der Grundton, der sich wieder nach der Höhe der Stimme richtet, wird nun

The said sling-ends are now inserted into this opening, threaded through the canal, and, after they have been pulled out of the other end of the canal, are fixed around the incision of the peg so that the foot of the peg leans firmly against the floor of the instrument and the aforementioned canal forms the extension of the openings in the floor of the koto. When the peg is turned on its longitudinal axle, then both parts of the sling wind themselves around each other and the string is tightened, more, or less. In fact, the mechanism is so devised that the string becomes tighter by twisting the peg around to the right, looser by twisting around to the left.

The kin-no-koto differs very substantially from the kotos considered thus far, in that:

1st, it has no moveable bridges, but rather, the strings are tuned with pegs;

2nd, the strings are unequally thick; the 4 lower are wound, the 3 upper, not; how to make the wound ones is not understood in Japan.

In olden times the instrument had only 5 strings which bore the five names "kyū" etc. given in Issue VI, p. 88; when later two more strings, which were in the higher octave, came in addition, these received the names little kyū or bung and little shō or bu, although these names hold good only for this instrument.

The ground-note, which again orients itself to the height of the voice, is

auf die mittlere Saite gebracht, und dann wird in folgender Weise gestimmt: Setzen wir z. B. den Grundton d', so ist die Reihenfolge der Töne

assigned to the middle string, and then tuning proceeds in the following manner: for example, if we set the ground-note as d', then the order of the notes is

1te Saite/1st string	a	der kleinen Octav. / of the small octave	
2te/2nd	"	g	" " " "
3te/3rd	"	c'	
4te/4th	"	d'	
5te/5th	"	a'	
6te/6th	"	g'	
7te/7th	"	c''	

Neben der dem Spieler zunächst liegenden Saite befinden sich 13 flache Perlmutterknöpfe, von denen der 7te das Instrument grade halbirt, er steht also von jedem Steg 55½ cm. ab. Die übrigen Stifte stehen symmetrisch in folgenden Entfernungen:

Alongside the string lying nearest the player[7] are 13 flat mother-of-pearl buttons, the 7th of which halves the instrument exactly; it stands therefore 55½ cm from each bridge. The other studs stand symmetrically in the following distances:

NUMMER DES STIFTS	ENTFERNUNG			
	VOM MITTEL-STIFT	VON EINANDER	VOM NÄCH-STEN STIFT	VOM ENTFERN-TESTEN ENDE

NUMBER OF STUD	DISTANCE			
	FROM CENTER STUD	FROM EACH OTHER	FROM NEXT STUD	FROM FURTHEST END
6 & 8	11 cm.	22 cm.	40.5	66.5
5 & 9	18.5 "	37 "	37	74
4 & 10	27.5 "	55 "	28	83
3 & 11	33.5 "	67 "	22	89
2 & 12	37 "	74 "	18.5	92.5
1 & 13	41[.5] "	83 "	14	97

---

7 This should be "furthest from the player." – Ed.

Die Distancen sind von der Mitte der Knöpfe aus gemessen, doch können Irrthümer um Millimeter vorgekommen sein, so daß zu weiterer genaueren Berechnung kleine Änderungen vorgenommen werden müssen, so z. B. berechnet der Japaner, daß von 1 und 13 die Entfernung nach dem nächsten Ende $\frac{1}{8}$ ist, während 8 × 14 = 112 ist. Von 5 nach 9 ist $\frac{1}{3}$, von 4 nach 10 rechnet er $\frac{1}{4}$, von 3 nach 11 = $\frac{1}{5}$, 2 nach 12 = $\frac{1}{6}$; $\frac{1}{7}$ findet sich nicht.

Die Beachtung dieser Verhältnisse ist aber deshalb wichtig, weil das Instrument auf zweierlei Weise gespielt wird:

1. Entweder wird der Finger auf der Gegend der Knöpfe fest aufgedrückt, und in diesem Falle wird die Saite mit dem Nagelrücken wegstoßend angeknippst, oder

2. ein Finger der linken Hand wird leise an denselben Stellen auf die Saite gelegt und werden so Schwingungsknoten und Flageolettöne erzeugt; in diesem Falle wird nur mit dem Ballen eines Fingers der rechten Hand auf die Saite geschlagen.

In beiden Fällen sind die erzeugten Töne leicht zu berechnen.

Für gewöhnlich wird nur eine Saite auf einmal angeschlagen u.zw. zur Begleitung der Stimme im Unisono; werden zwei Saiten zugleich gebraucht, so geschieht dies ebenfalls nur im Unisono.

The distances are measured from the middle of the buttons out. Still, mistakes in millimeters could have happened, so that for further, more precise calculation small alterations must be effected. So, for example, the Japanese calculates that from 1 and 13 the distance to the next is $\frac{1}{8}$, while 8 × 14 = 112. From 5 to 9 is $\frac{1}{3}$, from 4 to 10 he calculates $\frac{1}{4}$, from 3 to 11 = $\frac{1}{5}$, 2 to 12 = $\frac{1}{6}$; $\frac{1}{7}$ doesn't occur.

Attention to these relationships is important, however, because the instrument is played in two ways:

1. either the finger is pressed firmly onto the area of the button, and, in this case, the string flicked away outwards with the backside of the fingernail, or

2. one finger of the left hand is lightly laid in the same place on the string and so produces nodal points and flageol pitches [harmonics]; in this case, the string is struck just with the ball of one of the fingers of the right hand.

In both instances the notes produced are simple to calculate.

Usually only one string at a time is struck, in fact, for accompanying the voice in unison; should two strings be used together, this likewise happens only in unison.

Sollte für die 3te Saite ein anderer Grundton genommen werden, so würden die übrigen Töne in den entsprechenden Intervallen gestimmt werden und wird dann wie immer die der Stimmung nach dem Grundton, der sich auf der dritten Saite befindet, benannt. Ursprünglich sind wie bei der Sōno Koto alle Saiten gleich dick und gleich gespannt.

Die Biwa der Mikadomusik hatte nicht die im sechsten Hefte angegebene Stimmung, die ich früher in der Musik des Prinzen Hôta gefunden hatte. Die Saiten waren vielmehr folgendermaassen gestimmt: Prim, Secund, Quint, Octav. Als Prim können nun fünf verschiedene Töne genommen werden, und hat dann jede dieser Stimmungen einen besondern Namen:

Should another ground-note be taken for the 3rd string, then the remaining notes are tuned in the appropriate intervals, and, as always, the tuning is then named according to the ground-note, located on the 3rd string. Originally, as with the sō-no-koto, all strings are equally thick and under equal tension.

The biwa for the Mikado-music does not have the tuning given in the sixth issue, which I had found earlier in the music of Prince Hōta. The strings were tuned, rather, as follows: prime, second, fifth, octave. Five different notes can be taken as prime, and then each of these tunings has a special name:

Bei	Hiojo ist December	(d) Grundton.
"	Ichi ketsu ist Februar	(e) "
"	Sojo ist Mai	(g) "
"	Ohoshiki ist Juli	(a) "
"	Banshiki ist September	(h) "

For	hyōjō, December	(d) is ground-note.
"	ichikotsu, February	(e) is "[8]
"	sōjō, May	(g) is "
"	ōshiki, July	(a) is "
"	banshiki, September	(b) is "

Endlich giebt es noch eine 6te Stimmung, Suijo, bei welcher Juli (a) Grundton ist, der zweite Ton aber etwas niedriger.

Finally, there is still a 6th tuning, suijō, for which July (a) is the ground-note; the second note, however, is somewhat lower.

[8] Müller confuses the first two entries. – Ed.

Jede der Saiten hat eine verschiedene Dicke, alle gleiche Länge.Die Querleisten am Halse sind so gestellt, daß beim Aufdrücken der Saite auf dieselben der ursprüngliche Ton folgendermaassen verändert wird.

Each of the strings has a different thickness, all equal length. The horizontal bridges [frets] on the neck are so placed that by pressing the string on each, the original note is changed as follows:

Volle Länge		Prim.
1ter	Steg	Secund.
2ter	"	Kleine Terz.
3ter	"	Große Terz.
4ter	"	Quart.

Open string		prime.
1st	fret	major second.
2nd	"	minor third.
3rd	"	major third.
4th	"	perfect fourth.

Die Stellung dieser Stege ist also etwas anders, als sie auf Fig. 2, Taf. II dargestellt ist, welche Biwa zur Blindenmusik gehört, im Übrigen ist die Form dieselbe.

The placement of these frets is thus somewhat different from that set out in Fig. 2 Plate II (p. 118), which belongs to the biwa for music-of-the-blind. Otherwise the form is the same.

Die Saiten sind am untern Ende einfach so befestigt, daß jede Saite vermittelst eines Knotens am Ende eine Öse bildet, durch welche sie, nachdem sie durch das entsprechende Loch im Saitenhalter gesteckt ist, hindurch gezogen wird, so daß sie einfach mittelst einer Schlinge sich um den Saitenhalter befestigt.

The strings are fixed simply at the lower end so that each string by means of a knot at the end forms a loop through which, after having been pushed through the appropriate hole in the stringholder, it is drawn; then it simply ties itself with a loop around the stringholder.

Hiermit sind die in Japan gebräuchlichen Saiteninstrumente erledigt. Die chinesischen werde ich mit den übrigen chinesischen Instrumenten, die in Japan nicht üblich sind und höchstens von einzelnen Künstlern einmal gespielt werden, im Zusammenhang abhandeln.

Herewith all the stringed instruments in use in Japan have been dealt with. The Chinese, I shall treat in the conclusion, along with the other Chinese instruments that are not usual in Japan and are played at the most by single musicians.

Blase-Instrumente.

Wind instruments

Unter den Blase-Instumenten ist als das interessanteste und für ein europäisches Ohr angenehmste zu betrachten die Shō (Taf. VI, fig. 10). Sie ist auch des-

Among the wind instruments, the most interesting, and for a European ear to be regarded as most pleasant, is the shō (Plate VI, Fig. 10 [p. 122]). It is especially

halb besonders interessant, weil sie als Grundlage für die Stimmung des Orchesters dient und auf ihr zuweilen mehrere harmonische Töne zugleich erzeugt werden. Bei ihr, sowie bei allen japanischen Blase-Instrumenten besteht die Hauptkunst des Spielers darin, die Töne möglich lange anzuhalten.

Sie besteht aus folgenden Theilen:

1. Der *Windkasten* (Taf. IV., fig. 10.A) ist auf der Tafel von oben gesehen, d.h. von der Seite, wo die Pfeifen eingesteckt sind (das Profil s. Taf. VI, fig. 10) und in halber Größe gezeichnet. Er ist paukenförmig aus Holz geschnitzt, reich lackirt und mit dem Wappen des Besitzers geschmückt. In der einen Seite befindet sich das Mundstück, welches fest in den Windkasten eingesetzt ist; es ist von einer viereckigen Öffnung (Taf IV, fig. 10. C) durchbrochen und durch Metallbeschlag geschützt. An den bessern Instrumenten sind sämmtliche Beschläge von Silber. Durch das Mundstück, welches nur vor den Mund gesetzt, nicht in denselben genommen wird, kann man die Luft sowohl einblasen als ausziehen; beide Methoden sind üblich.

Die obere flache Seite des Windkastens (A) ist von 17 Löchern durchbrochen, welche stets so angeordnet sind, wie die Zeichnung es zeigt. In diese Öffnungen werden nun hineingesteckt:

interesting, as well, because it serves as basis for the tuning of the orchestra, and because, on occasions, multiple harmonious notes are produced simultaneously on it. For it [the *shō*], as for all Japanese wind instruments, the main art of the player lies in holding the notes for as long as possible.

It comprises the following parts:

1. The *wind-chest* (Plate IV, Fig. 10a [p. 120]) is seen from above on the plate, that is to say, from the side where the pipes are inserted (for the profile, see Plate VI, Fig. 10 [p. 122]), and is drawn in half size. It is carved out of wood in the shape of a kettledrum, generously lacquered, and decorated with the crest of the owner. On the one side is located the mouth-piece, which is permanently set into the wind-chest; it is broken through by a rectangular opening (Plate IV, Fig. 10c [p. 120]) and protected by a metal fitting. On the better instruments, all fittings are of silver. Through the mouth-piece, which is placed only before the mouth, not taken into it, one can both blow the air in and draw it out; both techniques are usual.

The upper, flat side of the wind-chest (a) is broken through by 17 holes which are always so ordered as the drawing shows. Into these holes are now inserted:

2. Die 17 *Pfeifen* von verschiedener Länge (Taf. X fig. 40). Jede Pfeife scheint aus einem Stück zu bestehen, in welches die Metallzunge eingefügt ist; erst dadurch, daß zufällig eine Pfeife zerbrach, fand ich aus, daß sie aus zwei Theilen besteht, die aber so fest in einander gefügt sind, daß man sie selbst bei sehr genauer Betrachtung für aus einem Stück geschnitzt halten sollte. Die einzelnen Theile jeder Pfeife sind also:

a. Ein oblong viereckiges *Messingplättchen* (Taf. X. fig. 40. a), das bei den verschiedenen Pfeifen verschieden groß ist. In der Mitte ist eine Zunge (b) auf drei Seiten ausgeschnitten und deren eine Fläche so dünn geschabt, daß sie wie die Zunge einer Harmonica beim Blasen frei schwingen kann. Ich bemerke aber ausdrücklich, daß das ganze Plättchen ein Stück ist, und daß die Zunge herausgearbeitet, nicht eingesetzt ist. Sollten die Zungen ihre ursprüngliche richtige Stimmung verlieren, so werden sie in der Nähe ihres freien Endes nach Bedürfnis mit einem Wachskügelchen (c) beschwert, in welchem ein kleines Metallkügelchen eingeschlossen ist.

b. Die eigentliche *Zungenpfeife* ist 5 cm. lang (Taf. X, Fig. 40. d). Sie ist aus Bambu geschnitten und

2. The 17 *pipes* of differing lengths (Plate X, Fig. 40 [p. 173]). Each pipe appears to consist of a single piece in which the metal tongue is infixed; only when one pipe broke by chance did I find out that it consists of two pieces, which are so tightly fitted, however, that even under very close scrutiny it would be taken as carved from one piece. The separate parts of each pipe are then:

a. A rectangular *brass platelet* (Plate X, Fig. 40a [p. 173]), which on the various pipes is of different size. In the middle a tongue (b) is cut out on three sides, and the surface of it so thinly shaved that when blown it can swing freely like the tongue on a harmonica. I note here explicitly, however, that the complete platelet is one piece, and that the tongue is carved out, not inserted. Should the tongues lose their original correct tuning, then they are weighted as needed, in the vicinity of their free end, with a little ball of wax (c) in which a tiny metal ball is enclosed.

b. The actual *tongued pipe* is 5 cm. long (Plate X, Fig 40d). It is cut from bamboo and completely

ganz lackirt und zwar in ihrem obern Theile, der außerhalb des Windkastens ist, mit mattem Goldlack, in ihrem untern, der sich im Windkasten befindet, mit schwarzem Lack; der Lack dient dazu, um die Pfeife gegen Feuchtigkeit zu schützen. Die eine Seite ist abgeflacht zur Aufnahme des Plättchens mit der Zunge; unten ist sie geschlossen, d.h. sie ist grade so geschnitzt, daß das untere Ende auf einen Knoten trifft. Das obere etwas dünnere Ende (e) ist nun genau eingepasst in (f.f').

c. Das *Ansatzrohr*, welches aus gebräuntem Bambus besteht. Die 17 Ansatzröhre sind in allen ihren frei sichtbaren Theilen rund (f); dagegen sind sie an allen ihren Berührungsstellen so schräg nach innen abgeflacht, daß sie fest an einander schließen (f') können. Sie sind von verschiedener Länge,

2	zu	45	cm.
4	,,	36	,,
4	,,	28	,,
4	,,	21	,,
3	,,	16	,,

doch ist diese Länge nur für das Auge berechnet, während die wirkliche Länge des Ansatzrohres ganz anders zu berechnen ist. Jedes Rohr hat nämlich etwas über 1 cm. oberhalb seines untern Endes, also dicht über der Endstelle der eingesetzten

lacquered, and actually, in its upper part, which is outside the wind-chest, with matte gold-lacquer, in its lower, which is located inside the windchest, with black lacquer; the lacquer serves to protect the pipes against moisture. The one side is leveled to accommodate the platelets with the tongues; underneath it is closed, that is to say, it is cut in a way so that the lower end coincides with a node. The upper, somewhat narrower end (e) is now tightly fitted into (f.f').

c. The *attached pipe*, which is made of fired bamboo. The 17 attached pipes are round in all of their clearly visible parts (f); in contrast, in all places where they meet they are flattened, slanting so much inwards that they can fit tightly one on the other (f'). They are of different lengths,

2	of	45	cm.
4	,,	36	,,
4	,,	28	,,
4	,,	21	,,
3	,,	16	,,

although this length is calculated for the eye only, while the actual length of the attached pipe is to be calculated completely differently. Each pipe has, in fact, a little more than 1 cm above its lower end, close in above the terminal point of the inserted

Zungenpfeife ein stecknadelkopf großes Loch (g); nur die Pfeifen N. 11 und 12 haben diese Öffnungen 2 cm. höher stehen, weil sie für den Zeige- und Mittelfinger der linken Hand bestimmt sind. Alle diese Löcher befinden sich an der Außenseite mit Ausnahme von 3 und 4, welche nach innen gerichtet sind und von 17, welches seitlich liegt. Die Richtung dieser drei Löcher ist in Fig. 39 durch kleine Striche angegeben. Dagegen befindet sich an jedem Ansatzrohr und zwar an dessen Innenseite eine zweite längliche Öffnung (Fig. 40, h), welche also die wirklich in Gebrauch kommende Länge des Rohrs bestimmt, während dessen weitere Länge nur des symmetrischen Aussehens wegen da ist.

Diese wirkliche Länge des Rohrs beträgt nun:

bei N.		
1,	ges$'''$	5 cm
2,	g$''$	13 "
3,	ges$''$	14.5 "
4,	e$''$	15 "
5,	des$''$	20 "
6,	as$''$	11 "
7,	blind	
8,	h$'$	6 "
9,	blind	
10,	e$'''$	8 "
11,	des$'''$	10 "
12,	h$''$	11 "
13,	a$''$	7 "
14,	d$'''$	17.5 "

tongued-pipe, a hole the size of a pin-head (g); only pipes No. 11 and 12 have these openings placed 2 cm higher because they are intended for the index- and middle-finger of the left hand. All these holes are located on the outer side with the exception of 3 and 4, which are set inside, and of 17, which is positioned to the side. The placing of these three holes is indicated in Fig. 39 by small lines. However, on each attached pipe, and actually on its inside, is to be found a second elongated, opening (Fig. 40h), which thus determines the length of the pipe really coming into use, whereas its extra length is there only for the sake of the symmetrical appearance.

This true pipe-length then comes out as:

for no.		
1,	g$\flat'''$	5 cm
2,	g$''$	13 "
3,	g$\flat''$	14.5 "
4,	e$''$	15 "
5,	d$\flat''$	20 "
6,	a$\flat''$	11 "
7,	mute	
8,	b$'$	6 "
9,	mute	
10,	e$'''$	8 "
11,	d$\flat'''$	10 "
12,	b$''$	11 "
13,	a$''$	7 "
14,	d$'''$	17.5 "

15,	d''	26"
16,	a'	22"
17,	c'''	10"9

15,	d''	26"
16,	a'	22"
17,	c'''	10"9

Zu diesen Längen ist dann noch die Entfernung der Zungenspitze vom Ansatzrohr hinzuzufügen, etwa 2 cm. Wo die Öffnung etwas zu tief angebracht war, wird der überflüssige Theil mit Schellack geschlossen. Die Pfeifen N. 9 und 10 haben, wie man auf Tafel VI Fig. 10 und Taf X Fig. 40 sieht, zwei oblonge mit Silber beschlagene Öffnungen (k) an der Außenseite, die aber nur als Zierrath dienen, denn N^r 10 hat noch eine innere Öffnung (h) tiefer und N^r 9 ist blind. Auch der obere Silberbeschlag (l), der sich gewöhnlich an 9, 10 und 1 befindet, ist nur Zierrath. Nimmt man nun die Zungenpfeife bis an die obere dünnere Stelle in den Mund und bläst, so entsteht kein Ton bis man das kleine oberhalb gelegene Loch (g) mit dem Finger schließt. Dann erst tritt die Länge der Luftsäule in das richtige Verhältnis zur Schwingungszahl der Zunge und es entsteht ein Ton. Dasselbe ist der Fall, wenn die Pfeife in dem Windkasten steckt.

Nachdem nun die Pfeifen ihrer Länge nach symmetrisch geordnet und in den Windkasten mit ihren untern Ende luftdicht eingesteckt sind, wird der Ring (Taf. IV, Fig. 10. b) von oben her über die Pfeifen geschoben und zwar so, daß die

9 Diese Angaben sind noch vor Vergleichung der Normalstimmgabeln gemacht und würden alle obenstehenden Angaben nach der neuen Pariser Stimmgabel um einen halben Ton zu erhöhen sein, also statt *ges g*. u.s.w.

To these lengths is then still to be added the distance of the tip of the tongue from the attached pipe – about 2 cm. Where the opening is made somewhat too low, the superfluous part is closed with shellac. Pipes 9 and 10 have, as one sees on Plate VI, Fig. 10 (p. 122) and Plate X, Fig. 40 (p. 173), two oblong, silver-gilded openings (k) on the outside, which serve, however, merely as decoration, since 10 has another inner opening (h) lower down, and 9 is mute. The upper silver-gilding (l), which is usually found on pipes 9, 10, and 1, is also only decoration. If one now takes the tongued pipe in the mouth as far as the upper thinner point and blows, then no note results until one closes the little hole lying above (g) with the finger. Only then does the length of the air-column come into the correct relationship with the vibration frequency of the tongue and a note results. The same is the case when the pipe is plugged into the wind-chest.

Once the pipes have been symmetrically ordered according to their length and inserted with their lower ends air-tight into the wind-chest, then

9 These specifications were made before comparing with the standard tuning fork, and all the above specifications, according to the new Parisian tuning-fork, should be raised by a semitone, i.e., *g* instead of *gb*, etc.
The assignation of mute pipes is corrected in the final installment. – Ed.

Einbiegung desselben genau der löcherfreien Stelle des Windkastens entspricht und sich hier zwischen die Pfeifen einschiebt. Der Ring wird so weit herabgeschoben, bis das ganze Instrument einen in allen seinen Theilen fest verbundenen Körper bildet. Durch die zwischen 1 und 17 gebliebene Lücke sind nun alle Pfeifen auch von der Innenseite dem Auge und dem Finger zugänglich.

Auf Tafel VI stellt die obere Figur das Instrument von rechts gesehen dar, wo sich die eben beschriebene freie Stelle findet; die untere Figur zeigt dasselbe von links, wenn das Mundstück dem Spieler zugewandt ist. An letzterer Figur kann man auch sehen, wie die Stelle, bis zu welcher der Ring vorgeschoben werden kann, durch den Silberbeschlag der beiden an N. 9 und 10 befindlichen Öffnungen (Taf. X, Fig. 40. k) limitirt wird.

Beim Nichtgebrauch wird, um eine Verbiegung der freien Enden zu verhindern, zwischen dieselben ein seidenes Kissen eingeschoben, wie es dieselbe Figur zeigt.

Um das Instrument zu reinigen, bedient man sich einer Kugel, die an einem Draht befestigt ist, und eines Läppchens. Außerdem hat der Spieler, während er das Instrument benutzt, einen Hibachi (japanisches Kohlenbecken, das allgemein als Ofen benutzt wird) neben sich stehen und benutzt jeden freien Augenblick, um das Instrument über dem Feuer zu trocknen, wobei er es beständig um seine Axe dreht, damit

the ring (Plate IV, Fig. 10b) is pushed from above down over the pipes, so that where it turns in coincides exactly with where there are no holes in the wind-chest, and here it pushes itself in between the pipes. The ring is pushed down far enough until the whole instrument forms a body tightly bound in all its parts. Through the gap left between 1 and 17, all pipes are now accessible also from the inside to eye and finger.

On Plate VI (p. 122), the upper figure displays the instrument seen from the right, where the open place just described is to be found; the lower figure shows the same seen from the left, when the mouth-piece is facing the player. From the latter figure one can also see how the place as far as which the ring can be pushed is limited by the silver-fittings on the two openings found on 9 and 10 (Plate X, Fig. 40k).

When not in use, so as to prevent bending of the free ends, a silk cushion is pushed in between them, as the same figure shows.

To clean the instrument one uses a metal ball, which is fixed to a wire, and a little rag. Moreover, while he uses the instrument, the player has standing next to him a hibachi (Japanese charcoal brazier used in general as stove) and uses every free moment to dry the instrument over the fire, whereby he turns it constantly on its axis so that one place doesn't perhaps warm too much and one of the waxballs (Fig. 40 c) mentioned

nicht etwa eine Stelle zu sehr erwärmt wird und vielleicht eins der oben erwähnten Wachskügelchen (Fig. 40 c) abschmilzt. Zur Vorsicht befinden sich aber noch in jedem Orchester eine Anzahl Reserveinstrumente, um gleich zur Hand zu sein, wenn eins ja unbrauchbar würde.

Behufs des Spielens fasst nun der Spieler den Windkasten in beide volle Hände so, daß die Pfeife und die Finger nach oben gerichtet sind und das Mundstück sich zwischen beiden Daumen befindet; das Instrument ruht nun auf beiden Handballen und wird durch die Ballen beider Daumen und durch die dicht an einander liegenden kleine Finger gehalten. Der rechte Zeigefinger wird zwischen Pfeife 1 und 17 (Taf. X, fig. 39) hindurchgesteckt und dient dazu, um mit seiner Spitze die nach innen mündenden Löcher von 3 und 4 und mit dem Rücken des ersten Fingergliedes die seitlich nach innen gerichtetet Öffnung von 17 schliessen zu können.

Der Spieler drückt nun das Mundstück an den Mund und bläst oder aspirirt, wodurch er selbstredend, indem er beides abwechselnd thut, die Töne ohne große Anstrengung sehr lange anhalten kann. Dabei tönen aber nur diejenigen Pfeifen, deren kleine Löcher (Fig. 40. g) mit den Fingerspitzen geschlossen sind. Wie die Finger auf die verschiedenen Pfeifen vertheilt sind ersieht man aus Fig. 39; auch kann man dort leicht herausfinden, warum die Reihenfolge der Töne so geordnet ist, und warum gewisse Töne (7 und 9) blind sind.

above perhaps melts. As a precaution, however, in each orchestra there are a number of reserve instruments, to be right there at hand should one indeed become unusable.

To play, the performer now takes the wind-chest cupped in both hands so that pipes and fingers are pointed upwards and the mouth-piece is between both thumbs; the instrument now rests on both heels of the hands, and is held by the balls of both thumbs and by the little fingers lying tightly next to each other. The right index finger is poked right through between pipes 1 and 17 (Plate X, Fig. 39 [p. 173]) and is used to enable closing the inwardly opening holes of 3 and 4 with its tip, and, with the back of the first phalanx, the lateral, inwardly poled opening of 17.

The player now presses the mouthpiece against the mouth and blows or inhales, whereby, in that he does the two alternatively, he of course is able to hold the notes for very long without great effort. Thereby only those pipes sound whose little holes (Fig. 40g) are closed with the fingertips. How the fingers are distributed on the various pipes, one can see from Fig. 39; there one can also easily find out why the sequence of notes is ordered so, and why certain notes (7 and 9) are mute. Apparently this happens only for easier orientation. Should, for

Es geschieht dies offenbar nur der leichtern Orientirung wegen. Schließen z. B. rechter Daumen und rechter Zeigefinger ihre nach rechts gelegenen Öffnungen, so erzeugen sie eine Octav, schließen sie die nach links gelegenen, so erzeugen sie eine Terz, und wenn der Rücken des Zeigefingers noch N. 17 schließt, einen Dreiklang.

Für den linken Daumen sind vier Töne bestimmt; legt er sich an das Mundstück dicht an, so schließt er N. 5, nimmt er dazu den linken Zeigefinger, so hat er die Octav. Entfernt sich der Daumen von dem Mundstück, so schließt er 6; N° 7, das blind ist, schützt ihn vor einem Missgriff; 6 und 11 bilden eine Quart. Geht der Daumen nach 8, so befindet er sich zwischen zwei blinden Pfeifen, kann also schwer fehlgreifen; mit dem Mittelfinger, 12, findet er wieder die Octav, geht der Daumen nach 10, so bilden 10 und 12 wieder die Quart. Da aber die Öffnungen von 11 und 12 viel höher liegen, so kann der Daumen nach dieser Seite nicht irren, ebensowenig kann dies der Ringfinger, der in den beiden Mittelpfeifen, (14 und 15) sowie in den beiden äußern (13 und 16) wo er sich an den Mittel- oder den kleinen Finger legt, je eine Octav hat; schließt er dagegen 13 und 14 oder 15 und 16, so erzeugt er eine Quart. So zeigt sich denn die Reihenfolge der Töne auf den Pfeifen als eine rationell ganz motivirte.

Wenn nun die Sho als für unser Ohr angenehm bezeichnet werden konnte, so gilt grade das Gegentheil von dem sich im Orchester am meisten hervorthuenden Blasinstrument, der Hichiriki

example, the right thumb and right index-finger close the openings lying to their right, then they would produce an octave, should they close those lying to the left, they produce a third, and if the back of the index-finger closes 17 as well, a triad.

Four notes are reserved for the left thumb: if it lays itself closely alongside the mouth-piece, it closes 5; if it adds [the note of] the left index-finger, it has the octave. Moving away from the mouth-piece, the thumb closes 6; 7, which is mute, protects it from a mistake; 6 and 11 form a perfect fourth. If the thumb goes to 8, it finds itself between two mute pipes, and so can err with difficulty; with the middle-finger, 12, it again finds the octave, and if the thumb goes to 10, then 10 and 12 again form the perfect fourth. However, since the openings of 11 and 12 lie much higher, the thumb cannot err towards this side; just as unlikely can the ring-finger which has an octave each in the two middle pipes (14 and 15) as well as in the two outer (13 and 16) where it lays itself on the middle - or the little finger. However, if it closes 13 and 14 or 15 and 16, it produces a perfect fourth. In this way, then, the order of the notes on the pipes reveals itself as one that is fully rationally motivated.

If the shō can be described as pleasing to our ears, then the exact opposite is true for the most dominant wind instrument in the orchestra, the hichiriki (Plate VI, Fig. 11 [p. 122]). It is a type of oboe, the body of

(Taf. VI. fig. 11); sie ist eine Art Hoboë, deren Körper aus Bambus besteht, 18 cm. lang; hat auf der Vorderseit 7 Öffnungen in Intervallen von 2 cm.; die erste steht 4 cm. vom obern Ende des Körpers ab; auf der Rückseite 2 Öffnungen 5 und 11 cm von eben da selbst. Das feine Mundstück besteht aus einem runden feinen, 6 cm. langen Stück Schilf, das mit Papier fest umwickelt und in das dickere Ende des Körpers gesteckt wird. Das freie Ende ist ganz dünn geschabt und flach gedrückt, so daß es auf diese Weise zwei Zungen bildet nach Art des Hoboë- oder Fagot-Mundstücks; beide Zungen werden durch einen übergeschobenen flachgedrückten Bambusring fest an einander gedrückt und werden beim Nichtgebrauch mit einem Deckel geschützt. Um das Instrument zu spielen, nimmt man es in beide Hände und zwar werden die Löcher geschlossen von oben her durch 2ten bis 4ten Finger der linken und durch 2ten bis 5ten der rechten Hand. Beide Daumen liegen auf den beiden Öffnungen der Rückseite.

Die auf derselben erzeugten Töne sind der Reihe nach: a''', g''', ges''', e'', des''', c''', (nicht ganz rein), h'', a'', g''. Sie werden alle durch Schließen der Finger der Reihe nach erzeugt, nur beim zweiten wird der linke Daumen geöffnet. In frühern Zeiten wurde die zweite Öffnung auf der Rückseite zur Modificirung des des''' gebraucht, jetzt bleibt dieselbe stets geschlossen. Beim Spielen wird das Mundstück erst stark mit Speichel angefeuchtet, dann bis an den Bambusring zwischen die Spitzen

which is made of bamboo, 18 cm long; has on the front 7 holes in intervals of 2 cm; the first stands back 4 cm from the upper end of the body; on the back, 2 holes, 5 and 11 cm, likewise from the end. The delicate mouth-piece consists of a round, thin, 6 cm long piece of reed, which is firmly wrapped in paper and pushed into the thicker end of the body. The free end is shaved very thin and pressed flat so that in this way it forms two tongues in the style of the oboe- or bassoon-mouth-piece; both tongues are firmly pressed together by a flattened bamboo-ring slid over them, and, when not in use, they are protected by a cover. To play the instrument, one takes it in both hands and, specifically, the holes are closed from top down with the 2nd to 4th fingers of the left hand, and with the 2nd to 5th of the right. Both thumbs lie on the two openings on the back.

The notes produced on same are in sequence: a''', g''', gb''', $e''[']$, db''', c''', (not quite pure), b'', a'', g''.[10] They are all produced by closing the fingers one after the other, only with the second, the left thumb is opened. In earlier times the second hole on the back was used for modifying the db''', now this always stays closed. When playing, the mouth-piece is first heavily moistened with saliva, then taken as far as the

---

[10] The sequence is an octave too high throughout. – Ed.

der Lippen genommen und mit starkem Aufblasen der Backen und großer Anstrengung geblasen; es bringt einen schrillenden, kreischenden Ton hervor, der um so unangenehmer wirkt, als er nicht rein angesetzt, sondern allmählich von unten unbestimmt hinauf gehend angeblasen wird.

bamboo ring between the cusp of the lips and blown with strong puffing-out of the cheeks and great effort; it yields a shrill, screeching note that is all the more unpleasant since it is not cleanly intoned, but blown gradually rising from somewhere below.

Flöten giebt es verschiedene Sorten:

There are various sorts of *flutes*:

a. Die *Ohteki* oder chinesische Flöte (Taf. VI. Fig. 12), welche auch in der Mikado-Musik gebraucht wird.
b. Die *Kagura Fuye* oder japanische Flöte. (Taf VI, Fig. 13).
c. Die *Komafuye* oder Koreanische Flöte (Taf VI. Fig. 14)[11]

a. The *ōteki* or Chinese flute (Plate VI, Fig. 12 [p. 122]), which also is used in the Mikado-music.
b. The *kagurabue* or Japanese flute (Plate VI, Fig. 13 [p. 122]).
c. The *komabue* or Korean flute (Plate VI, Fig. 14 [p. 122]).[11]

Außerdem giebt es sowohl in China, als in Japan verschiedene größere und kleinere Flöten bis zur Picoloflöte herab, die aber nicht bei größern Musikaufführungen, sondern auf der Straße und in Schaubuden von Gauklern u. dgl. benutzt werden. Zahl und Stellung der Löcher differiren sehr. Man unterscheidet die *Kusafuye* (wörtlich *Krautflöte*) für deren Namen man zwei etymologische Deutungen hat: a, daß sie ursprünglich aus Kraut (Schilf) geschnitten wurde; b, daß sie von

Besides, both in China and in Japan there are various bigger and smaller flutes right down to piccolo-flutes, which, however, are not used for major music performances, but by jugglers and the like on the streets and in fair booths. Number and positioning of the holes vary greatly. One distinguishes the *kusabue* (literally weed flute), for whose name there are two etymological interpretations: (a) that it was originally cut from weed (reed); (b) that it was played

---

[11] Bei der Angabe der Flöten ist im VI^{ten} Heft ein Irrthum vor sich gegangen; auf Pag. 14 sind sowohl die koreanische als die japanische mit N. 14 bezeichnet. Letztere muß N. 13 tragen; auf Seite 21 im Register sind beide Nummern grade zu verwechselt.

[11] In the description of the flutes a mistake occurred in the VIth issue: on p. 84, both the Korean and the Japanese are indicated with 14. The latter must bear 13; on page 112 the two numbers are downright mixed-up in the register. [Flutes are muddled here. Switch labels 13 and 14. – Ed.]

Hirten, die das Vieh ins Kraut (Gras) trieben, gespielt wurde.

2, Die *Shinō buye*, die in den Theatern, Schaubuden u. dgl. zur Begleitung der Stimme gebraucht wird. Um sich nun der Stimme adaptiren zu können, muß der Spieler ein Assortiment von 12 solchen Flöten, deren Stimmung stets um einen halben Ton höher geht, mit sich führen.

Die Ohteki misst 39½ cm., die *Kagura Fuye* 45, die *Komafuye* ist etwas kürzer. Die genaue Beschreibung kann ich unterlassen, da alle Verhältnisse aus Taf. VI, Fig. 12, 13, 14 bei fünfmaliger Vergrößerung leicht zu entnehmen sind.

Die *Ohteki* hat außer dem Mundloch 7 Löcher auf derselben Seite; jede der beiden andern nur 6. Die Stellung der Löcher an dem verschiedenen Flöten wird durch folgendes Paradigma erläutert:

by shepherds who drove livestock into the weeds (grass).

The *shinobue*, which is used to accompany the voice in the theaters, show booths, and the like. To be able to adapt himself to the voice, the player must carry with him an assortment of 12 such flutes, the tuning of which stepwise goes up a semitone higher.

The *ōteki* measures 39½ cm, the *kagurabue* 45, the *komabue* is somewhat shorter. I can omit exact description since with five-fold enlargement all relationships are easily to be taken from Plate VI, Figs. 12, 13, 14 (p. 122).

The *ōteki* has, aside from the mouthhole, 7 holes on the same side; each of the other two only 6. The positioning of the holes on the different flutes is explained by the following example:

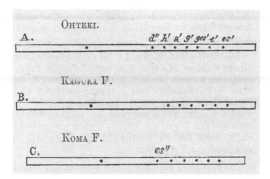

Ōteki, kagurabue, komabue

Der letzte Ton der Ohteki ist nicht rein und wird nicht gebraucht. Doch muß ich bemerken, daß alle diese Töne nicht rein sind, sondern je nach dem Blasen um fast einen halben Ton schwan-

The last note of the ōteki is not pure and is not used. Yet I must remark that all these notes are not pure, but, rather, fluctuate according to the blowing by almost a semitone. Likewise, the upper and the

ken. Ebenso werden die höhere und die tiefere Octav eines jeden Tons durch die Stärke des Anblasens erzeugt, so daß jeder Ton in drei Octaven geblasen werden kann; doch sagten mir die Spieler, daß der tiefere Ton sehr schwer zu blasen sei.

Die Benutzung der Finger ist grade so, wie bei der Hichiriki (2-4 der linken, 2-5 der rechten Hand, beide Daumen zum Stützen). Das Instrument wird nicht horizontal, sondern in einem Winkel von fast 45 Grad von links oben nach rechts unten gehalten. Beim Spielen lecken sie fortwährend über das Mundloch.

lower octave of a given note are produced by the force of blowing, so that each note can be blown in three octaves; the players told me, however, that the lower note is very difficult to blow.

The use of the fingers is exactly as for the hichiriki (2-4 of the left hand, 2-5 of the right, both thumbs for support). The instrument is not held horizontally but at an angle of almost 45 degrees from upper left to bottom right. When playing they lick constantly over the mouthpiece.

Schlaginstrumente

Das wichtigste dieser Instrument ist die Shaku Bioshi, die Holzklapper (Taf. V, Fig. 20). Sie besteht aus zwei länglich flachen Brettern und wird aus Biwa- (Eriobotrya japonica) oder Enjiu- (Sophora japonica) Holz gefertigt. Ihr Ursprung wird darauf zurückgeführt, daß früher die Daimios solche Brettchen hatten, die ihnen als Zierrath und Erkennungszeichen dienten, und die dann durchgeschnitten und, um Aufmerksamkeit zu erregen, zusammengeschlagen wurden. Auch jetzt noch kündigt der Ausrufer, welcher bei Schauspielen, Gaukelspielen u.s.w. die Annoncen und Erklärungen übernimmt, Anfang und Ende seiner Erklärungen, Verwandlungen u. dgl. durch Zusammenschlagen ähnlicher Brettchen an; sie spielen bei solchen Vorstellungen etwa die Rolle wie bei uns die Schelle oder Pfeife.

Percussion instruments

The most important of these instruments is the shakubyōshi, the wooden clapper (Plate V, Fig. 20 [p. 121]). It consists of two longish flat boards and is made of biwa- (Eriobotrya japonica) or enju- (Sophora japonica) wood: Its origin is traced back to the daimyōs' earlier having had such little boards which served them as ornament and identification, and which were then sliced through and beaten together to call attention. Still nowadays, too, the bell crier who undertakes at plays, juggling shows, and so on the announcements and explanations, signals the beginning and end of his explanations, transformations, and the like, through the hitting together of similar little boards: at such performances they play a role somewhat like the bell or whistle with us.

Beim Spielen werden die Brettchen so gehalten, daß der Länge nach das eine mit seiner Kante auf der Mitte der Fläche des andern steht; nun werden sie im Winkel mit den vom Körper des Spielenden entferntern Enden von einander entfernt und schnell zusammengeklappt.

Die Shōko (Taf. V. Fig. 18), ist ein Bronzebecken, das an zwei Henkeln in einem reichverzierten Holzrahmen frei aufgehängt ist. Das Becken selbst ist schüsselartig hohl und reicht mit Wappen verziert. In Fig. 18 befindet sich in der Mitte das Wappen des Mikado und darum drei concentrische Kreise, an welche sich dann die Henkel schließen; bei a zeigt die Figur links die Seitenansicht, die rechts den Durchschnitt der Mitte des Beckens.

Geschlagen wird es mit zwei Klöppeln, welche auf der Figur grade in der Mitte herunterhängen. Sie wird nur in der Mitte des Beckens, nie am Rande geschlagen.

Die Taiko Taf. V. fig. 15 ist eine ebenfalls in einem reichen Holzrahmen aufgehängte Trommel, mit 2 reich bemalten Fellen bespannt, die etwa 9 Centimeter von einaner entfernt und theils festgeklebt, theils angenagelt sind; sie wird mit den zwei Klöppeln geschlagen, welche man auf der Figur zu beiden Seiten aufgesteckt sieht. a ist die Seitenansicht der Trommel in neunmaliger Verkleinerung.

Die Kakko (Taf. VI, Fg. 16) besteht aus einer Art großen hohlen, hölzernen Doppelpokal; an jedem Ende desselben befindet sich ein fest in einen Rahmen

When played, the little boards are held so that the one stands lengthwise with its edge along the middle of the plane of the other; now they are parted from one another, forming an angle, and at the end distanced from the body of the player, and quickly clapped together.

The shōko (Plate V, Fig. 18 [p. 121]) is a bronze gong which is suspended on two handles in a richly decorated wooden frame. The gong itself is concave like a bowl and copiously ornamented with crests. In Fig. 18, the crest of the Mikado is to be found in the middle, and around it three concentric circles to which the handles then attach; in a the figure on the left shows the lateral view, the right, the cross-section of the middle of the gong.

It is struck with two beaters that, in the figure, hang down right in the middle. It is only struck in the middle of the bowl, never on the edge.

The taiko (Plate V, Fig. 15 [p. 121]) is a drum likewise suspended in a rich wooden frame, covered with 2 richly painted skins that are about 9 cm apart from one another and partly glued, partly nailed; it is struck with the two beaters to be seen in the figure mounted on either side; a is the lateral view in ninefold reduction.

The kakko (Plate VI, Fig. 16 [p. 122]) consists of a sort of big, hollow, wooden double-goblet; at each end of it there is a skin stretched fast in a frame. Both

gespanntes Fell. Beide Rahmen sind fest mit einander durch seidene Schnüre verbunden, ähnlich wie bei unsern Trommeln; die festere Anspannung geschieht nun entweder, wie es in der Figur angegeben ist, durch mehrfaches Umlegen und Anziehen einer starken, seidenen Schnur (so war es in der Musik des Prinzen von Hōta) oder es sind um je zwei Schnüre seidene Schlingen gezogen, welche, wie bei uns die ledernen Schlingen, verschoben werden können und so eine größere oder geringere Spannung erzeugen (so war es in der Kapelle des Mikado). Bei jener erstern Vorrichtung kann während des Spiels durch einen Druck mit der Hand auf die Längsschnüre der Ton noch etwas erhöht werden. Die *kakko* liegt auf einem Ständer und wird mit zwei Klöppeln so geschlagen, daß beide Felle zugleich benutzt werden; ein Wirbel wird also z. B. auf beiden Fellen executirt.

Die *Yōko* oder *Sanno tsuzumi* (Taf. VI Fig. 17) ist von der vorigen nur in der Größe verschieden.

DR. MÜLLER.
(*Forsetzung folgt.*)

frames are linked firmly to one another with a silken cord, as it is with our drums; stronger tension occurs, then, either, as given in the figure, through multiple winding and tightening of a strong silken lash (this is as it was in the music of the Prince of Hōta), or, there are silk slings threaded around two cords at a time, which – as with us the leather slings – can be shifted and so produce a bigger or lesser tension (this is as it was in the ensemble of the Mikado). With this first arrangement the note can be raised slightly further during the performance by pressure with the hand on the lengthwise cords. The *kakko* lies on a stand and is struck with two beaters in such way that both skins are used at the same time; a roll, for example, is executed on both skins.

The *yōko* or *san-no-tsuzumi* (Plate VI, Fig. 17 [p. 122]) differs from the former only in size.

DR. MÜLLER
(*To be continued*)

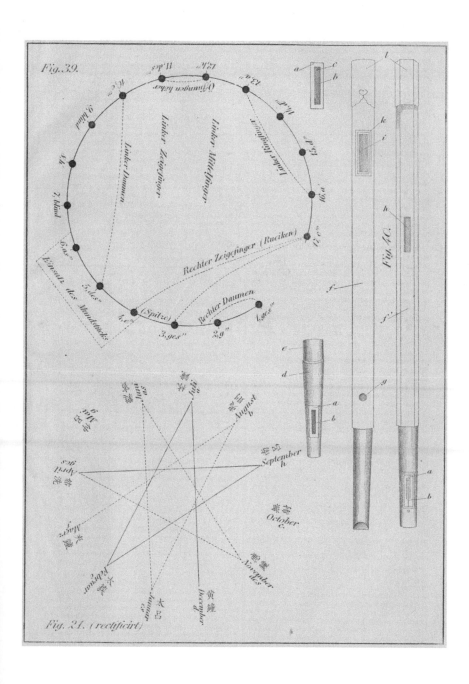

1875

第6号より続く

私が最初 [第6号] の文章の中で述べた、日本の中国音楽についてどうにかしてより深い理解を得たいという希望は実現したが、何らかの完璧を期すという要求を持ちながら、未だにそこからは遠く隔たっている。まず始めに、私は、新しく日本と中国の教養ある音楽家と知り合いになった。さらに私は、ミカドの侍医という立場を利用して、ミカドの専用楽団の楽器、演奏を詳しく調べるに至り、最終的には中国に短期間滞在し、中国楽器の完璧なコレクションを調達した。

　　私はここでまず、新しいことがらに移る前に、最初の論文の情報の一部を訂正し、補完することから始める。

　　まず、私はまた別の形の音叉 [調子笛] 見付けた。それは、外見は Fig. 27 (Taf. VIII) に似ているが、Fig. 25 (Taf. IX) のようなリード管からできている点が異なる。この楽器の調律は、後者のそれと一致しているが、1オクターヴ低い。

　　調子笛の原型は、しかし、リードのない Fig. 27 の楽器にそっくりで、各管の長さは、管長と質量の値[12] に一致するように数学的に計算されたものである。これはリツカン [律管](音の管) と呼ばれる。Taf. VII、Fig. 22 に描かれたものはシケツ [四穴] [4つの穴]」という。Taf. VIII, Fig. 24 と Taf. IX, Figs. 25 & 26 に描かれたものはチョウシブエ [調子笛] という。

　　標準の律管として京都に 1000 年間保存されてきた律管は大通寺で作られたもので、その正確な描写は公刊されている。

　　さらに古い律管は、雅楽(ミカドの音楽、第6号、13頁(p. 80)、脚注参照)で保有しているものである。それは入念に絹で包まれ、小箱に保管されている。決して使用に供されることはなく、聖蹟として守られ、他の律管を調整するために時たま使用されるだけである。管を束ねている絹糸だけは色褪せていて、この律管が疑いなく古いことを示している。管そのものはたいへんよく保存されているが、2つだけ時の流れの中で新しくされたと伝えられている。よく保存されている理由は、ひとえに、始めからいつも雅楽の楽人の手中にあり、彼らによって入念に手入れされてきたからに尽きるだろう。私は、この律管と私が所有している 160 年くらい古い律管と比べてみた。私が律管を取り出した時、そこに居合わせた楽人の1人が突然嬉しそうに言い出した。それを作ったのは彼の八代前の先祖・オオハタヒロタメ [太秦廣為] で、彼はまだ「オオハタ」と名乗っている[13] 律管は、標準のものとまったく一致することがわかった。新しいパリの律管と比べると、最低音が d で、よって第八管が a となる。従ってこれはミカドの音楽の標準調律である。これとは別の世

---

[12] ワグネル博士は中国と日本の長さと重さの単位に関する長い論文を第9号に発表する予定であるので、これらの関係の議論は、彼のより完全な説明に任せることにする。

[13] 日本の世代を考えるには、子供の養子制度を考慮しなければならない。それが家業の維持を助けるからだ。たとえば、ある音楽家が自分の実の息子が医者の養子となりその家を継いだとすると、[別の] 音楽家を息子として認めるのである。

俗音楽用の調子笛は、雅楽用とはほとんど全音 [長 2 度] 異なる。この律管に基づいて、Fig. 21, Taf.VII の「音の輪」の各音は Taf. X にあるように修正されなければならない。月の名前はあまり正確には対応しない。というのは、日本の暦計算は、我々のものと本質的に異なるからである。[14]

　私はまた気づいたのだが、Taf. VII にあがっている図を「右左を廻って」と表現するのは正しくない。私の元の下書きでは、12 月は底に来なければならないが、木版図では一番上に来ている。これもまた Taf. X で訂正した。「右左を廻る」という指示があると、読者は一番近い点を出発点と捉える。

　13 絃の箏に関しては、第 6 号 21 頁 (p. 98) に載せた調絃は雅楽では使われない。基音として使われるのは、12 月 = d、2 月 = e、5 月 = g、7 月 = a、9 月 = b である。もっとも一般的なのは、しかし、はじめの 2 つで、基音はいつも第 2 絃に来る。調子を記すには、基音の下に「調子」ということばをつける。

　音階は次の通り。

		黄鐘調子	太簇調子
		(12月) d	(2月) e
第 1 絃		12 月 d′	9 月 b′
第 2 絃		12 月 d′	2 月 e′
第 3 絃		7 月 a (小オクターヴ)	4 月 g♭′
第 4 絃		8 月 b (小オクターヴ)	7 月 a′
第 5 絃		12 月 d′	9 月 b′
第 6 絃		2 月 e′	11 月 d♭″
第 7 絃		4 月 g♭′	2 月 e″
第 8 絃		7 月 a′	4 月 g♭″
第 9 絃		10 月 c″	7 月 a″
第 10 絃		12 月 d″	9 月 b″
第 11 絃		2 月 e″	11 月 d♭‴
第 12 絃		4 月 g♭″	2 月 e‴
第 13 絃		7 月 a″	4 月 g♭‴

　この音階では、「音の輪」と対応させるために、c♯ と f♯ の代わりに d♭ と g♭ を入れた。

　和琴または 6 絃の日本のコトは、雅楽では次のように調絃する。

　演奏者から数えて

　　第 1 絃　＝　d (c″ – b″ のオクターヴ)
　　第 2 絃　＝　a (c′ – b′ のオクターヴ)

---

[14] 固定した点が冬至である。その前の新月が 11 番目の月の始まりなので、ゆえに私はそれを 12 月に当てた。律管の最低音はこれに当たる。以下の陰暦の各月は 1 つの月として数えられ、3 年ごとに、10 番目の月を 2 回重ねて最後の月とする必要が生じ、新しい出発点はその次に来る。

$$第_3絃 \quad = \quad (c' - b' \text{ のオクターヴ}) \text{ この音}$$
は最初に律管で調絃し、これに
よってその他全部を調絃する。
$$第_4絃 \quad = \quad b\,(c' - b' \text{ のオクターヴ})$$
$$第_5絃 \quad = \quad g\,(c' - b' \text{ のオクターヴ})$$
$$第_6絃 \quad = \quad e\,(c' - b' \text{ のオクターヴ})$$

第3絃にもう1つ基音を取らねばならないとすれば、残りの音は[それに合わせて] 適切な音程に調律される。いつもの如く、調絃は基音によって名付けられるが、それは第3絃にある。箏ノコトと同様に、絃は本来すべて同じ太さ、同じ張力で張られる。

雅楽では使われないが、日本の古い音楽で慣習的に用いられる他の調絃は、ほとんどの場合、恣意的に変えられている。[15] 基音は常に第3絃に置かれ、第1絃は低いオクターヴ、第2絃は5度、第6絃は2度、第4絃は6度または7度、第5絃は3度または4度に調絃する。これらの調絃は、場合によっては発生した地域、あるいは果たす機能によって名付けられる。例えば宗教的な舞の調絃はカグラ・チョウシ[神楽調子]と名付けられる。

正しい調絃はたいへん重要視されている。個々の絃は厳密に定められた順番、すなわちだいたいオクターヴ、五度上昇、四度下降、によって調絃されたのち、今一度調絃が完全かどうかチェックされる(ネトリ[音取]=「音を取る」)。それには2通りの方法がある。

1. 右手に持った鼈甲片が使われ、すばやく絃をかき鳴らす。動作はいちいち特別に定められている。

2. 一方左手は、a. 親指とその他の指1本を使い、2本の絃をはじく。これは「ツミ[摘み]」と言う。あるいは、b. 1本の指の爪の背ですばやく音をはじく(|オル[折る]」。

音取の決まりは非常に厳格だが、それ以外はとりたてて重要なことはない。[和琴は]2種類の方法で演奏される。

1. 鼈甲片[コトサギ[琴軋]] Fig. 34 (Taf. III) で龍角のそばですべての絃を掻き鳴らし、ただちに5本の指で5本の絃を押さえると、1絃だけ残って鳴る。特定のグループの音を消す手の技法にはそれぞれ名称があり、楽譜に書かれる。この演奏技法は、主な拍を明示するためにのみ使用される(下記参照)。

---

[15] (日本語訳者注) 和琴の絃の番号は、箏と異なり、奏者に近い方が第1絃。神楽、久米舞の調絃は d'-a-d-b-g-e / 東遊は、f♯-c♯-b-a'-e-a。東遊の前半と後半を入れ替えると、ミュルレルの説明と合致する。たとえば、第3絃と第5絃との関係が3度 (a-c♯) のものが東遊、4度 (d-g) のものが、神楽、久米舞の調絃となる。

2. 単音は、使える指の背または腹で弾かれる。ただしそれは左手のみである。この技法は一種の装飾として使われる。

もう1つ特に興味をそそるのは和琴の歴史である。和琴の起源神話はちょうどギリシャのハープの起源神話のようである。それによれば、アポロンがハープの音の豊かさと美しさにはじめて気がついたのは、姉妹のディアナの弓の弦がヒュンと鳴った時だった。そして、隣り合ういくつかの弦を意図的に弾いて、その組み合わせによって和音の効果を創り出したのだった [『発明の本』第2巻、407頁]。同様に、神武天皇 (紀元前665年) のはるか前、戦士のカナトモノミコトは6つの弓を並べて立てて演奏に用いた。どのようにしたのかはわからない。6つの弓の使用に関する最初の歴史的資料は、紀元205年である。ジングコング [神功皇后] の名の下に武内宿禰という有名な将軍がいて、その随員が宿禰にコトについて説明し、6つの弓 (弦) でどのように音楽を作れるのかを示した。彼はそれをきれいに組み立て、軍旗で囲み、演奏して大きな感銘を与えた。そこからどのように、いつ和琴が発展したのかは正確には不明だが、恐らく允恭天皇の死 (紀元453年) の直後であろう。というのも、朝鮮の君主がその時弔問品を積んだ80艘の舟を送り、それには80人の楽人が乗っていたからである。彼らは対馬から筑紫 (筑前) へ進み、大坂、京都を目指した。そして日本人に初めて、より発達した音楽を知らしめたのである。おそらく、日本人は自分たちの6本の弓弦を、輸入された (7絃と13絃の) コトに似た胴に張り、この6絃を「和琴」もしくは「大和琴」と名付けたのだろう。[16]

当時の天皇たちは輸入音楽の育成を推進した。特に、安閑天皇は (534年) 朝鮮の楽器をモデルに日本で楽器を制作させた。推古女帝の御代 (611年) には朝鮮の味摩之が来日し、中国の音楽を教えた。それから音楽の研究がより本格的に行われ出した。研究を奨励したその他の天皇は、天武天皇 (673年) と文武天皇 (697年) である。彼らの下で新しい笛がいくつか作られた。それ以降、天皇は音楽を特に育成することはやめ、そのままにしたため、新しいものはほとんど生まれなくなった。

奈良には紀元738年に作られた和琴があるが、それは幅がやや狭い以外は、だいたい今日のものと同じである。[それより] 200年くらい新しいものは、まったく今日のものと同じである。

和琴は今日、大きな合奏ではめったに使われない。にもかかわらず、時折、13絃の箏の代替となることができる。ふだんは非常に稀にしか演奏されない純粋な古い音楽に用いられ、神楽笛、笏拍子 [第6号14頁 (p. 84)] と組み合わされる。和琴の独奏曲は、「ニワビノキョク [庭燎の曲]」1曲しかないが、和琴は歌の伴奏でも演奏される。

7絃の琴ノコト [Taf. IV, Fig. 5] は、日本ではほとんど演奏されない。ある非常に教養ある音楽家が言うには、江戸、京都、大阪にこの楽器の弾き方を本当によく

---

16 和琴は wa-gong (ワゴン) と書かれるが、実際には wanggong (ワンゴン) と発音される。「ワ」と「ヤマト」は日本の古名、「ゴン」は中国語で音の鳴る楽器のことである。どちらも、外国から来た楽器が日本風に改められたことを表している。

知っている音楽家は一人くらいしかいない、とのことである。中国でもまた、この楽器は上流家庭だけで演奏される。ある物知りな中国人音楽家は、実践、理論ともにほとんどの中国楽器を知っていたが、低い階級であったので、この神秘的な楽器についてはほとんど述べることがない、ということだった。この楽器は、まったく特別な機会だけに使用される。たとえば、天気が良いにもかかわらず、ある身分の高い人が悲しんでいる時、彼の気を晴らすために、このような楽器が引っ張り出され演奏される。しかし下々の者はこれを全く知らない。

先に言及した学者の町田氏は、この楽器の実用法を説明してくれた。

琴ノコトは長さ 118 センチ。絃の長さは 111 センチ。絃は楽器の狭い方の端の下の 2 本の足のあたりに堅く巻きつけられ、この端のへりにある 7 つの溝を通っている。広い方の先端から 6 センチのところに、横向きに乗絃がついていて、その上を絃が走っている。その上部に 7 つの孔があいている。そこから丈夫な絹糸または紐でできた 7 本のループ状の紐が出ていて、そこに、絃が独特の結び方でしっかり結びつけられている。

今述べたループ状の紐の開いた両端は、楽器の下側の平面に対して垂直に立っている 7 つの糸巻に、次の様な方法で固定されている。

個々の糸巻きは長さ 4 センチで、我々の九柱戯 [のピン] とそっくりである。平らな足の上 1 センチのところに、右回りの深い切れこみがある。この切れこみから溝が出ていて、平らな足の真ん中に流れ出ている。

これらの出口に前述のループ紐が入れられ、溝を通って、溝の反対側の端から引っぱり出されて、糸巻きの切れこみの回りに固定される。その結果、糸巻きの足がしっかりと楽器の底に固定され、今言及した溝が、コトの底の開口部の延長線上にくるのである。糸巻きを縦軸に沿って回すと、ループ紐の両側が互いに巻き付き、絃の張りがきつくなったり緩んだりするのである。実際、糸巻きを右回りにねじると張りがきつくなり、左回りに回すと緩むような仕組みになっている。

琴ノコトはこれまで述べて来た箏とは、以下の点で本質的に異なる。

第一に、可動式の柱はなく、糸巻きによって絃を調律する。

第二に、絃は太さが異なる。低い方の 4 絃は細い絃を表面に巻いてあるが、上の 3 絃はそうではない。巻絃の作り方は日本では知られていない。

古い時代にはこの楽器は 5 絃だった。第 6 号 15 頁 [p. 88] に示したように、「宮」などの名前がついている。後になって高いオクターヴに 2 絃が追加され、「小さな宮」または「ブン [文]」、「小さな商」または「ブ [武]」という名前がつけられたが、これらの名前はこの楽器でのみ通用する。

基音は声の高さに基づき、真ん中の絃に当てられる。調絃は次の様な方法で行われる。たとえば、基音を d′ に設定すると、音の順番は

第 1 絃　　a　　小オクターヴ
第 2 絃　　g　　　〃〃
第 3 絃　　c′

第4絃　d′
第5絃　a′
第6絃　g′
第7絃　c″

　演奏者に近い側[17]に13個の平らな螺鈿のボタン [徽 [き]] があり、7番目のものがちょうど楽器の真ん中でに来る。つまり、それぞれの乗絃から55と½センチ隔たったところにある。それ以外の徽は、以下のような距離に対称的に置かれている。

徽の番号	距離			
	中央の徽から	相互	隣の徽から	最も遠い端から
6 & 8	11 cm.	22 cm.	40.5	66.5
5 & 9	18.5 ″	37 ″	37	74
4 & 10	27.5 ″	55 ″	28	83
3 & 11	33.5 ″	67 ″	22	89
2 & 12	37 ″	74 ″	18.5	92.5
1 & 13	41.5 ″	83 ″	14	97

　それぞれの距離は真ん中の徽から測ったが、ミリの単位では間違いがあるかもしれないので、さらに正確な計算のためには細かな修正をしなければならないだろう。たとえば、日本人は、1と13からまで、隣の徽との距離を ⅛ とするが、8 × 14は 112 である。5から9までは⅓、4から10までは¼、3から11までは⅕、2から12までは ⅙ としている。½ というのはない。

　この比率に注意することは、しかしながら、重要である。というのも、この楽器は以下のような2つの方法で演奏されるからである。

1. 徽の位置を指でしっかり押さえ、爪の裏側で絃を外側に弾く。または

2. 左手の指は軽く絃の上に置かれ、そこが振動の結節点となり、フラジオレット音 (ハーモニクス) が生じる。この場合、右手の指の腹で絃を弾く。

　どちらの場合も発せられた音は、簡単に算出できる。

　ふつう、歌の伴奏の場合はユニゾンで、一度に1本の絃が弾かれる。2絃が同時に弾かれる時も同じくユニゾンである。

---

[17] (英訳者補注) 正しくは演奏者から一番遠い側。

　　第3絃が基音となる場合は、残りの音も適切な音程に調絃される。そして、い
つものように、基音によって調絃は名付けられ、それは第3絃に位置する。元来、
箏ノコトと同様に、すべての絃は等しい太さで、等しい張力で張ってある。

　　ミカドの音楽の琵琶について、第6号では示さなかった調絃がある。それは、
以前オータ皇子の音楽の中で見付けたものである。絃は以下の様な方法で調律され
る。主音、第2度、第5度、オクターヴ。5つの異なる音を基音とすることができ、
個々の調絃には固有の名前がある。

平調は 12 月　　基音　　d(ママ)

壱越は 2 月　　基音　　e(ママ)[18]

双調は 5 月　　基音　　g

黄鐘は 7 月　　基音　　a

盤渉は 9 月　　基音　　b

　　最後にさらに第6の調絃、スイチョウ [水調] がある。基音 a(7月)だが、第2音
が少し低い。

　　絃は太さが異なり、長さは等しい。頸のところの水平の柱 [じゅう] は、絃をそ
の上に押し付けると、以下の様に音が変化するように作られている。

開放絃　　主音

第1柱　　長2度

第2柱　　短3度

第3柱　　長3度

第4柱　　完全4度

　　これらの柱の位置は、Fig. 2, Taf. II にある、盲人音楽の琵琶の柱とは少し異なっ
ている。その他の点では同じ形である。

　　絃は、下の端に単純に固定されている。各々の絃は端の結び目によって輪を
作っている。絃止め [覆手 (ふくじゅ)] の穴から押し出された後、その輪を通って、
引っ張られる。すると絃は簡単に、覆手のあたりに輪を作って自ら結ばれる。

　　これで、日本で使われているすべての絃楽器に触れた。中国の楽器については
結びのところで触れる。日本では一般的でない他の中国楽器や、せいぜい演奏者1
人で演奏される楽器等もそこで扱う。

管楽器

管楽器の中で、もっとも興味深く、ヨーロッパ人の耳に心地よく響くのは笙である
(Taf. VI, Fig. 10)。笙が特に面白いのは、雅楽合奏の音調の基盤となる役目があり、

---

[18] (英訳者、日本語訳者補注) ミユルレルは、最初の 2 つを逆に記している。

時折、様々な和音的な音が同時に鳴るからである。他のすべての日本の管楽器と同様、笙の演奏家の主たる技法は、音をできるだけ長く持続させることである。

笙は以下のような部分から成る。

1. 空気の部屋 [頭 (かしら)] (Taf. IV, Fig. 10a) は図では上から、つまり、管を差し込む側から見たところである (解説図 Taf. VI, Fig. 10 参照)。実物の半分の大きさである。頭は木を掘って半円球のような形に作られ、たっぷりと漆が塗られ、所有者の紋が描かれる。一方の側に吹き口があり、頭に常に固定されている。吹き口は四角い穴がくりぬかれ (Taf. IV, Fig. 10c)、金具で保護されている。上等な楽器だと金具はすべて銀である。吹き口は口の前に当てるだけで口にはくわえず、これに息を吹きこんだり吸ったりする。両方の奏法が通常用いられる。

   頭の上部の平らな面に、17 個の穴が開いており、挿絵に示したようにいつもこの配列である。これらの穴に [17 本の竹管が] 差し込まれる。

2. 17 本の管は異なる長さである (Taf. X, Fig. 40)。各管は金属製のリードがはめ込まれた単一の部品から出来ているように見える。偶然に 1 本の管が壊れてしまったために、私は管が 2 つの部品から成っていることを発見した。それは、非常にしっかりと互いに固定されるので、大変注意深く観察しても 1 つの部品に見えてしまう。各管の部品は以下のこごとくである。

a. 長方形の真鍮の小板は、管ごとに大きさが異なる (Taf. X, Fig. 40a)。真ん中 (Fig. 40b) に、三方に切り込みを入れて切り出された舌があり、表面は薄く削られていて、そのためハーモニカの舌のように息によって自由に振動する。しかし私ははっきり気づいたのだが、板全体は一つの部品であり、この舌は切り出されていて、差し込まれているのではないのである。本来の正しい音が出なくなった場合は、舌の開いた先端に近い方に蝋の小球 (Fig. 40c) を付けて必要な重さを加える。そこには小さな金属球が収まっている。

b. 舌がついた管の本来の長さは 5 センチである (Taf. X, Fig. 40d)。竹を切ったもので、全体に漆が塗られている。また、頭の上に出ている上部には金蒔絵が、頭に固定されている下部には黒漆が塗られている。漆は湿度から管を守る効果がある。一方の側は、舌がついた板をはめるために平らになっている。下部は閉じている。つまり、下の端は竹の節と一致するように切られている。上部の少し細い先端 (Fig. 40e) は、しっかりと f, f′ にはめ込まれている。

c. 取り付けられた管。燻した竹でできている。17 本の細竹は、目に見える部分は丸い (Fig. 40f)。それに対して、すべての管どうしが接触する内側部分は、しっかりと互いにくっつくことができるように、内側が斜めに面取りされている (Fig. 40f′)。管の長さはいろいろである

2 本	45cm
4 本	36cm
4 本	28cm
4 本	21cm
3 本	16cm

　これらの管長は見た目の長さであり、本当の管長はまったく別に算出される。それぞれの管は、実際には下の方の先端から1センチ上、つまりはめ込まれた舌の先の上あたりに、ピンの頭ほどの大きさの穴がある (Fig. 40g)。第11管と第12管のみはこれらの穴は2センチ高い位置にある。というのも、これらは、左手の人差し指と中指が当てられるからである。これらの穴はすべて外側についているが、第3と第4管は例外的に内側に、そして第17管は横についている。この3つの穴の方向は、Taf. X, Fig. 39 に点線で示してある。しかしながら、それぞれの管には、実際には内側に、第2の細長い穴がついている (Fig. 40h)。これが本当に使われる管長を決めているわけだが、その長さは単に見た目の対称性のためである。

　ゆえに、実際の管の長さは以下の如くである。

第 1 管	g♭′′′	5cm
第 2 管	g′′	13cm
第 3 管	g♭′′	14.5cm
第 4 管	e′′	15cm
第 5 管	d♭′′	20cm
第 6 管	a♭′′	11cm
第 7 管[19]	無音	
第 8 管	b′	6cm
第 9 管	無音	
第 10 管	e′′′	8cm
第 11 管	d♭′′′	10cm
第 12 管	h′′	11cm
第 13 管	a′′	7cm
第 14 管	d′′′	17.5cm
第 15 管	d′′	26cm
第 16 管	a′	22 cm
第 17 管	c′′′	10cm[20]

[19] (日本語訳者補注) 正しくは舌が無いのは第 9 管と 16 管。
[20] これらの詳細は、標準律管と比べる前に計測されたので、新しいパリの律管によれば、すべて半音上げられなければならない。たとえば、g♭は g になる。

この長さに、さらにとりつけられた管から舌までの距離、すなわち約2センチが加えられる。穴が低すぎる場合は、余った部分はシェラックワニスで閉じられる。第9と10管は、Taf. VI, Fig. 10とTaf. X, Fig. 40に見えるように、外側に銀で縁取られた2つの長方形の穴 (Fig. 40k) を持っている。しかしこれは単なる装飾の機能しかない。第10管には低いところに内側の穴 (Fig. 40h) がついている。第9管は使わない。第9、10、1管にある上部の銀の飾りもまた (Fig. 40l) 単なる飾りである。舌のついた管のできるだけ上部の薄いところを口のところに構え、息を吹き込んでも、小さな穴 (Fig. 40g) を指で塞がないと音が出ない。空気管の長さが舌の振動数に合った適切な比率になると初めて音が出る。これが、管が頭に差し込まれた時の状況である。

管を長さの順にシンメトリックに並べ、頭にその下の端を隙間なくきっちり差し込んだ後に、輪 (Taf. IV, Fig. 10b) を管の上から下に押し込む。[輪の] くびれた部分が頭の穴の無い位置に一致して、管と管の間にはまるようにする。この輪は楽器全体が、すべての部分が密着した1つの物体となるまで、しっかり奥まで差し込まれる。第1と17管の間の隙間から、すべての管の内側に、目と指が届く。

Taf. VIの、上の図は楽器を右から見たところで、今述べた開いた箇所が見える。下の図は左から見た図で、吹口が演奏者に向いたときである。後者は輪が押し込まれることができる位置が示されているが、第9と10管にある穴の銀飾りのところまでであることが見て取れる (Taf. X, Fig. 40k)。

使用しない時は、開いたほうの先端が曲がらないように、図に示したように、管の間に絹のクッションを押し込む。

この楽器を掃除するには、針金につないだ金属球とぼろ布を利用する。さらに、使用中は、演奏者はヒバチ [火鉢](日本の炭を使う火鉢で一般的にはストーブとして使用される) を隣に置き、吹いていない時は楽器を火の上にかざし乾かすために使用する。その際演奏者は、おそらく楽器の一カ所だけが熱くなりすぎないように、また、上記の蝋の小球 (Taf. X, Fig. 40c) が溶けないために、絶え間なく楽器を軸にそって回転させる。しかし、用心のために、各楽団では楽器が使えなくなった時のために、手元にいくつかの予備の楽器を備えている。

演奏するためには、演奏者は両手で包み込むように頭を持ち、管と指が上向きになり、両親指の間に吹き口が来るようにする。つまり、楽器が両手の丸い手のひらの中にあり、両方の親指の付け根と、互いにしっかりとくっついた [両手の] 小指の中に収まるのである。右手の人差し指は第1管と17管の間に突っ込まれ (Taf. X, Fig. 39)、その先端で第3と4管の内側に開いた穴を閉じたり、第1指骨の背で第17管の内側に横向きに開いた穴を塞ぐために使われる。

演奏者は、吹き口を口に押しあて、息を吹くか吸うかする。その両方を交互に行うことによって、それほど苦労しないで音を大変長く持続させることができる。その際、指先で小さな穴が塞がれた管だけが鳴る (Fig. 40g)。指がどのように管に割り当てられているのかは Fig. 39 でわかる。それを見るとまた、なぜ音がこの順番で

並べられているのか、なぜいくつかの音 (第 7 と第 9)[21] が使われないのかもわかるだろう。これがひとえに能率のためであることは明らかである。たとえば、右手の親指と人差し指は、その右側にある穴を閉じると 1 オクターヴ関係の音を作る。もし、左側にある穴を閉じると 3 度の音を作る。もし人差し指の背で 17 管を塞ぐと、三和音が作られる。

左の親指には 4 つの音が当てられる。吹き口のそばに置いて第 5 管 [db''] を閉じ、左手人差し指 [11 管 = db'''] を加えるとオクターヴが得られる。吹き口から離して、第 6 管を押さえる。音が出ない第 7 は押さえ間違いを避けるためのものである。第 6 管 [ab''] と第 11 管 [db'''] は完全 4 度の音程関係である。親指を第 8 管 [b'] に置くと、2 つの音の出ない管の間になり、間違って押さえることはほとんどない。中指で第 12 管を押さえるとオクターヴが出る。親指で第 10 管を押さえると、第 10[9,e'''] と 12 管 [b''] が、再び完全 4 度を作る。第 11[12]、12[13] 管はずっと高いところにあり、そこには親指は間違っても届かない。同様に薬指も届かない。薬指は間の 2 本の管 (第 14[d''']、15[d''] 管) を押さえるとオクターヴを作る。その外側の第 13 と 16 管には中指と小指が当てられ、同様にオクターヴを作る。しかし、第 13[a''] と 14[d'''] 管、または第 15[d''] と 16[a'] 管を閉じると、完全 4 度が得られる。このように、各管の音列の並びは、まったく合理的な理由からなのである。

笙が我々の耳を喜ばせると言うことができるとすれば、その正反対の、合奏の中でもっとも支配的な管楽器は篳篥である (Taf. VI, Fig. 11)。これはオーボエの一種で、本体は竹でできていて、長さは 18 センチである。前面に 2 センチ間隔で 7 孔あり、最初の孔は頭部から 4 センチのところにある。背面には、2 孔あり、同様に頭部から 5 センチと 11 センチのところについている。リードは丸く薄い 6 センチの長さの葦の小片で、紙がしっかり巻かれていて、楽器本体の太い方に差し込む。開いたほうの端は薄く削られていて、平に押しつぶされている。これによって、オーボエやファゴットのようなダブルリードになる。ダブルリードは、平たくつぶされた竹の輪 [セメ] をはめられて互いに密着し、使わない時は帽子をかぶせて保護される。この楽器を演奏するには、両手で持ち、上から、左手の 2 から 4 の指、右手の 2 から 5 の指で孔を押さえる。両方の親指は背面の 2 つの孔に置かれる。

この楽器から作られる音列は a'''、g'''、gb'''、e''(ママ)、db'''、c'''、(まったくぴったりではないが)、b''、a''、g'' である。これはすべて、孔を順番に閉じていって得られた音である。2 番目の音だけは親指を開ける。以前は、背面の第 2 孔は db''' の音を調整するために使用されたが、今では常に閉じられている。この楽器を演奏するには、まずリードをよく唾液で湿らせて、セメの位置まで唇にくわえさせ、頬を強く膨らませ、精一杯息を吹き込む。すると、甲高い金切り声のような音がし、さらに我々を不愉快にさせるのは、音程が合っておらず、何となく下から徐々に上がって行くように吹かれることである。

横笛には以下の様な種類がある。

---

[21] (日本語訳者補注) 前述の通り、無音の管の番号は正しくは第 9 と第 16。

a.　オウテキ [横笛]。または中国の笛 (Taf. VI, Fig. 12)。ミカドの音楽にも使用される。

b.　カグラブエ [神楽笛]。または日本の笛。(Taf. VI, Fig. 13)

c.　コマブエ [高麗笛]。または朝鮮の笛。(Taf. VI, Fig. 14)[22]

　　さらに、中国にも日本にも大小さまざまの笛、極小笛までいろいろある。しかし、あまり正式な音楽演奏には使われず、むしろ、路傍の曲芸師や見世物小屋等々で用いられる。指孔の数や位置はさまざまである。文字通り「草の笛」という意味のクサブエもある。その名前には語源的に 2 つの意味がある。a. もともと草 (葦) でできていた。b. 羊飼いが草原で家畜を追うために吹いた (草)。

2.　シノブエ [篠笛]。劇場、見世物小屋等々で声の伴奏として用いられる。声に合わせなければならないので、演奏者は半音ずつ高くなる 12 本の笛のセットを携えていなければならない。

　　横笛は 39 と ½ センチで、神楽笛は 45 センチである。高麗笛は少し短い。正確な描写はここでは割愛する。5 分の 1 の縮尺で、これらの笛の関係は Taf. VI, Figs. 12, 13, 14 で簡単にわかる。

　　横笛は、吹き口のほかに同じ側に 7 孔ある。その他の 2 つ [神楽笛と高麗笛] は 6 孔しかない。それぞれの笛の孔の位置は次の図で表される。

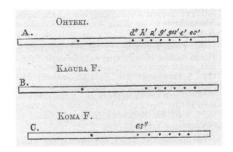

　　横笛の最後の音はきちんと合った音ではなく、使用されない。だが、ここで注意すべきは、すべての音がきちんと合っておらず、むしろ、吹き方によってほとんど半音程度変わることである。同様に、ある音の 1 オクターヴ高い音と低い音は、吹く強さによって生じる。つまり、それぞれの音は 3 オクターヴ出る。しかし、演奏者たちは、低い音を吹くのは非常に難しい、と語った。

　　指遣いは篳篥とまったく同様である (左手 2–4 指、右手 2–5 指、両方の親指は楽器を支える)。楽器は平行ではなく、左上から右下にかけて、だいたい 45 度の角度に構えられる。演奏する時は、吹口を絶え間なく舐めている。

22　第 6 号にあげた笛の説明には誤りがある。14 頁 (p. 84) で朝鮮の笛と日本の笛として No.14 に示したが、日本の笛は No.13 である。21 頁 (p. 112) の音域の 2 つの数字は混乱している。(英訳者補注: 3 つの笛が混乱している。)

打楽器

これらの楽器の中で最も重要なのは笏拍子、つまり木の拍子木である (Taf. V, Fig. 20)。2 枚の長い平らな木片から成り、琵琶もしくは槐 (えんじゅ) の木から作る。その起源は昔、大名が持っていた小さな板に遡る。その板は飾りと身分証のためだったが、2 つに割られ、注意を喚起するために打ち合わされるようになった。今日なお、劇場や曲芸ショーなどでお知らせや案内をする人によって、話、説明、転換などの始まり、終わりを合図するために、類似した小さな板が打ち鳴らされている。このような演奏において、彼らは西洋のベルや呼び笛のような役割を果たしているのである。

　演奏にあたっては、片方の木片の平面に、もう一方のふちを立てるような形で構える。そして、奏者の身体から遠いほうの端を、角度をつけて広げて離し、すばやく打ち合わせるのである。

　ショウコ [鉦鼓] (Taf. V, Fig. 18) は青銅製の盤で、豪華に装飾された木製の枠の 2 つの取手にぶら下がってる。この盤は鉢状に窪んでいて豪華な紋章で飾られている。Fig. 18 では、真ん中にミカドの紋章が見え、三重の同心円がついていて、そこに取手が付いている。a の図の左は側面図、右図は盤を真ん中から割った断面図である。

　2 本のバチで打たれるが、図ではバチは真ん中にぶら下がっている。鉦鼓は盤の真ん中が打たれ、縁は打たれない。

　タイコ [太鼓] (Taf. V, Fig. 15) は同様に、豪華な木製枠に吊るされた太鼓である。美しく絵が描かれた 2 枚の革が張られている。2 枚の革は約 9 センチ離れていて、部分的に糊付け、部分的に鋲留めされている。2 本のバチで打たれ、バチは図では [枠の] 両側に留められている。a は太鼓の側面図で 9 分の 1 の縮尺である。

　カッコ [鞨鼓] (Taf. VI, Fig. 16) は、大きな、中を剔り貫いた盃を 2 つ組み合わせたような木の胴から成り、両側に枠にしっかり固定された革が張ってある。2 つの枠は、我々の太鼓と同様に、絹の紐で互いにしっかり結ばれている。強い張力は、図に見えるように、丈夫な絹の紐を何回も折り返し引っ張るか [オータ皇子の音楽がそうだったように]、あるいは、絹の輪が 2 本の紐のまわりに通してあり、我々の革の紐と同様、時々それを動かして、より強い、あるいは弱い張力が得られる [ミカドの合奏音楽ではそうであった]。最初のやり方だと、音は演奏中に、長く渡してある紐に手で圧力を加えることにより、すこし上げることができる。鞨鼓は台の上に置き、2 本のバチで、両方の革を同時に使って打つ。たとえば、連打 [トレモロ＝来 [らい]] は両方の面を使って行われる。

　ヨウコ [腰鼓] または三の鼓 (Taf. VI, Fig. 17) は前述のもの [鞨鼓] と大きさの点だけ異なる。

　　　　　　　　　　　　　　　　ミュルレル博士 [続く]

1876

Einige Notizen über die japanische Musik

Some Notes on Japanese Music

(Forsetzung aus dem achten Heft und Schluss.) Ich muß den geehrten Leser um Entschuldigung bitten, wenn ich mich genöthigt sehe, auch diesen Aufsatz mit einigen Rectificationen von frühern Irrthümern zu beginnen; wer aber eine Einsicht in die ungeheuren Schwierigkeiten hat, welche das Studium von dergleichen Gegenständen in diesen Ländern bietet, wird mir kaum einen Vorwurf daraus machen, wenn ich manches Ungenaue publicirt habe; gewöhnlich haben die Leute, bei denen man sich informirt, selbst nur eine vage und sehr einseitige Kenntnis von der Sache, und nur durch Vergleichung einer Anzahl Aussagen und durch eigne Beobachtung kann man zu irgend welchen sichern Resultaten kommen. Ich bin ja auch kein Musiker von Fach und habe diese Reihe von Aufsätzen lediglich geschrieben, um zu dem Studium dieses bisher ganz unbekannten Gebiets anzuregen und die Wege zu eröffnen, nicht aber mit der Prätension, etwas Fertiges und Abgeschlossenes zu liefern.

(Continuation from Issue Eight and Ending.) I must beg forgiveness of the honored reader if I see myself compelled to begin this essay, too, with some rectifications of previous errors; but whoever has an insight into the enormous difficulties which the study of such topics presents in these lands will hardly chide me if I have published some imprecisions. Usually the people from whom one informs oneself have themselves only a vague and very one-sided knowledge of the matter, and only through comparison of a number of statements and through personal observation can one come to any sort of secure results. I am certainly no musician by profession and have written this series of essays merely to motivate the study of this so-far totally unknown field, and to open paths; not, however, with the pretension of delivering something complete and finished.

Zunächst hatte sich bei der Geschichte der Wanggong ein Irrthum eingeschlichen; die Kaiserin, unter welcher die sechs Bogen zusammengesetzt wurden, hieß Dsing go koku; der Feldherr, welcher die Zusammensetzung der Bogen befahl, hieß Takeno Udshino Sukune; der Name des Kriegers ist unbekannt.

Ich schließe hier gleich noch einige historische Notizen an, welche mir der bedeutende, japanische Gelehrte und Archaeologe, Herr Ninagawa gab:

Das Alter der Wanggong in Japan ist etwa 1,500 Jahr, das der Kanguro Fuye, und der Biwa 1,200; das der Musmeno Kōto (Mädchen-Koto, welche von der 13 saitigen Sôno-Koto nur durch die Dicke der Saiten differirt) 500, das der Samiseng 300, das der Kokin 160 Jahr. Die genauere Entstehungsart der Shaku Bioshi ist folgende: Die Adligen mussten früher, wenn sie vor dem Kaiser erschienen, mit beiden Händen vor ihrer Brust eine flache, längliche Holztafel von bestimmter Form halten, welche Shaku hieß und auch zum Aufschreiben von Notizen, Anreden u. dgl. für diese Gelegenheiten benutzt wurden. Nach dem Gebrauch wurden sie der Länge nach durchgesägt und die beiden Stücke dann zum Angeben des Taits (Hiyōshi) benutzt.[1] Das Zersägen

First of all, a mistake had slipped in over the history of the wagon; the Empress, under whom the six bows were assembled is called Jingū-kōgō; the general who ordered the the assembly of the bows is called Takenouchi-no-sukune; the name of the warrior is unknown.

I add right here a few further historical notes which the eminent Japanese scholar and archaeologist Herr Ninagawa gave me:

The age of the wagon in Japan is about 1,500 years; that of the kagurabue and of the biwa 1,200; that of the musumeno-koto (girls'-koto, which differs from the 13-stringed sō-no-koto only in the thickness of the strings) 500; that of the shamisen 300; that of the kokin 160 years. The more accurate evolution of the shakubyōshi is the following: earlier, when they appeared before the Emperor, the nobles had to hold with both hands in front of their chests a flat elongated wooden tablet of a prescribed form which was called shaku and for these occasions would be used, too, for the writing down of notes, forms of address, and the like. After use they would be sawn through lengthwise and the two pieces used then for giving the beat (hyōshi).[1] The sawing-up took place also so that the

---

[1] Das Angeben des Taits [Takts] mit der Hand heißt Te-biyôshi, mit dem Fuße Ashi-biyôshi; aus dem H wird durch den Nigori (sprich Ningori) bedeutet eigentlich unrein und bezeichnet die euphonisti[s]che Umwandlung der Consonanten bei Zusammensetzung ein B, ebenso wie Fuye sich bei Zusammensetzungen in Buye verwandelt, Wanggong statt Wagong ausgesprochen wird, u.s.w.

[1] Giving the beat with the hand is called te-byōshi, with the foot, ashi-byōshi; out of the h by means of the nigori (pronounced ningori), which means really impure, and indicates the euphonistic transformation of consonants in compounds, is made a b, just as fue is made to bue in compounds, and wang-gon is pronounced instead of wagong, etc.

geschah auch, damit die beiden Hälften als Legitimation, Erkennungszeichen, Pass und dgl. dienen konnten. Die Sitte, den Shaku zu tragen, existirt noch heute, wenn jemand in japanischer Tracht zu Hofe geht. Dieselbe Sitte herrschte in China seit Alters her, schon vor 2000 v. Ch. wird sie erwähnt. Nach dem heiligen Buche Chonking dienten sie dazu, daß die Großen in Gegenwart des Kaisers ihr Gesicht in Demuth verbergen konnten. Sie hießen dort Kouei, hatten für die verschiedenen Rangstufen verschiedene Formen und waren mit verschiedenen Emblemen geschmückt. Für den Kaiser existirten drei Sorten, mit denen er Audienz gab und sein Antlitz ebenfalls verbarg; die größte Sorte für ihn war 3 Fuß lang. Im Jahre 2042 erschienen die Großen bei Hofe mit schwarzen Koueis, um den Schrecken der Völker über eine statt gehabte große Wassersnoth kund zu thun. Endlich hörte ich noch als eine große antiquarische Merkwürdigkeit die Ishibuye (Steinflöte) anführen, von der bis vor Kurzem ein Exemplar in einem Tempel Yedo's existirte, aber auf unbekannte Art verschwunden ist, so daß ich sie nicht mehr selbst sehen, sondern nur eine ungefähre Beschreibung derselben erhalten konnte. Darnach scheint das Instrument mehr der Clarinette, als der Flöte geglichen zu haben. Es war ein etwa 2 Fuß langer, 4–5 Zoll im Durchmesser dicker Cylinder, der aus einem einzigen Steine bestand und wie ein Kanonenrohr ausgehölt war; die eine Seite des Mündungsendes war wie eine

two halves could serve as legitimation, identification, passport, and the like. The custom of carrying the *shaku* still exists today when someone goes to court in Japanese national dress. The same custom prevailed in China from of old; it is mentioned already before 2000 BCE. According to the sacred book *Shujing*, they served so that in the presence of the Emperor the Grandees could hide their faces in humility. There they were called *gui*, had various shapes for the different ranks, and were decorated with diverse emblems. For the Emperor there existed three types, with which he held audience and likewise concealed his countenance: the biggest sort for him was 3 feet long. In the year 2042 the Grandees appeared at court with black *gui* in order to make known the people's terror over a great flood that had happened. Finally, I heard mentioned as another major antiquarian curiosity the *ishibue* (stone flute), of which until recently an example existed in one of Edo's temples, but which has disappeared in unknown ways, so that I could no longer see it myself but could get only an approximate description of it. Accordingly, the instrument seems to have resembled the clarinet more than the flute. It was a cylinder about 2 feet long, 4–5 inches thick in diameter, which was made from a single stone, and was hollowed out like a cannon bore; one side of the mouth-end was obliquely and sharply levelled like a pipe and so formed the mouth-piece against which was blown; on one side of the cylinder several fingerholes were to be found.

Pfeife schräg und scharf abgeflacht und bildete so das Mundstück, gegen welches geblasen wurde; auf der einen Seite des Cylinders befanden sich dann mehrere Grifflöcher.

Die *Stellung der Pfeifen an der Shō*, die ich untersuchte, war nicht ganz richtig, vielmehr ist die Folge derselben, wie folgt:

The *setting of the pipes on the shō*, which I examined, was not quite correct; rather, the order of the same is as follows:

1te	Pfeife	fis$'''$	1st	pipe	fis$\sharp'''$
2te	„	g$''$	2nd	„	g$''$
3te	„	fis$''$	3rd	„	fis$\sharp''$
4te	„	e$''$	4th	„	e$''$
5te	„	cis$''$	5th	„	cis$\sharp''$
6te	„	gis$''$	6th	„	gis$\sharp''$
7te	„	h$'$	7th	„	b$'$
8te	„	e$'''$	8th	„	e$'''$
9te	„	blind	9th	„	mute
10te	„	cis$'''$	10th	„	cis$\sharp'''$
11te	„	h$''$	11th	„	b$''$
12te	„	a$''$	12th	„	a$''$
13te	„	d$'''$	13th	„	d$'''$
14te	„	d$'''$	14th	„	d$'''$ [d$''$]
15te	„	a$'$	15th	„	a$'$
16te	„	blind	16th	„	mute
17te	„	c$''$	17th	„	c$''$ [c$'''$]

Die fünfte Pfeife wird nicht mit dem linken, sondern mit dem rechten Daumen geschlossen, für die 14te und 15te wird zuweilen der rechte Mittel- oder Ringfinger benutzt. Auch bei Angabe der Stimmungen hatten sich noch einige Irrthümer eingeschlichen, Heft VIII, pag. 42 muss bei der Stimmung der Koscho Toshi der Monat der 3ten Saite Juli sein, für die 7te und 12te Saite ist Mai,

The fifth pipe is not closed with the left thumb, but with the right; for the 14th and 15th, sometimes the right middle- or ring-finger is used. Also when giving tunings, a few more mistakes had crept in; Issue VIII, page 42 (p. 147), for the tuning of *kōshō-chōshi*, the month of the 3rd string must be July; for the 7th and 12th string, May, *g*, instead of April, *g♭*, is to be written; on page 44 (p. 155),

g, statt April, ges, zu schreiben; auf Seite 44, muss die Stimmung für die Kino Kōto folgendermaßen abgeändert werden:

1te	Saite	a
2te	"	h
3te	"	d'
4te	"	e'
5te	"	ges'
6te	"	a'
7te	"	h'

Ich gehe nun über zu der nähern Besprechung des Gagakku, seiner Instrumente, Noten, u.s.w.

Das Gagakku ist, wie schon früher gesagt, ein Staatsinstitut, in welchem seit den Uranfängen der aus Korea eingeführten, gelehrten und heiligen Musik diese gepflegt und vererbt wird; es ist das einzige Institut, in welchem sich die alte Musik erhalten hat, die in China und Korea ganz verloren gegangen ist, und ist somit heute fast der einzige Ort, an welchem man noch Notizen über diese so merkwürdige Musik sammeln kann; aber auch hier fängt die Neigung zu Neuerungen an, sich bei den jüngern Musikern, von denen einige unter europäischem Einflusse stehen, geltend zu machen, und es ist daher äußerst wünschenswert, das wirklich Alte so schnell, als möglich, fest zustellen.

Die Lehrer des Gagakku sind vom Staate besoldet und geben außerhalb desselben keinen Unterricht; Schüler sind in diesem Augenblicke über 40. Es werden hier nur alte Stücke gelehrt,

the tuning for the kin-no-koto must be altered in the following way:

1st	string	a
2nd	"	b
3rd	"	d'
4th	"	e'
5th	"	g♭'
6th	"	a'
7th	"	b'

I pass on now to the more detailed description of Gagaku, its instruments, notations, and so forth.

Gagaku, as already stated earlier, is a state institution in which, since its very beginnings when introduced from Korea, the erudite and sacred music is maintained and handed down; it is the only institution in which the old music which has been completely lost in China and Korea survives, and is thus today nearly the only place where one can still collect notes about this such remarkable music; but here, too, the tendency for innovations is beginning to make itself felt among the younger musicians, a few of whom stand under European influences, and it is therefore exceedingly desirable to determine the really old as quickly as possible.

The teachers of Gagaku are in the employ of the state and give no instruction outside; right now there are over 40 students. Here only old pieces are taught, some with song; earlier, most, if not all,

zum Theil mit Gesang; früher haben
wohl die meisten, wo nicht alle, Gesangbegleitung gehabt, aber von vielen ist
merkwürdigerweise grade der Gesang
oder vielmehr der Text verloren gegangen, denn da der Gesang im Unisono mit
der Shō ist, so bleibt im Orchester immer
die Melodie. Das neuste Stück, was in der
Gagakku aufgeführt wird, ist 500 Jahre
alt.

 Der Unterricht geschieht nun in
der Weise, daß die Schüler zu Hause die
Noten und den Umriss der Melodie nach
den Katakanazeichen (s. unten und Taf.
21 Fig. 2, 3) auswendig lernen müssen;
erst nachher bekommen sie die Instrumente in die Hand und lernen deren
Handhabung für die einzelnen Stücke,
die immer auswendig gespielt werden.
Man wird schon aus dieser Lehrmethode
leicht begreifen, daß es sich nur um ein
mechanisches Abrichten handelt und
daß selbst in der Gagakku die wenigsten
Musiker im Stande sind, über ihre Kunst
irgend welchen Aufschluss zu geben.

 Von besonderen Interesse sind die
dort aufbewahrten uralten, kostbaren Instrumente; an das Alter derselben glaube ich, weil dieselben eben, wie ich schon
bei Gelegenheit der alten Stimmflöte sagte, seit uralten Zeiten den Händen besonders dazu bestimmter Pfleger als Reliqui-
en anvertraut waren. Sie sind alle kostbar
lackirt, mit Wappen versehen, in seidenen Hüllen und mehrfachen Kasten eingeschlossen, werden fast nie gebraucht
und auf das Äußerste gepflegt.

 Was nun die Zusammensetzung des
Orchesters betrifft so kann dasselbe in

were probably accompanied by song, but
curiously, for many it is precisely the
song that has been lost, or rather the text,
given that, since the song is in unison
with the shō, the melody thus always
remains in the orchestra. The newest
piece which is performed in gagaku is 500
years old.

 Instruction takes place in the way
that the pupils must learn the notes and
the contour of the melody by heart at
home from the katakana symbols (see below and Plate XXI, Figs. 2, 3 [p. 257]); only
after that do they get the instruments in
hand and learn their manipulation for
the individual pieces, which are always
played from memory. Already from this
teaching method one will easily grasp
that it is just a matter of mechanical
drill, and that even in gagaku the fewest
musicians are in a position to give any
sort of information about their art.

 Of particular interest are the age-
old, valuable instruments preserved
there. I believe in their antiquity because, as I stated already with regard to
the old tuning-flute (p. 145), since time
immemorial they were entrusted to the
hands of specially appointed curators
as relics. They are all sumptuously lacquered, furnished with crests, encased in
silken coverings and multiple boxes, are
almost never used, and cared for to the
utmost.

 Now, concerning the composition of
the orchestra, it can be put together in

verschiedenster Weise zusammengesetzt sein; doch können in demselben nur folgende Stimmen vorkommen:

1.– Die *menschliche Stimme;* es ist dann immer nur ein Sänger, der den Tact mit der *Shaku-bioshi* angiebt oder bei vollerm Orchester mehrere Sänger in Unisono, aber nur eine *Shaku-bioshi,* die andern Schlaginstrumente fallen dann weg. Die Stimme geht immer im Unisono mit der Shô. Höchst unangenehm ist der immer vorherrschende, gequetschte Gurgelton, das unreine Trillern (ich möchte es lieber ein Meckern nennen), kurz es ist eine Qual für uns, diesen Gesang mit anzuhören, den die Japaner doch sehr schön finden.[2] Gesang existirt nur bei ächt japanischen z.B. *Saibara* (Taf. XIX, Fig 6); das Stück wird dann nach den Anfangsworten benannt. Bei chinesischen und koreanischen heiligen Musikstücken existirt kein Gesang. Das Saibara ist in Katakana-Schrift auf der Tafel angegeben und daher leicht zu dechiffriren, Noten sind dabei nicht angegeben.

2.– Die Shō, welche eigentlich die Melodie führt; in chinesischen Stücken werden auf derselben für uns ganz unmögliche Harmonien gegriffen (s. unten), bei den japanischen Stücken wird nur immer ein Ton geblasen.

many different ways; yet in it only the following parts can occur:

1. The *human voice;* there is always only one singer who gives the beat with the *shakubyōshi,* or, with full orchestra, several singers in unison, but only one *shakubyōshi;* the other percussion instruments are then omitted. The voice always goes in unison with the *shō.* Highly unpleasant is the constantly dominating, strangulated gurgling-sound, the out-of-tune trilling (I would prefer to call it a bleating). In short, it is torture for us to listen to this singing which the Japanese, however, find very beautiful.[2] Singing exists only for genuine Japanese [pieces], for example, *saibara* (Plate XIX, Fig. 6 [p. 255]); the piece is then named after the opening words. For sacred Chinese and Korean pieces there is no song. The *saibara* is shown in *katakana*-script on the plate[3] and is therefore easy to decipher; notes are not specified with it.

2. The *shō,* which really carries the melody; in Chinese pieces, harmonies completely impossible for us are fingered on it (see below), for the Japanese pieces, always one note only is blown.

---

[2] Ich hatte erst kürzlich Gelegenheit, mich davon zu überzeugen, wie sehr unsere Musik den Japanern missfällt; es waren in Yedo ein paar sehr tüchtige italienische Coloratursängerinnen, und als ich nach dem Concert einen ganz gebildeten Japaner nach seinem Urtheil frug, meinte er, ein schöner getragener, japanischer Gesang sei doch weit angenehmer.

[2] Only recently I had the opportunity to see for myself how much our music displeases the Japanese; there were, in Edo, a couple of very competent Italian coloratura singers, and, after the concert, when I asked a very cultured Japanese his opinion, he held beautiful, solemn Japanese singing to be much more agreeable after all.

[3] The well-known *Ise no umi.* – Ed.

3.– Die Hidchiriki, die, wie ich schon früher sagte, für unsern Geschmack das im Übrigen schönste Stück durch seinen kreischenden und unreinen Ton verdirbt.

3. The hichiriki, which, as I stated earlier, for our taste spoils the otherwise most beautiful of pieces through its screeching and out-of-tune tone.

4.– Die Ohteki, eine ganz leidlich klingende, aber häufig unrein geblasene Flöte.

4. The ōteki, a quite tolerably sounding flute, frequently played out-of-tune, however.

Diese drei Instrumente sind im Orchester immer in gleicher Zahl vertreten; zu einem vollständigen Orchester gehören fünf und mehr von jedem derselben und wird das Orchester gradezu nach der Zahl der Flöten (was dann die gleiche Zahl von Shō's und Hidchiriki's eo ipso involvirt) benannt z.B. spricht man von einem fünfflötigen Orchester. Zu fünf von jeder Sorte Blase-Instrumenten gehören dann je zwei von jeder Art Saiteninstrumente und je eins von den Schlaginstrumenten.

These three instruments are always represented in the orchestra in the same number; to a full orchestra belong five and more of each of them, and the orchestra is named simply according to the number of flutes (which, by that very fact, then involves the same number of shōs and hichirikis); for example, one speaks of a "five-flute" orchestra. To five of each sort of wind instrument then belong two of each type of stringed instrument and one each of the percussion instruments.

5.– Die Biwa wird nur beim Anfang der Tacte benutzt, und zwar so, daß mit dem Batshi schnell über die Saiten gefahren wird. Häufig werden auch nur einzelne Saiten angeschlagen. Die Biwa ähnelt unserer Guittarre, ist aber aus sehr starken Holz gearbeitet, wodurch sie allerdings sehr schwer aber auch sehr volltönend wird.

5. The biwa is only used at the beginning of measures, and, namely, with the bachi being swiped quickly over the strings. Frequently, single strings alone are struck. The biwa is like our guitar, but is worked out of very heavy wood, whereby it becomes very weighty, but very sonorous.

6.– Die Koto hat sowohl die Bestimmung, mit der Biwa zusammen die Tactanfänge zu markiren dann aber auch, Fiorituren auszuführen. Diese Verzierungen haben ein ganzes Stück hindurch stets denselben Character, ähnliche dem, welchen man in dem Musikstück der Gagakku findet.

6. The koto has the purpose both to mark together with the biwa the beginning of the measure and also to execute fioriture. All the way through a piece these embellishments consistently have the same character, like that found in the musical piece of gagaku [pp. 242–244].

Diese beiden Instrument haben einen äußerst sonoren und angenehmen Klang und würden gewiss ebenso, wie die Shō, auch in Europa viel Anklang finden.

7.– Die Wanggong wird nur ausnahmsweise statt der viel reichern Koto benutzt.

8.– Kakko soll theoretisch in der Stimmung des Grundtons stehen, also in dem mitgetheilten Stücke z.B. in e, practisch wird dies aber nicht durchgeführt. Dieselbe hat 8 verschiedene Schlagarten, doch sind die gewöhnlichsten die drei in dem Stück vorkommenden.

9.– Die Taiko hat keine besondere Stimmung. Sie hat einen sehr vollen Klang und würde in vielen Fällen mit Vortheil unsere große Pauke ersetzen; besonders würde sie sich für Theater der Raumersparnis und der besondern Eleganz, mit der sie ausgestattet ist, wegen sehr gut eignen. Sie hat 10 verschiedene Schlagarten, die sich aber hauptsächlich, auf Piano forte, Doppelschläge, Einsatz nach 2, 4, 8 Tacten und dgl. beziehen. Ich hörte ein Stück, wo die ganze Zeit hindurch Taiko und Kakko eine Art Duett aufführten, während die andern Instrumente spielten, und zwar stand die Kakko in der höheren Quint gegen die Taiko, der Rhytmus war:

Both these instruments have a most sonorous and agreeable sound and, just as the shō, would certainly appeal in Europe, too.

7. The wagon is used only in exceptional circumstances instead of the much richer koto.

8. The kakko should theoretically stand in tune with the ground-note; so, in the piece made known here, for example, in e. Practically, however, this is never realized. It has 8 different ways of striking, yet the most common are the three occurring in the piece.

9. The taiko has no particular tuning. It has a very full sound and in many cases would replace our large kettledrum to advantage; it would be especially suited for theater because of its saving in space and the particular elegance with which it is endowed. It has 10 different ways of striking, which relate mainly, however, to piano/forte double-strokes, entry after 2, 4, 8 measures, and the like. I heard a piece in which for the whole time throughout, taiko and kakko performed a sort of duet, while the other instruments played, and, in fact, the kakko stood at the upper fifth to the taiko. The rhythm was:

Keine japanische oder chinesische Trommel oder Pauke hat Schnüre, die über das Fell laufen.

No Japanese or Chinese drum or kettledrum has cords that pass over the skin.

10.– Die Shōko hat keine besondere Stimmung; sie klingt sehr schwach, und um ihren Rhythmus zu erforschen, musste ich mich, da ich nicht dicht dabei saß, auf das Auge, nicht auf das Ohr verlassen.

Bei allen diesen drei Instrumenten heißt der linke Klöppel Mebatshi, der weibliche, und wird, mit Ausnahme der Wirbel auf der Kakko, immer piano oder als Vorschlag gebraucht, der rechte heißt Obatschi, der männliche[4] und wird zu einzelnen festen, kräftigen Schlägen benutzt.

11.– Die Yōko (Taf. VI Fig. 17) wird bei einigen koreanischen Stücken benutzt, auch bei feierlichen Aufzügen.

12.– Die Shaku bioshi (auf Taf. XII, Fig. y berichtigt dargestellt) tritt besonders bei Stücken mit Gesangbegleitung statt der oben angeführten drei Schlaginstrumente ein.

Wie schon oben bemerkt, gilt alles eben gesagte nur für die Gagakku, die meist nur chinesische und koreanische Stücke aufführt. Rein alt japanische, wie sie z.B. bei den No-Tänzen vorkommen, erfordern nur Kangura fuye, Wanggong und Shaku bioshi, werden dann aber mit Gesang begleitet. Nur einmal hatte ich Gelegenheit, diese Art der Musik genauer zu studieren. Mann und Frau sangen den langsamen eintönigen Gesang im Unisono und schlug der Mann jedesmal beim ersten Tacttheil die beiden

10. The shōko has no particular tuning; it sounds very faint, and in order to investigate its rhythm, since I wasn't sitting close beside it, I had to rely on the eye, not on the ear.

For all these three instruments, the left beater is called mebachi (the female), and, with the exception of the roll on the kakko, is always used piano or as an upbeat; the right is called obachi (the male)[4] and is used for single firm strong strokes.

11. The yōko (Plate VI, Fig. 17 [p. 122]) is used for some Korean pieces, also for ceremonial processions.

12. The shakubyōshi (on Plate XII, Fig. y [p. 247], shown corrected) comes in specially for pieces with song-accompaniment, instead of the three percussion instruments mentioned above.

As noted above already, all that has just been said applies solely for gagaku, which mostly performs only Chinese and Korean pieces. Pure old-Japanese [pieces], as they occur, for example for the nō-dances, require only kagurabue, wagon, and shakubyōshi, but are then accompanied by song. Only once did I have the opportunity to study this sort of music more closely. A man and a woman sang the slow, monotonous song in unison, and each time with the first beat of the measure, the man hit the two

---

[4]   Die Silben O und Me einem Worte vor oder nachgesetzt bedeuten immer männlich und weiblich, Batshi heißt der Schläger sowohl bei Saiten- als bei Schlaginstrumenten.

[4]   The syllables o and me set before or after a word always mean masculine and feminine; bachi is the name for the beater both for stringed and percussion instruments.

Theile der Shaku-bioshi zusammen; am Schluss des Tactes wurde der Ton immer mit einem Sforzando kurz abgestoßen, die Kangura fuye begleitete sehr unrein und meist im Unisono. Die Wanggong fehlte zwar, doch würde sie so benutzt worden sein, daß der Spieler beim ersten Tacttheil über sämmtliche Saiten mit dem Kotosangi strich und sofort fünf Saiten mit den fünf Fingern der linken Hand dämpfte und nur den sechsten, mit der Stimme übereinstimmenden Ton nachklingen ließ.

Doch kehren wir zur Gagakku zurück: Die genannten Instrumente können in den verschiedensten Weisen combinirt werden. So besitze ich z. B. eine Sammlung Melodieen für Sho und Taiko allein. Bei den Stücken, die ich außerdem in diesem Heft mitgetheilten Go Dshioh Raku betreffs der Zusammensetzung des Orchesters näher zu studieren Gelegenheit hatte, waren die Stimmen in folgender Weise besetzt:

1tes Stück: 2 *Sänger*, von denen der Hauptsänger die Shaku Bioshi schlug. Dann im Unisono damit 1 Hidchiriki, 1 Ohteki; gleichzeitig mit der Shaku bioshi setzten jedesmal 2 Biwa ein; 2 Kōto markirten den Tact und machten Fiorituren.

2tes Stück: *Shō, Ohteki* und *Hichiriki* je 3, Biwa, Koto, Taiko, Kakko Shōko je 1.

3tes Stück: Die *Blaseinstrumente* alle sechsfach, die *Saiteninstrumente* dreifach, die *Schlaginstrumente* einfach besetzt, im Ganzen also

parts of the *shakubyōshi* together; at the end of the measure, the note was always abruptly broken off *sforzando*; the *kagurabue* accompanied, very out-of-tune and mostly in unison. The *wagon* was missing, in fact, but it would have been used in such a way that, on the first beat, the player swept over all strings with the *kotosagi* and immediately dampened five strings with the five fingers of the left hand, letting only the sixth, with the note agreeing with the voice, linger on.

But let us now turn back to *gagaku*. The aforementioned instruments can be combined in all sorts of ways. So, for instance, I own a collection of melodies for *shō* and *taiko* on their own. For pieces other than *Goshōraku* given in this issue, which in respect of [ensemble-]constitution I had the opportunity to study more closely, the parts were filled in the following ways:

1st piece: 2 *singers*, of whom the main singer beat the *shakubyōshi*.Then in unison with them 1 *hichiriki*, 1 ōteki; simultaneously each time with the *shakubyōshi*, 2 *biwa* came in; 2 *koto* marked the measure and made *fioriture*.

2nd piece: *shō, ōteki*, and *hichiriki*, 3 of each; *biwa, koto, taiko, kakko, shōko*, 1 of each.

3rd piece: the *wind instruments* all filled sixfold, the *stringed instruments* threefold, the *percussion instruments* singly; so 27 musicians in

27 Musiker. Das Stück endet mit einem Solo der Hauptkünstler, u.z.w. 1 Hidchiriki, 1 Biwa und 3 Koto.

all. The piece ended with a solo by the three main artists, namely, 1 hichiriki, 1 biwa, and 3 koto.

Bei all diesen Stücken, die sämtlich auf der Quint mit nachgeschlagenem Grundton endeten, waren die Instrumente gleicher Art vollständig im Unisono; früher sollen sie zuweilen verschiedene Parthieen gespielt haben; jetzt aber nie.

In all these pieces, every one of which ended on the fifth with a delayed groundnote, the instruments of the same type were completely in unison; formerly, they are held to have sometimes played different parts; but now never.

Die Aufstellung der Instrumente ist nicht an bestimmte Regeln gebunden; bei öffentlichen Aufführungen eines kleinern Orchesters habe ich zwar die gleichartigen Instrumente zusammen sitzen sehen; bei der großen Aufführung im Gagakku aber saß das Orchester in Form eines Hufeisens, dessen offenen Seite wir Zuhörer einnahmen; die Spieler gleichartiger Instrumente saßen so, daß sie sich ansehen konnten und achteten genau auf einander.

The deployment of the instruments is not bound to fixed rules: for official performances of a small orchestra I have actually seen the instruments of the same type sitting together; for the large performances in Gagaku, however, the orchestra sat in the form of a horseshoe whose open side took in us listeners; the players of the same type of instrument sat so that they could see each other and paid precise heed to one another.

Ein Kapellmeister oder Dirigent ist nicht vorhanden; höchstens könnte bei den Stücken, wo eine Shaku Bioshi mitwirkt, der Spieler derselben als Angeber des Tacts angesehen werden; sonst folgen sämmtliche Spieler einfach dem Hauptinstrument, wobei sie genau wissen, auf welche Note sie einzusetzen haben; das Zusammenspiel der gleichartigen Instrumente ist ungemein exact.

A bandmaster or conductor is nonexistent; at most, for pieces where a shakubyōshi participates, the player of this could be seen as the one who gives the beat; otherwise all players simply follow the main instrument, whereby they know exactly on which note they are to enter; the interplay between same-type instruments is extraordinarily exact.

Alle Musiker spielen immer auswendig; eine Partitur existirt nicht, sondern nur die Stimmen der einzelnen Instrumente. Wie ich aber schon früher sagte ist es durchaus nicht nothwen-

All musicians always play from memory; a score does not exist, but only the parts for the individual instruments. As I said earlier, however, it is quite unnecessary that the performers them-

dig, daß die Ausführenden selbst die richtigen Noten kennen, sondern sie lernen nach dem Gehör und einfachen phonetischen Zeichen mechanisch erst ihre Parthie auswendig und dann erst lernen sie dieselbe spielen.

Sehen wir nun die Zeichen für die einzelnen Töne auf den verschiedenen Instrumenten näher an und zwar:

1.– Die Shō (Tafel XVIII Fig. 1.) Es sind hier auf dem Schema die Zeichen in die betreffenden Kreise eingeschrieben. Folgen wir nun der Nummerirung, wie sie auf Taf. X, Fig. 39, für die einzelnen Pfeifen angegeben ist, so stellen sich die Verhältnisse folgendermaßen:

selves know the proper notations. Rather, they first learn their part mechanically by ear and simple phonetic symbols, and only then do they learn to play it.

Let us now inspect more closely the symbols for the individual notes on the different instruments, namely:

1. The shō (Plate XVIII, Fig. 1 [p. 253]). On the diagram here, the symbols are written into the appropriate circle. If we now follow the numbering for the individual pipes, as it is given on Plate X, Fig. 39 (p. 173), the relationships present themselves in the following way:[5]

N. 1	heißt	Sen,	gehört zu	April	ist unser	fis'''
" 2	"	Jiu,	"	Mai,	"	g''
" 3	"	Gē	"	April	"	fis''
" 4	"	Otzu	"	Februar	"	e''
" 5	"	Ku	"	November	"	cis''
" 6	"	Bi	"	Juni	"	gis''
" 7	"	Ichi	"	September	"	h'
" 8	"	Hachi	"	Februar	"	e'''
" 9	"	Ya (blind)				
" 10	"	Gong	"	November	"	cis'''
" 11	"	Shihi	"	September	"	h''
" 12	"	Giyoh	"	Juli	"	a''
" 13	"	Djioh	"	December	"	d'''
" 14	"	Bō	"	December	"	d''
" 15	"	Kotou	"	Juli	"	a'
" 16	"	Mo				
" 17	"	Hi	"	October	"	c''

- -

[5] Here pitch-to-pipe relationships are in order, since the mute pipes are correctly identified as pipes 9 and 16. The reader needs to be aware that for Plate X, however, Müller had not yet corrected the placing of mute pipes; there pitch-to-pipe relationships are out of order from pipe 7 through to pipe 16. – Ed.

N. 1	is called	*sen*, belongs to	April	is our	♯′′′
" 2	"	jū,	"	May,	"	g′′
" 3	"	ge	"	April	"	♯′′
" 4	"	otsu	"	February	"	e′′
" 5	"	ku	"	November	"	♯′′
" 6	"	bi	"	June	"	g♯′′
" 7	"	ichi	"	September	"	b′
" 8	"	hachi	"	February	"	e′′′
" 9	"	ya [mute]	"			
" 10	"	gon	"	November	"	♯′′′
" 11	"	shichi	"	September	"	b′′
" 12	"	gyō	"	July	"	a′′
" 13	"	jō	"	December	"	d′′′
" 14	"	bō	"	December	"	d′′
" 15	"	kotsu	"	July	"	a′
" 16	"	mō [mute]	"			
" 17	"	hi	"	October	"	c′′ [c′′′]

Die Töne sind hier nach Vergleichung mit der neuen Pariser Stimmgabel rectificirt.

Bei japanischen Stücken wird nun einfach der angegebene Ton geblasen, bei chinesischen wird dagegen der volle Accord von 5 oder 6 Tönen geblasen und zwar nach folgendem Schema, Taf. XVIII. Fig 2.

The pitches are rectified here following comparison with the new Parisian tuning-fork.

For Japanese pieces, simply the note indicated is blown, for Chinese, in contrast, the full chord of 5 or 6 notes is blown and, namely, according to the following diagram, Plate XVIII, Fig. 2 (p. 253).

Zu	a′	als *Hauptton* gehören	a′′, h′′, e′′′, h′, fis′′′
"	cis′′	"	a′′, h′′, gis′′, d′′, e′′
"	e′′	"	a′′, h′′, d′′′, e′′′, fis′′′
"	g′′	"	a′′, h′′, d′′, fis′′
"	a′′	"	h′′, d′′′, e′′′, fis′′′
"	h′	"	a′′, h′′, d′′, e′′, fis′′′
"	d′′	"	a′′, h′′, e′′′, e′′, fis′′′
"	fis′′	"	a′′, h′′, gis′′, d′′′, fis′′′
"	gis′′	"	a′′, h′′, d′′′, c′′, fis′′′
"	c′′	"	a′′, h′′, d′′′, e′′′, fis′′′

To	a'	as ground-note belong	a'', b'', e''', b' [e''], $f\sharp'''$
"	$c\sharp''$	"	a'', b'', $g\sharp'''$, d'', e''
"	e''	"	a'', b'', d''', e''', $f\sharp'''$
"	g''	"	a'', b'', d'' [d'''], $f\sharp'''$, [e''']
"	a''	"	b'', d''', e''', $f\sharp'''$
"	b'	"	a'', b'', d'', e'', $f\sharp'''$
"	d''	"	a'', b'', e''', e'', $f\sharp'''$
"	$f\sharp''$	"	a'', b'', $g\sharp'''$, d''', $f\sharp'''$
"	$g\sharp''$	"	a'', b'', d''', c''', $f\sharp'''$
"	c'' [c''']	"	a'', b'', d''', e''', $f\sharp'''$

Nach welchem Gesetze diese sogenannten Accorde bestimmt werden, habe ich noch nicht ergründen können, wahrscheinlich wird man es durch Rechnung finden können. Ich glaubte Anfangs, von diesen Nebentönen würde nur einer oder zwei zu dem Hauptton genommen; der Spieler versicherte und zeigte mir dagegen, daß er alle 6 gleichzeitig anblies; ich konnte aber ebenso wenig, als zwei musikverständige Herrn, die mich begleiteten, die disharmonirenden Töne hören, so daß ich annehmen muss, sie werden durch die harmonischen Töne erdrückt, was im Orchester um so leichter geschehen kann, als der Hauptton noch durch die andern Instrumente unterstützt wird. Das Zeichen Shî-kū (Taf. XVIII Fig 1. a) bedeutet ein Langziehen der Note durch den folgenden Tact; bei Verbindung zweier Noten durch einen rothen Strich dient die erste als Vorschlag.

2.– Die Hidchiriki (Taf. XVIII Fig. 4). Hier wird einfach das Zeichen des Loches, welches offen bleiben soll, angegeben.

I have not yet been able to fathom out according to which rules these so-called chords are determined; one could probably find them through calculation. At first I believed that of these accessory notes only one or two were taken with the principal note; the player assured me and showed me that, to the contrary, he blows all 6 at once. However, I could just as barely hear the disharmonizing notes as the two musically knowledgeable gentlemen who accompanied me, so I must assume they are suppressed by the harmonious pitches, which could all the easier happen in the the orchestra, since the principal note is further supported by the other instruments. The symbol hiku (Plate XVIII, Fig. 1 a [p. 253]) signifies a prolongation of the note through the following bar; when two notes are linked by a red stroke, the first serves as a grace note.

2. The hichiriki (Plate XVIII, Fig. 4 [p. 253]). Indicated simply here is the symbol for the hole which should remain open. Be-

Unterhalb stehen die chinesischen Namen. Um die Zeichen richtig zu lesen, muss man die Abbildung so vor sich legen, daß das Mundstück nach rechts liegt, die 7 Grifflöcher nach oben, das eine nach unten. Man zählt dann von rechts nach links.

1tes Loch heißt	Gēh	gehört zu	Juli	= a''
Unteres " "	Djōh	"	Juni	= g''
2tes " "	Itchi	"	April	= fis''
3tes " "	Shi	"	Februar	= e''
4tes " "	Roku	"	December	= d''
5tes " "	Bō	"	October	= c''
6tes " "	Ku	"	September	= h'
7tes // "	Gō	"	Juli (erniedrigt)	= as'
Schlussöffnung	Setzu	"	Juni	= g'

- -

1st hole is called	ge	belongs to	July	= a''
beneath "	jō	"	June	= g''
2nd "	ichi	"	April	= ♯''
3rd "	shi	"	February	= e''
4th "	roku	"	December	= d''
5th "	bō	"	October	= c''
6th "	ku	"	September	= b'
7th "	go	"	July (lowered)	= ab'
open end "	zetsu	"	June	= g'

Wo die Noten kurz über einander sind, bedeutet dies einen kurzen Vorschlag. Noch ein Zeichen für die Hidchiriki ist Taf. XX Fig. 2.a, Udzu bedeutet kurz aufschlagen mit dem Finger.

3.– Die Ohteki (Taf. XVIII fig. 3.) hat eine ganz ähnliche Notirung, wie die vorige; auch hier werden nur die Zeichen der Grifflöcher, welche offen bleiben sollen, angegeben.

Where two notes occur closely one above the other, this means a short grace note. A further symbol for hichiriki is Plate XX, Fig. 2 a (p. 256), utsu, and indicates short flicking with the finger.

3. The ōteki (Plate XVIII, Fig. 3 [p. 253]) has a notation quite similar to the former; here, too, are indicated only the symbols for the holes which should remain open.

1tes Loch heißt	Roku	gehört zu	December	= d$''$
2tes " "	Tschiuh	"	September	= h$'$
3tes " "	Saku	"	Juli	= a$'$
4tes " "	Djōh	"	Juni	= g$'$
5tes " "	Gō	"	April	= fis$'$
6tes " "	Kang	"	Februar	= e$'$
7tes " "	Shi	"	Januar	= dis$'$

- - - - - - - - - - - - - - - - - -

1st hole is called	roku	belongs to	December	= d$''$
2nd "	chū	"	September	= b$'$
3rd "	shaku	"	July	= a$'$
4th "	jō	"	June	= g$'$
5th "	go	"	April	= f♯$'$
6th "	kan	"	February	= e$'$
7th "	ji	"	January	= d♯$'$

Zwischen dem 1ten und 2ten Loche befindet sich noch ein Zeichen, welches Gēh heißt, dem October (c$''$) entspricht und so erzeugt wird, daß man das erste und dritte Loch öffnet, das zweite aber schließt.

Wie schon früher gesagt, entspricht jedes Loch je nach dem Anblasen drei Octaven, und ist es entweder dem Geschmack des Spielers überlassen, in welcher Octav er blasen will, oder es ist bestimmt vorgeschrieben, wie bei der ersten Wiederholung in dem mitgettheilten Stück.

Noch andere Zeichen für die Ohteki sind:

1, Udzu (Taf. XVIII, Fig. 3 a) bedeutet, daß der Finger kurz aufgeschlagen werden soll;

2, Shiku (Ziehen, Taf. XVIII, Fig. 1 a) giebt an, daß der Ton lang angehalten werden soll.

Between the 1st and the 2nd hole is to be found a further symbol which is called ge, corresponds to October (c$''$), and is produced when one opens the first and third holes, but closes the second.

As already stated earlier, each hole, depending on (over-)blowing, accommodates three octaves, and either it is left to the taste of the player in which octave he wants to play, or it is prescribed, as for the first repeat in the piece given.

Further signs for the ōteki are:

(a) Utsu (Plate XVIII, Fig 3 a [p. 253]), means that the finger should be briefly flicked.

(b) Hiku (stretch, Plate XVIII, Fig. 1 a [p. 253]), indicates that the note should be held long.

3, Kůa (Feuer, Taf. XVIII, Fig. 3 b) bedeutet einen raschen Übergang zur folgenden Note, eine Art Vorschlag.

4, Für die Kakko (Taf. XIX, Fig. 2) werden die bei der Notirung üblichen rothen Punkte in die Mitte geschrieben. Die sieben obern Zeichen bedeuten Wirbel (Raï) und zwar werden die Zeichen rechts (vom Leser aus) von den Punkten mit der rechten Hand, die links von den Punkten mit der linken Hand geschlagen.

Bei den drei ersten Punkten schlagen also beide Hände einen Wirbel, nach dem dritten Punkt und ebenso nach dem 5ten und 7ten wirbelt die linke Hand allein, d.h. sie fängt langsam an und fährt accelerando fort.

Rechts von dem 4ten Punkt steht dann das Zeichen für einen kurzen Schlag (Seï). Je nach der Stärke und Schnelligkeit der Schläge und Wirbel giebt es 8 verschiedene Schlagarten, die aber nicht besonders bezeichnet werden, sondern von dem Character des Stücks, der Tradition und dem Geschmack des Spielers abhängen.

5, Die Schläge der Taiko (Taf. XIX, Fig. 3) werden durch dicke rothe Punkte angegeben und zwar giebt es deren zwei Arten:

1^{tens} – Rothe Doppelpunkte, die durch einen Strich verbunden sind, und von denen der linke etwas kleiner ist und höher steht. Der linke Punkt bedeutet den linken, weiblichen Klöppel, mit dem einen halben Tact vorher ein leiser Schlag gegeben wird; der rechte, dickere Punkt bedeutet den rechten, männlichen Klöp-

(c) Ka (fire, Plate XVIII, Fig. 3 b [p. 253]), means a quick change-over to the next note, a sort of grace note.

4. For the kakko (Plate XIX, Fig. 2 [p. 255]), the red dots usual for notating are written in the center. The seven upper symbols mean roll (rai) and, indeed, the signs to the right of the dots (from the reader's viewpoint) are beaten with the right hand, those to the left of the dots with the left hand.

For the first three dots, therefore, both hands beat a roll; after the third dot, and likewise after the 5th and 7th, the left hand rolls alone, that is, it begins slowly and carries on accelerando.

Right of the 4th dot then stands the symbol for a short stroke (sei). According to the strength and speed of the strokes and rolls there are 8 different types of striking, which are not specially named but depend on the character of the piece, the tradition, and the taste of the player.

5. The strokes of the taiko (Plate XIX, Fig. 3 [p. 255]) are indicated by thick red dots and are, namely, two types:

1st, red double-dots that are linked by a stroke, and of which the left is somewhat smaller and stands higher. The left dot signifies the left, female beater, with which a soft stroke is given a half-measure ahead; the right, thicker dot signifies the right, male beater with which a strong stroke is given on the

pel, mit dem beim ersten Tacttheil ein starker Schlag gegeben wird.

2^{tens} – Ein einzelner Punkt bedeutet den männlichen, starken Schlag allein, ohne den weiblichen Vorschlag.

6, Die *Shaku Bioshi* wird grade so, wie die *Taiko* durch dicke Punkte notiert, aber schwarz statt roth.

7, Das Zeichen für die *Shōko* heißt *Kin* (Taf. XIX, Fig. 4) und wird grade, wie bei der Kakko rechts und links von den Punkten geschrieben, je nachdem der starke *Obatshi* oder der schwache *Mebatshi* gebraucht werden soll. Wirbel u. dgl. existiren hier nicht. Wo auf beiden Seiten des Punktes ein Zeichen steht, hat der *Mebatshi* einen ganz kurzen, leisen Vorschlag zu machen.

8, Die *Biwa* hat je nach der Stimmung verschiedene Zeichen (Taf. XVIII, Fig. 5 und Taf. XVIIIa, Fig. 6–9). Die Namen und Töne sind:[*]

---

first beat [of the measure].

2nd, a single dot signifies the male strong stroke alone, without the female upbeat.

6. The *shakubyōshi*, just like the *taiko*, is notated with thick dots, but black instead of red.

7. The symbol for the *shōko* is called *kin* (Plate XIX, Fig. 4 [p. 255]) and is written, just as for the *kakko*, right and left of the dots according to whether the strong *obachi* or the weak *mebachi* should be used. Rolls and the like do not exist here. Where a symbol stands on both sides of the dot, the *mebachi* is to make a very short, quiet upbeat.

8. The *biwa* has different symbols depending on the tuning (Plate XVIII, Fig. 5 [p. 253] and Plate XVIIIa, Figs. 6–9 [p. 254]). The names and notes are:

Hiōdjo.[*]
Februar=Stimmung, e Grundton; Taf. XVIIIa Fig. 5.

Saite:	1	2	3	4
VOLLE LÄNGE	Itchi Februar e	Ôtsu September h	Pïô Februar e'	Dju Juli a'
1ter STEG	Ku April ges–fis	Geh November des'–cis'	Shitzi April ges'–fis'	Hachi September h'
2ter STEG	Bo Mai g	Djü December d'	Hi Mai g'	Boku October • c''
3ter STEG	Su Juni • as–gis	Bi Januar • dis'–es'	Gong Juni • as'–gis'	Sen November • des''–cis''
4ter STEG	To Juli a	Kō Februar e'	Shi Juli a'	Ja December d''

Hyōjō*
February=tuning, e ground-note; Plate XVIII, Fig. 5.[6]

Saite:	1	2	3	4
Full Length	ichi February e	otsu September b	gyō February e'	jō July a'
1st Fret	ku April $gb\text{-}f\sharp$	ge November $db'\text{-}c\sharp'$	shichi April $gb'\text{-}f\sharp'$	hachi September b'
2nd Fret	bō May g	jū December d'	hi May g'	boku October • c''
3rd Fret	shū June • $ab\text{-}g\sharp$	bi January • $d\sharp'\text{-}eb'$	gon June • $ab'\text{-}g\sharp'$	sen November • $db''\text{-}c\sharp''$
4th Fret	to July a	kō February e'	shi July a'	ya December d''

Itchikotsu.
December=Stimmung, d Grundton; Taf. XVIIIa Fig. 6.

Saite:	1	2	3	4
VOLLE LÄNGE	Juli a	December d	Februar e	Juli a
1ter STEG	September h	Februar e	April $ges\text{-}fis$	September h
2ter STEG	October • c	März • f	Mai • g	October • c
3ter STEG	November • $des\text{-}cis$	April $ges\text{-}fis$	Juni • $as\text{-}gis$	November • $des\text{-}cis$
4ter STEG	December • d	Mai • g	Juli a	December d

* Diejenigen Töne, welche mit Punkten versehen sind, werden zum Spielen nicht benutzt.

* Those notes which are marked with dots are not used for playing.
  Müller's biwa-tunings are pitched an octave too high. – Ed.

Ichikotsu
December=tuning, d ground-note; Plate XVIIIa, Fig. 6.[7]

Saite:	1	2	3	4
Full Length	July a	December d	February e	July a
1st Fret	September b	February e	April g♭–f♯	September b
2nd Fret	October • c	March • f	May • g	October • c
3rd Fret	November • d♭–c♯	April g♭–f♯	June • a♭–g♯	November • d♭–c♯
4th Fret	December • d	May • g	July a	December d

Sodjo.
Mai=Stimmung, g od. as Grundton; Taf. XVIIIa Fig. 7.

Saite:	1	2	3	4
VOLLE LÄNGE	Mai g	Juli a	December d′	Mai g′
1ter STEG	Juli a	September h	Februar e′	Juli a′
2ter STEG	August • b	October c′	März • f′	August • b′
3ter STEG	September h	November • des′–cis′	April ges′–fis′	September h′
4ter STEG	October c′	December d′	Mai g′	October c″

Sōjō
May=tuning, g or a♭ ground-note; Plate XVIIIa, Fig. 7.[8]

Saite:	1	2	3	4
Full Length	May g	July a	December d′	May g′
1st Fret	July a	September b	February e′	July a′
2nd Fret	August • b♭	October c′	March • f′	August • b♭′
3rd Fret	September b	November • d♭′–c♯′	April g♭′–f♯′	September b′
4th Fret	October c′	December d′	May g′	October c″

[7] P. 254
[8] P. 254

Oshiki.
Juli=Stimmung, a Grundton; Taf. XVIIIa Fig. 8.

Saite:	1	2	3	4
VOLLE LÄNGE	Juli a	October c'	Februar e'	Juli a'
1ter STEG	September h	December d'	April $ges'-fis'$	September h'
2ter STEG	October c'	Januar • $dis'-es'$	Mai g'	October c''
3ter STEG	November • $des'-cis'$	Februar e'	Juni • $gis'-as'$	November • $des''-cis''$
4ter STEG	December d'	März • f'	Juli a'	December d''

Ōshiki.
July=tuning, a ground-note; Plate XVIIIa, Fig. 8.[9]

Saite:	1	2	3	4
FULL LENGTH	July a	October c'	February e'	July a'
1st FRET	September b	December d'	April $gb'-f\sharp'$	September b'
2nd FRET	October c'	Januar • $d\sharp'-eb'$	May g'	October c''
3rd FRET	November • $db'-c\sharp'$	February e'	June • $g\sharp'-ab'$	November • $db''-c\sharp''$
4th FRET	December d'	March • f'	July a'	December d''

Banshiū.
September=Stimmung, h Grundton; Taf. XVIIIa Fig. 9.

Saite:	1	2	3	4
VOLLE LÄNGE	April $ges-fis$	September h	Februar e'	Juli a'
1ter STEG	Juni $gis-as$	November $des'-cis'$	April $ges'-fis'$	September h'
2ter STEG	Juli a	December d'	Mai • g'	October • c''
3ter STEG	August • b	Januar • $dis'-es'$	Juni $gis'-as'$	November $des''-cis''$
4ter STEG	September h	Februar e'	Juli a'	December d''

Banshiki
September=tuning, b ground-note; Plate XVIIIa, Fig. 9.[10]

Saite:	1	2	3	4
Full Length	April $gb–f\sharp$	September b	February e'	July a'
1st FRET	June $g\sharp–ab$	November $db'–c\sharp'$	April $gb'–f\sharp'$	September b'
2nd FRET	July a	December d'	May • g'	October • c''
3rd FRET	August • bb	January • $d\sharp'–eb'$	June $g\sharp'–ab'$	November $db''–c\sharp''$
4th FRET	September b	February e'	July a'	December d''

* Diejenigen Töne, welche mit Punkten versehen sind, werden zum Spielen nicht benutzt.

* Those notes which are marked with dots are not used for playing.

Beim Spielen wird auf den

1ten Steg der Zeigefinger
2ten ” ” Mittelfinger
3ten ” ” Ringfinger
4ten ” ” kleine Finger

When playing, on the

1st fret the index finger
2nd ” ” middle finger
3rd ” ” ring finger
4th ” ” little finger

der linken Hand aufgelegt. Nur auf dem 2ten Steg wird für die erste Saite der Daumen benutzt. Wenn nun eine Biwa-Note geschrieben steht, so heißt das, daß man von der bezeichneten Note aus, abwärts mit dem Batshi über die Saiten mehr oder weniger schnell streichen soll. Die höhern Saiten bleiben in ihrer vollen Länge. Sind zwei Noten in gleicher Grösse angegeben und durch einen rothen Haken (Taf. XVIII Fig. 5 f.) verbunden, so heißt das, daß diese beiden Noten gegriffen werden, die andern Saiten in voller Länge bleiben. Sind dagegen die Noten kleiner z.B. Fig. bei g' fis' g' so soll mit dem Batshi über g' und c'' gefahren, dann statt g' einen kurzen Augenblick fis' gegriffen und sofort wieder auf g' zurückgekehrt, ohne daß die Saite von

of the left hand is positioned. Only on the 2nd fret, for the first string, is the thumb used. Now, when one [single] biwa-note is written, this means that from the designated note out, one should sweep, more or less quickly, downwards over the strings with the bachi. The higher strings remain in their full length. If two same-sized notes are denoted and linked by a red hook (Plate XVIII, Fig. 5 f [p. 253]), then this means that these two notes are fingered, the other strings remain in full length. If, however, the notes are smaller, as for example with g', $f\sharp'$, g' (Plate XXI, Fig. 1 [p. 257]), g' and c'' should be swept over with the bachi, then instead of g', for a short moment $f\sharp'$ [should be] fingered

10 P. 254

neuem angeschlagen würde. Ein kleiner, rother Haken Fig. 5, g bedeutet, daß über die Saiten von unten nach oben, statt, wie gewöhnlich von oben nach unten gefahren werden soll. Die Accorde werden also auf der Biwa stets im Harpeggio gespielt.

9, Bei der *Koto* (Taf XIX Fig. 1) ist ganz einfach jede Saite numerirt, blos die drei letzten haben andere Zeichen, als die gewöhnlichen Ziffern. In welcher Stimmung nun auch die Koto stehen mag, bleibt die Bezeichnung der anzuschlagenden Saite dieselbe, so daß sich bestimmte Zeichen für bestimmte Noten nicht angeben lassen.

10, Bei der *Wanggong* ist die Notirung grade so, wie bei der Koto, nur grade in entgegengesetzter Richtung, so daß bei der Koto N.1 am entferntesten, bei der Wanggong am nächsten beim Spieler liegt.

11, Die *Kangura fuye* hat besondere Namen für jedes Loch, die dann als Noten gebraucht werden.

Außer den bloßen Noten sind nun folgende andern Angaben für ein Musikstück erforderlich:

1.– Das *Tempo*; man unterscheidet:

a, *Haya*, schnelles Tempo, was meist bei kürzeren Stücken angewandt wird.

b, *Nobe*, langsameres Tempo, das mehr bei feierlichen, längern Stücken angewendet wird.

Ich habe es versuchen wollen, das Tempo metronomisch festzustellen; das ist aber ganz unmöglich. Als ich mir *Haya* vorzählen ließ, bekam ich 92 Viertel auf

and immediately turned back again to g', without the string being plucked anew. A small red hook (Plate XVIII, Fig. 5 g [p. 253]) means that one is to go over the strings from bottom to top instead of, as usually, from top to bottom. The chords are thus always played *arpeggio* on the biwa.

9. For the *koto* (Plate XIX, Fig. 1 [p. 255]), each string is just simply numbered, only the last three have symbols other than the usual numbers. In whichever tuning the *koto* may stand, the indication of the string to be plucked is the same, so that specific symbols for specific notes cannot be given.

10. For the *wagon*, the notation is just as for the *koto* only exactly the other way round, so that for the *koto* No. 1 lies furthest from the player, for the *wagon*, closest.

11. The *kagurabue* has special names for each hole, which are then used as notation.

Aside from the bare notes, the following further specifications are necessary for a musical piece:

1. The *tempo*; one distinguishes:

a, *haya*, fast tempo, which is mostly applied in shorter pieces.

b, *nobe*, slow tempo, which is applied more for solemn, longer pieces.

I wanted to try to ascertain the tempo with the metronome; but that is completely impossible. When I had *haya* counted out for me, I got 92 crotchets per

die Minute; als ich die einzelnen Instrumente dann spielen ließ, wechselte das Tempo zwischen 60 und 80, und als später die Instrumente alle zusammen spielten, fand ich immer für dasselbe Stück nur 40–60 in der Minute. Ein bestimmtes Tempo wird also nicht inne gehalten, sondern, da das lange Anhalten der Töne auf den Blaseinstrumenten für besonders schön gilt, so hängt das Tempo haupsächlich von der größern oder geringern Langathmigkeit der Bläser ab; damit hängt auch zusammen, daß dasselbe Stück im Anfange langsamer, später schneller gespielt wird. Eine zweite Eigenthümlichkeit steht ebenfalls hiermit im Zusammenhang, daß nämlich für Kinder und alte Leute Noten und Tempo der Blasinstrumente kleine Veränderungen erleiden.

2.– Der Tact wird in doppelter Weise angegeben; die kleinen rothen Punkte bezeichnen jedesmal einen Tact-Anfang, und wird jeder Tact in vier gleiche Theile getheilt, die aber nicht weiter notirt, wohl aber beim Einstudieren, Vorsingen u. dgl. mit der Hand markirt werden und zwar so, daß der Sänger beim Tact-Anfang beide Hände vertical in einander schlägt, bei den drei andern Vierteln sie nur rhythmisch einander nähert. Bei profaner Musik habe ich wohl zuweilen 2/4 oder 2/8 Tact gehört; bei der Gagakku ist dagegen nur 4/4 Tact im Gebrauch.

Neben den rothen Punkten stehen zwischen den Noten noch kleine, schwarze Kreise (Taf. XIX, Fig. 5) welche in regelmäßigen Intervallen z.B. nach 2 oder

minute; when I then had the individual instruments play, the tempo fluctuated between 60 and 80; and when, later, the instruments played all together, I found for the same piece always only 40–60 per minute. So, an exact tempo is not held; rather, since the long holding-out of the notes on the wind-instruments is considered as especially beautiful, the tempo depends mainly on the greater or lesser long-windedness of the wind-players; also connected to this is that the same piece is played slower at the beginning, quicker later. A second peculiarity stands likewise in connection herewith, namely, that for children and old people notation and tempo of the wind instruments incur small alterations.

2. The *meter* is indicated in double fashion; the small red dots each time mark a beginning of a measure, and each measure is split into four equal parts which are not further notated, but of course, when studying, singing out loud and the like, are marked with the hand, and, namely, with the singer clapping both hands together vertically with the beginning of the measure, for the three other quarters, merely drawing them close to each other rhythmically. In secular music I have sometimes heard 2/4 or 2/8 meter; for *gagaku*, however, only 4/4 meter is in use.

Besides the red dots, standing between the notes are also small black circles (Plate XIX, Fig. 5 [p. 255]) that recur in regular intervals, for example after 2 or

4 Tacten wiederkehren und nur für das Auge einen Anhalt bilden sollen. Bei der Ohteki werden sie durch kleine Striche ersetzt, (Taf. XX, Fig. 1), bei der Koto und den Schlaginstrumenten fallen sie ganz weg.

Außer der Abtheilung durch Punkte existirt nur noch die zweite Eintheilung durch große Punkte, welche in allen Instrumenten angegeben sind und in regelmäßigen Perioden wiederkehren. Sie sind entweder *roth* und bedeuten dann das Aufschlagen des *Obatshi* auf der Taiko, oder *schwarz*, wo sie das Zusammenschlagen der *Shaku Bioshi* bezeichnen. Es können zwar auch Taiko Schläge eingelegt sein, wie z.b. bei der letzten Wiederholung des zweiten Theils in dem Stück; aber an der bestimmten Stelle müssen sie immer wiederkehren, und wird das Stück nach dieser rhythmischen Wiederkehr benannt; das mitgetheilte Stück ist achttheilig, weil die Taiko bei jedem 8ten Tacte wiederkehrt.

Ferner existirt noch eine Abtheilung in Theile; *Go dshioh raku*, z.B. besteht aus 2 Theilen zu 16 Tacten, hinter jedem Theile steht das Wiederholungszeichen, *Nikaishi* (Taf. XX Fig. 3 und bei allen Instrumenten). Da nun die Taiko zum ersten Male beim 3ten Tacte angeschlagen wird, so müssen nach dem zweiten Taikoschlage (8 Tacte später) noch drei Tacte folgen, bevor der Theil zu Ende ist und das *Nikaishi* gesetzt werden kann. Dasselbe wiederholt sich beim 2ten Theil.

Die Instrumente setzen nun beim 1ten Male nur nach einander ein, und hören beim Schluss nicht zusammen

4 measures, and should build a support for the eye only. For the *ōteki* they are replaced by small strokes (Plate XX, Fig. 1 [p. 256]), for the *koto* and the percussion instruments they fall out completely.

In addition to the partitioning with dots, there exists the second division with big dots which are indicated in all instruments and recur in regular periods. They are either *red*, and then stand for the striking of the *obachi* of the *taiko*, or *black*, where they mark the hitting together of the *shakubyōshi*. Although *taiko*-strokes can be inserted, as for example in the last repeat of the second part in the piece, they must, however, always recur at the prescribed place, and the piece is named according to this rhythmic recurrence; the piece given here is 8-part because the *taiko* recurs every 8 measures.

Moreover there exists yet another partitioning in sections; *Goshōraku*, for example, consists of 2 sections of 16 measures; after each section stands the repeat sign *ni kaeshi* (Plate XX, Fig. 3 [p. 256]), and for all instruments). Now, since the *taiko* is beaten for the first time in the 3rd [5th] measure, after the second *taiko*-beat (8 measures later) three more measures have to follow before the the section is at its end, and the *ni kaeshi* can be set. The same repeats in the 2nd section.

The instruments enter the first time around only one after the other, and stop not together at the end, so that the first

auf, so daß der erste Theil nur bei der zweiten, der zweite nur bei der ersten Ausführung so gespielt wird, wie er notirt ist. Ich habe in der europaeischen Notirung den Einsatz der einzelnen Instrumente durch ein E, das Aufhören durch Pausen bezeichnet; in der japanischen Notirung existirt nichts dergleichen, sondern diese Verhältnisse sind in einem besonderen Commentar für jedes Stück angegeben; dort heißt es auch, daß das Stück am Schlusse vom letzten Taikoschlage ad libitum gespielt wird, nur muss die Reihenfolge des Aufhörens der Instrumente strenge inne gehalten werden. Außerdem ist noch ein Zeichen Kwairu (zufügen, Taf. XIX Fig. 5h) welches bedeutet, daß bei der zweiten Wiederholung Schläge auf der Taiko und Shōko eingeschoben werden. Diese Modification ist angegeben Taf. XIX, Fig. 3 und 4b. Das Stück wird nur folgendermaßen notirt: Jedes Instrument wird apart geschrieben, Titel und rothe Punkte (kleine und große) sind bei allen gleich, so daß es leicht ist, nach diesen Punkten die zusammengehörigen Noten auf den einzelnen Instrumenten herauszufinden. Es versteht sich von selbst, daß die sämmtlichen Parthieen wie alle japanische und chinesische Schrift von oben nach unten für die Zeichen, von rechts nach links für die Reihen, von hinten nach vorn für die Seiten gelesen werden müssen.

Im Original sind die Noten viel größer und ist für jedes Instrument ein besonderes Doppel Blatt bestimmt.

section is played as it is notated only in the second statement, the second, only in the first. In the European notation, I have marked the entry of the individual instruments with an E, the stopping with a pause; in the Japanese notation nothing of the sort exists, but these relationships are indicated in a special commentary for each piece; there it is said, too, that from the final taiko-beat the piece is played ad libitum, exept that the order of the instruments' stopping must be strictly adhered to. In addition, there is a further sign, kuwaeru (to add, Plate XIX, Fig. 5 h [p. 255]), which means that, in the second repeat, beats on the taiko and shōko are inserted. This modification is indicated on Plate XIX, Figs. 3 and 4, b (p. 255). The piece is now notated in the following manner: each instrument is written separately, title and red dots (big and small) are the same for all, so that it is easy to figure out the notes that belong together on the individual instruments. It goes without saying that all parts, as all Japanese and Chinese script, must be read from top to bottom for the symbols, from right to left for the columns, and from back to front for the pages.

In the original the notation is much bigger, and for each instrument a special double-page is assigned.

Der Raumersparnis wegen sind auf den Tafeln XIX bis XXI sämmtliche Partheen kleiner und zusammengerückt, sonst aber genau wiedergegeben.

Sehen wir nun zunächst die Noten für die Shō etwas näher an (Taf. XIX Fig. 5). Das erste Zeichen rechts oben (a) heißt Shō, also der Name des Instruments. Links davon kommen 2 Zeichen (b) von denen das obere Hiodshō, Stimmung das untere Taisoku, Februar (e), bedeutet; d.h. also: Tonart e moll, denn Durtonarten haben die Japaner und Chinesen nicht.[11] Von der dritten Zeichenreihe (c) heißen die drei obern Go dshioh raku; dies ist der Name des Stücks, die Bedeutung konnte mir Niemand angeben. Das vierte Zeichen (d) heißt Kiu, jedes Stück ist entweder Dsio, wo kein Tempo angegeben ist oder Ha, ein ganz langes Stück oder Kiu, kurzes Stück; die folgenden Zeichen (e) heißen Shokioku, kleines Stück; (f) Haya, schnelles Tempo, (g) Hioshi hachi, 8 d.h., daß 8 Tacte eine Abtheilung bilden; (h) heißt kwairu zufügen und bezieht sich auf die Schlaginstrumente, s. oben.

Dieser ganze Titel wiederholt sich nun bei jedem einzelnen Instrument, natürlich mit Veränderung des 1ten Zeichens. Nun kommen die Noten, wie sie in die einzelnen Tacte gehören, links neben die rothen Tactpunkte geschrieben; der dicke rothe Punkt für die Taiko

In order to save on space, on Plates XIX to XXI (pp. 255–257), all parts are smaller and squeezed together, but otherwise reproduced exactly.

In the first instance, let us look at the notation of the shō a little more closely (Plate XIX, Fig. 5 [p. 255]). The first symbol on the top right (a) is read shō, that is, the name of the instrument. Left of that come 2 symbols (b) the upper of them means hyōjō, tuning, the lower, taizoku [taisō], February (e); so in other words: e-minor mode, for the Japanese and Chinese do not have major modes.[11] From the third column of symbols, the three upper are read Goshōraku; this is the name of the piece, the meaning [of which] no-one could give me. The fourth symbol (d) is read kyū, short piece. Each piece is either jo, in which no tempo is specified, or ha, a fairly long piece, or kyū, [a] short piece; the following symbols read (e) shō-kyoku, little piece; (f) haya, fast tempo, (g) hyōshi hachi, that is, that 8 measures form a section; (h) reads kuwaeru, add, and refers to the percussion instruments (above).

This complete title repeats for each individual instrument, needless to say with alteration of the first symbol. Now come the notes, as they belong in the individual measures, written to the left of the red measure-dots; the thick red dot for the taiko repeats for each instrument:

---

[11] Woher das kommt, kann man leicht aus dem Aufsatz des Herrn Dr. Wagner ersehen, wo er über die Entstehung der ersten fünf Töne spricht; man kommt da mit Nothwendigkeit auf die Molltonleiter; s. auch Heft VI, Pag. 15 und 16.

[11] From where that comes one can easily see from Dr. Wagner's [Wagener] essay in which he speaks about the origin of the first five notes; one comes necessarily to the minor scale; see also Issue VI, pp. 15–16 (p. 96).

wiederholt sich bei jedem Instrument. Taf. XX, Fig. 1, Noten für die Ohteki; Fig. 2. für Hidchiriki, fahren auf der untern Hälfte der Tafel (B) fort bei Fig. 2.; Taf. XXI, Fig. 1, Noten für die Biwa; Taf. XIX, Fig. 2, Kakko; Fig. 3, Taiko, a, wie sie zuerst geschlagen wird, b, wie die zwei letzten Abtheilungen beim Schluss geschlagen werden; Fig. 4, Shōko, a und b haben dieselbe Bedeutung wie bei Taiko.

Da die Reihen der rothen Punkte auf der europäisch-geschriebenen Partitur über der Parthie der Sho angegeben sind, so glaube ich, wird es mit Hülfe der Tafeln XVIII bis XXI und der eben gegebenen Erläuterungen nicht sehr schwer fallen, nun die einzelnen Stimmen zu dechiffriren und etwaige kleine Irrthümer zu rectificiren.

Nur eins muß ich noch näher erläutern; wenn bei den Koto-Noten zwei Noten durch einen rothen Strich verbunden sind, (Taf. XIX. B. Fig. 4.) z.B. 3 und 8, (Taf. XIX Fig. 1a.) so soll die Ausführung so sein, wie sie in der Partitur angegeben ist, u. zw. wird erst die 4te Saite mit dem Zeigefinger gegriffen und 1/4 angehalten, dann läßt man den Mittelfinger in Achteln über die 3te und 4te Saite gleiten, derselbe gleitet dann ganz kurz über die 5te und nach diesem kurzen Vorschlag greifen Zeigefinger und Daumen zugleich die 6te und 8te Saite; die 7te fällt aus. Um dies genauer zu bezeichnen, macht man einen verticalen rothen Strich, schreibt grade auf demselben die Hauptnoten und die Nebennoten rechts und links davon kleiner. Dies geschieht aber nicht in der gewöhnlichen Noti-

Plate XX, Fig. 1 (p. 256), notation for the ōteki; Fig. 2 for hichiriki, continuing on the lower half of the Plate (B); Plate XXI, Fig. 1 (p. 257), notation for the biwa; Plate XIX, Fig. 2 (p. 255), kakko; Fig. 3, taiko, a as it is beaten at first, b as the two last sections are beaten at the end; Fig. 4, shōko, a and b have the same meaning as for the taiko.

As the series of red dots are indicated above the part for shō in the score written in European style, I believe that, with the help of Plates XVIII to XXI (pp. 253–257) and the explanations just given, it will not be very difficult to now decipher the individual parts and to rectify possible small errors.

One more thing I must explain further; if in koto-notation two notes are linked with a red stroke (Plate XX, B. Fig. 4 [p. 256]), for example, [the symbols for] 3 and 8 (Plate XIX, Fig. 1 a [p. 255]), then the execution is to be as shown in the full-score, that is, first, the 4th string is plucked with the index finger and held for [a] 1/4 [note], then one has the middle-finger glide over the 3rd and 4th strings in eighth-notes, the same [finger] glides very briefly over the 5th string and after this short grace note, index finger and thumb pluck the 6th and the 8th string at the same time; the 7th string drops out. In order to indicate this more precisely, one makes a vertical red stroke, writes the main notes right on it, and the accessory notes smaller, right and left of it. This does not occur in

rung, sondern nur in dem schon früher erwähnten Commentar.

Wie ich schon früher sagte, lernen die Schüler aber nicht nach diesen Noten die Stücke auswendig, sondern für sie sind die Stücke so aufgeschrieben, wie Taf. XXI, Fig. 2, für die Hidchiriki und Fig. 3 für die Ohteki. Die Tactzeichen sind wie bei den andern Noten; dann kommen links gewöhnliche Katakanazeichen (die eine Art der 72 japanischen, phonetischen Schriftzeichen), und links davon kommen dann, kleiner die richtigen Noten, wie man sich durch Vergleichung leicht überzeugen kann. Die Katakanazeichen lauten bei der Hidchiriki (Fig. 2) von oben bis exclusive dem 1ten Taikozeichen: Fe e rū, rē ē, t^a ā, re ^{e}; wobei das Komma jedesmal den rothen Punkt bedeutet. Diese Laute werden nun dem Schüler unter Angabe des Tacts mit der Hand in der oben beschriebenen Weise vorgesungen und er muss sie sich zu Hause einüben, bis er sie auswendig kann.

Die richtigen Noten sind also eigentlich nur als Anhalt für den Lehrer bestimmt. Bei der Ohteki (Fig. 3) ist am Anfang noch eine Reihe Katakanazeichen vorausgeschrieben, der erste Tact lautet statt tō ō rō hō hier ti i ra ha u.s.w. und bedeutet, daß beim ersten Male diese Noten eine Octav höher genommen werden sollen.

Nachdem ich nun die heilige Musik so weit es mir möglich war erläutert habe, will ich noch eine Liste der im Kriege und bei Religionsgebräuchen üblichen, sowie der chinesischen Instrumente hier

the regular notation, however, but only in the commentary, mentioned earlier.

As I stated earlier, the pupils, however, do not learn the pieces by heart from these notations, but the pieces are written down for them as on Plate XXI, Fig. 2 (p. 257) for the *hichiriki* and Fig. 3 for the *ōteki*. The signs for the measure are as for the other notations; then to the left are normal *katakana* signs (one type of the 72 Japanese phonetic script-characters), and left of them come next, smaller, the real notes, as one can easily see for oneself through comparison. The *katakana* signs for the *hichiriki* (Fig. 2) read from the top until, but excluding, the *taiko* symbol: Te e rū, rē ē, ta ā, re e, whereby the comma indicates the red dot each time. These sounds are sung to the pupil, while giving the beat with the hand in the manner described above, and he must practice them at home until he knows them by heart.

The real notations, therefore, are actually only intended as support for the teacher. For the *ōteki* (Fig. 3 (p. 257)), another row of *katakana* signs is written beforehand; the first measure reads, instead of tō ō rō hō, here *chi* i ra ha, and so on, and means that, for the first time around, these notes should be taken an octave higher.

Because I have now explained the sacred music, to the extent it was possible for me, I want to affix yet another list of the instruments which are customary for war and religious purposes, as well as of

anschließen und zum Schluss einen Auszug aus dem von Confucius gesammelten alten heiligen Buche der Chinesen dem Chouking[12] mittheilen.

those that are Chinese, and, to end with, to convey an excerpt out of the old sacred book of the Chinese compiled by Confucius, the Shujing.[12]

I.– Die Kriegsinstrumente.

Taf. XI, Fig. J. Dzin daiko wird in der Hand gehalten und mit dem Klöppel (I') geschlagen.

Fig. L, heißt ebenso, wird aber auf dem Rücken getragen.

Fig. K. Dzingane aus Metall; der Klöppel (K') ist daneben, der Durchschnitt (K") darunter gezeichnet.

Fig. M, Dzin-gai, große Muschel mit einem Mundstück aus Metall; sie giebt angeblasen einen sehr weit schallenden Ton.

Alle diese Instrumente werden sowohl zum Sammeln der Truppen als für verschiedene Signale gebraucht; diese bestehen aus langsamen, rhythmischen Tönen. Sie sind auch notirt, doch habe ich die Noten nicht erhalten können;

Die Trommeln und die Muscheln werden beim Marschieren benutzt, das Metallbecken zum Aufhören des Kampfs.

I. The Instruments of War

Plate XI, Fig. J (p. 246). Jindaiko is held in the hand and struck with the beater (J').

Fig. L, is called the same, but is carried on the back.

Fig. K. Jingane, [made] out of metal; the beater (K') is beside it, the side-view (K") drawn beneath.

Fig. M. Jingai,[13] large conch with a mouth-piece of metal; blown, it produces a very far-resounding tone.

All these instruments are used both for mustering the troops and for various signals; these consist of slow, rhythmical notes. They are also notated, but I have not been able to obtain the notation.

The drums and the conches are used when marching, the metal gong for the cessation of the battle.

---

[12] Le Chou-king, un des livres sacrés des Chinois, qui renferme les principes de leur gouvernement et de leur moral; ouvrage recueilli par Confucius, traduit par le père Gaubil, missionaire en Chine, revu et corrigé sur le texte Chinois par M. de Guignes, Paris, Tilliard, 1770.

[12] Le Chou-king, un des livres sacrés des Chinois, qui renferme les principes de leur gouvernement et de leur moral; ouvrage recueilli par Confucius, traduit par le père Antoine Gaubil, missionaire en Chine, revu et corrigé sur le texte Chinois par M. de Guignes, Paris, Tilliard, 1770. (Electronic copy http://babel.hathitrust.org/cgi/pt?id=hvd.hxkew5).

[13] Also known as horagai – Ed.

II.– Profane Instrumente.

Sie werden zuweilen zur *Samiseng* und *Koto* von Blinden und Mädchen benutzt, bes. in Theatern u. dgl.

Taf. XI, Fig. N, Shaku-hachi (d.h. ein Fuß acht Zoll) eine Art Clarinette aber ohne Mundstück; sie ist aus Bambu gefertigt, u. zw. aus dem untersten Theil über der Wurzel wegen der Stellung der Knoten; die Biegung ist die natürliche. *Hito yō giri* (einknotige Flöte) ist dieser ganz ähnlich, aber ohne die Biegung.

Fig. O, Shime-daiko (Zusammengeschnürte Trommel) wird mit 2 Holzklöppeln geschlagen. O″ ist die Oberfläche, O‴ der Durchschnitt.

III.– Instrumente, die beim Buddhadienst benutzt werden

Je nach der Höhe der Bezahlung nimmt die Anzahl der Instrumente und der ausführenden Priester zu. Bei geringer Bezahlung schlägt ein Priester zuweilen 2–3 Instrumente.

Taf. III, Fig. x, Han Shō (halbe Glocke) ist die kleine Glocke; sie ist hinter dem Tempel aufgehängt; sie wird geschlagen zum Sammeln der Priester, ferner bei Beerdigungen, wenn der Sarg in den Tempel gebracht wird; bei den Tönen dieser Glocke verlässt der Todte den irdischen Leib und gehört von da ab der anderen Welt an. X′ ist der obere Theil, X″ der Durchschnitt, X‴ die Ansicht von Unten. XX⁗ der Klöppel *Shu-moku* (Schlagholz).

Taf. XIII, Fig. n. und n′ sind zwei Metallbecken nach Art der in der türkischen

II. *Secular Instruments*

They are used sometimes, along with the *shamisen* and *koto*, by the blind and by girls, especially in theaters and the like.

Plate XI, Fig. N (p. 246). *Shakuhachi* (that is, one-foot-eight-inches), a type of clarinet but without mouth-piece; it is made of bamboo, and in fact out of the lowermost part above the root because of the positioning of the nodes; the curve is natural. *Hitoyogiri* (one-node flute) is quite similar to this, without the curve, however.

Fig. O (p. 246). *Shimedaiko* (braced drum) is struck with two wooden beaters; O″ is the surface area, O‴, the side-view.

III. *Instruments which are used in the Buddhist Service*

According to the amount of the payment, the number of instruments and performing priests increases. For low payment, sometimes one priest beats 2–3 instruments.

Plate XII, Fig. x (p. 247). *Hanshō* (half-bell) is the small bell; it is hung up behind the temple; it is beaten to gather the priests; furthermore, at funerals when the coffin is brought into the temple; with the sounds of this bell the dead person leaves this earthly body and from then on belongs to the other world. x′ is the upper part, x″ the cross-section, x‴ the view from below, xⁱᵛ the beater, *shumoku* (beating-wood).

Plate XIII, Figs. n and n′[14] (p. 248) are

Musik üblichen. n" ist der Durchschnitt, n"' die innere Ansicht.

two metal cymbals in the style of those common in Turkish music; n" is the side-view, n"', the inner view.

Fig. o, Die Dora ist das chinesische Metallbecken, wird mit O' geschlagen; o" Durchschnitt.

Fig. o (p. 248). The dora is the Chinese metal gong, is beaten with o'; o" side-view.

Fig. p, Wani gutsi (Wani ist der Name eines Fisches, Kutsi der Mund) hängt am Eingang der Tempel; sie wird mit dem lang herunterhängenden Strick p" geschlagen, um den Buddha zur An-hörung des Gebets herbeizurufen. p"' Seitenansicht, p^{iv} Durchschnitt.

Fig. p. Waniguchi (wani is the name of a fish, kuchi, the mouth) hangs at the entrance of the temples; it is struck with the long rope p" that hangs downwards to summon the Buddha to listen to the praying. p"' side-view, p^{iv} cross-section.

Fig. q, Kleine Trommel, auch Taiko genannt, steht im Tempel, wird zum buddhistischen Psalmodiren benutzt; sie wird benutzt, um die Seelen der Verstorbenen aus dem Fegefeuer zu erlösen. q', Seitenansicht, q" der Batsi.

Fig. q. Small drum, also called taiko, stands in the temple, is used for Buddhist psalmody; it is used to release the souls of the dead from purgatory; q' side-view, q" the bachi.

Fig. r, Hioshigi (Rhythmus-Holz) wird wie der Shaku-bioshi benutzt, aber in schnellerm Tempo; r' Querdurchschnitt.

Fig. r. Hyōshigi (rhythm-wood) is used like the shakubyōshi, only in quicker tempo; r' cross-section.

Taf. XIV, Fig. s. Nio hashi ist ein Metallgefäß, das auf einem Kissen und einem Holz-Untersatz ruht; s' Durchschnitt; s" obere Ansicht, s"' Klöppel, dessen eine Hälfte (zum Aufschlagen) mit Leder überzogen ist.

Plate XIV (p. 249), Fig. s. Nyō-hachi is a metal bowl that rests on a cushion and a wooden pedestal; s' cross-section; s" view from above, s"' beater, one half (with which to beat) is covered in leather.

Fig. T, Shōko ist wie die im Gagakku, nur flach gelegt und mit einem andern Klöppel (F'); t" Seitenansicht, t"' Durchschnitt; t"" untere Ansicht.

Fig. t. Shōko, is like that in Gagaku, only that it is laid flat and is with another beater (t'); t", side-view, t"' cross-section, t^{iv} view from below.

Fig. u, Lin ist die Nio hashi im verkleinerten Maßstabe zum Hausgebrauch; der Klöppel ist angebunden, damit er

Fig. u. Rin is the nyō-hachi in reduced scale for home-use; the beater is fastened

---

[14] n' ommitted on plate. – Ed.

nicht verloren geht; u' obere Ansicht, u" Durchschnitt.

Fig. v. ist eine kleine Shōko zum Hausgebrauch und von Pilgern benutzt; letztere legen sie auf die Genitalien und schlagen sie dann; v' obere Ansicht, v" untere Ansicht, v'" Durchschnitt, v"" der Untersatz, v""' der Klöppel Shumoku.

Fig. w, Rēi Schelle, wird von Pilgern benutzt, z.B. bei der Besteigung des Fujiyama.

Taf. XV, Fig. A Ban-gi hölzerne Platte, wird zum Versammeln der Priester gebraucht.

Fig. X. Tsuri gane. Große Glocke, die neben jedem Tempel in einem besondern Gerüst (Shuro) aufgehängt ist und mit dem schweren hölzernen Balken (Shimoku) angeschlagen wird. In einigen Tempeln (Shiba in Tokeï, in Kioto pp.) erreicht sie colossale Grössen (12 Fuß hoch). Sie wird zum Angeben der Zeit benutzt und am Ende des Jahres schlug jede solche Glocke 108 Schläge.[17]

to it, so that it does not get lost; u' view from above, u" cross-section.

Fig. v is a small shōko used for domestic purposes and by pilgrims; the latter lay it on their genitals and then beat it; v' view from above, v" view from below, v'" cross-section, v^{iv} the pedestal, v^{v} the beater, shumoku.

Fig. w. Rei, slit-bell, used by pilgrims, for example, on the ascent of Fujiyama.

Plate XV (p. 250),[15] Fig. A. Bangi, wooden slab, is used to gather the priests.

Fig. X. Tsurigane, big bell, which is hung in a special frame (shuro) next to every temple and is struck with a heavy wooden bar (shimoku). In some temples (Shiba in Tokei,[16] in Kyoto, etc.) it reaches a colossal size (12 feet high). It is used to state the time, and at the end of the year each such bell struck 108 strokes.[17]

---

[17] Bis Januar 1873 wurde immer die japanische Zeit angegeben. Von Sonnenuntergang bis Sonnenaufgang wurde die Zeit in 6 gleiche Teile (Toki) getheilt; ebenso die Zeit von Sonnenaufgang bis Sonnenuntergang. Zur Zeit der Aequinoctien betrug also jede Toki 2 Stunden, sonst variirten sie alle 14 Tage. Die Zeit wurde nun so angegeben daß erst als Avertissement 3 Schläge kamen u. zw. 2 langsame und der 3te schnell. Dann kamen wieder langsam 3 bis 8 langsame und zum Schluss ein schnellerer Schlag. Nehmen wir der Einfachheit wegen die Toki gleich an, so schlug man

um	12	Uhr	9	Schläge
"	2	"	8	"
"	4	"	7	"
"	6	"	6	"

[15] Superscripts omitted on plate. – Ed.
[16] Probably the Zōjōji temple in Shiba. – Ed.
[17] Until January 1873, the Japanese time was always given. The time from sunset to sunrise was divided into 6 equal parts (toki); the time from sunrise to sunset, likewise. At the time of the Equinox, therefore, each toki came to 2 hours, otherwise they varied every 14 days. Now, the time was stated in such way that first came three beats as announcement, namely two slow, the third quick. Then came again three to eight slow [beats], and at the end one quicker beat. If we take, for simplicity, the toki as equal, then one would beat:

at	12	o'clock	9	strokes
"	2	"	8	"
"	4	"	7	"
"	6	"	6	"

Fig. B, Metallbecken

Fig. C, Kleines Tambourin für Pilger, Bettler, pp; wird mit einem Holzstabe geschlagen.

Fig. D., Fisch aus Holz oder Metal, wird statt des Bangi gebraucht. D' Klöppel.

Fig. E, Yu ist ein liegender Tiger; über die gewulsteten Falten des Rückens wird mit dem Bambu E' hin und her gestrichen; der Bambu ist pinselartig gespalten.

Taf. XVI, Fig. b, Taiko und 1 Batsi

Fig. 2 [z]. Taiko mit 2 Batsi.

Taf. XVII, Fig. I. Ke eigentlich aus Stein, aber auch zuweilen aus Bronze.

Fig. H, Moku-gio (Holz-Fischmaul), die Schuppen sind durch Schnitzwerk angedeutet, und golden oder grün lackirt, während das übrige Instrument gewöhnlich roth ist; die Größe ist sehr verschieden, bis 2 Fuß groß. Innen ist es hohl, durch den Lack werden die Fugen verdeckt. H', der mit Leder bezogene Batsi.

Fig. B. Metal cymbals.

Fig. C. Small tambourine for pilgrims, beggars, and so on; is beaten with a wooden rod.

Fig. D. Fish made of wood or metal, is used instead of the bangi; D', beater.

Fig. E. Yu [gyo] is a recumbent tiger; the jagged furrows of the back are scraped over to and fro with the bamboo E'; the bamboo is fissured like a brush.

Plate XVI (p. 251), Fig. b. Taiko and 1 bachi.

Fig. z. Taiko with 2 bachi.

Plate XVII (p. 252), Fig. I. Kei, really out of stone, but sometimes out of bronze.

Fig. H. Mokugyō (wooden fishmouth); the scales are indicated by carving, and are lacquered gold or green, while the rest of the instrument is usually red; the size is very varied, up to 2 feet high. It is hollow inside, the joints are hidden by the lacquer; H',[18] the leather-covered bachi.

um	8	Uhr	5	Schläge
„	10	„	4	„

ohne die Vorschläge; dann fing es wieder von vorne an.

Seit 1873 wird europäische Zeitrechnung angenommen, und kommen erst die 3 Schläge, dann die europäische Stundenzahl, der letzte Schlag immer schnell.

Der Balken hängt an einem Gerüst mit 4 Stricken befestigt und wird durch einen besonders dazu angestellten Priester in Schwingungen versetzt; die Zahl der Schwingungen zwischen 2 Schlägen oder vielmehr Stößen bestimmt deren Tempo.

at	8	o'clock	5	strokes
„	10	„	4	„

without the anticipatory strokes; then it would start again from the beginning.

Since 1873 the European calculation of time is adopted, and first come the three strokes, then the European number of the hour, the last stroke always fast.

The pole hangs from a frame anchored with four ropes and is set in motion by a priest especially appointed for this; the number of swings between two strokes, or rather blows, determines their tempo.

[18] Superscript omitted on plate. – Ed.

Fig. G, Shaku dsiō sind Metallringe die auf einem langen Stock befestigt sind, und beim Aufstoßen klappern; Priester brauchen sie.

IV.– Zum Shinto dienst wird nur das Instrument Taf. XVII, Fig. F. benutzt; es heißt Su dzu und ist eine hohle Metallkugel in welcher andere kleine Metallkörner lose liegen.

V.– Jetzt noch in China übliche Instrumente.

Da die alte heilige Musik in China verloren gegangen ist, so sind dies alles profane Instrumente:

Taf. XXII, a. Die Ya misen in zwei Ansichten. Sie ist der japanischen Samiseng ganz ähnlich, aber abgerundet und mit Schlangenhaut statt Katzenfell überzogen.

Die Schlangenhaut wird allgemein in China und den Liu-kiu Inseln[19] zu solchem Zwecke benutzt, in Japan dagegen niemals. Sie wird ohne Batsi mit den blossen Fingern gespielt.

Der Steg ist auf Taf. XXIII, a, in 2 Ansichten dargestellt.

Fig. b, Die Kokin in Seiten und Vorderansicht, dazwischen die untere Ansicht des Körpers, der Steg auf Taf. XXIII, b. Der Körper des Bogens besteht aus einem gebogenen Stück Holz, der Haarbezug ist oben durchgesteckt, unten festgebunden. Er läuft zwischen den 2

Fig. G. Shakujō are metal rings which are attached to a long staff and clatter when jerked; priests use them.

IV. For the Shinto Service, only the instrument, Plate XVII, Fig. F (p. 252), is used; it is called suzu and is a hollow metalball, in which other small metal grains lie loosely.

V. Instruments still common in China

Since the old sacred music has been lost in China, these are all secular instruments:

Plate XXII, a (p. 258). The jamisen [sanxian], in two views. It is quite similar to the Japanese shamisen, only rounded and covered with snakeskin in place of catskin.

Snakeskin is used in general for such purposes in China and the Ryūkyū Islands;[19] in Japan, by contrast, never. It is played without bachi, with the bare fingers.

The bridge is depicted on Plate XXIII, a (p. 259), in two views.

Fig. b (Plate XXII, p. 258). The kokin (huqin) in lateral and face-view; in between, the view of the body from below, the bridge on Plate XXIII, b (p. 259). The body of the bow consists of a curved piece of wood; the bow-hairs are threaded through at the top and tied on at the

---

[19] Ich hatte Gelegenheit eine Rolle mit Abbildungen der in Liu-kiu gebräuchlichen Instrumente zu sehen und fand, daß sie von den chinesischen gar nicht differiren.

[19] I had the opportunity to see a scroll with illustrations of the instruments common in the Ryūkyū and found that they do not differ at all from the Chinese instruments.

Saiten durch. Diese sind zwischen Bogen und Wirbel durch eine Schlinge oder einen Ring etwas näher an den Hals des Instruments gezogen. Der Hals selbst hat die Form, welche die beiden Querchnitte (D-D) zeigen. Beim Spielen wird das Instrument aufrecht auf die Knie gestellt, und die beiden Saiten, welche von ungleicher Dicke und in der Sexte gestimmt sind, mit dem Mittel- und dem Ringfinger verschieden gespannt und aus einander gedrückt; der Bogen wird für die untere Saite mit der Vorder-, für die obere mit der Rückseite benutzt. Der Spieler klebt oben an dem Körper des Instruments ein Stück Colophonium an, über welches er beim Spielen fortwährend streicht. Sie spielen auf diesem Instrument ganz muntere Melodieen, z.B. spielte einer das Musikstück für die beiden Gekings (s. Musikanlage) mit; der Ton ist aber ein widerwärtiger. Ich sah ein solches ganz altes Instrument, bei dem der Körper aus einem dickern Stück Bambu bestand, durch welchen ein zweiter dünnerer Bambu durchgesteckt war. Die eine Seite war mit Fell bezogen, die andere durch den natürlichen Knoten des Bambu geschlossen, aber dieser war durchbrochen; Wirbel existirten daran nicht.

Fig. c, Die Biwa oder von den Chinesen Pipa genannt, ist eine Vervollkommnung der japanischen Biwa. Die 4 ersten Stege stehen grade so, wie bei dieser, durch die hinzugefügten Stege ist aber eine weitere Erhöhung der Töne möglich.

bottom. They pass between the two strings. These are drawn a little closer in to the neck of the instrument with a loop or a ring between bow and peg. The neck itself has the shape shown by the two cross-sections [A–A and] D–D. When playing, the instrument is placed upright on the knee, and the two strings, which are of unequal thickness and tuned to a sixth, are differently tensioned and forced apart by the middle and the ring finger; the bow is used with the front side for the lower string, with the backside for the upper. The player sticks a piece of resin atop the body of the instrument over which he bows all the time when playing. On this instrument they play very lively melodies; for example, one played along in the musical piece for the two gekkin (yueqin) (see musical attachment [Transcription 2, p. 245]); the tone, however, is abominable. I saw one such, quite old instrument, the body of which consisted of a thick piece of bamboo, through which a second thinner bamboo was stuck. One side was covered with skin, the other closed by the natural node of the bamboo, although this was open-worked; pegs did not exist on it.

Fig. c. The biwa or, called by the Chinese, pipa, is a refinement of the Japanese biwa. The 4 first frets stand just as for this [biwa], but through those added, a further increase in pitches is possible.

Fig. d, Tsalmera, ist eine Art Clarinette, aber ohne Mundstück mehr pfeifenartig; sie hat unten auf der Rückseite noch eine Öffnung, wodurch sie auch als Flöte gebraucht werden könnte.

Fig. e, Rapa; der Körper ist ähnlich der Hidchiriki, nur daß oben und unten Metallansätze sind; das Mundstück ist ähnlich dem der Hidchiriki, aber viel kleiner, in der Mitte mit einem Faden zusammengeschnürt; es besteht aus dünnem Schilf (e"), e' ist die untere Ansicht.

Fig. f, ist dem vorigen ganz ähnlich, nur kleiner.

Fig. g, ähnelt der Shaku-Bioshi und wird ebenso gebraucht.

Fig. h, Moku-gio, cf, Taf. XVII, Fig. H, ist aber nicht lackirt, und wird von Verkäufern pp. zur Erregung der Aufmerksamkeit bei den Vorübergehenden benutzt.

Taf. XXIII, Fig. i. Die Yanking oder westliche Kôto wird nur von Töchtern vornehmer Häuser gespielt. Es ist daher sehr schwer, sich über dies Instrument Notizen zu verschaffen. Der Körper des Instruments ähnelt unserer Cither; die Saiten sind aus Stahl. Dieser Umstand sowohl, wie der Name sprechen für einen fremden, jedenfalls westlichen Ursprung des Instruments. Die Saiten sind an je zwei Stiften (i' und i") befestigt, von denen der eine durch den Stimmhammer (Tototsi, i'") gedreht und die Saite gestimmt werden kann. Auf dem Resonanzboden befinden sich zwei lange, durchlöcherte Stege. Die Saiten laufen immer durch die runden Öff-

Fig. d. Charumera is a type of clarinet, but without mouth-piece, more like a pipe; it has at the bottom on the back side another opening by which it can also be used as a flute.

Fig. e. Laba. The body is similar to the hichiriki, only that at the top and bottom there are metal attachments; the mouth-piece is like that of the hichiriki, but much smaller, tied together in the middle with a thread; it consists of thin reeds e"; e' is the view from below.[20]

Fig. f is very like the preceding, only smaller.

Fig. g resembles the shakubyōshi and is used in the same way.

Fig. h. Mokugyō [muyu], see Plate XVII, Fig. H (p. 252), is not lacquered, however, and is used by vendors and so on to attract the attention of passers-by.

Plate XXIII, Fig. i (p. 259). The yangqin or Western koto is played only by daughters of genteel households. It is therefore very difficult to acquire notes about this instrument. The body of the instrument resembles our zither; the strings are of steel. This fact, as well as the name, speak for a foreign, in any case Western, origin for the instrument. The strings are attached to each of two pins (i' and i"), one of which can be turned with a tuning-hammer (chō-tsuchi [diaochui], i'") and the string tuned. On the sounding board are found two long, perforated bridges. The strings always run through

[20] The superscripts for e" and e' are missing on the plate. – Ed.

nungen des zunächst liegenden Steges hindurch und über den entferntern weg, so daß die Saiten sich über dem Mitteltheil des Resonanzbodens kreuzen. Die tiefern, dickern Saiten sind immer nur eine, die höhern je zwei für einen Ton. Das Instrument wird so vor den Spieler hingestellt, daß die breitere Seite dem Spieler zugewandt ist. Nun sagte mir der Chinese (niedern Standes), welcher mir das Instrument erklärte, man gebrauchte nur die mittlere Abtheilung für die tieferen, einsaitigen Töne, die linke für die höheren; das scheint mir aber nicht ganz richtig; ich habe nämlich eine Yanking gesehen, bei welcher die beweglichen Stege so gestellt waren, daß die Theile der tiefern Saiten rechts und links vom Stege grade um 2 Octaven differirten, die der höhern um eine Quart, so daß also 28 verschiedene Töne erzeugt werden konnten.

Die Stimmung, wie sie mir der Chinese zeigte, war für die tieferen Saiten D E F G A H c, für die höhern g a h b d', dis', g'.

Gespielt wird das Instrument mit zwei Hämmerchen aus Bambu oder Schildpatt (i'''', i''''' Rückseite); i'''''' zeigt den Deckel des Instruments, i''''''' das geschlossene Instrument; i'''''''' dasselbe von der schmalen Seite mit dem herausgezogenen Kasten für den Stimmhammer.

Taf. XXIV, Fig k.'' und l, die tenko (Punkttrommel) und die Hanko (Bretttrommel) gehören zusammen. Sie sind feste hölzerne, nur mit Fell überzogene Trommeln, die in der Quart gestimmt sind, aber keinen sonoren, sondern nur

the round openings of the nearest-lying bridge and out over the more distant [bridge] so that the strings cross over the middle part of the sounding board. The lower, thicker strings are always one per note; the higher, two each [per note]. The instrument is placed in front of the player so that the broader side is facing the player. Now, the Chinese (of low class) who explained the instrument to me, told me one uses only the middle section for the lower one-stringed notes, the left for the higher; however, that seems not quite right to me; to wit, I have seen a yangqin on which the moveable bridges were so placed that the sections of the lower strings right and left of the bridge differed by exactly two octaves, those of the higher by a fourth, so that consequently 28 different notes could be produced.

The tuning, as the Chinese showed it to me, was for the lower strings, D E F G A B c, for the higher, g a b bb d', d#', g'.

The instrument is played with two little hammers of bamboo or tortoiseshell (i^{iv}, i^{iv} backside); i^{vii} shows the lid of the instrument, i^{vi} the instrument closed, i^{v21} the same from the narrow side with the drawer for the tuning-hammer pulled out.

Plate XXIV, Figs. k[22] and l (p. 260).

[21] Discrepancy in figure-labelling between text and plate. Translation follows plate. – Ed.
[22] Superscript-labelling is again confused for this instrument-pair; editorial rectifications. – Ed.

einen klappenden Ton von sich geben. Sie ruhen auf einem Gestell, das aus 6 Bambus gebildet ist, die durch 3 Schnüre (k') zusammengehalten werden, auf welchen die Trommel ruht; k", l" geben die Flächenansichten der Instrumente, l''' den Durchschnitt von 1. Geschlagen werden sie mit zwei Bambusstäbchen, l' oder k'''.

Fig. j, Shōkun, eine Trompete, deren beide Stücke in einander geschoben werden können. Sie wird bei Mandarinenzügen, Ausrufen pp. benutzt und giebt einen schreienden Ton von sich. j' ist das Mundstück von oben, j" das Schallrohr von unten gesehen.

Fig. m, ist die Dora aus Metall, welche mit dem Klöppel m' geschlagen wird; m" und m''' sind die Durchschnitte.

Außerdem ist noch gebräuchlich:

Die Dōko, eine flache Felltrommel, die an drei Ringen aufgehängt ist und mit einem Bambusstab geschlagen wird und die Getsiura ganz ähnlich wie Taf. XIV, Fig. v.

Endlich muss ich unter den chinesischen Instrumenten noch etwas näher eingehen auf die Geking (Heft VI, Taf. IV, Fig. 7). Sie besteht ganz aus Holz, innen ist quer durch den Körper ein Metalldraht gesteckt, der mit einem Ende in der Seitenwand befestigt ist, mit dem andern Ende frei in der Nähe der andern Seitenwand schwingt. Dieser Draht giebt dem Instrument einen mehr metallischen Klang und unterstützt den

The *tenko* [diangu] (dot drum) and the *hanko* [bangu] (board drum) belong together. They are hard wooden drums, covered only with skin, which are tuned in a fourth, but give out no sonorous sound, only a clacking [sound]. They rest on a frame which is built from 6 bamboo [rods] held together by three laces (k') on which the drum rests; k" (h"), l" give the surface views of the instruments, l''' the cross-section of l. They are struck with two bamboo-sticks l' or k''' (k").

Fig. j. *Shōkun* [suona?], a trumpet, the two pieces of which can be slid into each other. It is used for Mandarin-processions, proclamations, and so on, and issues a shrieking sound; j' is the mouth-piece seen from above, j" the sounding-tube, from below.

Fig. m is the *dora* [tongluo], of metal, which is struck with the beater m'; m" and m''' are cross-sections.

In addition, still in use are:

The *dōko* [taogu?], a flat skin-drum, which is suspended on three rings and is struck with a bamboo stick, and the *getsiura* [tongba?] very like Plate XIV, Fig. v (p. 249).

Finally, among the Chinese instruments, I must go in a little more detail into the *gekkin* [yueqin] (Issue VI, Plate IV, Fig. 7 [p. 120]). It is completely made of wood; inside, diagonally across the body, is inserted a metal-wire which with one end is fixed to the side-wall, with the other end swings free near the other side-wall. This wire gives the instrument a more metallic sound and supports the singer in his bleat-

Sänger bei seinem meckernden Trillern. Bespannt ist es mit 2 Paar Saiten, das eine Paar eine Quint höher als das andere gestimmt. Gespielt wird es mit einem kleinen Batshi. Ich theile als Anlage ein Stück (Manpan Riusui) mit, das erst von 2 Gekin's und dann von denselben und einer kōkin aufgeführt wurde.

Ich kann die Reihe der ostasiatischen Instrumente nicht abschließen, ohne noch eines eigenthümlichen Instruments zu gedenken, das in Yezo unter den Aino's gebräuchlich ist; eine Art Maultrommel. Es ist dies ein ganz dünnes Holzbrettchen von etwa 4 Zoll Länge und 2 Zoll Breite. In der Mitte ist eine etwa 1 Linie breite, 15 Linien lange, am freien Ende zugespitzte Holzzunge auf drei Seiten ausgeschnitten, ganz ähnlich wie die Metallzungen der Shō (Taf. XX, Fig. 5.) Das Brettchen wird vor den Mund gehalten und die Zunge durch Blasen und Singen in Schwingungen versetzt. Auch eine eiserne Maultrommel habe ich gesehen, die bei den Aino's gebraucht wird; sie ähnelt ganz der unsrigen, nur ist der äußere Bügel vor der Zunge geschlossen, hat keine freien Enden, wie die unsrige; trotzdem glaube ich, daß dies Instrument westlichen Ursprungs ist.

ing trilling. It is strung with 2 pairs of strings, the one pair tuned a fifth higher than the other. It is played with a small bachi. I give as attachment a piece (Manban liushui [Transcription 2, p. 245]), which was performed first by 2 gekkin [yueqin] and then by the same plus a kokin [huqin].

I cannot end the series of East Asian instruments without making mention of a further, singular instrument that is common in Yezo among the Ainu; a kind of jaw harp. This is a very thin little wooden board of about 4 inches length and 2 inches width. In the middle an approximately 1-line-wide,[23] 15-line-long wooden tongue, pointed at its free end, is carved out on three sides, very similiarly as for the metal-tongues of the shō (Plate XX, Fig. 5[24] [p. 256]), held in front of the mouth and the tongue set into vibration through blowing and singing. I have also seen an iron jaw harp which is used by the Ainu; it is just like ours, only that the outer frame is closed in front of the tongue, has no free ends, as ours does; nonetheless, I believe that this instrument is of Western origin.

[23] 1 line = 1/12 inch = 2.174 mm. – Ed.
[24] Labelled in Japanese as Yezo no fue. – Ed.

Ich lasse nun zum Schlusse Auszüge aus dem oben erwähnten Chu-King folgen, welche die Entstehung und Bedeutung der altchinesischen Musik etwas erläutern. Dann theile ich noch einige Notizen über japanische und chinesische Musik mit, die HERR STEIN nebst 3 Musikanlagen eingesandt hat.

Die Chinesen haben eine sehr hohe Meinung von ihrer alten Musik, die ihnen verloren gegangen ist; sie nennen dieselbe Yo, und setzten ihren Ursprung in die ältesten, fabelhaften Zeiten. Sie sagen, daß einer ihrer Könige, Namens Tcho-yang, der lange vor Foki (ungefähr 3000 v. Chr; die Angaben variiren zwischen 2952 und 3300) lebte, auf den Gesang der Vögel lauschte, und danach eine Musik zusammensetzte, deren Harmonie überall eindrang, den intelligenten Geist rührte und die Leidenschaften beruhigte; so wurden die äußern Sinne gesund, die Säfte (humores) des Körpers kamen in das Gleichgewicht und das Leben der Menschen verlängerte sich. Diese Musik hieß Tsie-ven, Mäßigkeit und Anmuth.

Der Hauptzweck dieser alten Musik war die Harmonie aller Tugenden; so daß diese Harmonie erst dann vollständig war, wenn Körper und Seele übereinstimmten und die Leidenschaften der Vernunft unterworfen waren.

To conclude, I append extracts from the above-mentioned Shujing that elucidate somewhat the emergence and meaning of the old Chinese music. Then I convey a few more notes on Japanese and Chinese music[25] which Herr Stein submitted along with three music attachments.[26]

The Chinese have a very high estimation of their old music, which has become lost to them; they name this yue and place its origin in the oldest, mythical times. They say that one of their kings by the name of Choyong,[27] who lived long before Fuxi (about 3000 BCE; the details vary between 2952 and 3300), listened to the song of birds and afterwards put together music whose harmony penetrated everywhere, stirred the intelligent mind, and calmed the passions; so the outer senses became healthy, the fluids (humors) of the body came into balance, and the life of the people was prolonged. This music was called jie-en, temperance and grace.

The principal purpose of this old music was the harmony of all virtues; so that this harmony was only then complete when body and soul were in accord and the passions were subject to reason.

This music was always one with courtesy; this courtesy, they say, which reveals itself to the outside must come

---

[25] Likely based on Confucius, Le Chou-king, – Ed.

[27] Confucius, Le Chou-king, 332. – Ed.

Diese Musik war immer mit der Höflichkeit vereint; diese Höflichkeit, sagen sie, die sich nach außen offenbart, muss von innen herauskommen, wie die Harmonie, die im Herzen ruht, sich nach außen verbreiten soll.

Im Allgemeinen sprechen die Chinesen von dieser alten Musik, wie die Griechen von der des Orpheus und der Lyra des Mercur (?), deren Theile denen des Weltalls entsprachen. Sie hatten besondere Beamte, welche beauftragt waren, sie den in den religiösen Festen beschäftigten Musikern zu lehren.

Der Abbé Arnaud, welcher Einsicht in eine Abhandlung über die altchinesische Musik gehabt hat, wovon er einen Auszug in seinen "Variétés littéraires" veröffentlicht hat, hat bemerkt, daß das System dieser Musik dasselbe ist, wie das des Pythagoras und der Egypter. "Der Hauptzweck der Musik, haben alle Pythagoräer gesagt, ist, die Leidenschaften zu beruhigen, das Verständnis zu erleuchten und die Liebe zur Tugend einzuflößen. Seine Seele in Gleichmuth erhalten, sagen die Chinesen, bescheiden und aufrichtig sein, Rechtlichkeit und Beständigkeit sich aneignen, alle Welt lieben und vor Allem die, denen man das Leben verdankt, das sind die Tugenden, welche die Musik einflößen soll, und die man durchaus erlangen muss, wenn man den Namen eines Musikers verdienen will." So sind, abgesehen vom System der Musik Pythagoräer und Chinesen über die hohe Idee einig, welche sie sich über die Musik gebildet haben.

from the inside, as the harmony that rests in the heart should spread outwards.

In general, the Chinese speak of this old music as the Greeks do that of Orpheus and the Lyre of Mercury (?)[28] whose parts corresponded with those of the universe. They had special officials who were charged with teaching it to the musicians involved in the religious ceremonies.

Abbé Arnaud, who had had access to a treatise on the old-Chinese music, an abstract of which he published in his *Variétés littéraires*, remarked that the system of this music is the same as that of Pythagoras and the Egyptians; "The main purpose of music, all Pythagoreans have said, is to calm the passions, to elucidate understanding, and to infuse the love for virtue. To keep one's soul in equanimity, say the Chinese, to be modest and sincere, to acquire lawfulness and steadfastness, to love the whole world and, above all, those to whom one owes one's life, these are the virtues which music should infuse, and which one must achieve by all means, if one wants to earn the name of musician."[29] Irrespective of musical system, Pythagoreans and Chinese, then, are at one in the elevated idea which they have formed about music.

[28] See the early fifth-century Saturnalia I.19.15 in Macrobius, *Macrobii Ambrosii Theodosii Opera, vol. II*, 183. – Ed.

[29] Suard and Arnaud, *Variétés littéraires*, II, 309–310. – Ed.

Aber diese vollkommene Musik ent-
artete bald, und man sieht im Chouking,
daß eine Musik getadelt wird, welche die
Sittenverderbnis beförderte, eine unan-
ständige Musik.[30] Ohne Zweifel trugen
die schlüpfrigen Lieder, die man zu der
Musik sang, zu der Sittenverderbniss bei.

Heute haben die Chinesen ein "Pe-
pang" genanntes Instrument; es besteht
aus mehreren Brettchen aus Hartholz, einen Fuss lang und vier Finger breit, oben
schmaler und dort zusammengeheftet;
sie bedienen sich derselben, wie wir der

But this perfect music soon de-
generated, and one sees in the *Shujing*
that a music which corrupts morals, an
obscene music,[30] is reproached. Without
doubt the lewd songs that were sung to
the music contributed to the decline of
morals.

Today the Chinese have an instrument named *paiban*; it consists of several
small boards of hardwood, one foot long
and four fingers wide, narrower at the
top, and threaded together there; they
use this as we the castanets, and mark the
beat with it.

[30] Dies wiederholt sich im Chouking immer;
ein grosser Theil der guten Kaiser erfand
eine specielle Musik; den schlechten Kai-
sern wird dagegen oft vorgeworfen, dass
sie schlechte Musik liebten oder die Musik unterdrückten. s. auch: Das schöne
Mädchen von Pau Kapit. II.
Der Kaiser Chou (2255 v. Ch.) erfand eine
Musik, die alle Thiere bändigte; sie hiess
Tachao. Eine ähnliche Wichtigkeit wird der
Verbindung von Musik und Tanz beige-
legt. *Lo-pi* sagt, dass das Leben des Menschen von der Vereinigung von Himmel
und Erde abhängt und von der Benutzung
alles Geschaffenen. Die *feine Materie* (auch
der *Geist* oder *Dunst* genannt) circulirt im
Körper. Ist der Körper also nicht in Bewe-
gung, so fliesst die *Materie* nicht, sammelt
sich an, und daher die Krankheiten, die
alle nur von Stauung (Obstruction) herrühren. Unter einer ruhigen Regierung
sieht man nichts Krankes, aber unter einem schlechten König ist Alles in Unord-
nung; deshalb sagt das *Li-ki* (eines der heiligen Bücher) dass man über eine Regierung nach den unter ihr üblichen Tänzen
urtheilen kann. Mann sagt auch, dass man
die Tugend eines Mannes nach der Art
und Weise beurtheilen kann, wie er die *Se*
spielt. So ist denn der Tanz eine Körperbe-
wegung, die aber gleichzeitig in Verbindung mit der Regierung steht, grade so,
wie dies von der Musik gilt.

[30] This is repeated over and over in *Shujing*;
a large number of the good emperors invented a special music; bad emperors, by
contrast, are often accused of liking bad
music or of suppressing music. See also,
"The Beautiful Girl from Pao," chap. II.
(Arendt, Carl (1876). "Das schöne Mädchen
von Pao.") Emperor Chou [Shun] (2255 BCE)
invented a music that restrained all animals; it was called *dashao*. A similar importance is attached to the association of
music with dance. Luo Bi (On Luo Bi, see
Shaughnessy, *Rewriting Early Chinese Texts*,
161. – Ed.) says that the life of man depends
on the unification of heaven and earth and
on the use of all things created. The *fine
matter* (also named the *spirit* or *vapour*) cir-
culates in the body. If the body is not in
movement, then the *matter* does not flow,
accumulates, and thence originate sick-
nesses that all derive only from stasis (obstruction). Under a peaceful rule one sees
nothing sick, but under a bad king everything is in disorder; thus the *Liji* (one of
the sacred books) states that one can judge
a rule according to the dances customary
under it. It is also said that one can judge
the virtue of a man according to the way
in which he plays the *se*. So, then, dance is
a body-movement that at the same time
stands in relation to ruling, exactly as this
holds good also of music.

Castagnetten, und geben den Tact damit an.

Taf. XVII, Fig. 1. Man sagt von diesem Instrument, Kin genannt, dessen Erfindung dem Fohi zugeschrieben wird, wunderbare Dinge. Man sagt, dass dieser Fürst die Gesetzte der Musik gab, und nachdem er den Fischfang organisirt hatte, soll er ein Lied für die Fischer componirt haben, ebenso, wie Chin-nong, der Erfinder des Pflügens, ein Lied für die Ackerbauer machte.

Fohi nahm von dem Holze, Tong genannt, höhlte es aus und machte daraus die Kin,[31] 7 Fuss 2 Zoll lang. Die Saiten waren aus Seide verfertigt, 27 an der Zahl; er nannte das Instrument Li.

Die Chinesen stimmen über die Saitenzahl des Instrumentes nicht überein; Einige geben ihm 27, Andere 25, Andere 20, 10, endlich sogar nur 5. Man sagt, dass Venvang oder Vouvang zwei andere hinzufügte, was 7 macht. Was die Länge betrifft, so geben die Einen ihm 7 Fuss, 2 Zoll, die andern 3 Fuss, 6 Zoll, 6 Linien. Man sagt, daß die Oberfläche rund war, wie der Himmel, die untere Fläche flach, wie die Erde; daß der See des Long oder Drachen (eine Stelle an dem Instrument) 8 Zoll maß, um mit den 8 Winden zu communiciren, der See des Fong oder Phoenix 4 Zoll, um die 4 Jahreszeiten zu repräsentiren. Diejenigen, die ihm nur 5 Saiten geben,[32] sagen, sie seien die Repräsentanten der 5 Planeten gewesen. Als Fohi diese Lyra erfand, gab sie einen himmlischen Ton. Er spielte darauf ein Stück, Kia-pien

Plate XVII, Fig. 1 (p. 252). Marvelous things are said about this instrument, named qin, whose invention is attributed to Fuxi. It is said that this prince established the rules of music, and after he had organized fishing, he is held to have composed a song for the fishermen, in the same way as Shennong, the inventor of the plow, made a song for the farmers.

Fuxi took some of the wood named tong, hollowed it out and made out of it the qin,[31] 7 feet 2 inches long. The strings were made from silk, 27 in number; he named the instrument li.

The Chinese do not agree on the number of strings of the instrument; some give it 27, others 25, [still] others 20, 10, and, finally, only 5. It is said that Wen Wang or Wu Wang added two others, making 7. Regarding the length, some give it as 7 feet 2 inches, others 3 feet, 6 inches, 6 lines. The upper surface is said to have been round, like the heavens, the lower surface flat, like the earth; the lake of the long or dragon (a place on the instrument) to have been 8 inches in size in order to communicate with the 8 winds, the lake of the feng or phoenix, 4 inches, to represent the four seasons of the year. Those who give it only 5 strings[32] say they were the representatives of the 5 planets. When Fuxi invented this lyre, it gave forth a heavenly tone. He played on it a piece named Jiabian in order to praise

---

[31] Früher als Kino Kōto beschrieben.
[32] Dies ist wahrscheinlich das Richtige.

[31] Referred to earlier as kin-no-koto.
[32] This is probably correct.

genannt, um die Wohlthaten des intelligenten Geistes zu preisen und um den
Himmel mit dem Menschen zu verbinden. Andere sagen, daß dies Instrument
die bösen Zauber abwandte und unreine
Gesinnung vom Herzen entfernte.

Die Chinesen stimmen über dieses
Instrument ebenso wenig, wie über das
Folgende überein, sowohl was die Form
als den Erfinder betrifft.

Ich habe gesagt, daß die Saiten aus
Seide waren, und man hat bis heute in
China keine andern für alle Saiteninstrument,[33] aber man trifft eine Auswahl in
der Seide und behauptet, daß diejenige,
welche von Seidenwürmern kommt, die
mit den Blättern eines Baums, Namens
Uche, gefüttert wurden, bei weitem die
beste ist, und daß diese Saiten einen vol-
leren Klang haben. Dieser Baum ist dem
Maulbeerbaum ähnlich, trägt Früchte
von der Dicke der Avelines, die Schale ist
schwarz, das Fleisch weiß und essbar.
Man bedient sich dieses Baums auch,
um rothgelb zu färben.

Der Baum, dessen sich Fohi bediente,
um den Kin zu verfertigen, heißt Tong; es
giebt deren mehrere Arten; der schwarze
Tsin-tong trägt keine Früchte; Blätter und
Zweige sind schwärzlich.

Der weiße Pe-tong, dessen Blätter
weiß sind, trägt im Anfang des Frühlings
gelbe und violette Blumen; die Blätter
kommen erst um die Tag- und Nacht-
gleiche; die Blumen und Blätter werden
in der Medicin angewandt. Es giebt an-

the benefaction of the intelligent mind
and to link heaven with man. Others
say that this instrument averts wicked
magic and removes impure dispositions
from the heart.

In respect both of form and founder,
the Chinese agree about this instrument
just as little as they do about what follows.

I have said that the strings were
of silk, and to this day in China, for all
stringed-instruments,[33] no others are to
be had. A selection in the silk is made,
however, and it is maintained that that
which comes from silkworms which
were fed on the leaves of a tree, zhe, is
by far and wide the best, and that these
strings have a fuller sound. This tree is
similar to the mulberry tree, bears fruit
the thickness of the cob-nut; the skin is
black, the flesh white and edible. One
uses this tree also to dye red-gold.

The tree which Fuxi used to make
the qin is called tong; there are many
types; the black qingtong bears no fruit;
leaves and branches are blackish.

The white baitong, whose leaves are
white, bears yellow and purple flowers
at the beginning of spring; the leaves
come only at the equinox; the flowers
and leaves are applied in medicine. There
are other types whose leaves and bark are

---

[33] Die Yangking mit Stahlseiten scheint dem
Verfasser noch unbekannt gewesen zu
sein.

[33] The yangqin with steel-strings seems to
have been still unknown to the author.
(Presumably Herr Stein – Ed.)

dere Arten, deren Blätter und Rinde grau sind und die eine Frucht von der Dicke eines Pfirsichs tragen, aus welchen man ein Öl zum Anreiben der Farben bereitet; die Frucht ist nicht essbar.

Es giebt andere welche grüne Blätter und Rinde haben deren Frucht von der Größe einer Haselnuss und essbar ist; andere haben Früchte ohne Blüthen, andere Blüthen ohne Früchte.

Abgesehen von diesem Baume bedient man sich noch zu demselben Gebrauche eines Baums Namens Ye, den die Chinesen den König der Bäume nennen.

Taf. XVII, Fig. 2. Die Se.[34]. Dieses

grey and which bear a fruit the thickness of a peach out of which an oil for the rubbing on of colours is prepared; the fruit is inedible.

There are others which have green leaves and bark, whose fruit is the size of a hazelnut and is edible: others have fruits without flowers, others flowers without fruits.

Aside from this tree, for the same purpose a tree by the name of *ye*, which the Chinese call the king of the trees, is also used.

Plate XVII, Fig. 2 (p. 252). The *se*.[34]

[34] Lopi (zwischen 954 und 1279 p. Ch. unter der Song Dynastie) sagt in seiner Geschichte des Kaisers *Tchusiangchi* (vor Fohi), daß der Kaiser dem *Se-kouei* befahl, eine *Se* mit 5 Saiten zu machen, um die durch Stürme und unregelmässigen Eintritt der Jahreszeiten gestörte Harmonie des Weltalls herzustellen. Es ist dies das erste musikalische Instrument, das erwähnt wird; Lopi sagt bei dieser Gelegenheit, daß die Musik nur die Übereinstimmung der beiden Principien ist, das eine actif, *Yang*, das andere passif, *Yn*, auf denen die Erhaltung der sichtbaren Welt beruht. In der That ist die schöne Ordnung der Welt eine Harmonie, und mag man nun die physische Welt d.h. Himmel und Erde, oder die moralische Welt d.h. den Menschen, oder die politische Welt, d.h. das Königreich oder alle drei verkettet betrachten, so begegnet man immer diesen beiden Principien, die übereinstimmen müssen, sonst ist keine Harmonie möglich. Lopi fügt hinzu, daß der Weise die falschen Ac-

[34] Luo Bi [see footnote on p. 232] (between 954 [960] and 1279 CE, under the Song dynasty) says in his history of the Emperor *Chuxiang ji* (before *Fuxi*) that the Emperor ordered *Se-kui* to make a *se* with 5 strings, in order to establish the harmony of the universe, destroyed through storms and irregular entry of the four seasons. This is the first musical instrument to be mentioned; Luo Bi said on this occasion that music is just an agreement of the two principles, the one active, *yang*, the other passive, *yin*, on which the preservation of the visible world depends. In fact, the beautiful order of the world is a harmony, and should one reflect upon the physical world, i.e., heaven and earth, or the moral world, i.e., humanity, or the political world, i.e., the kingdom, or all three linked, then one always encounters these two principles, which must be in agreement, otherwise no harmony is possible. *Luo Bi* added to this that the sage brings the faulty ac-

Instrument wird ebenfalls dem Fohi zugeschrieben. Er soll sie aus einem Holze, Namens *Sang* angefertigt und mit 36 Saiten versehen haben. Das Instrument diente dazu, die Menschen tugendhafter und gerechter zu machen. Einige behaupten, daß das Instrument 50 Saiten hatte, daß aber *Hoang-ti* eins von 25 Saiten anfertigte, weil das von Fohi einen zu traurigen Ton hatte. Noch andere sagen, daß *Niu-va*, Fohi's Frau, die Verminderung vornahm, und daß darauf Alles im Weltall in Ordnung war.

Das Instrument war 8 Fuß, 1 Zoll lang, 1 Fuß, 8 Zoll breit.

Taf. XVII, Fig. 3. Die *Ming-kieou* oder einfach *Kieou* war ein dreieckiges Instrument; zuweilen aber auch rund, denn man findet in chinesischen Büchern beide Formen. Es bestand aus Stein und gab einen harmonischen Ton; im Capitel *Y-tsi* des *Chouking* ist die Rede davon.[35]

This instrument is likewise attributed to Fuxi. He is held to have made it from a wood by the name of *sang*, and to have furnished it with 36 strings. The instrument served to make the people more virtuous and fair-minded. Some maintain that the instrument had 50 strings, but that *Huang-di* made one of 25 strings because that of Fuxi had too sad a tone. Still others say that *Nüwa*, Fuxi's wife, carried out the reduction and that thereupon everything in the universe was in order.

The instrument was 8 feet, 1 inch long, 1 foot, 8 inches wide.

Plate XVII, Fig. 3 (p. 252). The *bianqing*, or simply *qing*, was a triangular instrument; sometimes round, however, for one finds both forms in Chinese books. It was made of stone and gave out a harmonious tone; it is discussed in the chapter "Yi ji" of *Shujing*.[35] This

---

corde des *Yn* und *Yang* zur Übereinstimmung bringt, und daß er Instrumente erfindet, um ihre Einigkeit darzustellen. Von allen Instrumenten, von denen er spricht, sind die hauptsächlichsten die *Kin* und die *Se*; beide sind für das harmonische Concert wesentlich. Die erstere beherrscht das *active*, die letztere das *passive* Princip. Der König hat beide. Die tributairen Fürsten haben nur die *Se* und können die *Kin* nicht haben. Diese *Kin* steht dem Leben vor und flößt deshalb Freude ein; die *Se* beherrscht den Tod und erregt deshalb Traurigkeit und Mitleid.

[35] Dies Kapitel behandelt die Zeit 2253-2049 v. Ch. Der Kaiser *Yu* sagt darin: Wenn ich Musik hören will, die 5 Töne, die 8 Modulationen, so untersuche ich mein gu-

cord of *yin* and *yang* into agreement, and that he invents instruments in order to represent their unity. Of all the instruments he speaks of, the most important are the qin and the se; both are essential for the harmonious concert. The former rules the *active* principle, the latter the *passive*. The king has both. The tributary princes only have the se and cannot have the qin. This qin presides over life and therefore instills joy; the se presides over death and therefore arouses sadness and compassion.

[35] This chapter deals with the time 2253–1049 BCE. Emperor *Yu* says therein: if I want to listen to music, the 5 tones, the 8 modulations, I thus examine my

Dieser Stein war so aufgehängt, wie man es auf der Tafel sieht. In dem *Lo-king-tou* oder Inhaltsverzeichnis der Heiligen Bücher sieht man solche Instrumente, welche zwei Reihen von je acht solcher Steine in Form eines Dreiecks ohne Basis aufgehängt tragen. Man nannte dies *Pieng-king*.

Es gab noch ein zweites viel größeres Instrument, welches man *Ta-king* nannte.

Die Chinesen hatten mehrere Arten Flöten. Die einfachste, *Yo* genannt, hatte nur drei Löcher und wurde wie unsere Flöte quer gehalten.

Die *Tchong* war auch eine Art Pfeife oder Trompete, denn es ist schwer, diese Instrumente richtig zu unterscheiden.

stone was suspended as one sees on the plate. In the *Luojing tu*, or the table of contents for the sacred books, one sees instruments which carry two rows each of eight such suspended stones, [stones] in the form of a triangle without base. This was called *bianqing*.

There was a second, much bigger instrument named *daqing*.

The Chinese had several types of flute. The simplest, named *yue*, had only three holes and was held horizontally like our flute.

The *zhong* was also a type of pipe or trumpet, for it is difficult to distinguish these instruments correctly. It was made

---

tes oder schlechtes Betragen und wünsche, daß man mir die Lieder, die den fünf Tönen adaptirt sind, darbringe. Der Minister, welcher der Musik vorstand, hieß *Kouei*; er sagte: Wenn man die *Ming-kieou* tönen läßt oder die *Kin* oder die *Se* spielt und sie mit Liedern begleitet, so kommen Vater und Großvater (d.h. die Todten nehmen an dem Fest Theil). Der Gast *Yu's* (der verstorbene Kaiser *Tan-tchou*) nimmt seinen Sitz ein, alle Vasallenfürsten nehmen ihren Platz ein; unter den Tönen der Flöten und der kleinen Trommel (*Tao-kou*) beginnen und enden gleichzeitig die *Tchou* (eine Art Shaku Bioshi) und die *Yu* (ebenfalls eine Art Castagnetten). Die Glocken und Orgeln tönen abwechselnd; der *Toang-hoang* (fabelhafter Vogel) schlägt vor Freude mit den Flügeln wenn er die neun Accorde der *Siao Chao* (Taf. XVII, Fig. 6) hört. Wenn ich meinen Stein (*Kieou*) schlage, stark oder schwach, springen die wilden Thiere vor Freude, die Beamtenhäupter stimmen überein.

good or bad conduct and wish that I am presented with the songs which are adapted to the five tones. The Minister who presided over the music was called *Kui*; he said: when one has the *mingjiu* sound, or accompanies the *qin* or the *se* with songs, then come father and grandfather (i.e., the dead take part in the feast). *Yu*'s guest (the deceased Emperor *Tan*) takes his seat; all vassal princes take their seats; amidst the sounding of the flutes and the small drum (*taogu*), begin and end simultaneously the *zhu* (a type of *shakubyōshi*) and the *yu* (likewise a sort of castanet). The bells and the [mouth-]organs sound by turns; the *fenghuang* (mythical bird) beats with its wings for joy, when it hears the nine chords of the *xiaoshao* (Plate XVII, Fig. 6 [p. 252]). When I strike my stone (*qing*), strongly or weakly, the wild animals jump for joy, the heads of the officials are in agreement.

Sie bestand aus Metall, hatte 5 Löcher auf der einen Seite und eins auf der andern.

Dieses selbe Zeichen *Tchong* war der Name eines alten Musikers, der einen Bruder, Namens *Pe*, hatte, der ebenfalls in der Musik bewandert war. Die vereinigten Namen *Tchong-Pe* werden symbolisch, wie *Castor und Pollux* zur Bezeichnung eines Brüderpaars gebraucht.

Die *Tië* war eine andere Flöte, die sich ebenso spielte und 5 Löcher hatte (Taf. XVII, Fig. 4).

Die *Kuon* war eine Doppelflöte; jede der beiden Flöten hatte 6 Löcher (Taf. XVII, Fig. 5).

Die *Tchi* war eine andere Flöte, wie die vorigen aus Schilf gemacht. Es gab deren zwei Sorten; die großen waren 1 Fuß, 4 Zoll lang und maßen 3 Zoll Umfang; die kleinen waren 1 Fuß, 2 Zoll lang. Einige behaupten, daß sie 8 Löcher hatte, andere nur sieben.

Das Instrument Namens *Siao* (Taf. XVII, Fig. 6) bestand aus 23 Pfeifen und war 4 Fuß lang. Es gab ein kleineres Namens *Tchao*, welches nur 16 Pfeifen hatte und 1 Fuß 2 Zoll lang war. Der Ton dieses Instruments, sagt man, glich dem Gesang des *Fong-hoang*[36] und die Form seinen Flügeln.

Das Instrument (Taf. XVII Fig. 7) hieß *Seng* und war eine Art tragbare Orgel von 4 Fuß Höhe; es gab deren zwei Sorten mit 19 und 13 Pfeifen. Man schreibt dessen Erfindung der *Niu-va*,

of metal, had 5 holes on the one side and one on the other.

The same character *Zhong* was the name of an old musician who had a brother named *Bai*, who was likewise versed in music. The names combined, *Zhong-Bai*, were used symbolically, like *Castor and Pollux*, for indicating a pair of brothers.

The *di* was another flute, which was played in the same way, and had 5 holes (Plate XVII, Fig. 4 [p. 252]).

The *guan* was a double flute; each of the two flutes had 6 holes (Plate XVII, Fig. 5 [p. 252]).

The *chi* was another flute, made from reed like the former. There were two kinds; the large were 1 foot 4 inches long and measured 3 inches in circumference; the small were 1 foot 2 inches long. Some maintain that it had 8 holes, others only seven.

The instrument by the name of *xiao* (Plate XVII, Fig. 6 [p. 252]) consisted of 23 pipes and was 4 feet long. There was a smaller one named *zhao* which had only 16 pipes and was 1 foot 2 inches long. The tone of this instrument, it was said, resembled the sound of the *fenghuang*,[36] and the form its wings.

The instrument (Plate XVII, Fig. 7 [p. 252]) is called *sheng* and was a sort of portable organ, 4 feet in height; there were two sorts, with 19 and 13 pipes. Its invention is ascribed to *Nüwa*, wife of

---

[36] Fabelhafter Vogel, der vor dem Drachen das Symbol der Kaiser, später das der Kaiserinnen war und vielfach z. B. im Haar u. dgl. getragen wurde

[36] Mythical bird, which before the dragon was the symbol for the Emperor, later that of the Empress, and was frequently worn, for example, in the hair.

Frau des Fohi, zu und sagt, daß sie dasselbe auf Hügeln und Gewässern spielte und daß es einen sehr zarten Ton hatte.

Die Yu war gleichfalls eine Art Orgel mit 36 Pfeifen von 4 Fuß 2 Zoll Länge.

Die Taoku war eine kleine Trommel (Taf. XVII Fig. 8), deren man sich bei religiösen Feierlichkeiten bediente. Außer ihr hatten die Chinesen noch mehrere andere Trommeln, deren man sich je nach den Geisten oder Göttern, denen man die Feier darbrachte, bediente. Es waren:

Die Feng-ku oder Fuen-ku, die man bei militairischen Expeditionen schlug, sie war 8 Fuß lang und an einem Gerüste aufgehängt.

Die Lui-ku oder Donnertrommel, hatte 8 Flächen, auf die man schlug und wurde bei den Festen für die obern Götter, Chin, benutzt.

Die Lu-ku war eine andere Trommel mit 4 Seiten, deren man sich bei den Festen für die Kuei oder niedern Götter und die Vorfahren bediente.

Die Ling-ku hatte 6 Seiten und diente bei den Festen für die Erde; alle diese Trommeln waren aufgehängt.

Es gab noch mehrere Trommeln, deren man sich im gewöhnlichen Leben bediente und die man trug z.B. die Tongleao, eine Art Tambourin.

Die Tcho (Taf. XVII, Fig. 9) war ein hölzernes, lakkirtes Gefäß, an dessen innere Wände man mit dem Tchi (Fig. 10) schlug, was dann einen Ton gab. Man bediente sich dieses Instruments, wenn man die Musik begann, es war äusserlich

Fuxi, and it is said she played the same on hills and stretches of water and that it had a very delicate sound.

The yu was likewise a type of organ with 36 pipes of 4 feet 2 inches length.

The taogu was a small drum (Plate XVII, Fig. 8 [p. 252]), which would be used for religious festivities. Aside from it, the Chinese had several other drums which were used according to the spirits or gods for whom the feast was presented. They were:

The feng'gu or fen'gu, which was struck on military expeditions; it was 8 feet long and suspended in a frame.

The leigu, or thunder-drum, had 8 surfaces which were struck upon, and was used for feasts for the upper god, shen.

The lugu was another drum with 4 sides, which was used for the feasts of the gui or lower gods, and for the ancestors.

The ling'gu had 6 sides and was used for the feasts of the earth; all these drums were suspended.

There were still other drums which were used in everyday life and which were carried, for example, the tongluo, a type of tambourine.

The zhu (Plate XVII, Fig. 9 [p. 252]) was a wooden lacquered vessel, the inside walls of which were beaten with the qi (Fig. 10), which then produced a sound. This instrument was used when the music began; externally it was 4 feet 2 inches

4 Fuß 2 Zoll groß und innen 1 Fuß, 2 Zoll tief.

Die Yu (Taf. XVII Fig. 11) war ein anderes Instrument, welches einem liegenden lauernden Tiger aus Bronze glich; die Haare seines Rückens waren ziemlich hoch und 27 an der Zahl bildeten[37] eine Art Tasten; man schlug auf dieselben mit einem hölzernen, einen Fuß langen Klöppel, Tchin genannt. Man schlug das Instrument kurz vor dem Schlusse der Musik.

Es gab noch ein Instrument aus gebranntem Thon Namens Hien oder Hiuen, dessen man sich in der alten Musik bediente und dessen Erfindung man dem Fohi zuschreibt. Es glich einer Schale und war mit 6 Öffnungen versehen.

Ein anderes Gefäß, die Ting, das Fohi für die Himmelsopfer (Kino-chen oder Fong-chen) bestimmte, wird von Lo-pi in einer besondern Dissertation besprochen; er sagt, daß dieses Instrument der Anfang der Harmonie ist, denn wenn es die Öffnung nach unten hat, ist es eine Glocke, welche die Basis und das Fundament der Musik ist, hat es dagegen die Öffnung nach oben, so ist es ein Opfergefäß. Die drei Füsse sind das Bild der Dreieinigkeit.

Die Glocke (Taf. XVII Fig. 12) heißt Yong und ist aus Metall. Die Chinese hatten noch eine andere Namens Tchong. Man hing in einem ähnlichen Gestell,

tall, and inside 1 foot, 2 inches deep.

The yu (Plate XVII, Fig. 11 [p. 252]) was another instrument which resembled a crouching, preying tiger made of bronze; the hair on its back was fairly lengthy and 27 in number, and formed[37] a sort of keyboard; these were struck with a one-foot-long wooden beater, named qin. The instrument was struck shortly before the end of the music.

There was another instrument out of fired clay, by the name of xian or xun, which was used in the old music and whose invention is attributed to Fuxi. It resembled a bowl and was equipped with 6 openings.

Another vessel, the ting, which Fuxi assigned for the Heavenly Offering (jiaoshen or fengshen), is discussed by Luo Bi in a separate dissertation; he says that this instrument is the beginning of harmony, for when it has the opening facing downwards it is a bell, which is the basis and the fundamental of music; if, however, it has the opening facing upwards then it is an offering vessel. The three feet are the image of the Trinity.

The bell (Plate XVII, Fig. 12 [p. 252]) is called called yong and is of metal. The Chinese had another by the name of zhong. Two rows each of eight bells were sus-

---

[37] Diese Lesart differirt von der, welche ich oben bei den buddhistischen Instrumenten gegeben; ich halte aber die meinige für die richtige, weil sie jetzt noch üblich ist und auch der Abbildung mehr entspricht.– DER VERFASSER.

[37] This reading differs from that which I gave above (p. 223) for the Buddhist instruments; I consider mine correct, however, because it is still common and also better matches the illustration. –The Author.

wie das Fig. zwei Reihen von je acht kleinen Glocken auf. Dies Instrument hieß Pientchong.

Po war eine Art Schelle. Eine andere Art Glöckchen befestigten sie an den Trommeln; es gab deren mehrere Sorten, Tcho, Chao, und To.

Die Klöppel der Glocken hiessen Che, die Zunge, die Glocken mit hölzernem Klöppel hießen Moto, die mit metallenem Kin-to.

Ich bemerke noch, daß merkwürdigerweise im Chu-king überall die Glocke als das Urinstrument betrachtet wird. Ling-lung nahm im Thale Hiai-ki ein Stück Schilf, machte Löcher hinein und blies hinein, um die Töne der Glocke nachzumachen. Er unterschied die verschiedenen Töne der Musik, von denen 6 Liu und 6 Lu hießen; mit diesen Tönen ahmte er den Gesang des Fonghoang nach.- Der Minister Yong-yueng erfand 12 Glocken im Verhältniß zu den 12 Monden; da stimmten die 5 Töne überein, die Jahreszeiten wurden abgetheilt.

Von Kiu (1900 v. Ch.) wird gesagt, daß er westliche Musik machte, wie? wird nicht angegeben.

pended in a frame similar to the Figure. This instrument was called bian zhong.

Bo was a type of slit-bell. Another type of little bell was attached to the drums; there were several sorts, zhuo, zhao, and duo.

The beaters for the bells were called she (the tongue); the bells with wooden beaters were called muduo; those with metal ones, jinduo.

I note further, that, curiously, everywhere in the Shujing the bell is considered as the Ur-instrument. Ling Lun, in the valley of Xiexi took a piece of reed, made holes in it, and blew into it to copy the notes of the bell. He differentiated the different notes of music, 6 of which were called lü, and 6 lü;[38] with these notes he imitated the song of the fenghuang. Minister Xuan Yuan invented 12 bells in relation to the 12 months; there the 5 notes were in agreement, the seasons of the year were partitioned.

It is said of Kui (1900 BCE) that he made Western music. How, is not indicated.

[38] These are written 律 and 吕, respectively. – Ed.

The layout of transnotation on the following pages follows Müller's intent. It rearranges his recto—verso—recto pages so as to read the landscape-format score here over verso—recto—verso pages. It begins over two pages, finishing overleaf with one. – Ed.

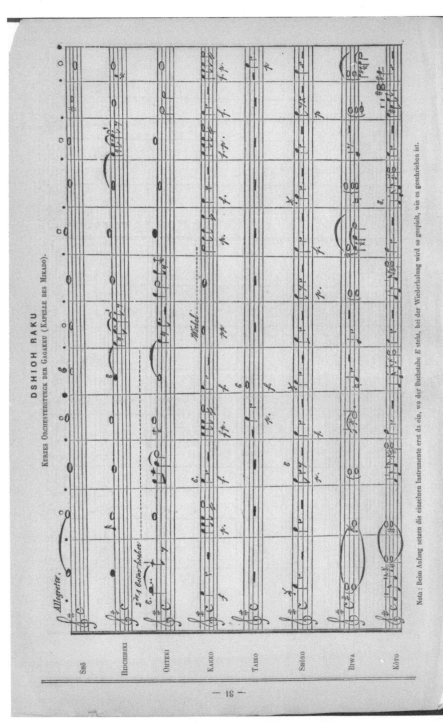

Transnotation: Goshōraku-no-kyū (1)

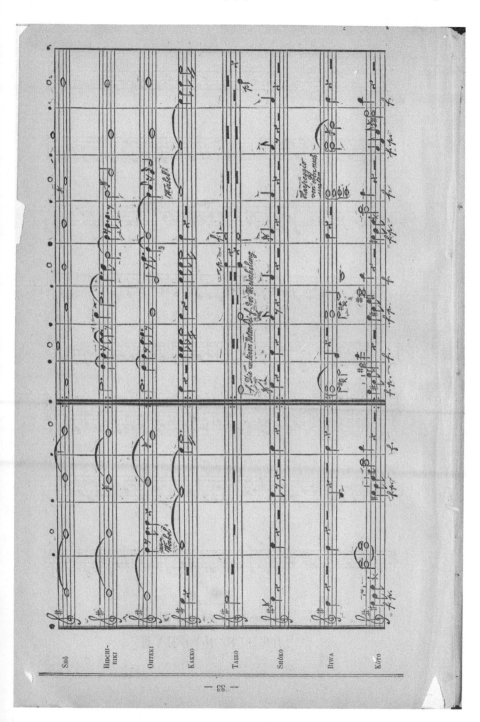

Transnotation: Goshōraku-no-kyū (2)

Transnotation: Goshōraku-no-kyū (3)

MANPAN RIUSUI.

Gespielt auf zwei Geking.

– Transcription 2: Manban liushui –

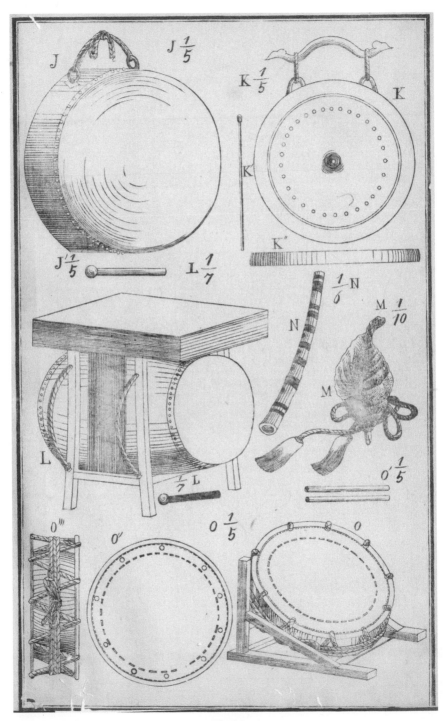

– Tafel/Plate XI –

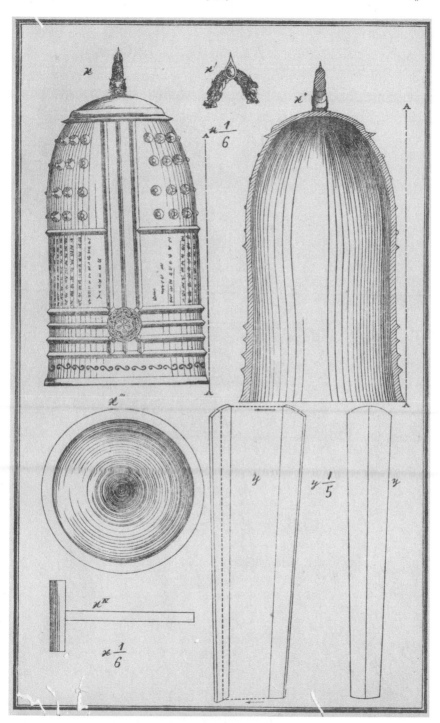

– Tafel/Plate XII –

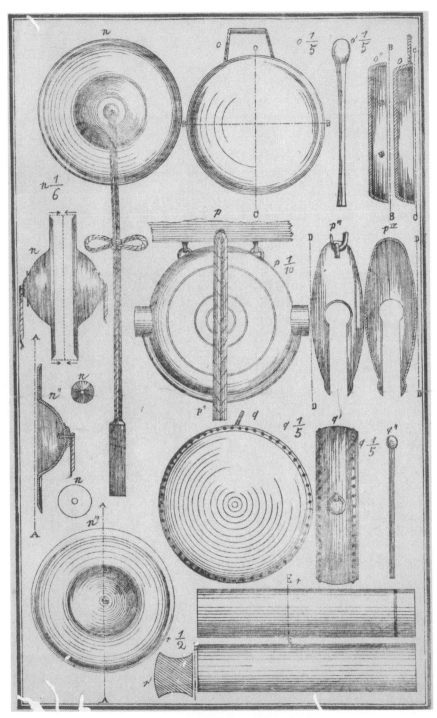

– Tafel/Plate XIII –

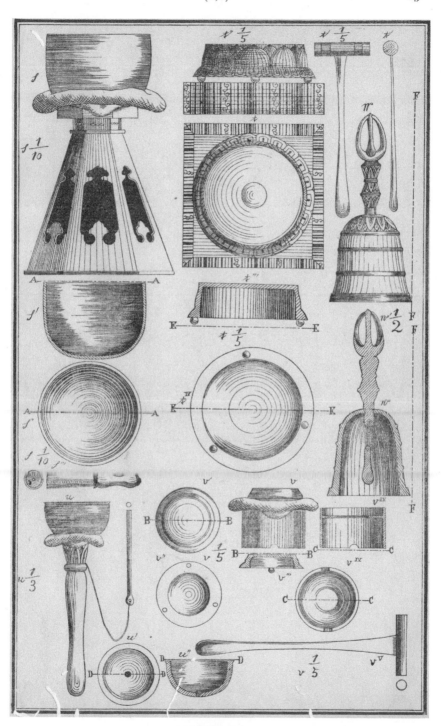

– Tafel/Plate XIV –

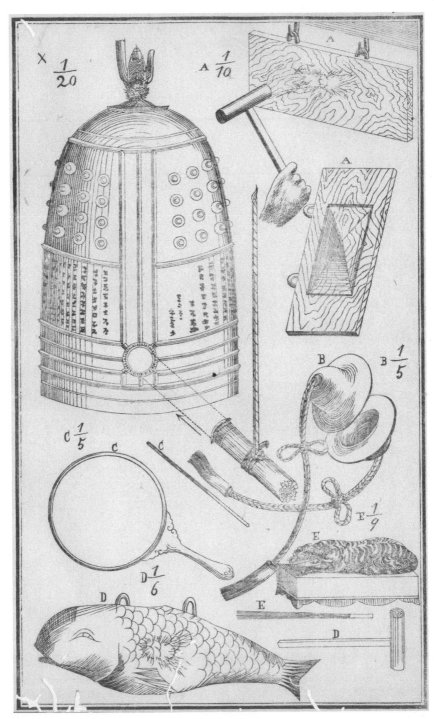

– Tafel/Plate XV –

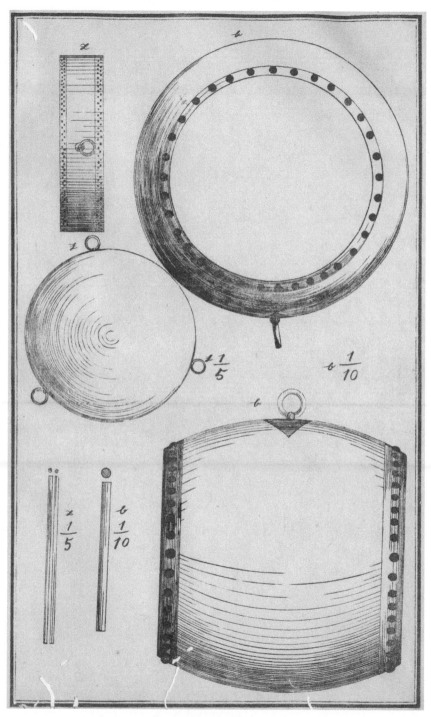

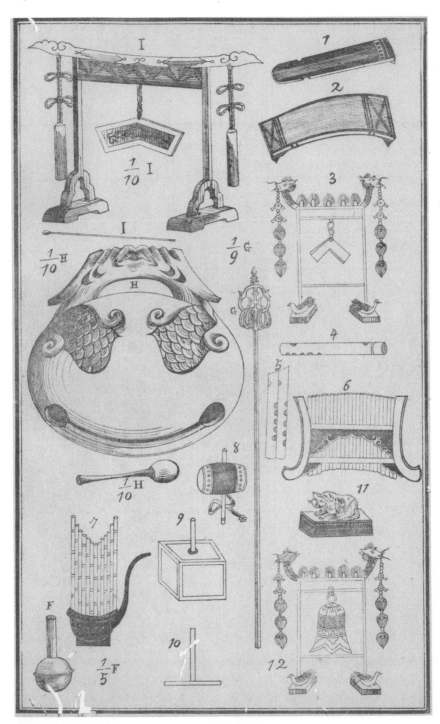

– Tafel/Plate XVII –

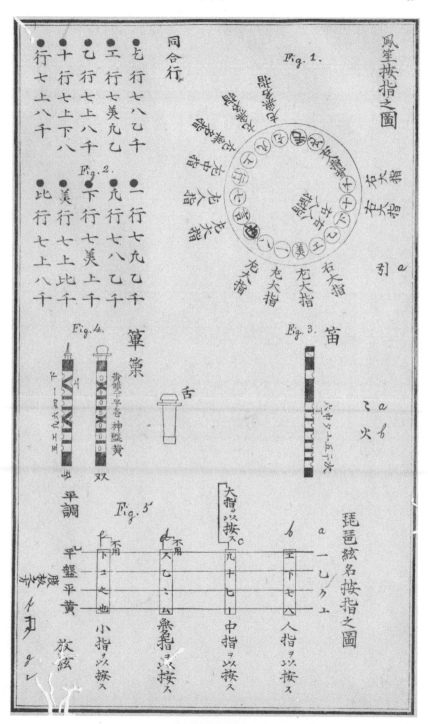

Fig. 1.

Fig. 2.

Fig. 3. 笛

Fig. 4. 篳篥

Fig. 5.

鳳笙按指之圖

琵琶絃名按指之圖

– Tafel/Plate XVIII –

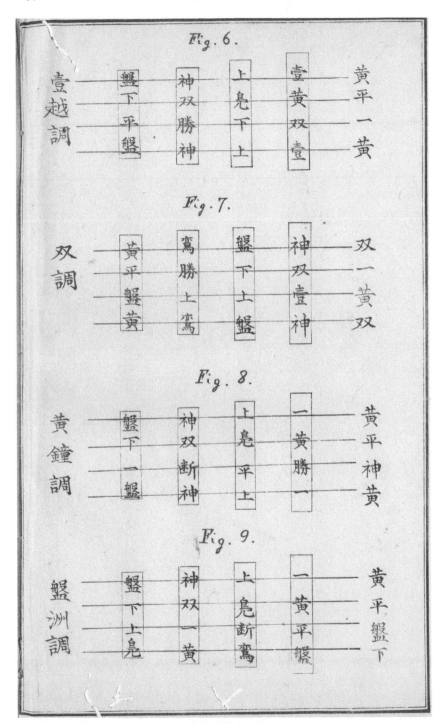

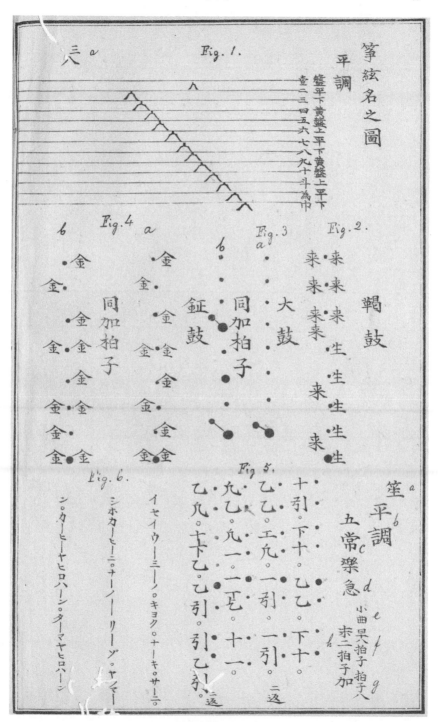

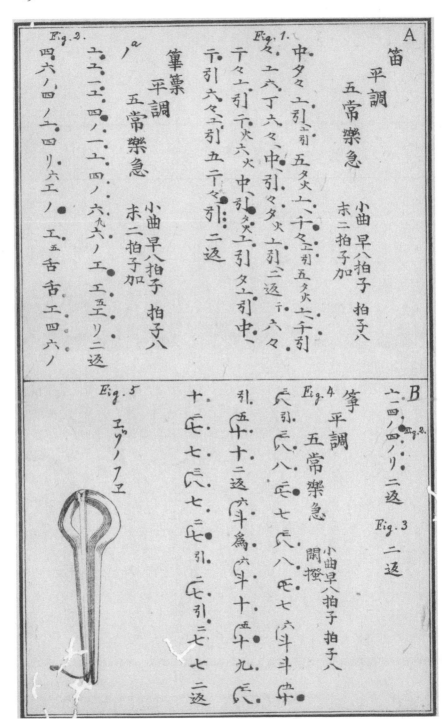

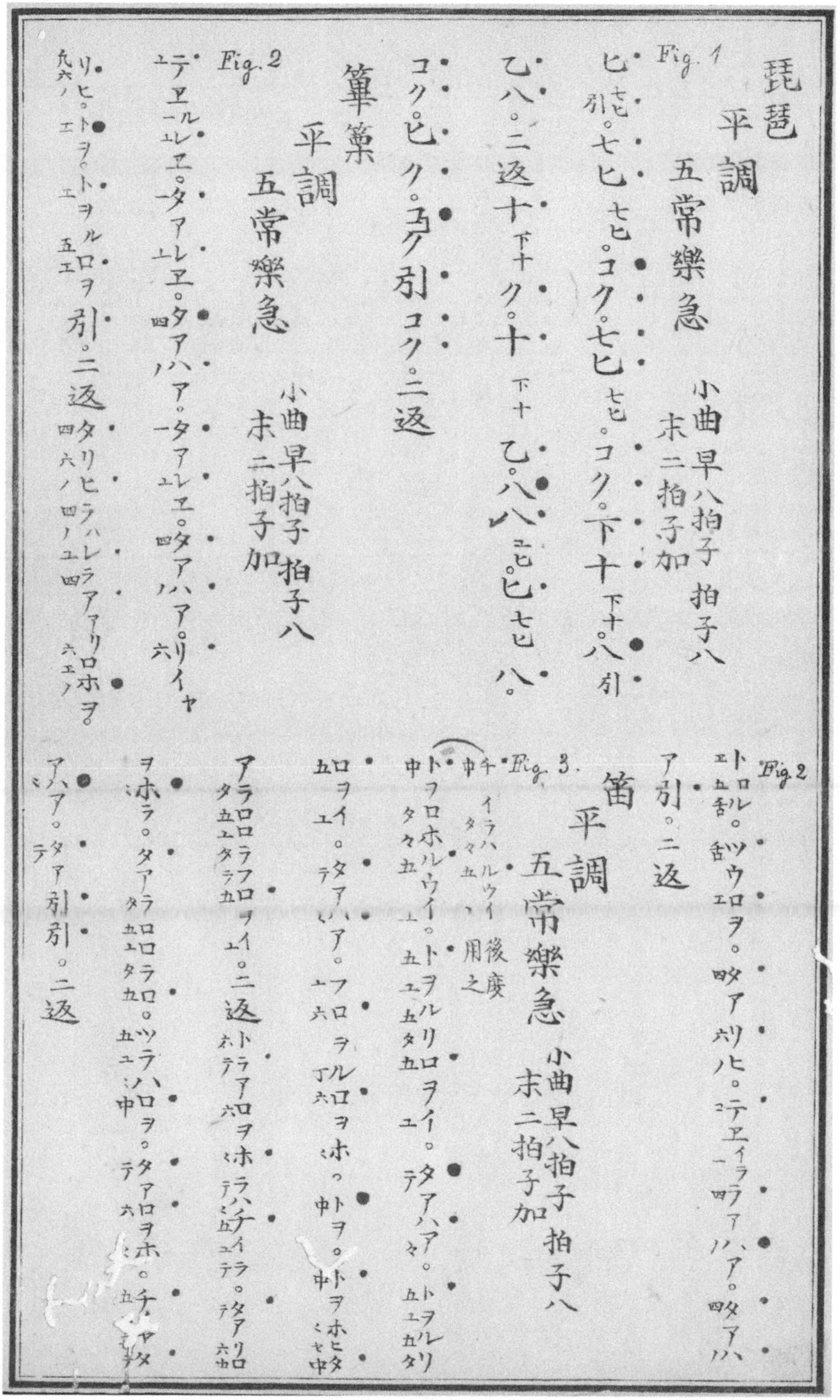

琵琶

平調

五常樂急　小曲早八拍子　拍子八
　　　　　　末二拍子加

Fig. 1

ヒ𛀙。七ヒ。コク。七ヒ。コク。下十下八引
乙八。二返十下ク。十　下十　乙八八七ヒ七ヒ。八。

コク。ヒ　ク。ユク引コク。二返

篳篥

平調

五常樂急　小曲早八拍子　拍子八
　　　　　　末二拍子加

Fig. 2

テヱルレヱ。タアレヱ。タアハア。タアヱレヱ。四ハ
ユ　四ノ　　タアハア。タアリイ。ャ
タリヒラハレラ　アアリロホヲ
リ。ヒ。トヲ。トヲルロヲ　別。二返
九六八　エ　五エ　　四六八四ユ四　六エノ

ア別。二返

Fig. 3

笛

平調

五常樂急　小曲早八拍子　拍子八
　　　　　　末二拍子加

Fig. 2

ア別。二返

– Tafel/Plate XXI –

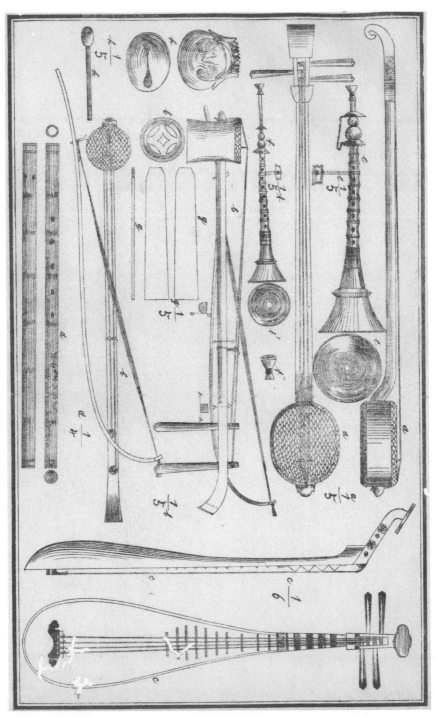

− Tafel/Plate XXII −

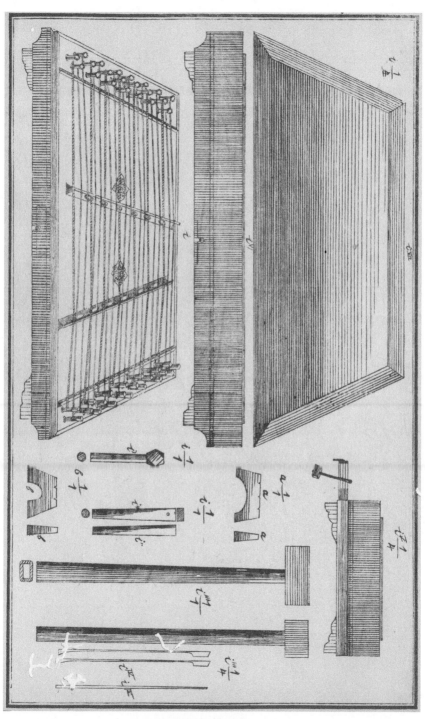

– Tafel/Plate XXIII –

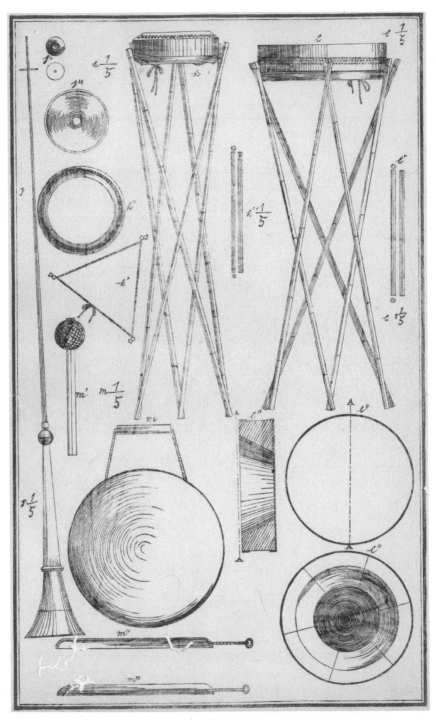

– Tafel/Plate XXIV –

SAIBARA.

(Japanisches Lied, UTA.*)*

———

イゼイウーミーノ。キョキ。ナーキ。サーニ。
シホカーヒーニ。ナーノーリーゾ。ヤッ
マーシ。カーヒーヤヒロハーシ。ターマヤ
ヒロハーシ

— Saibara: Ise no umi —

1876

第8号からの続き、完結編

私はまず、名誉ある読者のみなさんにお詫びしなければならい。というのも、以前におかした間違いをまず修正することから文章を始めなければならないと思われるからである。しかし、およそ誰でも、このような場所でこのような物事に関する研究をする時は途方もない困難さに直面するものであり、私が多少不正確なものを発表してしまったとしても、それは仕方がないことである。ふつう情報をくれる人々というのは、彼ら自身が物事に関して曖昧な、一面的な知識しか持っていないので、たくさんの記述を比べ、自分で観察を行わないと、何らかの確固とした結果にたどり着くことはできない。私はまちがいなく専門の音楽家ではなく、このまったく知られていない分野の研究のきっかけとなるためだけに、この連続エッセイを書いている。道を開くため、ではあるが、完璧で完結したものを述べるなどという野心はない。

まず始めに、私は和琴の歴史について間違いを忍びこませてしまった。女帝はジンゴ・コク [神功皇后] と言い、彼女のもとに6つの弓が集められた。6つの弓を集めさせた将軍はタケノ・ウチノ・スクネ [竹内宿禰] という。戦士の名前は不明である。

私はここでもう少し歴史に関するメモを付け加える。それは、高名な日本の学者であり考古学者であるニナガワ [蜷川] 氏が提供してくれたものである。

日本における和琴の歴史は約1500年、神楽笛と琵琶は1200年、「ムスメノコト」[13絃の [雅楽の] 箏ノコトと絃の太さだけが違う] は500年、三味線は300年、コキン [胡琴]38 は160年である。笏拍子の正確な起源は次のようなものである。貴族たちは昔、天皇の前に出る時、平らで長い決まった形の板を胸の前に両手で持たなければならなかった。これを笏という。メモを書き留めたり、名前を呼ぶなどの機会に使われていたということである。使われているうちに、縦長に2枚に切断されして、拍 (拍子)39 をとるために使われるようになった。切断された2枚の木片はまた、認証、身分証、通行証などとしても機能した。笏を持つという風習は今日もあり、日本で宮廷に行く時の服装はいつもそうである。同様の習慣は中国でも古くからあった。紀元前2000年以前にすでに言及されている。神聖な本『シュキン [詩経]』によると、皇帝の御前では諸侯たちは畏まって顔を隠す、とのことである。中国では「クイ」と呼ばれ、位階ごとに様々な形があり、それぞれ違った紋章で飾られる。皇帝用には3種類あり、臣下に拝謁する時は笏で顔を隠す。一番大きなものは、長さ3フィートのものである。2042年には、諸侯は黒いクイを持って宮廷に参内し、大

---

38 (日本語訳者補注) 胡弓のことか。

39 手で拍子をとることを「手拍子」といい、足でとることを「足拍子」と言う。hの音は濁ってbになる。「濁り」とは純粋でない、という意味だが、単語の結合による子音の音変化を意味する。「ふえ」は複合形では「ぶえ」に変わるのと同様である。和琴は「わごん」ではなく「わんごん」と発音される。

洪水に対する民衆の恐怖を知らせた。最後に、私は、おおいなる古代の骨董品とし
てイシブエ (石笛) があると聞いた。それについては、最近まで江戸のある寺に遺品
があった。しかし、知らないうちになくなってしまったので、私自身でもう見るこ
とはできず、おおよその記述を入手することしかできなかった。それによると、そ
の楽器はフルートと言うよりはクラリネットのように見え、2 フィートくらいの長
さで、厚みは 4-5 インチである。1 個の石からできていて、大砲の砲身のように中
空である。開いた口の一端は、管のように斜めに鋭く削られていて、そこに向かっ
て息を吹き込むように吹き口が作られている。筒の脇には、いくつかの指孔がつい
ている。

    (前に) 調べた笙の管の配置は不正確であった。むしろ以下の様な順番である。

第 1 管	f♯'''
第 2 管	g''
第 3 管	f♯''
第 4 管	e''
第 5 管	c♯''
第 6 管	g♯'
第 7 管	b'
第 8 管	e'''
第 9 管	無音
第 10 管	c♯'''
第 11 管	b''
第 12 管	a''
第 13 管	d'''
第 14 管	d''' [d'']
第 15 管	a'
第 16 管	無音
第 17 管	c'' [c''']

    第 5 管は、左ではなく右手の親指で閉じる。第 14 と 15 管には時々右手の中指
または薬指が使われる。調律についても 2、3 誤りがある。第 8 号 42 頁 (p. 147) の黄
鐘調子の調律については、第 3 絃の月 ＝ 7 月でなければならない。第 7 と 12 絃は、
4 月 g♭ではなく、5 月 g と書かれなければならない。44 頁 (p. 155) の琴ノコトの調絃
は、以下のように修正されなければならない。

第 1 絃	a
第 2 絃	b
第 3 絃	d'
第 4 絃	e'
第 5 絃	g♭'

第 6 絃　　a′
第 7 絃　　b′

　私はここで、雅楽についてもっと詳しく、その楽器や楽譜などについて述べる。
　雅楽は、すでに以前に述べたように、国家制度であり、その制度の中で、朝鮮
から輸入された当初から、教養を必要とする神聖な音楽が保護され伝承されてきた。
雅楽にだけ、朝鮮と中国ではまったく失われてしまった古い音楽が残っており、そ
れゆえ、今日この驚くべき音楽に関する情報を集めることができるほとんど唯一の
場所になっている。しかし、ここでもまた、若い音楽家たちの間で新しいものへの
傾斜が始まっていて、何人かはヨーロッパの影響下にある。ゆえに、何にも増して
望まれることは、本当に古いものをできる限り早く見極めることである。
　雅楽の教師は国家に雇われていて、外部では教習しない。生徒は現在 40 人であ
る。ここでは古い楽曲ばかりが教習される。いくつかは歌である。以前は、全部で
はないが大部分に歌がついていた。しかし不思議なことに、多くの場合、失われた
のは歌、というか歌詞である。歌 |の旋律| は笙と同音であるとすれば、かくして、
旋律は器楽合奏の中に残ることになったのである。雅楽で演奏される最も新しい楽
曲でも、500 年の歴史がある。
　教習は以下のような方法で行われる。生徒たちは家で、旋律の音符と輪郭をカ
タカナ記号で暗記して学ばなければならない〔以下の Taf. 21, Figs. 2, 3 参照〕。その後
初めて楽器を手に取り、個々の楽曲の演奏の仕方を学ぶ。演奏は常に暗譜である。
この教習方法から容易にわかるのは、練習は機械的な訓練でしかなく、雅楽におい
てさえ、自分たちの芸術について何らかの説明ができる立場にいる音楽家はわずか
しかいない、ということだろう。
　就中、興味を引かれるのは、そこで保存されている非常に古く貴重な楽器であ
る。私はそれらの古さを信用している。というのも、すでに古い調子笛の時に述べ
たように、これらの古楽器は太古から特別に定められた保護者の手に、聖なる遺物
として委ねられて来たからである。それらはすべて高価な漆塗りで、紋章で飾られ、
絹の袋入りで、何重にも箱に入っている。ほとんど未使用で、細心の注意を払って
管理されて来た。
　オーケストラの構成に関係してはさまざまな組み合わせが可能だが、以下のよ
うな要素がある。

1.　人間の声。笏拍子で拍子をとりながら独唱するか、オーケストラと一緒に数
　　人の歌い手が斉唱する。しかし、笏拍子のみで、他の打楽器は省略される。
　　声はいつも笙の伴奏と一緒のユニゾンである。非常に不快なのは、つねに支
　　配的な押しつぶしたような咽声や、調子はずれのトリルのような声である
　　〔動物の囀き声と呼びたい〕。要するに、我々にとってはこれらの歌を聞くの

は苦痛であるが、日本人にとってはとても美しいと感じられるのである[40]歌は、純粋な日本の楽曲、たとえば催馬楽 (Taf. XIX, Fig. 6) にしかない。楽曲は歌いだしによって曲名が名付けられている。中国と朝鮮の楽曲 [唐楽と高麗楽] には歌はない。催馬楽はカタカナ文字によって図に示されていて、容易に解読することができるが、音は記されていない。

2. 笙。本来旋律を受け持つ。中国の楽曲では、我々にとってはまったく不可能な和音が演奏される [下記参照]。日本の楽曲ではつねに単音が吹かれる。

3. 篳篥。すでに述べたが、我々の好みからすると、その叫ぶような調子外れの音は、それがなければ美しいはずの作品を、台無しにしている。

4. 横笛は充分許容範囲の響きであるが、しばしば調子外れに吹かれるフルートである。

この3つの楽器は合奏では同じ数ずつ参加する。大編成ではそれぞれの楽器が5管かそれ以上ずつ含まれ、横笛の数 (当然、笙と篳篥も同じ数だけ含まれる) で、たとえば「五管通り」などと、合奏が呼ばれるのである。「五管通り」では、管楽器それぞれ5つ、絃楽器はそれぞれ2つ、打楽器はそれぞれ1つ含まれる。

5. 琵琶は小節の出だしだけで弾かれる。つまりバチで絃を素早く掻き鳴らすのである。しばしば1絃だけ弾かれることもある。琵琶は我々のギターと似ているが、たいへん頑丈な木で作られている。そのため非常に重いが、よく通る音がする。

6. 箏もまた琵琶とともに小節の出だしを明示するが、装飾するという役割も持っている。楽曲全体を通してこの装飾がつねに同じ性質を持っていることは、[付属の] 雅楽曲の譜例に見える通りである。

これらの2つの楽器は、最も朗々とした心地よい響きを持っているので、笙のように、きっとヨーロッパでも大いに気に入られるだろう。

7. 和琴は非常に例外的な場合のみ、はるかに豊かな [音色と音域を持つ] 箏の代わりに使われることがある。

8. 鞨鼓は、理論的には基音と同音に調律されるべきである。たとえば例にあげた楽曲では e である。しかし実践ではこれは実行されたことはない。8種類の打ち方があるが、最も日常的なものは譜例に出てくる3種類である。

---

[40] 私はついこの間、いかに我々の音楽が日本人に気に入らないかについて納得する機会があった。江戸に、本当にすばらしいイタリアのコロラトゥーラ歌手が2、3人ほどいたのだが、コンサートの後で、ある非常に教養のある日本人に感想を尋ねてみると、彼は、結局、美しく荘重な日本の歌のほうがずっと心地よい、と言ったのである。

9. 太鼓には特別な調律はまったくない。太鼓は大きな音がして、それを活か
   して、多くの場合、我々の大きなティンパニーの代替になり得る。特に、ス
   ペースの節約や、太鼓が備えている優美さのゆえに劇場にふさわしい。太
   鼓には 10 種類の打ち方があるが、主に弱音/強音の両手の二重音と結びつい
   て、2、4、8 小節の出だし等に打つ。私はある楽曲を聴いたが、そこでは、
   他の楽器が演奏している間、ずっと太鼓と鞨鼓が二重奏をしていた。鞨鼓は
   太鼓に対して 5 度上の音程であった。リズムは以下の通りであった。

41

日本や中国の太鼓、ティンパニーで、革の上に紐が走っているものはない。

10. 鉦鼓には特別な調律はない。非常に弱い音なので、そのリズムを調べるに
    は、私はまだそのそばに座ったことがないので、耳ではなく、目を頼りにし
    なければならないだろう。

これら 3 つの楽器では、左手のバチをメバチ [雌桴] といい、女性的という意味
である。鞨鼓の連打 [トレモロ＝「来 (らい)」] を除いて、いつもピアノ [小さい音
量] で、もしくは、前打音として使われる。右はオバチ [雄桴] といい、男性的[42] と
いう意味で、独立した硬い、力強い音で打たれる。

11. 腰鼓 (Taf. VI, Fig. 17) は朝鮮の楽曲 [高麗楽] に用いられ、儀式的な行列 [道行]
    の時にも用いられる。

12. 笏拍子 (Taf. XII, Fig. y、訂正版) は、歌のついている楽曲のために、上記の 3
    つの打楽器の代わりに、特別に使われる。

すでに示した通り、今述べたことは、ほとんど中国と朝鮮の楽曲ばかり演奏す
る雅楽にのみ当てはまることである。日本固有の古い楽曲は、ちょうど能の仕舞に
見られるように、神楽笛、和琴、笏拍子だけを要し、歌が付いている。私は、かつ
て一度だけこの種の音楽をじっくりと学ぶ機会があった。男性と女性がゆっくりし
た単調なユニゾンの歌を歌い、男性が小節の頭ごとに笏拍子を打ち合わせた。拍子
の終わりは、いつもスフォルサァンドによって音が突然終わった。神楽笛は調子は
ずれの音で、だいたいユニゾンで伴奏していた。和琴はなかったが、次のように用
いられたはずである。演奏者は、最初の拍ですべての絃をコトサギ [琴軋] で一気に

---

[41] (日本語訳者補注)「陵王乱序」と思われる。
[42] 単語の前後につく「お」と「め」という音節は、常に「男の」と「女の」という意味がある。「バ
チ」は絃楽器と打楽器を弾く/打つもののことを言う。

掻き鳴らし、ただちに左手の5本の指で5つの絃の音を止め、声と同じ [高さの] 音に調絃された6つ目の音だけが響き続けるようにする。

　雅楽にまた戻ってみよう。上に掲げた楽器はさまざまな方法で組み合わせることができる。たとえば、私は笙と太鼓の楽譜集を持っている。この号に紹介した「五常楽」以外の楽曲についても、その [合奏] 構成についてより詳しく研究する機会を得たが、以下のようなパートを持っていた。

　最初の楽曲は2人の歌い手がおり、主唱者が笏拍子を打った。

　そして篳篥1人、横笛1人がユニゾンで加わる。毎回笏拍子と同時に琵琶2面が加わる。筝2面は拍を示し、装飾する。

　第2曲目。笙、横笛、篳篥は各3。琵琶、筝、太鼓、鞨鼓、鉦鼓は各1。

　第3曲目。管楽器各6人、絃楽器各3人、打楽器各1人、計27人編成。楽曲は3つの主要楽器奏者、すなわち篳篥1人、琵琶1人、筝3人で終った。

　これらの楽曲ではみな5度のあとに基音が来て終るが、同種の楽器は完全にユニゾンであった。昔は時たま違うことを吹いたと言われているが、今はそのようなことはない。

　楽器の配置は決まった法則に縛られているわけではない。小編成の正式演奏の時は、同種の楽器が一緒に座っているのを見た。雅楽の大規模な演奏の時は、オーケストラは蹄鉄型に座り、その開いた側に我々聴衆が座る。同種の楽器の演奏者は、互いに見えて、よく注意が払えるように座る。

　楽長もしくは指揮者はいない。せいぜい、笏拍子がある楽曲では、その演奏者が拍子をとる人として指揮者と見なせるかもしれない。その他では、一同は単純に主たる楽器に従う。そこでは、彼らはどの音から [合奏に] 加わるのかを正確に知っている。つまり、同種の楽器のチームワークが並外れて正確なのである。

　すべての音楽家はいつも暗譜で演奏する。総譜はなく、ただ個々の楽器のパート譜があるのみである。しかし私が前に言ったように、演奏者たちはみずから適切な楽譜を持つことがどうしても必要だったわけではない。むしろ、彼らはまず機械的に耳で聴き取ることと簡単な音声記号によって自分のパートを暗記し、そのあと実際の演奏の仕方を習うのである。

　ここで、それぞれの楽器の個々の音の記号について、もう少し詳しく見て行くことにしよう。

1. 笙 (Taf. XVIII, Fig. 1)。図では、各記号がちょうど良い輪の中に示されている。Taf. X, Fig. 39 に示されている各管の番号に従うと、その関係は以下のようになる。

| 第1管 | セン [千] という。 | 4月に属し西洋の | ♯''' になる。 |
| 第2管 | ジュウ [十] | 5月 | g'' |

（1876）

第3管	ゲ [下]	4月	f♯''
第4管	オツ [乙]	2月	e''
第5管	ク [工]	11月	c♯''
第6管	ビ [美]	6月	g♯''
第7管	イチ [一]	9月	b'
第8管	ハチ [八]	2月	e'''
第9管	ヤ [也]	無音	
第10管	ゴン [言]	11月	c♯'''
第11管	シチ [七]	9月	b''
第12管	ギョウ [行]	7月	a''
第13管	ジョウ [上]	12月	d'''
第14管	ボウ [凡]	12月	d''
第15管	コツ [乞]	7月	a'
第16管	モウ [毛]	無音	
第17管	ヒ [比]	10月	c''[43]

新しいパリの音叉と比較し、音は修正されている。

日本の楽曲では単純に表示されている音が吹かれるが、中国の楽曲 [唐楽] では5または6音の和音が吹かれる。以下の表になる (Taf. XVIII, Fig. 2)。

a'	[乞] は	a'', b'', e''', b'[44] f♯''' を含む
c♯''	[工]	a'', b'', g♯'', d'', e''
e''	[乙]	a'', b'', d''', e''', f♯''
g''	[十]	a'', b'', d'', f♯''[45]
a''	[行]	b'', d''', e''', f♯'''
b'	[ ]	a'', b'', d'', e'', f♯''
d''	[凡]	a'', b'', e''', e'', f♯''
f♯''	[下]	a'', b'', g♯'', d''', f♯'''
g♯''	[美]	a'', b'', d''', c''', f♯'''
c''	[比]	a'', b'', d''', e''', f♯'''

何らかの法則によってこれらのいわゆる和音は決まっているのだが、私はまだそれを究明できていない。おそらく計算によって発見できるだろう。私は最初、主音と、これらの隣り合う音から1つまたは2つの音をとるのだと思ったが、ある演奏者が断言し、演奏してくれたことによれば、その反対

---

43 (日本語訳者補注) 比は正しくは c''' とするべき。以下の和音の説明においても同様。
44 (日本語訳者補注) この b' は正しくは e''。
45 (日本語訳者補注) 十の和音 (合竹) は正しくは a'', b'', d''', f♯'', e'''。

に、6つの音を同時に吹くのである。しかし、私に同行してくれた音楽に
詣が深い2人の紳士と同様に、私はこれらの音にほとんど不協和音を聞きと
ることができなかった。よって私は、それらの [不協和] 音は、協和音によっ
て消されてしまうと考えるべきだろう。そのようなことは合奏では容易に起
こりうる。というのも、合奏では主たる音は他の楽器によって保たれるから
だ。「引 (ひく)」の記号 (Taf. XVIII, Fig. 1a) は、次の小節まで音を長く延ばす
ことを意味している。赤線で2音を結ぶ場合は、最初の音が装飾音であるこ
とを示す。

2. 篳篥 (Taf. XVIII, Fig. 4)。この楽器では単に開けるべき孔の記号を書く。以下
は中国名である。記号を正しく読むためには、自分の前に図を置き、舌を右
に、7つの指孔が上に、1つは下に来るようにする。そして、右から左へ数
える。

第1孔	ゲ	[下]	7月 = a″
裏	ジョウ	[上]	6月 = g″
第2孔	イチ [イツ]	[一]	4月 = f#″
第3孔	シ	[四]	2月 = e″
第4孔	ロク [リク]	[六]	12月 = d″
第5孔	ボウ [ハン]	[凡]	10月 = c″
第6孔	ク [コウ]	[工]	9月 = b′
第7孔	ゴ	[五]	7月 (下がった) = ab′
全部閉孔	ゼツ	[舌]	6月 = g′

2つの音符が上下に接近している場合は、短い装飾音を意味している。篳篥
の (Taf. XX, Fig. 2a) の記号 [〃]「ウツ [打]」は、指で短く叩くことを意味し
ている。

3. 横笛 (Taf. XVIII, Fig. 3) は篳篥とよく似た記譜法である。ここでもまた開ける
べき孔の記号が示されている。

第1孔	ロク	[六]	12月 = d″
第2孔	チュウ	[中]	9月 = b′
第3孔	サク⁴⁶	[夕]	7月 = a′
第4孔	ジョウ	[上]	6月 = g′
第5孔	ゴ	[五]	4月 = f#′
第6孔	カン	[テ]	2月 = e′
第7孔	シ	[次]	1月 = d#′

---

46 (日本語訳者補注) 現在では「シャク」と発音する。

第1と第2孔の間には、さらに「ゲ [下 (丁)]」という記号があり、10月 (c'') に一致し、第1と第3孔は開け、第2孔を閉じるとその音が出る。

以前すでに述べたように、各孔は息の吹き込みによって3オクターヴ出すことができるが、演奏者の好みによってどのオクターヴを吹くか、あるいは、例に示した楽曲の初回の吹き方のように、あらかじめ規定された通りに吹くかのどちらかになる。[47]

横笛のその他の記号は、

(a) ウツ [打] (Taf. XVIII, Fig. 3a) は指で素早く叩くことを意味する。

(b) ヒク [引] (延ばす、Taf. XVIII, Fig. 1a) は音が長く保たれることを示す。

(c) カ [火] (火、Taf. XVIII, Fig. 3b) は次の音へ素早く移ることを意味する。装飾音の一種。

4. 鞨鼓 (Taf. XIX, Fig. 2) では、通常、記譜のために真ん中に赤い点が書かれる。上部の7つの記号は連打「ライ [来]」で、読者から見て点の右側にある記号は右手で、左にある記号は左手で打たれる。

最初の3つの点は、3つ目の点のうしろまで両手で連打 [「諸来 (もろらい)」] を打つ。同様に5つ目と7つ目の点の後は連打を左手だけで打つ。「来」は、始めはゆっくり、先に行くに従って加速する。

4つ目の点の右には、短く打つ「セイ [生 (正)]」の記号がある。「生」と「来」の強さと速さによって、8種類の異なるリズムパタンを作る。それらには特別な名前は付いていないが、楽曲の性質や伝統、それに演奏者の好みによって名付けられることがある。

5. 太鼓 (Taf. XIX, Fig. 3) の打点は大きな赤い点で示され、2種類ある。

第一に、線で結ばれた赤い2つの点がある。左の方が少し小さく、より高い位置にある。左の点は左手の女性的な拍 [雌桴] で、半小節早く打たれる。右のより大きな点は右手の男性的な拍 [雄桴] で、小節の1拍目に強く打たれる。

第二に、独立した点は、雄桴で強く打つのみで、雌桴の前打音は伴わない。

6. 笏拍子も太鼓と同様に大きい点で表されるが、赤でなく黒点である。

7. 鉦鼓の記号は「キン [金]」(Taf. XIX, Fig. 4) といい、鞨鼓と同様に点の右と左に書かれるが、[太鼓の] 強い雄桴か弱い雌桴のどちらが使われるかによる。連打 [来] などは鉦鼓にはない。点の両側に記号があるところで、雌桴が短く弱く前打音で打たれる。

---

[47] (日本語訳者補注) Taf. XXI, Fig. 3 の「五常楽急」のことを指すと思われる。「五常楽急」冒頭の龍笛は、初回は低い音域、2回目はその1オクターヴ上の音域で演奏される。

8. 琵琶は調子によってさまざまな記号がある (Taf. XVIII, Fig. 5 と Taf. XVIIIa, Figs. 6–9)。名前と記号は以下の通り。

平調
二月, *e* 基音; Tafel XVIII Fig. 5.[48]

絃	1	2	3	4
開放絃	一 二月 *e*	凵 九月 *b*	ク 二月 *e′*	上 七月 *a′*
第1柱	工 四月 *g♭–f♯*	下 十一月 *d♭′–c♯′*	七 四月 *g♭′–f♯′*	八 九月 *b′*
第2柱	几 五月 *g*	十 十二月 *d′*	ヒ 五月 *g′*	丨 十月 *c″*
第3柱	フ 六月 • *a♭–g♯*	乙 一月 • *d♯′–e♭′*	ミ 六月 • *a♭′–g♯′*	ム 十一月 • *d♭″–c♯″*
第4柱	斗 七月 *a*	ユ 二月 *e′*	之 七月 *a′*	也 十二月 *d″*

点 (•) のついた音は演奏には使用されない。

壱越調
十二月, *d* 基音; Tafel XVIIIa Fig. 6.[49]

絃	1	2	3	4
開放絃	七月 *a*	十二月 *d*	二月 *e*	七月 *a*
第1絃	九月 *b*	二月 *e*	四月 *g♭–f♯*	九月 *b*
第2柱	十月 • *c*	三月 • *f*	五月 • *g*	十月 • *c*
第3柱	十一月 • *d♭–c♯*	四月 *g♭–f♯*	六月 • *a♭–g♯*	十一月 • *d♭–c♯*
第4柱	十二月 • *d*	五月 • *g*	七月 *a*	十二月 *d*

48 P. 253
49 P. 254

雙調

五月, g または a♭ 基音; Tafel XVIIIa Fig. 7.[50]

絃	1	2	3	4
開放絃	五月 g	七月 a	十二月 d'	五月 g'
第 1 絃	七月 a	九月 b	二月 e'	七月 a'
第 2 柱	八月 • $b♭$	十月 c'	三月 • f'	八月 • $b♭'$
第 3 柱	九月 b	十一月 • $d♭'-c♯'$	四月 $g♭'-f♯'$	九月 b'
第 4 柱	十月 c'	十二月 d'	五月 g'	十月 c''

黄鐘調

七月, a 基音; Tafel XVIIIa Fig. 8.[51]

絃	1	2	3	4
開放絃	七月 a	十月 c'	二月 e'	七月 a'
第 1 絃	九月 b	十二月 d'	四月 $g♭'-f♯'$	九月 b'
第 2 柱	十月 c'	一月 $d♯'-e♭'$	五月 g'	十月 c''
第 3 柱	十一月 • $d♭'-c♯'$	二月 e'	六月 • $g♯'-a♭'$	十一月 • $d♭''-c♯''$
第 4 柱	十二月 d'	三月 • f'	七月 a'	十二月 d''

[50] P. 254
[51] P. 254

盤渉調

九月, b 基音; Tafel XVIIIa Fig. 9.[52]

絃	1	2	3	4
開放絃	四月 *gb–f#*	九月 *b*	二月 *e'*	七月 *a'*
第 1 絃	六月 *g#–ab*	十一月 *db'–c#'*	四月 *gb'–f#'*	九月 *b'*
第 2 柱	七月 *a*	十二月 *d'*	五月 • *g'*	十月 • *c''*
第 3 柱	八月 • *bb*	一月 • *d#'–eb'*	六月 *g#–ab'*	十一月 *db''–c#''*
第 4 柱	九月 *b*	二月 *e'*	七月 *a'*	十二月 *d''*

演奏に際しては、

> 第 1 柱に左手の人差し指
> 第 2 柱に中指
> 第 3 柱に薬指
> 第 4 柱に小指

を置く。第 1 絃の第 2 柱だけは親指が使われる。琵琶の音符が単独で書かれている時は、指示されている音符から（ママ）下に向かって[53] バチで絃を多少素早く掻き鳴らさなければならないことを意味している。上の方の絃は開放絃のままである。同じ大きさの音符が赤いカギで結ばれている場合は〔Taf. XVIII, Fig. 5f〕両方のポジションを押さえるというが、その他は開放絃である。これに対して、たとえば Fig. 1, Taf. XXI の *g' f#' g'* のように、音符が小さく書かれている場合は、バチで *g'* と *c''* を弾き、*g'* の代わりに *f#'* の音を指で押さえて瞬間的に出し、すぐにまた *g'* にもどるが、絃を改めて掻き鳴らすことはない。小さい赤いカギ〔Taf. XVIII, Fig. 5g〕は上から下に弾く通

[52] P. 254
[53] （日本語訳者補注）正しくは、書かれている音符に向かって絃をかき鳴らす。つまり、書かれている音がアルペジオの最後に鳴る。

常の奏法の代わりに、下から上へ絃を弾くことを意味している。琵琶では、このように和音はいつもアルペジオで演奏される。

9. 箏では (Taf. XIX, Fig. 1)、各絃に単純に番号が振られている。ただし、最後の3つは通常の数字とは別の記号である。どの調絃でもはじかれる絃の記号は同じで、よって特定の記号が特定の音高を意味するわけではない。

10. 和琴の記譜法も箏とまったく同様だが、一つだけ正反対なのは、箏では第1絃が演奏者から最も遠いのに対し、和琴では、最も近い絃が第1絃であることである。

11. 神楽笛はそれぞれの孔に固有の名がついていて、楽譜に使われている。

音の記号以外に、以下のようなさらなる説明が楽曲のためには必要だろう。

1. テンポについては、以下の様な区別がある。

　　a, ハヤ [早]」＝ 速いテンポ。短い楽曲の大部分に使われる。
　　b, ノベ [延]」＝ ゆっくりのテンポ。厳粛で長い楽曲に用いられる。

テンポをメトロノームで確認したかったが、それはまったく不可能だった。「早」を測ったところ、1分間に四分音符92個であった。楽器別に演奏してもらった時は、テンポは60から80の間であった。後にすべての楽器で一緒に演奏してもらったところ、同じ楽曲がいつも1分間40–60であることがわかった。よって、決まったテンポはない。むしろ、管楽器の長い持続音は特に美しいと見なされているため、テンポは主に、管楽器奏者の息の続き加減に左右されるのである。それと関連して、この楽曲は始めはゆっくり、後に速く演奏される。同様にこれに関連した第二の変わった特徴は、子供や年配者においては管楽器の音符とテンポは変化が少ない、ということである。

2. 拍子は二重のやり方で記されている。小さい赤い点は小節の始まりを表す。それぞれの小節は等しい4部分に分けられるが、それは楽譜には記されない。しかしもちろん、勉強や唱歌などの時には手で拍を刻む。すなわち、歌い手は小節の始めに両手を縦に打ち合わせ、あとの3拍は両手を近づけてリズムをとる。世俗音楽では、2/4 や 2/8 拍子を聞いたが、雅楽では 4/4 拍子のみ用いられる。

赤い点の他に、音符の間に黒い点がある (Taf. XIX, Fig. 5)。これは、たとえば、2または4小節ごとに規則正しく現れるが、見た目を整えるためだけのものである。横笛では小さな句点によって表され (Taf. XX, Fig. 1)、箏と打楽器ではまったく省略される。

点による分割のほかに、大きな点による第二の区分がある。それはすべての楽器にあり、規則正しく現れる。それは、太鼓の雄枠の打たれる拍を表す赤点か、笏拍子を打ち合わせるところを表す黒点である。たとえば、楽曲 [譜例の「五常楽急」] の第 2 部分の最後の繰り返しのように、太鼓の打点は加えることができるが、決まった場所につねに来なければならず、楽曲はこのリズム反復 [の種類] によって名付けられている。譜例の楽曲は 8 部分から成るが、それは太鼓が 8 小節ごとに打たれるからである。

さらに、もう 1 つの分割がある。たとえば「ゴショウラク [五常楽]」は 16 小節からなる 2 部分から出来ている。それぞれの部分の下には、繰り返しを表す「ニカエシ [二返]」がある (Taf. XX, Fig. 3)。これはすべての楽器に当てはまる。最初の太鼓は第 3 小節目で打たれ (ママ)、2 度目の太鼓 (8 小節後) の後ろにあと 3 小節続き、この部分が終わる。そして「二返」が来る。同様に第 2 部分も繰り返す。

楽器は [楽曲の]1 巡目に次々と加わって行き、やめる時は一緒ではない。そのため、第 1 部が楽譜に示されている通りに演奏されるのは 2 巡目の時であり、第 2 部は 1 巡目の時から [楽譜の通り] である。私は、五線譜の中で個々の楽器の始まりを E で示し、終わりを休符で示した。日本の楽譜にはこのようなものはなく、これらの関係は楽曲ごとの固有の解説で示される。また、楽曲は最後の太鼓以降アド・リブで演奏されるが、楽器がやめる順番は厳格に守られなければならないと言われている。そのほか、「クワエル [加]」(加えるの意。Taf. XIX, Fig. 5h) がある。これは、繰り返しの時に太鼓と鉦鼓に、打音を挿入することである。この変化形は Taf. XIX, Figs. 3 と 4 の b に示した。この楽曲は次のようなやり方で記譜されている。個々の楽器は別に書かれる。曲名と赤い点 (小と大) はすべて [の楽器] に対して共通である。そのため [それらの点を目安に] 同じ位置に来る各楽器の音符を見つけることは容易である。当然のことながら、すべての日本語と中国語の書物のように、楽譜はみな文字は上から下へ、行は右から左へ、ページは [西洋の] 後ろから前へ読まれなければならない。

もとの楽譜はずっと大きく、各楽器は、特別な二重ページ [袋とじの紙] に書かれている。

スペースの節約のために、Taf. XIX から Taf. XXI までは、全部を小さく、間隔をつめている。しかしそれ以外は正確に再現されている。

初めに、笙の楽譜についてもうすこし詳しく見てみよう (Taf. XIX, Fig. 5)。右上の最初の記号 (a) は「ショウ [笙]」と書いてあり、楽器の名前である。その左に 2 つの記号がある (b)。上は調子の「ヒョウデョウ [平調]」、下は「タイゾク [太簇]」[54] といい、2 月 (e) の音を意味する。言い換えるとホ短調である。というのも、日本と中国には長調がないからである。[55]3 行目の記号 (c) は上から 3 文字は「ゴ・ジョウ・

---

[54] (日本語訳者補注) Fig. 5 の中には「太簇」の文字は見えない。

[55] その出処はどこかといえば、ワグネル博士の書いたものに簡単に見つけることができる。博士は最初に生まれる五音の起源を説いていて、人は必然的に短調の音階に到達するのである。第 6 号の 15, 16 頁 (p. 96) 参照。

ラク」と読め、曲名である。名前の意味については誰も説明できなかった。4つ目の記号 (d) は「キュウ [急]」で、短い曲を意味する。各曲は、テンポがない「ジョ [序]」か、長々しい「ハ [破]」か、短い「急」のどれかである。それに続く記号 (e) は「ショウキョク [小曲]」といい、小さい曲のことである。(f) の「ハヤ [早]」は速いテンポ、(g) の「ヒョウシ・ハチ [拍子八]」は、つまり、8小節で1区分を構成するということである。(h) は「クワエル [加]」と読み、「加える」意味で、打楽器に関係している (上記参照)。

以上の表題部分全部がすべての楽器それぞれに表記されている。言うまでもなく、最初の記号 [楽器名] は変わってくる。音符はそれぞれの小節に属し、小節を表す赤い点の左側に書かれる。大きな赤い点は太鼓のためのもので、各楽器で繰り返し記される。Taf. XX, Fig. 1 は横笛の楽譜、Fig. 2 は篳篥の楽譜で、下半分が Tafel (B) に続く。Taf. XXI, Fig. 1 は琵琶譜、Taf. XIX, Fig. 2 は鞨鼓譜である。Fig. 3 は太鼓譜で、a は始めに打たれるもの、b は最後の2部分で打たれるものである。Fig. 4 は鉦鼓譜で、a と b は太鼓と同様の意味である。

連続する赤い点は、西洋五線譜の笙のパートの上に明記されているので、Taf. XVIII から XXI まで、今述べた説明の助けを借りれば、個々のパートを解読し、もしかしてありうる小さな間違いを訂正することは、さほど難しくないと思う。

さらに説明しなければならないことがある。箏の楽譜で (Taf. XXB, Fig. 4)、たとえば「三」と「八」のように2つの音が赤い線で結ばれているとき (Taf. XIX, Fig. 1a)[56] 総譜に記されているように弾かなければならない。すなわち、まず第4絃を人差し指で掻き、四分音符分留まる。次に、中指で第3と第4絃を八分音符で鳴らす。同じ指で第5絃をとても短く鳴らし、この短い装飾音のあとで、人差し指と親指で第6と第8絃を同時につかむように弾く。第7絃は使わない。これをより正確に表すために、赤い垂直の線を書き、その上に中心の音を書き、隣接する音は小さく右左に書く。しかし、このようなことは通常の楽譜には書かれず、あらかじめ述べられる説明の中にだけ現れる。

すでに以前に述べたように、生徒たちは楽曲をこれらの楽譜から覚えるわけではない。むしろ、彼らのためには、楽曲は Taf. XXI, Fig. 2[篳篥] や Taf. XXI, Fig. 3[横笛] のように書き表される。[57] 小節の記号はさきほどの楽譜と同じである。左に、普通のカタカナ文字 (日本語の 72 の音声表記文字) が来て、さらに左に小さい実際の音を表す記号が来る。これらは自分で対照させることにより、簡単に理解できる。カタカナ記号の読みは、篳篥の場合 (Taf. XXI, Fig. 2)、上から最初の太鼓の前まで、「テ エル、レ エ、タ ア、レ エ、」となる。コンマ [、の区切りの単位] は [原典では] 赤い点に当る。これらの音韻は生徒たちに向かって歌われる。その際、前述のように手で拍子とる。生徒は家で暗記するまで練習しなければならない。

---

[56] (日本語訳者補注) 図では実際には赤い線は脱落している。
[57] (日本語訳者補注) 暗記用の歌「唱歌」の音節を書いた「仮名譜」。

ゆえに、本当の楽譜[58]は教師の手助けのためでしかない。横笛 (Taf. XVIII, Fig. 3) では、冒頭の前にもう 1 行カタカナが書かれていて、最初の小節は「トヲロホ」の代わりに「チイラハ」などとなっている。これは、初度はオクターヴ高い音で吹かねばならないことを意味している[59]。

ここまで、神聖な音楽について自分にできる限り詳しく説明したので、今度は戦争や宗教で使われる楽器や中国の楽器を一覧したい。最後は、孔子によって編纂された古代中国の聖なる本『シュキン [詩経]』[60] からの例を紹介して終わりたい。

I. 戦の楽器

Taf. XI,

Fig. J ジンダイコ [陣太鼓] は片手に持ち、バチで打つ (I′)。

Fig. L も同じ名前だが、背中に背負う。

Fig. K ジンガネ [陣鉦]。金属製。そばにあるのはバチ (K′)。側面図 (K″) は下に示されている。

Fig. M ジンガイ [陣貝]。金属の吹き口をつけた大きなホラ貝。吹くと非常に遠くまで響く音が出る。

これらの楽器はすべて兵を集合させたり、さまざまな信号のために使われる。これらはゆっくりしたリズミカルな音からなっている。楽譜があるが、私はそれを入手できていない。

太鼓と貝は行進に使われ、鉦は戦いをやめるときに使われる。

II. 世俗楽器

世俗楽器は、時々盲人や娘による三味線と箏とともに使われるが、特に劇場などで使われる。

Taf. XI,

Fig. N はシャクハチ [尺八]（「1 尺 8 寸」の意）。リードのないクラリネットの類いである。竹から作る。根のすぐ上の低い部分を使うが、これは節の位置の理由からである。カーブは自然のものである。ヒトヨギリ [一節切]（節が 1 つある笛) はこれとよく似ているが、曲がっていない。

Taf. XI,

---

[58] (日本語訳者補注) 雅楽では唱歌を記した「仮名譜」に対して、指孔記号の楽譜を「本譜」という。ここでは、die richtigen Noten は「本譜」のことを指すか。

[59] (日本語訳者補注) 正しくはオクターヴ高く吹かれるのは「後度」＝二巡目。

[60] 『シュキン [詩経]』は中国の神聖な本で、その統治や道徳の原理が詰まっている。孔子が編纂した著作で、中国派遣の宣教使ゴビル神父によって [フランス語] 訳された。ド・ギニュによって本文が [さらに] 校閲、添削され、1770 年にパリで Tilliard から出版された。

Fig. O はシメダイコ [締太鼓](紐で締めた太鼓) で、2 本の木製バチで打つ。O″ は上の部分、O‴ は側面図である。

III. 仏教儀礼で使われる楽器

報酬次第で、楽器の数とそれを演奏する僧侶の数はふえる。報酬が安いと、1 人の僧侶が 2、3 の楽器を演奏する。

Taf. XII,

Fig. X ハンショウ [半鐘](半分の鐘) は小さな鐘である。寺の裏に吊るされる。僧侶の集合や、葬式で寺に棺が運び込まれる時に鳴らされる。この鐘の音で、死者はこの世の肉体から離れ、あの世に行く。X′ は上部、X″ は断面図、X‴ は下からの図。X‴′ はシュモク [鐘木](鐘を打つ木)。

Taf. XIII,

Fig. n と n′ は金属の 2 枚のシンバルで、トルコ音楽でよく使われている形である。n″ は側面図、n‴ は内側の図。

Fig. o はドラ [銅鑼]。中国の金属のカネ。o′ で打たれる、o″ は側面図。

Fig. p はワニグチ [鰐口](ワニは魚の一種、クチは口)。寺の入り口に吊るされる。長くつり下がった紐 (p′) で、仏が願を聞いてくれるように注意を引くために打たれる。P‴ は側面図、p‴′ は断面図。

Fig. q 小さな太鼓。タイコ [太鼓] ともいう。寺にある。仏教の祈りに使われる。地獄から死者の魂を救うために使用される。q′ は側面図、q″ はバチ。

Fig. r はヒョウシギ [拍子木](拍子をとる木)で、笏拍子のように使われるが、テンポは速い。r′ は断面図。

Taf. XIV,

Fig. s ニョウハチ [饒鉢] は金属製の器である。クッションと木の台の上にのっている。s′ は断面図、s″ は上からの図、s‴ はバチである。打つ側は革で覆われている。

Fig. t 雅楽と同様の鉦鼓であるが、平に置かれ、違うバチ (t′) で打つ。t″ は側面図、t‴ は断面図、t‴′ は下からの図である。

Fig. u リン [鈴]。家庭用の縮小サイズの饒鉢。バチはなくならないように [楽器本体に] 結んである。u′ は上からの図、u″ は断面図である。

Fig. v 小さな鉦鼓で、家の中と巡礼で使用される。後者は股の上に置かれ、打たれる。v′ は上からの図、v″ は下からの図、v‴ は断面図、v‴′ は台、v‴″ はバチ「シュモク [鐘木]」である。

Fig. w レイ [鈴]。呼鈴で、たとえば富士山の巡礼登山などで使われる。

Taf. XV,

Fig. A　バンギ [板木]。木のプレートで、僧侶たちを呼び集めるのに使われる。

Fig. X　ツリガネ [釣鐘]。大きな鐘で、寺に隣接してある特別な架 [シュロウ [鐘楼]) につり下げられている。重い角材 [シュモク [鐘木]) で打たれる。いくつかの寺 (トーケイのシバ[61] や京都など) の鐘は巨大な大きさに達している [高さ 12 フィート]。鐘は時刻を告げるのに使われ[62] 年末には各寺でこのような鐘が 108 回鳴らされる。

Fig. B　金属製のシンバル。

Fig. C　巡礼や乞食などが持つ小さな太鼓。木のバチで打たれる。

Fig. D　木か金属の魚で、版木の代わりに打たれる。D′ はバチ。

Fig. E　ユ [ギョ [敔]] は横たわる虎である。背中の褶曲したぎざぎざの部分を竹 (E′) で擦る。竹は刷毛のように細かく割かれている。

Taf. XVI,

Fig. b　太鼓と 1 本のバチ。

Fig. c　太鼓と 2 本のバチ。

Taf. XVII,

Fig. I、ケ [磬] はもっぱら石で作られるが、時折ブロンズのこともある。

Fig. H　モクギョウ [木魚](木の魚の口)。鱗は彫刻する。金や緑の漆塗りのものもあるが、普通は赤である。大きさはさまざまで 2 フィートの大きさまである。内側は空洞である。漆によって継ぎ目は隠されている。H′ は革で覆われたバチ。

Fig. G　シャクジョウ [錫杖] は金属製の輪が長い杖につけられたもので、揺らして打ち合わせて鳴らす。僧侶が使う。

---

[61] (日本語訳者補注) 東京、芝の増上寺のことか。

[62] 1873 年 1 月以前は、日本の時刻を [鐘] が告げていた。日の出から日の入りまでを 6 つの等しい部分 (トキ [刻]) に分ける。日の入りから日の出までも同様。春分・秋分の時は、ゆえに各刻は 2 時間になるが、その他は 14 日ごとに異なる。時刻は、始めの 3 つは前触れとして、2 つはゆっくり、3 つ目は速く、というふうに鳴らして知らされる。次に、ゆっくり 3〜8 つ打ち、最後に 1 打、少し速く打つ。わかりやすくするために刻を等しくすると、次のように打つ。前触れの打音は除いて、12 時は 9 打、2 時は 8 打、4 時は 7 打、6 時は 6 打、8 時は 5 打、10 時は 4 打である。そして、また頭から打ち始める。1873 年からヨーロッパの時間計算法が導入された。始めに 3 打あり、次にヨーロッパの時間の数が打たれ、最後に少し速い打音が来る。棒は 4 本の紐で固定された枠にぶら下がっていて、特別に任命された僧侶によって振られる。鳴らす数が 2 もしくはそれ以上の場合はその数によってテンポが決まる。

IV. 神道の儀礼には、

Taf. XVII, Fig. F の楽器だけが使われる。スズ [鈴] という。金属製の中空の球の中
に金属の小球が固定されずに入っている。

V. 中国で今も使われている楽器
　　中国では古い神聖な音楽は失われてしまったので、これらはすべて世俗的な楽
器である。

Taf. XXII,

　　　　Fig. a ジャミセンを 2 つの方向から見た図。日本のシャミセン [三味線] と
　　　　　　　よく似ているが、形は丸く、猫革の代わりに蛇革が張ってある。
　　　　　　　蛇革は中国と琉球諸島[63] ではこのような用途に一般的に使われるが、
　　　　　　　日本本土ではまったく見かけない。この楽器は、バチではなく自分の
　　　　　　　爪で弾く。

　　　　コマは Taf. XXIII, a で、2 つの方向からの図である。

　　　　Fig. b はフチン [胡琴] で、側面と前からの図である。その間に、胴の下か
　　　　　　　らの図、コマの図がある (Taf. XXIII, Fig. b)。弓の本体は曲がった木片
　　　　　　　からできている。弓の毛は上部を貫いていて、下部にしっかりと固定
　　　　　　　されている。弓は 2 つの絃の間を通っている。絃は、弓と糸巻きの間
　　　　　　　で、紐や輪によって棹の方に少し寄せられている。棹は、2 つの断面
　　　　　　　図 (A–A と D–D) が示すような形をしている。演奏する時は、膝の上
　　　　　　　にたてて置く。太さが異なる 2 絃は 6 度に調絃されて、張りの強さも
　　　　　　　異なり、中指と薬指で隔てられる。弓の前側は低いほうの絃に、裏側
　　　　　　　は高い方の絃に当てる。演奏者は楽器の胴の上に松ヤニをつけ、演奏
　　　　　　　中はその上を絶え間なく擦っている。この楽器ではたいへん快活な旋
　　　　　　　律が演奏される。たとえば、ある楽曲は 2 つのユエチン [月琴] のため
　　　　　　　の作品であった。しかし、音はひどいものだった。私は、たいへん古
　　　　　　　い楽器を見たが、胴は分厚い竹でできていて、それに 2 つ目の細い竹
　　　　　　　が差し込まれていた。片面は動物の革が張られていて、もう一方は透
　　　　　　　かし彫りがある竹の自然の節で閉じていた。糸巻きはついていない。

　　　　Fig. c ビワ [琵琶]。中国語では「ピパ」と呼ばれている。日本の琵琶を改良
　　　　　　　した形である。当初の 4 つの柱は [日本の琵琶のように] ついている
　　　　　　　が、さらに加えられた柱によって、音の数を増やすことが可能となる。

　　　　Fig. d チャルメラはクラリネットの類である。リードはなく、ただの管に近
　　　　　　　い。裏側の下部に穴が開いていて、フルートとして使うこともできる。

[63] 私は、琉球で一般的な楽器の絵巻を見る機会を得たが、それらの楽器が中国楽器とまったく異な
　　らないことを発見した。

Fig. e　ラッパ [喇叭]。胴は篳篥に似ているが、上部と下部は金属がついている。リードも篳篥と似ているがずっと小さい。真ん中が紐で結ばれている。リードは薄い葦 (e'') でできている。e' は下から見た図である。

Fig. f　Fig. e と同じで、大きさが小さいだけ。

Fig. g　笏拍子と似ていて、同じように使われる。

Fig. h　モクギョ [木魚] (Taf. XVII, Fig. H も参照のこと)。ただし漆塗りではない。物売りが通行人の注意を引くのに使う。

Taf. XXIII,

Fig. i　ヤンチン [楊琴] または「西の琴」。上流の令嬢たちだけが演奏する。ゆえに、この楽器について説明を入手することはたいへん難しい。楽器の胴は西洋のツィターに似ている。弦は鋼鉄である。この事実は、名前とともに、この楽器が外国の、ともかく西に起源があることを示している。弦は2つのピンのそれぞれ $(i'$ と $i'')$ に固定されていて、片方をハンマー (トトチ [調槌]、$i''')$ で回転させて調律する。共鳴胴には2つの長い穴があいたコマがある。弦は、つねに近いほうにあるコマの丸い穴を通り、遠いほうのコマの上を通る。それにより、弦は共鳴胴の中央部分で交差する。低い、太い弦はつねに1弦1音だが、高い方の弦は2弦1音になる。この楽器は幅の広い方が演奏者側になるように置く。私に説明してくれたある身分の低い中国人によると、低い、単独弦の音には中央の部分を使い、高い音には左の方の弦を使う。しかし、私にはこれは正しいと思えない。すなわち、私は楊琴をみたことがあるが、可動式のコマは、コマの左右の低音弦の領域は2オクターヴ異なり、高い弦は4度の音程になるように据えられるので、都合28の異なる音を生じさせることができる。

その中国人が説明するには、調律は、低音弦はDEFGABcで、高音弦は $g, a, b, b\flat, d', d\sharp', g'$ だという。

この楽器は2本の竹もしくは鼈甲のハンマーで演奏される $(i'''', i''''$ 裏側)。i'''''' は楽器のふた。i''''' は閉めたところ。i'''''' は狭い幅 [横] からの図で、ハンマーを入れておく引き出しを出した状態。

Taf. XXIV,

Fig. k と Fig. l はテンコ [点鼓] とハンコ [板鼓] で、一組を成している。硬い木でできていて、革がかぶさっている。4度に調律されているが、音が響かず、カタカタという音がする。それらは、6本の竹の棒を3本の紐 (k')[64] で結んだ枠の上に乗っている。k'' と l'' は平面図、l''' は l の断面図、l' または k''' の竹のバチで打たれる。

---

[64] (英訳者補注) 番号が少し混乱している。

Fig. j　ショークンといい、トランペットである。二つの部品を互いに押し込んで組み立てる。貴族の行列や点呼などに用いられ、叫ぶような音がする。j′はマウスピースを上から見た所、j″は本体を下から見たところである。

Fig. m　ドラ [銅鑼] で金属製である。バチ (m′) で打たれる。m″とm‴は断面図と側面図である。

さらに、他に使われている楽器。

ドウコ [胴鼓?] は平らな革の鼓である。3つの輪でつり下げられ、竹の棒で打つ。グチュラ [??鑼] は Taf. XIV, Fig. v にそっくりである。

最後に私は、中国楽器の中で月琴について少し詳しく見なければならない [第6号、Taf. IV, Fig. 7]。これは木でできていて、胴体の内側に斜めに金属線が差し込まれている。一方の端は側面に固定され、他方の端は反対の側面の近くで自由に振動する。この金属線は楽器に金属的な響きをもたらし、歌手の甲高いビブラート声を助ける。ダブルコースの弦を 2 組張り、一方が他方の 5 度上になるように調弦する。小さなバチで演奏する。私は「漫板流水」という作品を附録につけておいたが、最初は月琴 2 つ、次はそれに胡琴を加えた演奏だった。

私は、エゾ [蝦夷] のアイヌの人々でよく使われるある楽器に触れることなしに、東アジアの楽器シリーズを閉じることはできない。それは口の鼓 [口琴] である。長さ 4 インチ、幅 2 インチの薄い木片である。真ん中に、幅約 1 ライン[65] 長さ約 15 ラインの先の尖った舌が、三方から切り出されている。笙の金属リードとよく似ている (Taf. XX, Fig. 5)。この木片は口の前にくわえられ、息を吹き込んだり、歌ったりすることによって舌が振動する。もう一つ、アイヌで使われている鉄製の口琴を見たことがある。それは西洋のものとそっくりであるが、舌の前の外側の枠が閉じていて、西洋のもののように端は開いていない。にもかかわらず、この楽器は西側起源であると私は思う。

最後に私は、前述の『書経』からの抜粋をたどり、古代中国音楽の起こりと意味を多少明らかにする。その後、日本音楽と中国音楽に関する記述をさらに 2、3 述べるが、中国音楽の記述は、スタイン氏が 3 つの音楽例とともに私に送ってくれたものである。

中国人は自らの古い音楽について非常に高尚な思想を持っているが、それは彼らにとっては失われたものとなっている。彼らはそれをヨ [ユエ、楽] と名付け、その起源を最古の神話時代に置いている。彼らが言うには、フシ [伏義][紀元前 3000 年頃だが、細かくは 2952 年から 3300 年まで諸説ある] よりずっと前にいた王の一人チョヤンが、鳥の囀りに耳を澄まし、後に音楽を組み合わせた。その和音はいたるところに響きわたり、知性を目覚めさせ、感情を鎮めた。それによって、外側の感覚が健康的になり、身体の体液がバランスを得て、人間の寿命が長くなるのであ

---

[65] (英訳者補注) 1 ラインは 1/12 のインチ = 2.174mm。

る。このような音楽をジエ・ウェン [節文] というが、すなわち節度と優美さのことである。

この古代音楽の主たる目的は、あらゆる美徳の調和であった。身体と精神が一致し、感情が理性に従った時のみ調和が完成する。

この音楽は常に礼節を伴っている。この礼節とは、彼らが言うには、外面に表れるものだが、内面から湧き出るものでなくてはならない。なぜなら、心の中にある調和が外に向かって広がらなければならないからである。

一般的に、古代音楽について中国人は、まるでギリシア人がオルフェウスとメルキュールのリラ (?)[66] などの古い音楽について語るのと同様に語り、その部分は宇宙に関する部分と一致している。彼らは、宗教儀礼に従事する音楽家にそれを教えるための、特別な役人を雇っていた。

アーノ神父は、古代中国音楽に関する論考を読み、その要約を自らの著書「文学の多様性」 Variétés littéraires で発表したが、この音楽のシステムはピタゴラスやエジプト人のそれと同じである、と述べている。「すべてのピタゴラス派の人々が言うには、音楽の主たる目的は、熱情を鎮め、理解を明快にし、美徳への愛を涵養することである。中国人が言うには、人が平静さを保ち、慎み深く誠実であり、法に適い、安定していて、世の中全体、なかんずく自分の人生で世話になっている人々を愛すること、これらは、音楽によって満たされるべき美徳であり、いやしくも音楽家を名乗らんとする者は、必ずそれを達成しなければならない」[67] であるから、音楽のシステムに関係なく、ピタゴラス派の人々と中国人は、音楽に関して彼らが生み出した崇高な思想においては同一なのである。

しかしながら、この完全な音楽はすぐに退化するもので、『書経』においても風紀を乱す音楽、淫らな音楽[68] が非難されているのが見える。間違いなく、音楽につけて歌われる淫らな歌が、道徳の劣化をもたらした。

今日、中国人は、ペパン [パイパン、拍板] という名の楽器を持っている。それは硬い木から作られた数枚の小さい木片で、1フィートの長さ、指 4 本分の幅である。上部が幅が狭く、そこが糸で止められている。拍を刻む。

---

[66] (英訳者補注) 5 世紀初頭の Saturnalia I.19.15 in Macrobius, Macrobii Ambrosii Theodosii Opera, vol. II, 183 参照のこと

[67] (英訳者補注) Suard and Arnaud, Variétés littéraires, 309–310.

[68] このことは、『書経』に繰り返し現れる。良い皇帝の大部分は特別な音楽を作り出すが、悪い皇帝はその反対に、悪い音楽を好むか、音楽を弾圧するとして、非難される。「パオの美しい娘」第二章も参照のこと (Arendt, "Das schöne Mädchen von Pao. Eine Erzählung aus der Geschichte Chinas im achten Jahrhundert v. Chr.")。紀元 2255 年の皇帝・舜は、すべての動物が従う音楽「ダシャオ」を考えだした。音楽と舞踊の結合にも、同様の重要性がある。ロピ (ルオビ)[羅泌]は言う。人間の生は天と地の結合に依拠しており、すべての創造物を使用することに依っている。よい物質 (「心」または「気」と呼ばれる) は身体を巡る。もし、身体が動かないと物質も流れず、溜まり、その停滞がすべて病気のもととなるのである。安定した統治下では人は病気にならないが、悪い王のもとではすべてが混乱する。それゆえに、『礼記』(聖典の一つ) では、その治世下で慣例的に行われる舞踊によって、治世が評価されるのだと言う。また、人の徳は、その人の瑟の弾き方によって判断されるとも言う。であるから、身体の動きである舞踊は、同時に統治と関係しており、そしてこれはまさに音楽にも当てはまるのである。

Taf. XVII, Fig.1 チン [琴] と名付けられたこの楽器については、驚くべきことが言われている。それを発明したのは伏羲だと言うのだ。人々が言うには、この君主は音楽の法則を作り、漁業を調えた後、漁師のために歌を作った。ちょうど、鋤の発明者であるシンノン [神農] が、農耕民のための歌を作ったように。

伏羲はトン [桐] という木を用い、それを穿って琴を作った。[69] 琴は7フィート2インチの長さである。絃は絹から作り、27本である。彼はその楽器を「リ」と名付けた。

中国人は、この楽器の絃の数について、一致しているわけではない。ある人は27、別の人は25、さらに別の人は20、10といい、最後にはわずか5という人まであった。ウェンワン [文王] またはウワン [武王] がさらに2絃加え、7絃になったという。長さについて言えば、あるものは7フィート2インチ、また別のものは3フィート6インチ6ラインである。上の面は天と同様に丸く、下の面は地のように平だと言う。龍池 (楽器上の場所) は8インチで、八つの風 [八風] と通じる。鳳池は4インチで、四季 [四気] を表している。5絃説を唱える者は、5絃が五星を表しているという。[70] 伏羲がこの琴を発明した時、天の音が生まれた。彼はその楽器で、キア・ピエン [ジア・ビエン] という曲を演奏して、知性の恵みを讃え、天と人間を結びつけた。また別の人が言うには、この楽器は悪い呪術を防ぎ、不純な考えを心から追い出すという。

この楽器の形式と発明者に関して、中国人はほとんど意見が一致しないが、同様に、以下のことについても一致しない。

私は、絃は絹であると述べた。そして今日まで、中国ではすべての楽器の絃は絹で、その他の材質は用いない。[71] しかし、絹の品質を選ぶ時は以下のように言われている。チェ [榛 [はしばみ]] という木の葉を餌として育った蚕からとれるものが断然優れていて、それらの絃は豊かな響きがすると言われている。この木は桑の木と似ていて、セイヨウハシバミを厚くしたような実がなる。皮は黒く、果肉は白く、食べられる。赤黄色を染める時にもこの木を使う。

伏羲が琴を作るのに用いた木はトン [桐] という。さまざまな種類がある。黒いチントン [青桐] は実は成らない。葉と枝は黒っぽい。

白いペィトン [白桐] は、葉が白く、春の始めに黄色と紫の花が咲く。葉は春分の頃にならないと出て来ない。花と葉は薬として用いられる。葉と樹皮が灰色の別の種類もある。桃のような実が生り、その実から、絵の具を延ばすための油がとれる。実は食べられない。

---

[69] 以前は琴ノコトと記述したものである。
[70] 恐らく正しいだろう。
[71] スチール弦のヤンチンはいまだ見た事がないように筆者には思われる。

また別に、緑の葉と樹皮のものもある。ヘーゼルナッツのような大きさの実が生り、食べられる。別のものは、花が咲かずに実が生る。また、花は咲くが実が生らないものもある。

これと別に、イェ[72]という名前の木も同じ目的に用いる。この木を中国人は木の王様と呼んでいる。

Taf. XVII, Fig. 2 は瑟[73]である。この楽器も同様に伏羲に帰されている。桑という名の木から作られ、36 絃そなえている。人間をより道徳的に、善意に満ちた状態にするために用いられる。ある人が言うには、この楽器は 50 絃であったが、黄帝が 25 絃にした。というのも、伏羲のものはあまり悲しげな音だったからである。また別の者が言うには、伏羲の妻・女媧が [絃を] 減らし、それによってこの世のすべてのものが秩序だったという。

この楽器は 8 フィート 1 インチの長さで、1 フィート 8 インチの幅である。

Taf. XVII, Fig. 3 は、編磬 あるいは、単に磬といい、三角の楽器である。しかし、時々丸い形もある。中国の書物には両方の形が出てくる。石でできており、調和のとれた音がする。『書経』の一章「イチ [益稷]」[74] には、これについて話がある。この石は図に示したように、ぶら下げる。ラキントゥ (ルオジントゥ)[羅経図] あるいは、聖なる本の目次には、三角形の底の無い [への字型の] 石が 8 枚、2 列につり下げられているのが見える。これを編磬という。

もう一つのずっと大きなものはタキン (ダチン)[大磬] と言う。

---

[72] (日本語訳者補注) 梓は「木王」と呼ばれるので梓のことか。

[73] 羅泌 (954–1279 宋時代) は、皇帝の歴史「チュシャンチ」(伏羲以前) の中でこういう。皇帝はセクェイに命じて、5 絃の瑟を作らせた。それは嵐や予期せぬ四季の到来によって乱された宇宙の調和をとり戻すためである。これが最初に言及されるべき楽器である。羅泌はここでこう言っている。音楽とはひとえに、能動的な「陽」と受動的な「陰」という二つの原理の一致である。その上に、目に見える世界が保持されているのである。実際に、この世の美しい秩序とは調和であり、例えば天と地という物理的世界、あるいは人間性という道徳的世界、あるいは王国という政治的世界、あるいはこの三つが連関したものについて熟考するならば、人は常にこの二つの原理に向き合い、この二つは一致せられなければならない。そうでないと調和は不可能なのである。羅泌はさらに加えて言う。賢人が陰と陽の誤った結合を一致へと導き、その者が [二つの原理の] 統合を表す楽器を発明した。彼が言及するすべての楽器の中で、最も重要なのは琴と瑟である。両方とも調和的合奏のための根本となるものである。琴は能動的なものを、瑟は受動的なものを支配する。王は両方を有するが、臣下の諸侯は瑟しか持たず、琴を持つことができない。琴は生を司り、喜びを注ぎこむが、瑟は死を司り、ゆえに悲しみと同情を呼び起こす。

[74] この章は紀元前 2253–1049 の時期を扱っている。皇帝・禹はこう言った。5 音と 8 調の音楽が聴きたい時は、私は自分の良い行い、悪い行いを調べ、そして、5 音を採用している歌を歌ってもらいたいと思う。音楽を統括する大臣が呼ばれ、こう言った。もし編磬 [?] を響かせたり、琴または瑟に歌を伴奏させる時は、父または祖父がやって来る (つまり、死者が祭りに参加する)。禹の客人 (故・皇帝タン [湯] の霊) は座につき、家来の諸候も所定の位置に着く。笛と小さな太鼓 (鼗鼓) の音が響く中、柷 (笏拍子の一種) と敔 (カスタネットの一種) が同時に始めと終わりに鳴る。鐘とオルガン [笙] が交互に鳴る。シャオチャオ (Taf. XVII. Fig. 6) の 9 つの和音が聞こえる時、トァンホァン [鳳凰?](空想上の鳥) が、喜びに羽を羽ばたかせる。私が自分の石 (磬) を強く、あるいは弱く打つと、野生の動物たちは喜びのあまり跳ね上がり、役人の長たちは意気投合した。

　中国には笛もいくつかある。一番単純なものはヨ [籥] というもので、孔は3つしかなく、西洋のフルートと同様、水平に構える。

　チョンは管かトランペットのようなものである。これらの楽器を正しく区別するのは難しい。金属でできており、一方の側面に孔が5つあり、他方に1つある。

　同じ漢字で書くチョン [鐘] は、昔の音楽家の名前で、彼には、同じく音楽に従事するペ (バイ)[伯] という名前の兄弟がいた。チョン・ペという複合名称は、双子座のカストールとポリュデウケース兄弟のような一組の兄弟を象徴的に表している[75]

ディ [笛] はまた別の笛で、同じように吹かれ、5つの孔がある (Taf. XVII, Fig. 4)。

クワン [管] は双管の笛で、それぞれの管に6孔ある (Taf. XVII, Fig. 5)。

　チ [篪] はまた別の笛で、前のものと同じく蘆でできている。二種類ある。大きい方は1フィート4インチの長さで、周囲は3インチである。小さい方は1フィート2インチの長さである。8孔あるという者もあれば、7孔しかないという者もいる。

シャオ [簫] (Taf. XVII, Fig. 6) という名前の笛は、23の管からなり、4フィートの長さである。小さいものもあり、チャオといい、16管で1フィート2インチの長さである。この楽器の音は鳳凰[76] の声に似ていて、形はその翼のようだと言われている。

Taf. XVII, Fig. 7 の楽器はシェン [笙] と呼ばれ、携帯用のオルガンのようなものである。4フィートの高さの19管と13管の二種類ある。その発明は伏羲の妻・女媧に帰せられていて、彼女自身が丘の上や水上で演奏し、その音は非常に繊細だったという。

　ユ [竽] も同様にオルガンの類で、36管あり、長さ4フィート2インチである。

タオグ [鼗鼓] は小さな鼓 (Taf. XVII. Fig. 8) である。宗教的な儀式で使う。それ以外に中国には太鼓がいくつかあり、それらは、儀式で祀る霊や神のために使われる。以下の様なものがある。

　フェング [鳳鼓] またはフエングは、軍隊の遠征の時に打つ。8フィートの長さで、枠にぶら下がっている。

　レイグ [雷鼓] は8面あり、人が打つ。より上位の神様シン [神] のための祭りで使われる。

---

[75] (日本語訳者補注) 真に自分の琴を理解してくれる友人・鍾子期の死とともに、琴を弾くのを止めた「伯牙絶弦」の故事を指すか (『呂氏春秋』)。

[76] 空想の鳥で、龍が皇帝のシンボルになる前は、皇帝のシンボルだった。鳳凰は後に皇后のシンボルとなり、しばしば髪などに飾られた。

ルグ [路鼓] はまた別の太鼓で、4面あり、クィ [鬼] あるいは下位の神様や先祖のための祭りで使われる。

リング [輪鼓] は6面あり、大地の祭りで使われる。これらの鼓はすべて吊るされる。

さらに、日常生活に使う鼓がたくさんあり、持ち運びされる。たとえば、タンバリンのようなトンリャオというものもある。

チョ [柷] (Taf. XVII, Fig. 9) は木の漆塗りの箱で、その内側をチ [槌] (Taf. XVII, Fig. 10) で打つと音が出る。

この楽器 [Fig. 10] は、音楽を始める時に用いる。外側は4フィート2インチの大きさで、内側は1フィート2インチの深さである。

ユ [敔] (Taf. XVII, Fig.11) はまた別の楽器で、横たわり、待ち伏せする虎の形を模したブロンズ製の楽器である。その背中の毛はかなり高く、数にすると27本で77 鍵盤のようになっている。チンという木製の1フィートの長さのバチで打つ。音楽が終る直前にこの楽器を短く演奏する。

また別に、火で焼いた粘土製の楽器がある。シュェンまたはシュン [塤] という。これは古い音楽に用いられ、伏羲の発明とされている。椀のような形をしていて、孔が6つある。

また別の楽器ティン [鼎] は、伏羲が天神の供物 (ジャオシェン [交神] またはフェンシェン [封神]) のために定めたもので、羅泌のまた別の論文に描写されている。それによると、この楽器は調和の始まりである。この器を下向きにすると音楽の土台や基礎となる鐘となり、器を上向きにすると供物の容器となる。三足は三才 [天地人] の象徴である。

カネ (Taf. XVII, Fig. 12) はヨンと呼ばれ、金属製である。中国人はチョン [鐘] という別の楽器も持っている。Fig. 12 と同じような枠に、鐘を八個ずつ二列に吊るす。これを編鐘という。

ポ (ボ)[鈸] は鈴の類である。別の小型の鈴は太鼓に結ばれている。いくつか種類があり、チョ、チャオ、トなどという。

カネを打つバチはチェ (シェ)[舌] といい、舌状で、木製のバチで打つ鐘はムト [木搥] といい、金属製のバチで打つものはキント [金搥] という。

私は、興味深いことに、『書経』ではいたるところで鐘が楽器の根源と見なされていることに気づいた。リン・ルン [伶倫] は、ヒエ・キ (シエ・チ)[嶰谿] という谷で蘆の小片を切取り、孔を開け、鐘の音に似せて吹いてみた。

---

77 この解釈は、私が仏教楽器のところで挙げたものと異なる。しかし、私は自分のものが正しいと思う。というのは、これは現在でも普通であり、図版のイラストにもより近いからだ (著者)。

彼はいろいろな音を識別し、六つは律、六つは呂と名付けた。これらの音で、鳳凰の声をまねしてみた。宰相ヨン・ユエンは、12 の月に相関する 12 の鐘を作った。五音が調和し、四季が分けられた。

紀元前 1900 年の夔については彼が西方の音楽を作ったと言われているが、その方法については説明されていない。

Postface: A Remark on Müller's Interactive Gagaku Study Score

Elizabeth J. Markham & Rembrandt F. Wolpert

> As the series of red dots are indicated above the part for *shō* in the score written in European style, I believe that, with the help of Plates XVIII to XXI (pp. 253–257) and the explanations just given, it will not be very difficult to now decipher the individual parts and to rectify possible small errors.[1]

Müller had no precedent to go by for his study score of Dshioh-raku/Goshōraku [no kyū].[2] He opted to lay out his representations of the eight individual parts in the *tōgaku* ensemble according to the format of the Western orchestral score, with the wind-parts (above) separated from the string-parts (below) by the percussion section (middle) (see Transnotations 1–3, pp. 242, 243, 244). Alignment of one part beneath the other is in any case in keeping with their shared notated metric-grid of (red) dots (running along the top); further mensural support for alignment comes (albeit not for all his notations) from the small intracolumnary circles that show double-bar[3] segmentation of a notation (also marked across the top).[4] Reading the landscape-format score from top downwards (moving as designed from p. 242, down to p. 243, then flipping over to p. 244) gives the eight parts for *Goshōraku no kyū* ordered on the pages as:

[1] "Da die Reihen der rothen Punkte auf der europäisch-geschriebenen Partitur über der Parthie der Sho angegeben sind, so glaube ich, wird es mit Hülfe der Tafeln XVIII bis XXI und der eben gegebenen Erläuterungen nicht sehr schwer fallen, nun die einzelnen Stimmen zu dechiffriren und etwaige kleine Irrthümer zu rectificiren." (P. 217)

[2] "Kurzes Orchesterstück der Gagakku (Kapelle des Mikado)" ("Short orchestral piece of *gagaku* [Ensemble of the Mikado]") as he subtitles the score.

[3] We use "bar" rather than "measure" in this note for clarity in a context much concerned with various aspects of "measuring" time.

[4] For dots and circles as mensural notation, see p. 34f.

1. *shō* mouth-organ
2. *hichiriki* reed-pipe
3. *ōteki* flute
4. *kakko* small drum
5. *taiko* large drum
6. *shōko* bronze gong
7. *biwa* lute
8. *koto* zither

The principles Müller followed for his readings and amplifications of the set of notations he used (and provided in facsimile) for *Goshōraku no kyū* have been addressed (pp. 27–38). Here we add an essential note of clarification for *shō* (the mouth-organ, on the very top stave of the score) and, more urgently, for *biwa* (the lute, second from the bottom). Our reason for drawing these two parts out from the rest is that Müller's transnotational slips and misunderstandings – and, too, his printer's errors – are of such a nature that they may mask what he intended and cloud what ought to be visible now as a starting point for an important line of thought in the history of *gagaku* scholarship. It is these two parts in the *tōgaku* ensemble that have been vital for the historical study of *gagaku* in general, and *Goshōraku no kyū*, for *shō* and *biwa* in particular, has featured repeatedly along the way in specifically *tōgaku* research ever since Müller's facsimile-notations were unearthed again in the mid-1950s.[5]

Müller's time signature and note-values

Müller conducted experiments on the musical speed of *gagaku* performance. He used a metronome and reports in terms of quarter-notes per minute. The speeds he then gives are considerably faster than ones nowadays.[6] He also observed and reports on the role of *shōga* syllabaries for instrumental *gagaku*, the singing-while-keeping-time traditions for transmitting, learning, recalling, and rehearsing.[7] He affirms that pupils are singing the *shōga* while physically marking with the hand what he elsewhere defines as the "four equal parts" of a slice of time (a bar) marked by mensural notation ("the series of red dots") only at its beginning. Müller settles on a

---

[5] Shiba, *Gosen-fu*, 181; Picken and Wolpert, "Mouth-organ and Lute Parts of Tōgaku and their Interrelationships," 82; Wolpert, "Tang-music (Tōgaku) Manuscripts for Lute and their Interrelationships," 84; Picken et al., *Music from the Tang Court 1*, 5–6; Markham, "Contrafactum and a Buddhist neumatic notation from medieval Japan," 76; Terauchi, *Gagaku no rizumu kōzō*; Yang, "Japonifying the Qin," 141–218, especially 203 and 207; Nelson, "Court and Religious Music (2)," 52–61; Wolpert, "Tang Music Theory of Ritual Calendrical Transposition Applied," 77–80.

[6] *Idem*, "Metronomes, Matrices, and Other Musical Monsters," 63–65; Terauchi, "Tempo and Phrasing of the Gagaku in 1940s"; Nelson, "Court and Religious Music (2)," 58.

[7] Markham, "The Concept of a 'Basic Melody'," 62.

common-time signature for his score; eight common-time bars correspond to a complete combinatory percussion ostinato, a complete statement of a mensural "series of red dots" in a notation; two ostinati make a section; there are two sections, each of which is played twice. The piece thus claims an overall dimension of eight × eight common-time bars (excluding the *ad libitum* ending, a terminal convention which is not notated). A note to the opening of the score itself explains that it represents the first section of the piece as played on repeat; in the first statement, performance convention entails staggered entry of individual instrumental parts; Müller nevertheless marks these into his score by using the letter E for *Eintritt* ("entry"). And for section two, represented as played first in this case, he likewise still shows the terminating *ad libitum* pattern as four extra bars right at the end of the score.

Choice of time-signature carries with it connotations for performance speed;[8] choice of note-duration assigned to tablature-signs in a transnotation of measured instrumental notations for *gagaku* likewise. Müller's common-time meter assigns a complete bar of "four equal parts" (four quarter-notes) to each of the mensural dots (along the top), and hence a duration of a whole-note to the individual (non-annotated) tablature-signs in *shō-* and *biwa*-parts. His deciding on the whole-note as the basic transnotational time-unit is significant, for Laurence Picken would also assign a common-time signature and take a whole-note as the unit for his historic comparative transcription in 1957 of *shō-* and *biwa*-parts for the opening of the *tōgaku* item *Butokuraku* "Military Virtue Music."[9] This first transcription (Picken's term then for our "transnotation" now), showing only the notes as written, without their unwritten chordal additions (as Müller also had done for the *shō*-part, in fact), demonstrated the heterophonic relationship between melodic lines inherent in modern parts for *shō* and *biwa*. That these melodies function in the *shō-* and *biwa*-parts like a *cantus firmus* in *tōgaku* texture, but can be retrieved as the lively tunes of the Chinese Tang dynasty (which the name *tōgaku* "Music of Tang" announces) by speeding them up and expressing this increase in tempo by four-fold reduction of the basic transnotational unit (from whole-note to quarter-note), was, in 1957, a proposition still to come.

With that proposition published ten years later,[10] however, we confront a major issue in *gagaku* research between (1) a conception of "measure" and performance tempo that follows Picken and his later Cambridge Group and takes the quarter-note as its basic time-unit in order to express a lively performance speed (see Example 9, p. 299), and (2) a conception that follows modern performance practice, also for an historical notation, and takes a whole-note (complete bar of four quarter-notes) as the

---

[8] Fallows, "Tempo and Expression Marks."
[9] Picken, "The New Oxford History of Music: Ancient and Oriental Music," 147.
[10] *Idem*, "Central Asian Tunes in the Gagaku Tradition," 546–547.

unit, thereby expressing in terms of durational expansion vis-à-vis the Cambridge stance a markedly – even extremely – slow speed. In fact, performance tempo in tōgaku nowadays is typically so slow as to render the shō- and biwa-parts imperceptible as coherent melody. Regarding matters of tempo and note-duration in representations of Japanese gagaku in staff-notation, such differences in musical orthography are not just cosmetic: they show a fundamental polarity in conception and perception of melody and form, and thus in understanding of their historical evolution, all sharing of actual pitches notwithstanding.

Müller's transnotations for mouth-organ shō and lute biwa

In his transnotation of the notated shō-part (Plate XIX, Fig. 5, p. 255) (top stave in the full-score on pages 242–244), Müller makes one mistake over and over (see Example 4, p. 294). He systematically misreads two different notational symbols as one (bō 几 and kotsu 乙 both as kotsu 乙), with the result that for the mouth-organ each intended d'' comes out as an an a'; and he misses a "grace-note" (p. 203), g' leaning into f♯', in bar 3 on the bottom stave in Example 4. Otherwise his whole-note melody, representing only the notes of the written tablature and ignoring the cluster-chords, which are added in performance and are described in his essay in detail from a Japanese chart, is consistent with later transnotations that follow the view of Picken and the Cam-

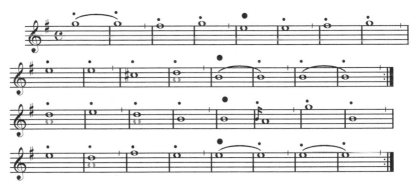

Example 4 – Müller's shō transnotation emended. A grey note denotes his misreading of a tablature-sign.

bridge Group (see top line in Example 9, p. 299). To put it another way, these later Cambridge transnotations are made, independently, on principles essentially the same as those Müller set up for himself for the shō in his full score for Goshōraku no kyū; significantly, however, they are reduced to quarter-note durations with all the implications for the perception of melody at increased performance speed that this choice entails.

The transnotation of the notated *biwa*-part (Plate XXI, Fig. 1, p. 257) is contained in the lowest-pitched notes on the full-score stave BIWA (second from bottom), with the exception of the note distinguished as "reverse plucked" by a "small red hook" (p. 212) in the Japanese notation, and marked by "*arpeggio* from top to bottom"[11] in the score; here it is the highest-pitched note that is part of the transnotation. The notation itself has three instances of misprinting Japanese tablature-signs: twice a misprint of *bi* 乙 for *otsu* 𝐋 (d♯ for B), which Müller ignores in both cases, transnotating each correctly as B; and there is a misprint in the figure 八ユヒ, which should be the common figure 八ㄴヒ. Since, for whatever reason, Müller omits transnotation of these small tablature-signs ユヒ, he unwittingly sidesteps a further mistake. Six bars before the end of the second section (Transnotation 3, p. 244), however, he himself adds an "ornament" to the *g* (*g-f♯-g*), a diminution which is not in his Japanese notation.[12] And an obvious error is his systematic transnotation of the tablature-sign *ko* ユ (*e*) as *f*♮; the pitch *f*♮ is simply not available in the tuning for *hyōjō*. Puzzlingly, this would have been clear from his own tuning-diagram (pp. 207–208).

Example 5 – Performance practice today: *arpeggio*-chord for notated note *g*

Example 6 – Müller's full-score (p. 242): *arpeggio*-chord for notated note d♯

Where Müller went more seriously wrong, though, was in his attempt to include in his full-score the unwritten *arpeggio*-chords of *biwa* performance idiom; and his transnotation, like that for *koto*, is confusingly pitched an octave higher than it sounds. His verbal descriptions of the chords (p. 211) and his amplifications in the score are incompatible with each other. And both are also incompatible with known performance practice,[13] namely, as we have elucidated (Example 3, p. 33), to excite all open strings that are pitch-wise below the string of the notated note (Example 5). Müller incorrectly conveys that each that is higher pitch-wise is to be fingered at an adjacent position on the same fret as that for the notated note (Example 6). He seems

---

[11] "Harpeggio von oben nach unten."

[12] The court music scores published in 1876 have a ligature *g-f♯* at this place; certain historical versions do have the *g-f♯-g* ornament, however.

[13] For a modern full-score transnotation of *Goshōraku no kyū* with some amplification of performance practice by a Japanese Court musician, see Shiba, *Gosen-fu*, 181.

to have thought that the performer lays his finger across the fret and excites stopped rather than open strings. This misunderstanding is made clear when a Westernized lute-tablature is laid under Müller's full-score representation for biwa (Example 7 on the next page): his chords are fingered there predominantly with the one finger that stops the single fret-position that is notated. However, Müller's inconsistent use of c♯′ (and two fingers) in two of his added chords (bars 1 and 8 in Example 7) may be an attempt (then aborted) to circumvent a "disallowed" pitch (c♮′) that this interpretation produces (see the annotation to his tuning-diagram, p. 208).[14] Five other chords retain c♮′ (bar 12 in Example 7 on the facing page, for instance), and his own verbal description incorrectly calls for a c♮′.

Remaining with the non-written convention of adding arpeggiated chords, we came to suspect that Müller's remark that "the higher strings remain full length"[15] may reveal that he later interpreted "higher" as indicating pitch, rather than indicating the physical position of the strings on the instrument as held. (Compare Example 3a, p. 33.) And so we confront a second issue in gagaku research of biwa convention: Müller no longer reads the numbering of strings according to Japanese practice as he gives it in his own tuning-diagrams (pp. 207–211, also Plate XVIII, p. 253 and Plate XVIIIa, p. 254), that is, starting from the lowest-tuned as number 1 and moving upwards pitch-wise. Rather, when working with staff-notation he falls back into ingrained European practice, which starts numerically from the highest-tuned string as number 1, moving from there downwards.[16] His "string 1" becomes the highest-pitched open string, whereas it is the lowest-pitched open string in Japanese usage, and in his diagrams. As convoluted as it may seem, from watching the biwa performers – holding their instruments horizontally – Müller must have confused what is physically "higher" from the ground with what is "higher" in pitch. He saw the performers sweeping across the open strings, from that highest from the ground downwards to the string that is notated. But once he had started thinking intuitively in European practice – presumably when making his full-score – what he had seen interfered with his now "inverted" string associations. In his imagination he now starts at the string stipulated by the notated tablature, and also strikes downwards towards the ground, with the disastrous result that his imagined chords are now the notes on the strings pitch-wise above that of the string notated. Compare chordal

---

[14] "Diejenigen Töne, welche mit Punkten versehen sind, werden zum Spielen nicht benutzt." "Those notes which are marked with dots are not used for playing."

[15] "Die höheren Saiten bleiben in ihrer vollen Länge" (p. 211).

[16] For numbering of strings on Western stringed instruments, see for example http://de.wikipedia.org/wiki/Violoncello; Müller's son was trained as a 'cellist. Specifically for lute-courses: http://www.lutesociety.org/pages/lute-stringing, for guitar stringing: http://howtotuneaguitar.org/tuning/how-to-tune/; a lute tuning-diagram with Western staff notation is in http://www.tenstringguitar.info/index.php?p=1_3.

structures in both staff- and tablature-notation in Müller (Example 7) and Shiba Sukehiro (Example 8). Indeed, Müller's own annotation, "*arpeggio* from top to bottom" (Transnotation (2), p. 243), for the single instance of a chord "reverse plucked" suggests we are right.

Example 7 – Excerpt from Müller's *Goshōraku no kyū*: transnotation (in corrected octave) in black, (wrongly) added chords in grey (facsimile of tablature, p. 257).

Example 8 – Excerpt from *Goshōraku no kyū* from Shiba, *Gosen-fu*, 181, with Westernized *biwa*-tablature underlaid.

Müller's misfortune here might well serve as a recommendation for following Western convention when writing about the *biwa* in a Western language (and for a Western audience). In other words, when making a choice to follow Japanese or European practice for numbering the strings, perhaps we ought to take into account the potential pitfalls of automatic string-ordering assumptions – assumptions triggered unconsciously in Western readers who are familiar with conventions for classical Western stringed instruments, and who are faced with reading unfamiliar conven-

tions in a text in which a realization of biwa-notation is represented in Western staff-notation.

It seems likely that Müller had not spent much time questioning (or observing) the biwa performers. The biwa is the weak point in his textual description of unwritten performance details and, consequently, also in his amplification of his transnotation. However, that transnotation of the plain, written Japanese notation – that is to say, transnotation exclusively of the notated tablature-signs – is only significantly marred by one systematic misreading (ʃ♮ for e, as in bars 5 and 9 in Example 7). It is surprising that he did not follow the same practice as for his mouth-organ transnotation, and omit the unwritten completely.[17]

Steps in musical thinking

Müller's suggestion in our motto to this note that the reader might want – indeed, is encouraged – to retrace for herself the steps which lead to the transnotation (-cum-amplification) of the tablatures offered in conjunction with the full-score of Goshōraku no kyū (Transnotations 1–3, on pages 242–244) was prudent. Even though we now see that nobody, except for Picken, seems to have seriously taken him up on it. Picken engaged with Müller's full set of facsimile notations in the 1950s, when these were almost all he had to work with in Cambridge. Sometime later he acquired modern tōgaku part-books for shō, and for the other two winds, hichiriki reed-pipe and ryūteki flute. But for biwa, his first encounter with more than Müller's facsimile and the single published specimen of biwa-tablature that supported his 1957 proposal[18] seems to have occurred only when he obtained copies of string parts of Meiji date (1876)[19] in 1969 and purchased part of the Kikutei-ke collection of musical manuscripts in 1970.[20] This part of the collection is much concerned with the biwa tradition.[21]

[17] To further confound the issue of Müller's string-ordering and arpeggiated chords, in the four bars of the ad libitum ending, they are in the right order. And Müller's chord in bars five to six in the final ostinato (p. 244), notated with a "large hook," gathers up all four strings, above and below.

[18] See p. 3.

[19] See NT's account, pp. 70–71.

[20] Koyama, "An introduction to the Kikutei Manuscripts of Japanese Music in the Lawrence [sic] Picken Collection at Cambridge University Library"; Ota, "Kenburijji no kikuteike kyūzō gagaku kankei shiryō mokuroku 1"; idem, "Kenburijji no kikuteike kyūzō gagaku kankei shiryō mokuroku 2."

[21] See Introduction in Picken et al., Music from the Tang Court 1, 5–14, and Picken's autobiographical account of these steps, available in a documentary film, Knott, Markham, and Wolpert, On the Road to Tang through Cambridge, in the Library of Congress.

Wuchang yue ji/Goshōraku no kyū
'Music of the Five Constant Virtues. Quick'

五　常　樂　急

Example 9 – *Goshōraku no kyū*: Picken and Wolpert, "Mouth-organ and Lute Parts of Tōgaku and their Interrelationships," 82. (Top line) Modern *shō*-part; (D) *Sango-yōroku* (ca. 1180); (C) *Biwa-fu* (1566); (B) *Biwa* (n.d.); (A) Meiji *biwa*-part (1876).

One tiny Kikutei-ke manuscript for biwa, titled simply Biwa and containing ten simplified[22] tōgaku items, including Goshōraku no kyū, became foundational for the Tang Music Project in a collaborative paper written by Picken with one of us (RFW) in 1972 (expanded in 1973, available in 1975,[23] but published only in 1981).[24] In fact, it was

Example 10 – Computer-generated[25] transnotation of a Meiji biwa-part for Go-shōraku no kyū (The Picken Collection, Cambridge University Library).

<hr/>

22 Only notes sounded by the right-hand are notated; notes sounded by the left hand alone are absent in the tablatures.

23 As Appendix 3 in Wolpert, "Lute Music and Tablatures of the Tang Period," 238–256.

24 Picken and Wolpert, "Mouth-organ and Lute Parts of Tōgaku and their Interrelationships." The manuscript was given to me (RFW) by Laurence Picken in 1976 to mark our collaboration and my election that year as William Stone Fellow of Peterhouse, Cambridge.

25 Wolpert, BiwaPrinter.

this study that enabled Picken to state that his hypothesis in 1957 that the basic tunes of the parts for mouth-organ and lute are essentially identical could be "regarded as confirmed."[26] Testimony to the centrality of *Goshōraku no kyū* in our thinking back then lies in its selection as a "test-piece" for the paper and its placement there as the first of the ten items (Example 9, p. 299); choice and placement were perhaps determined by Picken's prior experience with Müller's facsimile and, presumably, with the version in the Meiji parts he had acquired in 1969. Unnoticed[27] though, a reduction from an early stage in the research for the paper, when Picken was still concerned with the 1957 proposition that the basic tunes for mouth-organ and lute are essentially identical, had crept in and remained undetected in my published transnotation of the Meiji *biwa*-part for *Goshōraku no kyū*. We had decided to include this, along with other lute-parts by then available to us, for the sake of comparison with the version in the little *Kikutei-ke* manuscript, *Biwa*.

I had reduced my transnotation of the written Meiji *biwa*-part for *Goshōraku no kyū* ([A] in Example 9), stripping away diminutions fingered-plucked by the left hand (identical with ornaments in the late twelfth-century version [D], absent from the version in *Biwa* [B]), to reveal in quarter-notes that it carries the same basic melody as that carried by the simpler, written part for *shō* (top line).[28] It is this experimental reduction that made its way to publication. "Full" transnotations of this Meiji part for *Goshōraku no kyū* were included elsewhere in my dissertation[29] and/or have been available in other published papers.[30] But it seems mandatory that, in Müller's spirit of self-correction in his essays, I too offer the reader interested in tracking further steps in the history of *gagaku* scholarship a rectified transnotation (in quarter-notes) of the Meiji *biwa*-part for *Goshōraku no kyū* (Example 10), of a part only minimally different from the one that Müller himself used for his interactive full-score.[31]

It is to be hoped that our disentangling some of these transnotational knots will enable a better appreciation of just what a mine of information Müller offered the Western musicological world back there in the mid-1870s, in his innovative, interactive study score for *Goshōraku no kyū*, its generating facsimile notations, and their verbal explanations. 🔊

---

[26] Picken and Wolpert, "Mouth-organ and Lute Parts of Tōgaku and their Interrelationships," 80.

[27] And unnoticed as well in Appendix 3 to my (RFW) doctoral dissertation.

[28] I (RFW) note, herewith, that in the reduction (A) in Example 9, *b* on beat 6 in the penultimate measure should read as *a*. In the same place my diminution as a mordent for *Sango-yōroku* (D) should be, rather, the conventional run *bag* (Example 10).

[29] Wolpert, "Lute Music and Tablatures of the Tang Period," 155, 318.

[30] *Idem*, "Tang-music (Tōgaku) Manuscripts for Lute and their Interrelationships," 84.

[31] See NT's discussion above, on pages 71–72.

Bibliography

Abraham, Otto, and Erich M. von Hornbostel. "Studien über das Tonsystem und die Musik der Japaner." *Sammelbände der Internationalen Musikgesellschaft* 4, no. 2 (1903): 302–360.

———. "Über die Bedeutung des Phonographen für vergleichende Musikwissenschaft." *Zeitschrift für Ethnologie* 36 (1904): 222–233.

Adler, Guido. "Über Heterophonie." *Jahrbuch der Musikbibliothek Peters*, 1908, 17–27.

Amiot, Joseph M. *Mémoire sur la musique des Chinois: tant anciens et modernes*. Edited by Pierre J. Roussier. Paris: Nyon l'aîné, 1779. http://gallica.bnf.fr/ark:/12148/bpt6k54211858/f4.image.

Arendt, Carl. "Das schöne Mädchen von Pao. Eine Erzählung aus der Geschichte Chinas im achten Jahrhundert v. Chr." *Mitteilungen der deutschen Gesellschaft für Natur- und Völkerkunde Ostasiens* 2, nos. 11–20 (Beilage 1. 1876).

Barrow, John. *Travels in China: Containing Descriptions, Observations, and Comparisons, Made and Collected in the Course of a Short Residence at the Imperial Palace of Yuen-Min-Yuen, and on a Subsequent Journey through the Country from Pekin to Canton, in which it is Attempted to Appreciate the Rank that this Extra-ordinary Empire may be Considered to Hold in the Scale of Civilized Nations*. London: T. Cadell / W. Davies, 1806.

Bird, Isabella L. *Unbeaten Tracks in Japan: An Account of Travels in the Interior Including Visits to the Aborigines of Yezo and the Shrines of Nikkō and Isé*. 2 vols. London: John Murray, 1880. Rutland, VT: C. E. Tuttle, 1973.

Bowers, John Z. "The Adoption of German Medicine in Japan: The Decision and the Beginning." *Bulletin of the History of Medicine* 53 (1979): 57–80.

———. *When the Twain Meet: The Rise of Western Medicine in Japan*. Baltimore, MD: The John Hopkins University Press, 1980.

Boxer, Charles R. *The Christian Century in Japan 1549–1650*. Berkeley: University of California Press, 1951.

Brandt, Max von. *Dreiunddreissig Jahre in Ost-Asien: Erinnerungen eines deutschen Diplomaten*. Leipzig: Georg Wigand, 1901.

————. *Doitsu kōshi no mita Meiji ishin* ドイツ公使の見た明治維新. Translated by Hara Kiyoshi 原潔 and Nagaoka Atsushi 永岡敦. Tōkyō: Shin Jinbutsu Ōraisha 新人物往来社, 1987. Originally published as *Dreiunddreissig Jahre in Ost-Asien: Erinnerungen eines deutschen Diplomaten* (Leipzig: Georg Wigand, 1901).

Bray, Francesca, ed. *Graphics and Text in the Production of Technical Knowledge in China: The Warp and the Weft*. Leiden: Brill, 2007.

Brown, Yu-Ying. "The Von Siebold Collection from Tokugawa Japan: Dr Philipp Franz von Siebold's Career in the Orient." *The Electronic British Library Journal*, 1975, 163–170. http://www.bl.uk/eblj/1975articles/pdf/article16.pdf.

Chamberlain, Basil H. *Things Japanese, Being Notes on Various Subjects Connected with Japan*. London: Kegan Paul, Trench, Trübner & Co., 1890.

Charlevoix, Pierre F. X. de. *Histoire de l'établissement, des progrès et de la décadence du christianisme dans l'empire du Japon : ou l'on voit les différentes révolutions qui ont agité cette monarchie pendant plus d'un siècle*. 2 vols. Rouen: Jacques Joseph Le Boullenger, 1715.

Courant, Maurice. "Chine et Corée: Essai Historique sur la Musique Classique des Chinois avec un Appendice Relatif a la Musique Coréenne." In *Encyclopédie de la musique et dictionnaire du Conservatoire*, edited by Albert Lavignac, 77–241. Paris: Charles Delagrave, 1913.

————. "Japon: Notice Historique." In *Encyclopédie de la musique et dictionnaire du Conservatoire*, edited by Albert Lavignac and Lionel de La Laurencie, 242–256. Paris: C. Delagrave, 1913.

Deutsche Gesellschaft für Natur- und Völkerkunde Ostasiens (OAG), ed. "Mitteilungen der OAG seit 1873." n.d. http://www.oag.jp/digitale-bibliothek/mitteilungen/.

Dittrich, R. "Beiträge zur Kentniss der japanischen Musik." *Mittheilungen der Deutschen Gesellschaft für Natur- und Völkerkunde Ostasiens* 6, no. 58 (1893–1897): 376–391.

Du Bois, Francis. "The Gekkin Musical Scale." *Transactions of the Asiatic Society of Japan* 19 (1891): 369–371.

Dumitrescu, Theodor, Karl Kügle, and Marnix van Berchum, eds. *Early Music Editing: Principles, Historiography, Future Directions*. Turnhout: Centre d'études

supérieures de la Renaissance, Université François-Rabelais de Tours, Brepols, 2013.

Eckert, Franz. "Japanische Liedcr." *Mittheilungen der Deutschen Gesellschaft für Natur- und Völkerkunde Ostasiens* 2, no. 20 (1876–1880): 423–428.

———. "Die japanische Nationalhymne." *Mittheilungen der Deutschen Gesellschaft für Natur- und Völkerkunde Ostasiens* 3, no. 23 (1880–1884): 131.

Ellis, Alexander J. "On the Musical Scales of Various Nations." *The Journal of the Society of Arts* 33, no. 1688 (March 1885): 485–527.

———. *Shominzoku no onkai : hikaku ongakuron* 諸民族の音階：比較音楽論. Translated by Monma Naomi 門馬直美. 1885. Tōkyō: Ongaku no tomosha 音楽之友社, 1951. Originally published as "On the Musical Scales of Various Nations," *The Journal of the Society of Arts* 33, no. 1688 (March 1885): 485–527.

Endō, Hirosi. *Bibliography of Oriental and Primitive Music.* Tōkyō: The Nanki Music Library, 1929.

Eppstein, Ury. *The Beginnings of Western Music in Meiji Era Japan.* Lewiston, NY: The Edwin Mellen Press, 1994.

Fallows, David. "Tempo and Expression Marks." In *The New Grove Dictionary of Music and Musicians,* edited by John Tyrell and Stanley Sadie. Oxford Music Online, 2001. http://www.oxfordmusiconline.com:80/subscriber/article/grove/music/27650.

Fritsch, Ingrid. "Walzenaufnahmen japanischer Musik (1901–1913) / Wax Cylinder Recordings of Japanese Music (1901–1913)." In *Historische Klangdokumente BPhA-WA 1,* edited by Artur Simon and Susanne Ziegler. Historische Klangdokumente / Historical Sound Documents. CD and Commentary. Berlin: Staatliche Museen zu Berlin – Stiftung Preußischer Kulturbesitz, 2003.

———. "Some Reflections on the Early Wax Cylinder Recordings of Japanese Music in the Berlin Phonogramm Archive (Germany)." In *Musicology and Globalization,* 224–228. The Musicological Society of Japan, 2004.

———. "Japan Ahead in Music? Zur Wertschätzung japanischer Musik im Westen." In *Japan immer wieder neu gesehen. Perspektiven der Japanforschung an der Universität zu Köln,* edited by Antje Weber Chantal u. Lemberg, 249–271. Berlin: LIT Verlag, 2013.

Fujio Tadashi 藤尾直史. "Miyake korekushon no sekai 三宅コレクションの世界." *Ouroboros: Museum of the University of Tokyo* 17 (May 10, 2002). http://www.um.u-tokyo.ac.jp/museum/ouroboros/07_01/shinki-syuzou.html.

Funk, Hermann. "Über die japanischen Theegesellschaften Cha no ju." *Mittheilungen der deutschen Gesellschaft für Natur- und Völkerkunde Ostasiens* 1, no. 6 (1874): 41–45.

―――. "Über japanische Gebete." *Mittheilungen der deutschen Gesellschaft für Natur- und Völkerkunde Ostasiens* 1, no. 9 (1876): 40–42.

―――. "Über Wahrsagung aus dem Panzer der Schildkroete." *Mittheilungen der deutschen Gesellschaft für Natur- und Völkerkunde Ostasiens* 1, no. 9 (1876): 36–40.

Gamō Mitsuko 蒲生美津子. "Meiji sentei-fu no seiritsu jijō 明治選定譜の成立事情." In *Ongaku to ongakugaku* 音楽と音楽学: *Hattori Kozo sensei kanreki kinen ronbunshū* 服部幸三先生還暦記念論文集, edited by Sumikura Ichiro 角倉一朗. Tōkyō: Ongaku no tomosha 音楽之友社, 1986.

Garfias, Robert A. *Music of a Thousand Autumns: The Tōgaku Style of Japanese Court Music.* Los Angeles, CA: University of California Press, 1975.

Gottschewski, Hermann. "Nineteenth-Century Gagaku Songs as a Subject of Musical Analysis: An Early Example of Musical Creativity in Modern Japan." *Nineteenth-Century Music Review* 10 (2013): 239–264.

Groneman, Isaak. *De gamelan te Jogjakarta, uitgegeven, met eene voorrede over onze kennis der Javaansche muziek.* With an introduction by Jan P. N. Land. Amsterdam: Johannes Müller, 1890.

Harich-Schneider, Eta. "The Present Condition of Japanese Court Music." *The Musical Quarterly* 39, no. 1 (January 1953): 49–74.

―――. *A History of Japanese Music.* London: Oxford University Press, 1973.

―――. *Musikalische Impressionen aus Japan 1941–1957.* Edited by Ingrid Fritsch. München: Iudicium, 2006.

Harrison, LeRon J. "Gagaku in Place and Practice: A Philosophical Inquiry into the Place of Japanese Imperial Court Music in Contemporary Culture." *Asian Music* 48, no. 1 (2017): 4–27.

Hayashi Kenzō 林謙三. "Hakuga no fue-fu kō 博雅笛譜考." *Gagaku: Kogaku-fu no kaidoku* 雅樂 – 古樂譜の解読, 1969, 285–308.

Helmholtz, Hermann. *On the Sensations of Tone as a Physiological Basis for the Theory of Music.* Edited and translated by Alexander J. Ellis. London: Longmans, Green & Co., 1875. Originally published as *Die Lehre von den Tonempfindungen als physiologische Grundlage für die Theorie der Musik* (1863; Braunschweig: F. Vieweg und Sohn, 1877), http://www.mdz-nbn-resolving.de/urn/resolver.pl?urn=urn:nbn:de:bvb:12-bsb10598685-7.

————. *Die Lehre von den Tonempfindungen als physiologische Grundlage für die Theorie der Musik.* 1863. Braunschweig: F. Vieweg und Sohn, 1877. http://www.mdz-nbn-resolving.de/urn/resolver.pl?urn=urn:nbn:de:bvb:12-bsb10598685-7.

Herzog, Avigdor. "Transcription and Transnotation in Ethnomusicology." *Journal of the International Folk Music Council* 16 (1964): 100–101. http://www.jstor.org/stable/835092.

Hiebert, Erwin N. *The Helmholtz Legacy in Physiological Acoustics.* New York, NY: Springer, 2014.

Hirschfeld, Mattias. *Beethoven in Japan: zur Einführung und Verbreitung westlicher Musik in der japanischen Gesellschaft.* Hamburg: Von Bockel, 2005.

Hoffman, Johann J. *A Japanese Grammar.* Leiden: A. W. Sÿthoff, 1867.

Holtz, Viktor. "Zwei japanische Lieder." *Mittheilungen der deutschen Gesellschaft für Natur- und Völkerkunde Ostasiens* I, no. 3 (1873): 13–14.

————. "Das japanische Schachspiel." *Mittheilungen der deutschen Gesellschaft für Natur- und Völkerkunde Ostasiens* I, no. 5 (1874): 10–12.

————. "Japanische Lieder." *Mittheilungen der deutschen Gesellschaft für Natur- und Völkerkunde Ostasiens* I, no. 4 (1874): 45–47.

Hornbostel, Erich M. von. "Über Mehrstimmigkeit in der außereuropäischen Musik." In *3. Kongreß der Internationalen Musikgesellschaft. Wien 25. bis 29. Mai 1909: Bericht,* edited by Guido Adler, 298–303. Leipzig: Breitkopf & Härtel, 1909.

————. "Melodie und Skala." *Jahrbuch der Musikbibliothek Peters* 20 (1912): 11–23.

Howard, Keith. "Contested Contextualization: The Historical Constructions of East Asian Music." Chap. 10 in McCollum and Hebert, *Theory and Method in Historical Ethnomusicology,* 337–360.

————. "Foreword: The Past Is No Longer a Foreign Country." In McCollum and Hebert, *Theory and Method in Historical Ethnomusicology,* ix–xv.

Hughes, David W. "The Picken School and East Asia: China, Japan and Korea." *Ethnomusicology Forum* 19, no. 2 (2010): 231–239.

Hunter, Justin R. "Redefining Western Military Drumming: A Look at Re-representation Techniques of Western Style Military Music in Late Edo Period Japan." *Studia instrumentorum musicae popularis* 1 (New Series) (2009): 67–78.

Imamiya Shin 今宮新. "Alexander von Siebold アレキサンダー・フォンー・シ ボル ト." *Shigaku* 史學 (Keiō University 慶應義塾大学) 15, no. 4 (1937): 115–155.

Isawa Shūji 伊澤修二. *Extracts from the Report of S. Isawa, Director of the Institute of Music, on the Result of the Investigations Concerning Music Undertaken by Order of the Department of Education, Tokio, Japan.* Translated by The Institute of Music. Tokyo: Department of Education, The Institute of Music, 1884.

Jackson, Myles W. "From Scientific Instrument to Musical Instruments: The Tuning Fork, the Metronome, and the Siren." Chap. 8 in *The Oxford Handbook of Sound Studies*, edited by Trevor Pinch and Karin Bijsterveld, 201–223. Oxford: Oxford University Press, 2012.

Johnson, Henry. "A Koto By Any Other Name: Exploring Japanese Systems of Musical Instrument Classification." *Asian Music* 28, no. 1 (1997): 43–59.

Kadota Akira 門田明. "Machida Hisanari ryakuden 町田久成略伝." *Kagoshima-kenritsu tanki daigaku kiyō* 鹿児島県立短期大学紀要 48 (1997): 1–6.

Kajino, Ena. "A Lost Opportunity for Tradition: The Violin in Early Twentieth-Century Japanese Traditional Music." *Nineteenth-Century Music Review* 10 (2013): 293–321.

Kämpfer, Engelbert. *Engelbert Kämpfers Geschichte und Beschreibung von Japan: Aus den Originalhandschriften des Verfassers.* Edited by Christian W. von Dohm. 2 vols. Lemgo: Verlag der Meyerschen Buchhandlung, 1777–1779.

Kapri, B. M. "Ueber japanische Musik." *Neue Zeitschrift für Musik* 71, no. 15 (1875): 146–148.

————. "Ueber japanische Musik." *Neue Zeitschrift für Musik* 71, no. 16 (1875): 159–161.

————. "Ueber japanische Musik." *Neue Zeitschrift für Musik* 72, no. 4 (1876): 33–35, Extra–Beilage.

Kim, Hoi-eun. "Physicians on the Move: German Physicians in Meiji Japan and Japanese Medical Students in Imperial Germany, 1868–1914." Ph.D., Harvard, 2006.

————. *Doctors of Empire: Medical and Anthropological Encounters between Imperial Germany and Meiji Japan.* Toronto, ON: University of Toronto Press, 2014.

Knechtges, David R., and Tong Xiao. *Wen Xuan or Selections of Refined Literature. Volume One: Rhapsodies on Metropolises and Capitals.* Vol. 1. Princeton, NJ: Princeton University Press, 1982.

Knott, Cargill G. "Remarks on Japanese Musical Scales." *Transactions of the Asiatic Society of Japan* 19, no. 2 (1891): 373–391.

Knott, Thomas, Elizabeth J. Markham, and Rembrandt F. Wolpert, eds. *On the Road to Tang.* Directed by Sarah Caldwell, Camera Dan Hnatio. Washington DC and

Fayetteville AR: Library of Congress / Center for the Study of Early Asian & Middle Eastern Musics, University of Arkansas, 2003.

————, eds. *On the Road to Tang through Cambridge*. Directed by Sarah Caldwell, Camera Dan Hnatio. (DVD). Washington, DC and Fayetteville, AR: Library of Congress & Center for the Study of Early Asian / Middle Eastern Musics, University of Arkansas, [2004] 2011.

Kong Qiu (Confucius). *Le Chou-king, un des livres sacrés des Chinois: qui renferme les fondements de leur ancienne histoire, les principes de leur gouvernement & de leur morale.* Edited by Joseph de Guignes. Translated by Antoine Gaubil. Paris: Tilliard, 1770. http://www.mdz-nbn-resolving.de/urn/resolver.pl?urn=urn:nbn:de:bvb:12-bsb10219776-2.

Koseki Tsuneo 小関恒雄. "御雇教師ミユルレルとホフマン, 'Notes on Leopold Müller and Theodor E. Hoffmann, Founders of the Medical School of Tokyo in the Early Meiji Era'." *Nihon Ishigaku Zasshi* 日本医史学雑誌 29, no. 3 (1983): 276–290.

Koyama, Noboru. "An introduction to the Kikutei Manuscripts of Japanese Music in the Lawrence [sic] Picken Collection at Cambridge University Library." In *European Association of Japanese Resource Specialists*, 1–9. 18. Rome, 2007. ==Dead_Link:==http://japanesestudies.arts.kuleuven.be/pub/bscw.cgi/17313.

Kraas, Ernst. "German Physicians in Japan: Personal, Medical and Cultural Characteristics." In Thiede, Hiki, and Keil, *Philipp Franz von Siebold and His Era*, 135–148.

Kraus, Alessandro. *La musique au Japon*. Florence: Impr. de l'Arte della stampa, 1879.

Lachmann, Robert. *Musik des Orients*. Breslau: F. Hirt, 1929.

Levy, Jim. "Joseph Amiot and Enlightenment Speculation on the Origins of Pythagorean Tuning." *THEORIA, University of North Texas Journal of Music Theory* 4 (1989): 63–88.

Long yun 龍雲. *Qian Deming : 18 shiji Zhong-Fa jian de wenhua shizhe* 錢德明: 18 世紀中法間的文化使者. Zhong-Fa wenxue guanxi yanjiu congshu 中法文學關係研究叢書. Beijing: Beijing daxue chubanshe 北京大學出版社, 2015. Originally published as "Un jésuite à la croisée de deux cultures: le rôle du père Joseph-Marie Amiot (1718–1793) comme intermédiaire culturel entre la Chine et la France" (Ph.D., Université Paris-Sorbonne (Paris IV), 2010), http://www.theses.fr/2010PA040068.

Long, Yun. "Un jésuite à la croisée de deux cultures: le rôle du père Joseph-Marie Amiot (1718–1793) comme intermédiaire culturel entre la Chine et la France." Ph.D., Université Paris-Sorbonne (Paris IV), 2010. http://www.theses.fr/2010PA040068.

Luo Bi 羅秘. *Lu shi* 路史. 1170. Shanghai: Hanfenlou 涵芬樓, 1920.

Macrobius, Ambrosius Aurelius Theodosius. *Macrobii Ambrosii Theodosii Opera quae supersunt : excussis exemplaribus tam manu exaratis quam typis descriptis emendavit: prolegomena, apparatum criticum, adnotationes, cum aliorum selectas tum suas, indicesque adiecit Ludovicus Janus: Saturnaliorum libri VII et indices.* Edited by Ludwig von Jan. Vol. 2. Quedlinburg and Leipzig: Gottfried Bass, 1852. https://archive. org/details/macrobiiambrosii02macr.

Marett, Allan J. "Tunes Notated in Flute Tablature from a Japanese Source of the Tenth Century." *Musica Asiatica* 1 (1977): 1–59.

———. "Tōgaku: Where Have the Tang Melodies Gone, and Where Have the New Melodies Come From?" *Ethnomusicology* 29, no. 3 (1985): 409–431.

———. "Modal Practice in the Tenth-Century Japanese Flute Source Hakuga no fue-fu 博雅笛譜 and Its Implications for our Understanding of Present-day tōgaku." In *PNC 2001 Annual Conference and Joint Meetings in HK*, edited by Pacific Neighborhood Consortium. Hong Kong, 2001. http://pnclink.org/annual/ annual2001/hk%5C%20pdf/allan%5C%20marett.pdf.

———. "Mode, § V, 5(ii): Japanese chōshi: Scales and Modes in Court Music." In *The New Grove Dictionary of Music and Musicians*, edited by Stanley Sadie, vol. 16, 853b–858b, 860b. London: Macmillan Publishers, 2001.

Markham, Elizabeth J. "The Concept of a 'Basic Melody' in Early Japanese Court Music: Evidence in a Buddhist Notation?" In *Studia Instrumentorum Musicae Popularis XII: Conference of the Study Group for Folk Musical Instruments, International Council for Traditional Music, Terschelling 1995*, edited by Eszter Fontana, Andreas Michel, and Erich Stockmann, 12:67–73. 1995. Halle: Janos Stekovics, 2004.

———. "*Contrafactum* and a Buddhist neumatic notation from medieval Japan." *Cantus Planus*, 2006, 53–82.

———. *Saibara: Japanese Court Songs of the Heian Period*. 2 vols. 1983. Cambridge: Cambridge University Press, 2009.

———. "Extrapolating Intent in Leopold Müller's Empirical Study of Gagaku in Early Meiji Japan." *International Musicological Society - 2nd Biennial Conference of the East Asian Regional Association* 國際音樂學學會東亞分會第二屆雙年會 (National Taiwan University, Taipei, Taiwan): Musics in the Shifting Global Order, 2013.

———. "Review of Carl Stumpf, *The Origins of Music*. Translated and edited by David Trippett. Oxford (Oxford University Press). 2012." *Ethnomusicology Forum* 23, no. 3 (2014): 459–462. doi:10.1080/17411912.2014.958512.

McCollum, Jonathan, and David G. Hebert, eds. *Theory and Method in Historical Ethnomusicology*. With a foreword by Keith Howard. Lanham, MD: Lexington Books, 2014.

McDermott, Joseph P., and Peter Burke, eds. *The Book Worlds of East Asia and Europe, 1450–1850: Connections and Comparisons*. Hong Kong: Hong Kong University Press, 2015.

Meyer, Hermann J., ed. *Neues Konservation-Lexikon, ein Wörterbuch des allgemeinen Wissens*. 2nd ed. 16 vols. Hildburghausen: Bibliographisches Institut, 1861–1873.

Mikami Kagefumi 三上景文. *Jige kaden* 地下家伝. Edited by Nihon koten zenshū kankō-kai 日本古典全集刊行会. Vol. 33. Nihon koten zenshū 日本古典全集. [1844] 1938.

Mittheilungen der Deutschen Gesellschaft für Natur- und Völkerkunde Ostasiens. Vol. 1. Tōkyō and Yokohama: Deutsche Gesellschaft für Natur- und Völkerkunde Ostasiens, 1873–1876.

Miyake, B., and Leopold Müller. "Ueber die japanische Geburtshuelfe (1)." *Mittheilungen der deutschen Gesellschaft für Natur- und Völkerkunde Ostasiens* 1, no. 5 (1873): 21–27.

———. "Ueber die japanische Geburtshuelfe (2)." *Mittheilungen der deutschen Gesellschaft für Natur- und Völkerkunde Ostasiens* 1, no. 8 (1875): 9–13.

———. "Ueber die japanische Geburtshuelfe (3)." *Mittheilungen der deutschen Gesellschaft für Natur- und Völkerkunde Ostasiens* 1, no. 10 (1876): 9–16.

Mizler von Kolof, Lorenz Christoph. "Abbildung und kurze Erklärung der musikalischen Instrumenten der Japoneser." *Musikalische Bibliothek* (Mizler) 3, no. 1 (1746): 160–168. Based on Pierre F. X. de Charlevoix's (1715), http.//www.mdz-nbn-resolving.de/urn/resolver.pl?urn=urn:nbn:de:bvb:12-bsb10599091-6.

Morse, Edward S. *Japan Day by Day: 1877, 1878–79, 1882–83*. 2 vols. Boston MA: Houghton Mifflin, 1917. https : / / ia802702 . us . archive . org / 13 / items / japandaybyday04morsgoog/japandaybyday04morsgoog.pdf.

———. *Nihon, sonohi sonohi* 日本その日その日. Translated by Ishikawa Kin'ichi 石川欣一. Tōkyō: Heibonsha 平凡社, 1970. Originally published as *Japan Day by Day: 1877, 1878–79, 1882–83*, 2 vols. (Boston MA: Houghton Mifflin, 1917), https://ia802702.us.archive.org/13/items/japandaybyday04morsgoog/japandaybyday04morsgoog.pdf.

Müller, Leopold. *Die Typhus-Epidemie des Jahres 1868 im Kreise Lötzen, Regierungs-Bezirk Gumbinnen, besonders vom ätiologischen und sanitäts-polizeilichen Standpunkte aus*

dargestellt. Berlin: August Hirschwald, 1869. http://hdl.handle.net/2027/uc1. b3362777.

Müller, Leopold. "Einige Notizen über die japanische Musik 1." *Mittheilungen der deutschen Gesellschaft für Natur- und Völkerkunde Ostasiens* 1, no. 6 (December 1874): 13–31.

―――. "Einige Notizen über die japanische Musik 2." *Mittheilungen der deutschen Gesellschaft für Natur- und Völkerkunde Ostasiens* 1, no. 8 (September 1875): 41–48.

―――. "Einige Notizen über die japanische Musik 3." *Mittheilungen der deutschen Gesellschaft für Natur- und Völkerkunde Ostasiens* 1, no. 9 (March 1876): 19–35.

―――. *Katalog der im langen Saal der Kunst-Akademie zum Besten des unter dem Protectorate Ihrer K. K. Hoheit der Frau Kronprinzessin stehenden Friedrichsstifts vom 16. Januar bis 11. Februar 1877 stattfindenden Austellung japanischer Gegenstände.* (Copy held in Landesarchiv Berlin, E Rep. 200-35, Nr. 51). Berlin: Gedruckt in der Königlichen Geheimen Ober-Hofdruckerei (R. v. Decker), 1877.

―――. "Tokio-Igaku. Skizzen und Erinnerungen aus der Zeit des geistigen Umschwungs in Japan, 1871–1876." *Deutsche Rundschau* 57, no. 2 (November 1888): 312–329.

―――. "Tokio-Igaku. Skizzen und Erinnerungen aus der Zeit des geistigen Umschwungs in Japan, 1871–1876." *Deutsche Rundschau* 57, no. 3 (December 1888): 441–459.

―――. *Tōkyō-Igaku* 東京一医学. Translated by Ishibashi Nagahide 石橋長英, Ogawa Teizō 小川鼎三, and Imai Tadashi 今井正. (Copy held in Landesarchiv Berlin, E Rep. 200-35, Nr. 51). Tōkyō: Hekisuto Japan (Hoechst Japan Co., Ltd.) ヘキストジャパン, 1975. Originally published as "Tokio-Igaku. Skizzen und Erinnerungen aus der Zeit des geistigen Umschwungs in Japan, 1871–1876," *Deutsche Rundschau* 57, no. 2 (November 1888): 312–329.

Nakamura Kōsuke 中村洪介. *Kindai Nihon yōgakushi josetsu* 近代日本洋楽史序說. Tōkyō: Tōkyō Shoseki 東京書籍, 2003.

Nakamura Rihei 中村理平. *Yōgaku dōnyūsha no kiseki: Nihon kindai yōgakushi josetsu.* 洋楽導入者の軌跡 : 日本近代洋楽史序說. Tōkyō: Tōsui Shobō. 刀水書房, 1993.

Nelson, Steven G. "Court and Religious Music (1): History of *gagaku* and *shōmyō*." In *The Ashgate Research Companion to Japanese Music,* edited by Alison Tokita and David W. Hughes, 35–48. SOAS Musicology Series. Aldershot, Hants: Ashgate, 2008.

————. "Court and Religious Music (2): Music of *gagaku* and *shōmyō*." In *The Ashgate Research Companion to Japanese Music*, edited by Alison Tokita and David W. Hughes, 49–76. SOAS Musicology Series. Aldershot, Hants: Ashgate, 2008.

Nettl, Bruno. *Nettl's Elephant: On the History of Ethnomusicology*. With a foreword by Anthony Seeger. Champaign, IL: University of Illinois Press, 2010.

————, ed. *Following the Elephant: Ethnomusicologists Contemplate Their Discipline*. Urbana-Champaign, IL: University of Illinois Press, 2016.

Ng, Kwok-Wai. "In Search of the Historical Development of Double-Reed Pipe Melodies in Japanese *Tōgaku*: Early Hypotheses and New Perspectives." *Asian Music* 42, no. 2 (2011): 88–111.

Nineteenth-Century Music Review 10 (2013).

Okunaka Yasuto 奥中康人. *Kokka to ongaku : Isawa Shūji ga mezashita Nihon Kindai* 国家と音楽：伊澤修二がめざした日本近代. Tōkyō: Shunjūsha 春秋社, 2008.

Ota Akiko 太田暁子. "Kenburijji daigaku toshokan shozō no kikuteike kyūzō gagaku kankei shiryō mokuroku 1 ケンブリッジ大学図書館所蔵の菊亭家旧蔵雅楽関係資料目録 其ノ一." *Tōkyō Ongaku Daigaku kenkyū kiyō* 東京音楽大学研究紀要, no. 36 (2012): 1–21.

————. "Kenburijji daigaku toshokan shozō no kikuteike kyūzō gagaku kankei shiryō mokuroku 2 ケンブリッジ大学図書館所蔵の菊亭家旧蔵雅楽関係資料目録 其ノ一." *Tōkyō Ongaku Daigaku kenkyū kiyō* 東京音楽大学研究紀要, no. 37 (2013): 1–23.

Ozawa Takeshi 小澤健志. "Tōkyō Kaisei Gakkō: oyatoi doitsujin sūgakukyōshi Alfred Westphal no sokuseki (Agora) 東京成学校お雇い独逸人数学教師アルフレット・ウエストフアルの足跡 (アゴラ) [Tōkyō Kaisei Gakkō. Life of Alfred Westphal, A German Mathematics Teacher of Tōkyō Kaisei Gakkō]." *Kagakushi Kenkyū* 科学史研究 50, no. 3 (2011): 224–228.

Picken, Laurence E. R. "The New Oxford History of Music: Ancient and Oriental Music." Chap. Music of Far Eastern Asia, 82–194. Oxford: Oxford University Press, 1957.

————. "The New Oxford History of Music: Ancient and Oriental Music." Chap. Music of Far Eastern Asia: 2. Other Countries, 135–194. Oxford: Oxford University Press, 1957.

————. "Central Asian Tunes in the Gagaku Tradition." In *Festschrift Walter Wiora*, edited by Ludwig Finscher and Christoph-Hellmut Mahling, 545–551. Kassel: Bärenreiter, 1967.

Picken, Laurence E. R., Noël J. Nickson, Rembrandt F. Wolpert, Allan J. Marett, Elizabeth J. Markham, Yōko Mitani, and Steven Jones, eds. *Music from the Tang Court: A Primary Study of the Original, Unpublished, Sino-Japanese Manuscripts, Together with a Survey of Relevant Historical Sources, Both Chinese and Japanese, and a Full Critical Commentary*. Vol. 5. 1990. Cambridge: Cambridge University Press, 2009.

Picken, Laurence E. R., and Rembrandt F. Wolpert. "Mouth-organ and Lute Parts of Tōgaku and their Interrelationships." *Musica Asiatica* 3 (1981): 79–95.

Picken, Laurence E. R., Rembrandt F. Wolpert, Allan J. Marett, Jonathan Condit, Elizabeth J. Markham, and Yōko Mitani. *Music from the Tang Court: Transcribed from the Original Unpublished Sino-Japanese Manuscripts together with a Survey of Relevant Historical Sources (both Chinese and Japanese) and with Editorial comments*. Vol. 1. London: Oxford University Press, 1981.

Picken, Laurence E. R., Rembrandt F. Wolpert, Allan J. Marett, Jonathan Condit, Elizabeth J. Markham, Yōko Mitani, Steven Jones, and Noël Nickson. *Music from the Tang Court*. 7 vols. London, Oxford and Cambridge: Oxford / Cambridge University Presses, 1981–2000.

Piggott, Francis T. "The Music of the Japanese, with Plates and Specimens of the Melody." *Transactions of the Asiatic Society of Japan* 19, no. 2 (May 1891): 271–368.

———. "The Music of Japan." *Proceedings of the Musical Association*, no. 18 (1892): 103–120.

———. "Principal Tunings of the Modern Japanese Koto." In *The Music and Musical Instruments of Japan*, with annotations by Thomas L. Southgate. London: B. T. Batsford, 1893.

———. "The Japanese Musical Scale." *Transactions of the Asiatic Society of Japan*, 1893.

———. *The Music and Musical Instruments of Japan*. With annotations by Thomas L. Southgate. London: B. T. Batsford, 1893.

———. *Nihon no ongaku to gakki: Meiji nijūnendai ni rainichi shita eijin no kiroku to kenkyū* 日本の音楽と楽器：明治二十年代に来日した英人の記録と研究. Translated by Hattori Ryūtarō 服部龍太郎. Tōkyō: Ongaku no tomosha 音楽之友社, 1967. Originally published as *The Music and Musical Instruments of Japan*, with annots. by Thomas L. Southgate (London: B. T. Batsford, 1893).

Pilinski, Stanislaw. "Memoire sur la Musique au Japon (1-2)." *Revue Orientale et Americaine* 2 (1878): 317–330.

———. "Memoire sur la Musique au Japon (3)." *Revue Orientale et Americaine* 3 (1879): 335–346.

The Garland Encyclopedia of World Music / East Asia: China, Japan, and Korea. Edited by Robert C. Provine, Yosihiko Tokumaru, and J. Lawrence Witzleben, vol. 7. Garland Pub, 2002.

Reed, Marcia, and Paola Demattè. *China on Paper: European and Chinese Works from the Late Sixteenth to the Early Nineteenth Century.* Los Angeles, CA: Getty Research Institute, 2007.

Revers, Peter. *Das Fremde und das Vertraute: Studien zur musiktheoretischen und musikdramatischen Ostasienrezeption.* Stuttgart: Franz Steiner, 1997.

———. "Jean-Joseph Marie Amiot in Beijing: Entdeckung und Erforschung chinesischer Musik im 18. Jahrhundert." In *Musik und Globalisierung: Zwischen kultureller Homogenisierung und kultureller Differenz, Bericht des Symposions an der Kunstuniversität Graz, 17. – 18.10.2006,* edited by Christian Utz, 50–58. Saarbrücken: Pfau, 2007.

Rieger, Matthias. *Helmholtz Musicus. Die Objektivierung der Musik im 19. Jahrhundert durch Helmholtz' Lehre von den Tonempfindungen.* Darmstadt: Wissenschaftliche Buchgesellschaft, 2006.

Rossi Rognoni, Gabriele, ed. *Alessandro Kraus: musicologo e antropologo.* Guida alla mostra. Florence: Firenze Musei, Galleria dell' Academia, Museo degli Strumenti Musicali, March 2004.

Sachs, Curt. *The Rise of Music in the Ancient World, East and West.* New York, NY: W. W. Norton, 1943.

———. *A Short History of World Music.* London: D. Dobson, 1956.

———. *Vergleichende Musikwissenschaft in ihren Grundzügen.* Musikpädagogische Bibliothek 1930 Leipzig: Quelle & Meyer, 1959.

———. *Hikaku ongakugaku* 比較音楽学. Translated by Nomura Yoshio 野村良雄 and Kishibe Shigeo 岸辺成雄. Tōkyō: Zenon gakufu shuppansha 全音楽譜出版社, 1966. Originally published as *Vergleichende Musikwissenschaft in ihren Grundzügen,* Musikpädagogische Bibliothek (1930; Leipzig: Quelle & Meyer, 1959).

Sadie, Stanley, ed. *The New Grove Dictionary of Music and Musicians.* Vol. 9. London: Macmillan, 1980.

Savage, Patrick E., and Steven Brown. "Toward a New Comparative Musicology." *Analytical Approaches To World Music* 2, no. 2 (2013): 148–197. http://aawmjournal.com/articles/2013b/Savage_Brown_AAWM_Vol_2_2.pdf.

Scheer, Christian. "Dr. med. Leopold Müller (1824–1893): Chef des Militärsanitätswesens der Republik Haiti, Leibarzt des Kaisers von Japan, Leitender Arzt des königlich preußischen Garnisonlazaretts in Berlin – Eine nichtalltägliche Bio-

graphie aus der Geschichte des Invalidenfriedhofes." In *Stadtgeschichte im Fokus von Kultur- und Sozialgeschichte: Festschrift für Laurenz Demps*, edited by Wolfgang Voigt and Kurt Wernicke, 285–325. Berlin: Trafo Verlag, 2006.

Schneider, Albrecht. "Comparative and Systematic Musicology in Relation to Ethnomusicology: A Historical and Methodological Survey." *Ethnomusicology* 50, no. 2 (2006): 236–258.

Seki Hideo 関秀夫. *Hakubutsukan no tanjō: Machida Hisanari to Tōkyō Teishitsu Hakubutsukan* 博物館の誕生 : 町田久成と東京帝室博物館. Tōkyō: Iwanami shoten 岩波書店, 2005.

Sestili, Daniele. "A Pioneer Work on Japanese Music: La Musique au Japon and its Author. Alessandro Kraus the Younger." *Asian Music* 33, no. 2 (2002): 83–110.

Shaughnessy, Edward L. *Rewriting Early Chinese Texts*. SUNY series in Chinese Philosophy and Culture. Albany, NY: SUNY Press, 2006.

Shiba Sukehiro 芝祐泰. *Gosen-fu ni yoru gagaku sōfu* 五線譜による雅楽総譜. 4 vols. Tōkyō: Kawai Gakufu カワイ楽譜, 1968–1972.

Shumway, Larry V. "'Gagaku' in the Provinces: Imperial Court Music at the Ikeda Fief at Bizen." *Asian Music*, 2001, 119–141.

Siebold, Philipp Franz von. *Nippon – Archiv zur Beschreibung von Japan und dessen Neben- und Schutzländern Jezo mit den südlichen Kurilen, Krafto, Kooraï und den Liukiu-Inseln: nach japanischen und europäischen Schriften und eigenen Beobachtungen.* Leiden: van der Hoek, 1832.

————. *Nippon* 日本. Translated by Nakai Akio 中井晶夫 and Saitō Makoto 斉藤信 et al. 9 vols. Tōkyō: Yūshōdō shoten 雄松堂書店, 1977. Originally published as *Nippon – Archiv zur Beschreibung von Japan und dessen Neben- und Schutzländern Jezo mit den südlichen Kurilen, Krafto, Kooraï und den Liukiu-Inseln: nach japanischen und europäischen Schriften und eigenen Beobachtungen* (Leiden: van der Hoek, 1832).

Spang, Christian W. "Anmerkungen zur frühen OAG-Geschichte bis zur Eintragung als 'japanischer Verein' (1904)." *Nachrichten der Gesellschaft für Natur- und Völkerkunde Ostasiens / Hamburg: Zeitschrift für Kultur und Geschichte Ost- und Südostasiens* 179–80 (2006): 67–91.

Steege, Benjamin. "Music Theory in the Public Sphere. The Case of Hermann von Helmholtz." *ZGMTH – Zeitschrift der Gesellschaft für Musiktheorie ZGMTH* Sonderausgabe (2010): 9–30. http://www.gmth.de/zeitschrift/artikel/557.aspx.

————. *Helmholtz and the Modern Listener*. Cambridge: Cambridge University Press, 2012.

Stein, F. "Zur Vergleichung chinesischer und japanischer Musik." *Mittheilungen der deutschen Gesellschaft für Natur- und Völkerkunde Ostasiens* I, no. 9 (1876): 60–62.

Stock, Jonathan P. J. "Alexander J. Ellis and His Place in the History of Ethnomusicology." *Ethnomusicology* 51, no. 2 (2007): 306–325.

Stone, Anne, and Marianne Wheeldon, eds. *Abstracts of Papers Read at the American Musicological Society (Eighty-second Annual Meeting) and the Society for Music Theory (Thirty-ninth Annual Meeting)*. 2016.

Stumpf, Carl. *Tonpsychologie*. 2 vols. Leipzig: S. Hirzel, 1883–1890.

———. Review of Alexander J. Ellis, *On the Musical Scales of Various Nations*. *Vierteljahresschrift für Musikwissenschaft* 2 (1886): 511–524.

———. "Tonsystem und Musik der Siamesen." *Beiträge zur Akustik und Musikwissenschaft* 3 (1901): 69–138.

———. *Die Anfänge der Musik*. Mit 6 Figuren, 60 Melodiebeispielen und 11 Abbildungen. Leipzig: J. A. Barth, 1911. Hildesheim: G. Olms, 1979.

———. *The Origins of Music*. Edited and translated by David Trippett. Classic European Music Science Monographs. Oxford: Oxford University Press, 2012.

Stumpf, Carl, and Erich M. von Hornbostel. "Über die Bedeutung ethnologischer Untersuchungen für die Psychologie und Ästhetik der Tonkunst." *Beiträge zur Akustik und Musikwissenschaft* 6 (1911): 102–115. http://vlp.mpiwg-berlin.mpg.de/pdf/lit38498_Hi.pdf.

———. "On the Significance of Ethnological Studies for the Psychology and Aesthetics of Musical Art." Translated by Gerd Grupe. *Translingual Discourse in Ethnomusicology* 1 (2015): 1–12. https://www.tde-journal.org/index.php/tde/article/view/984/831.

Suard, Jean-Baptiste A., and Abbé François Arnaud. *Variétés littéraires ou Recueil de pièces tant originales que traduites concernant la philosophie, la littérature et les arts*. 4 vols. 1768. Paris: La Jay, 1770.

———. *Variétés littéraires ou Recueil de pièces tant originales que traduites concernant la philosophie, la littérature et les arts*. Vol. 2. Paris: La Jay, 1770. http://reader.digitale-sammlungen.de/de/fs1/object/goToPage/bsb10135547.html?pageNo=1.

Syle, Edward W. "On Primitive Music: Especially that of Japan." *Transactions of the Asiatic Society of Japan* 5, no. 1 (1877): 170–179.

Takazawa Hiroshi. "ANEXCDOTA 32." *Chiba Iryō Center News* 46 (2011): 9.

Terauchi Naoko 寺内直子. *Gagaku no rizumu kōzō: Heian jidai sue ni okeru tōgaku kyoku ni tsuite* 雅楽のリズム構造：平安時代末における唐楽曲について [Rhythmic Structure

of Gagaku: Concerning Tōgaku Pieces in the Late Heian Period]. Tokyo: Daiichi shobō 第一書房, 1996.

Terauchi Naoko 寺内直子. "Nijuseiki ni okeru gagaku no tempo to fure–zingu no henyū: Gaisberg rokuon to Hōgaku chōsa gagari no gosenfu, 20 世紀における 雅楽のテンポとフレージングの変容: ガイスバーグ録音と邦楽調査掛の五線譜." *Kokusai Bunkagaku Kenkyū: Kobe Daigaku Kokusai Bunka Gakubu Kiyō* 国際文化学 研究: 神戸大学国際文化学部紀要 17 (2002–2003): 85–111.

———. "Western Impact on Traditional Music: 'Reform' and 'Universalization' in the Modern Period of Japan." *Journal of Chinese Ritual, Theatre and Folklore*, no. 141 (September 2003): 13–53.

———. "Tempo and Phrasing of the Gagaku in 1940s: Focusing on the 78-rpm Records 'The Album of Japanese Music' Produced by Kokusai Bunka Shinkokai 1940 年代前半の雅楽録音における 唐楽のテンポ: 国際文化振興会制作レコード 『日本音楽集』をめぐって." *Journal of Cross-cultural Studies* 国際文化学研究 30 (2008): 1–29. http://ci.nii.ac.jp/naid/110006979192/en/.

———. "Surface and Deep Structure in the Tōgaku Ensemble of Japanese Court Music (Gagaku)." In *Analytical and Cross-cultural Studies in World Music*, edited by Michael Tenzer and John Roeder, 19–55. New York, NY: Oxford University Press, 2011.

———. "Leopold Muller no「Nihon ongaku ni kansuru no–to」ni tsuite レオポル ト・ミュルレルの「日本音楽に関するノート」について [A Study on 'Einige Notizen über japanische Musik' written by Benjamin Karl Leopold Müller]." *Kokusai Bunkagaku Kenkyū: Kobe Daigaku Kokusai Bunka Gakubu Kiyō (Departmental Bulletin Paper)* 国際文化学研究: 神戸大学国際文化学部紀要 40 (2013): 25–72. http://www.lib.kobe-u.ac.jp/repository/81005419.pdf.

Terwen, Jan W. "De Lange en de gamelan: een negentiende-eeuwse ontmoeting tussen Oost en West." Doctoraalscriptie, Universiteit van Amsterdam, 2003.

Thiede, Arnulf, Yoshihiki Hiki, and Gundolf Keil, eds. *Philipp Franz von Siebold and His Era: Prerequisites, Developments, Consequences and Perspectives*. Berlin: Springer, 2000.

Tokita, Alison, and David W. Hughes, eds. *The Ashgate Research Companion to Japanese Music*. SOAS Musicology Series. Aldershot, Hants: Ashgate, 2008.

Tōkyō kokuritsu bunkazai kenkyūjo 東京国立文化財研究所. *Meijiki bankoku hakurankai bijutsuhin shuppin mokuroku* 明治期万国博覧会美術品出品目録. Tōkyō: Chūō Kōron Bijutsu Shuppan 中央公論美術出版, 1997.

Tokyo National Museum, ed. "140th Anniversary Thematic Exhibitions: The Protection of Cultural Properties by the Museum Founder, Ninagawa Noritane." 2012. http://www.tnm.jp/modules/r_free_page/index.php?id=1460.

Traynor, Leo M. "Shō-fu no moto ni sakanobotte 笙譜の本に遡って [Retracing the Origin of the Shō Notation]." Gagaku-kai 48 (1969): 28–31.

Traynor, Leo M., and Shigeo Kishibe. "The Four Unknown Pipes of the Shō (Mouthorgan) used in Ancient Japanese Court Music." Tōyō Ongaku Kenkyū – Journal of the Society for Research in Asiatic Music, 1951, 26–53.

Tsuge Gen'ichi 柘植元一. Japanese Music: An Annotated Bibliography. Garland Bibliographies in Ethnomusicology. New York, NY: Garland Publishing, 1986.

Tsuge Gen'ichi 柘植元一, Sun Xuanling 孫玄齢, and Tokita Alison 時田アリソン. "Kaigai ni okeru nihon ongaku kenkyū 海外における日本音楽研究." Tōyō ongaku kenkyū 東洋音楽研究 59 (1994): 102–115.

Tsukahara Yasuko 塚原康子. Jūkyū seiki no Nihon ni okeru seiyō ongaku no juyō 十九世紀の日本における西洋音楽の受容. Tōkyō: Taga Shuppan 多賀出版, 1993.

———. Kindai gagaku seido no kenkyū: Senzen no Kunaishō Shikibushoku Gakubu o chūshin ni 近代雅楽制度の研究　戦前期の宮内省式部職楽部を中心に. Report of Grant-in-Aid for Scientific Research 1998–1999 平成 10–11 年度科学研究費補助金研究成果報告書. Tōkyō Geijutsu Daigaku 東京藝術大学, 2001.

———. Meiji kokka to gagaku: dentō no kindaika / kokka no sōsei 明治国家と雅楽: 伝統の近代化／国楽の創成. Tōkyō: Yūshisha 有志舎, 2009.

———. "State Ceremony and Music in Meiji-era Japan." Nineteenth-Century Music Review 10 (2013): 223–238.

Veeder, P. V. "Some Japanese Musical Intervals." Transactions of the Asiatic Society of Japan 7 (1879): 76–85.

Völkerkunde Museum. Berichte des Museums für Völkerkunde Leipzig 1873-1900. Bound bundle of annual reports (catalogued under Eu Mus D 7a [1-28]). Leipzig: Grassi: Museum für Völkerkunde Leipzig, 1873–1900.

———. Sechster Bericht des Museums für Völkerkunde Leipzig 1878. Report. Leipzig, 1878.

———. Siebter Bericht des Museums für Völkerkunde Leipzig 1879. Report. Leipzig, 1879.

Wagener, Gottfried. "Bemerkungen ueber die Theorie der chinesischen Musik und ihren Zusammenhang mit der Philosophie." Mittheilungen der deutschen Gesellschaft für Natur- und Völkerkunde Ostasiens 2, no. 12 (1876): 42–61.

Weegmann, Carl von. "85 Jahre OAG." Mittheilungen der Deutschen Gesellschaft für Natur- und Völkerkunde Ostasiens 36 (1961): 1–39.

Weinstein, Jerry L. "Musical Pitch and International Agreement." *The American Journal of International Law* 46, no. 2 (1952): 341–343.

Wernich, Albrecht. "Über die Fortschritte der modernen Medicin in Japan." *Berliner Klinische Wochenschrift* 12 (1875): 447, 474, 590, 655, 667.

————. "Über die Fortschritte der modernen Medicin in Japan (Schluß)." *Berliner Klinische Wochenschrift* 13 (1876): 107.

Westphal, Alfred. "Fudjiyu auf der Kokiu." *Mittheilungen der deutschen Gesellschaft für Natur- und Völkerkunde Ostasiens* 1, no. 6 (1874): 19–21.

————. "Über das Wahrsagen auf der Rechenmaschine." *Mittheilungen der deutschen Gesellschaft für Natur- und Völkerkunde Ostasiens* 1, no. 8 (1875): 48–49.

————. "Über die chinesisch-japanische Rechenmaschine." *Mittheilungen der deutschen Gesellschaft für Natur- und Völkerkunde Ostasiens* 1, no. 8 (1875): 27–35.

————. "Beitrag zur Geschichte der Mathematik in Japan." *Mittheilungen der deutschen Gesellschaft für Natur- und Völkerkunde Ostasiens* 1, no. 9 (1876): 54–55.

————. "Über die chinesische Swan-Pan." *Mittheilungen der deutschen Gesellschaft für Natur- und Völkerkunde Ostasiens* 1, no. 9 (1876): 43–53.

Widdess, D. Richard. "Review of 'Laurence Picken with Rembrandt Wolpert, Allan Marett, Jonathan Condit, Elizabeth Markham and Yoko Mitani: *Music from the Tang Court. Fasc. 1.* 82 pp. Oxford: Oxford University Press, 1981.idem and Noel J. Nickson: *Music from the Tang Court. Fasc 2, 3.* 108 pp.; 98 pp. Cambridge, etc.: Cambridge University Press, 1985.'" *Bulletin of the School of Oriental and African Studies* 50, no. 1 (1987): 176–178.

————. "Historical Ethnomusicology." In *Ethnomusicology: An Introduction*, edited by H. Myers, 219–237. London: Macmillan, 1992.

————. "Laurence Ernest Rowland Picken 1909–2007: Biographical Memoirs of Fellows." In *Proceedings of the British Academy*, edited by Ron Johnston, IX:226–255. Oxford University Press, 2010.

Wieck, Friedrich G. *Das Buch der Erfindungen, Gewerbe und Industrien.* 4 vols. Leipzig: Otto Spamer, 1861.

Wolpert, Rembrandt F. "Lute Music and Tablatures of the Tang Period." Ph.D., Cambridge University, 1975.

————. "Tang-music (Tōgaku) Manuscripts for Lute and their Interrelationships." In *Music and Tradition: Essays on Asian and Other Musics Presented to Laurence Picken*, edited by D. Richard Widdess and Rembrandt F. Wolpert, 69–121. Cambridge University Press, 1981.

———. "Metronomes, Matrices, and Other Musical Monsters." In 10th *International CHIME Meeting, Amsterdam 5–9 October, 2005*. Keynote-paper. Amsterdam, October 2005.

———. "Metronomes, Matrices, and Other Musical Monsters: Editions of Japanese 'Táng Music' in Retrospect." In *Vom Erkennen des Erkannten. Musikalische Analyse und Editionsphilologie. Festschrift für Christian Martin Schmidt*, 59–77. Leipzig: Breitkopf & Härtel, 2007.

———. "'Einige Notizen über die japanische Musik': Dr. Leopold Müller's Account of Music in Early Meiji Japan." *International Musicological Society – 2nd Biennial Conference of the East Asian Regional Association* 國際音樂學學會東亞分會第二屆 雙年會 (*National Taiwan University, Taipei, Taiwan*): *Musics in the Shifting Global Order*, 2013.

———. "Tang Music Theory of Ritual Calendrical Transposition Applied." *CHIME: Journal of the European Foundation For Chinese Music Research* 18–19 (2013): 68–82.

———. *BiwaPrinter: Biwa Notation and Tablature Printer [Computer Software, v. 2.9dev]*. Fayetteville: Center for the Study of Early Asian and Middle Eastern Musics, University of Arkansas, 2017.

Yang Yuanzheng 楊元錚. "Japonifying the Qin: The Appropriation of Chinese Qin Music in Tokugawa Japan." PhD diss., The University of Hong Kong, 2008.

Yokohama Archives of History, ed. *The Japan Weekly Mail: A Political, Commercial, and Literary Journal* (Yokohama), Reprint Series 1: 1870–1899, 1, no. 1 (1870–1874) (2006).

———, ed. *The Japan Weekly Mail: A Political, Commercial, and Literary Journal* (Yokohama), Reprint Series 1: 1870–1899, 1, no. 2 (1875–1879) (2006).

Yokoyama, Toshio. *Japan in the Victorian Mind: A Study of Stereotyped Images of a Nation, 1850–80*. London: Palgrave Macmillan UK, 1987.

Yonezaki Kiyomi 米崎清実. *Ninagawa Noritane Nara no sujimichi* 蜷川式胤奈良の筋道. Tōkyō: Chūō kōron bijutsu shuppan 中央公論美術出版, 2005.

Yunesuko Higashi Ajia Bunka Kenkyū Senta ユネスコ東アジア文化研究センタ, ed. *Shiryō oyatoi gaikokujin* 資料御雇外国人. Tōkyō: Shōgakukan 小学館, 1975.

Zedtwitz, Moritz K. von. "Japanische Musikstücke." *Mittheilungen der Deutschen Gesellschaft für Natur- und Völkerkunde Ostasiens* 4, no. 33 (1884–1888): 129–145.

Organization of Plates and Figures

Each installment of Müller's "Notes" displays his musical examples and illustrations at the end of his essay, except for two in-text illustrations, one each in essays two and three. Appended transcriptions and transnotations of musical pieces are unnumbered but paginated to directly follow the essay. Appended illustrations, facsimiles of musical notations, and one song-text are given as figures, which are enumerated – with Arabic numerals, but also with upper and lower-case letters – and distributed over one or more plates. The plates are paginated and numbered with Roman numerals. On a given plate, the distribution of figures follows in principle a left-to right Western layout for depictions of instruments (although there are many exceptions), but a right-to-left East Asian layout for facsimiles of notations, and so on. Neither in-text illustration is numbered. The single song-text – for a *saibara*, a Japanese court-song – given first as a regular figure in the final installment, is repeated at the close of that installment, paginated but unnumbered.

Exceptionally, installment one is provided with a "Guide to the Illustrations." The "Guide" is paginated and placed after a musical transcription, but before the set of thirty-eight figures it refers to. The thirty-eight figures – some of which are multipart – are set out over nine plates. Installment two includes one plate only, but the essay relies heavily on the illustrations in the preceding installment. The final installment, the longest of the three, includes two musical pieces, as many as fifteen plates containing seventy-seven densely distributed figures (some again multipart), and the closing, repeated *saibara* song-text. Regrettably, however, this installment is not provided with a "Guide to the Illustrations."

Our table on pages 328–329 is intended to help the reader navigate the terrain between, on the one hand, Müller's pervasive reliance on his illustrations in his essays – in particular, his reliance on his own "Guide" as touchstone throughout, and on a complicated system for distinguishing the sets of figures he uses in the last essay – and, on the other hand, his printer's space-saving concerns and eventual, partially out-of-sequence display of those illustrations in the actual publications of the "Notes." For Müller's own references to his figures in the three installments, see the "References to Plates and Figures in 'Notes'" (pp. 331ff).

1874

Müller numbers and labels the thirty-eight illustrations on the plates in installment one (as far as and including Plate IX on our Table, p. 328) as continuous figures (Fig.

1., Fig. 2., etc.); and he uses lower-case letters to deal with multipart figures (for example, Fig. 35. a). In the body of the essay, he refers to the illustrations exclusively as figures, without locating them on their respective plates (for example, "Biwa, eine Art Guitarre, Fig. N° 2.", "siebensaitige Koto, Fig. N° 5.", pages 118 and 120 respectively). Indeed, Roman plate-numberings are not actually provided for the opening three plates that contain Figs. 1 to 4, and Figs. 34 to 38. His "Guide" is likewise ordered sequentially according to figure-number; but here each figure is also located (now from "Taf. III" onwards) on its appropriate plate (for example, Fig.10. – (Taf. VI). Shio [Shō]).

Our table (p. 328 down as far as the first double line) shows where Müller's order of figures over the nine plates was broken in the publication of this first installment: Plates V and VI were published in reverse order, with consequent out-of-sequence figures; and arrows show where space-saving concerns evidently meant that certain other figures were reallocated to plates with room to take them. The chart does not list components of multipart figures unless these have been separated, as is the case for Fig. 10 and Fig. 10a,b,c.

1875

The single plate in installment two (Plate X) continues the numbering and labelling of figures from installment one (p. 328). It adds two figures (Fig. 39. and multipart Fig. 40.); and it provides a rectified version of one previous figure (Fig. 21. [rectificirt]). The essay itself refers to the illustrations in the two installments by both figure and plate, predominantly in that order at the outset (for example, Fig. 27, Taf. VIII, p. 143), then mainly in the reverse order when dealing later, list-like, with depictions of instruments in installment one (for example, Taf. VI, Fig. 17, p. 172). To be noted is that a reference to Fig. 2 is now also given a plate number (Fig. 2, Taf. II, p. 158); we take our lead from Müller's retrospective numbering of plates for our table (for Plates II and III), but we leave "Plate I" unnumbered.

1876

The final installment of "Notes" departs from the system of numbering and labelling illustrations shared by the other two. The essay, with its important internal treatise on gagaku notation, ends with two musical pieces, Müller's gagaku full-score of Goshōraku no kyū and a transcription of a Chinese instrumental piece Manban liushui. The seventy-seven illustrations follow, on fifteen plates (Plates XI to XXIV).[32] In an introductory section in his essay, Müller refers both back to illustrations from the

---

[32] Two plates share ordinal number XVIII.

preceding issues and forward to some that will come; he gives both plate and figure (in that order) in his references in this essay. He then proceeds to his focal discussion of the *gagaku* notations that support his *gagaku* full-score. However, the facsimiles of notation he addresses (on Plates XVIII to XXI) are delayed in the series of plates; seven plates with musical instruments (Plates XI to XVII) are placed out ahead, even though they are not discussed in the essay until the *gagaku* coverage is completed. After the *gagaku*-tract comes a section on East Asian musical instruments, first on Japanese instruments mainly used for war and in religious contexts (Plates XI to XVII), followed by an account of some instruments known also in China (Plates XXII to XXIV). Then are included a section on ancient Chinese musical thought, and a final add-on on yet another list of twelve Chinese musical instruments (Plate XVII, 1 to 12).

The second page in our table (p. 329) tracks how the illustrations in installment three are numbered, labelled, and displayed on the fifteen plates. Four different types of enumeration are involved: one that uses upper-case letters, numbered continuously but broken up into chunks, set out over several discontinuous plates, and labelled without the designation "Fig." (Plates XI, XV, and XVII); one that uses lower-case letters, also numbered continuously but set out over several discontinuous plates, and also labelled without "Fig." (Plates XII to XIV, Plate XVI, and Plates XXII to XXIV); one that numbers and also labels illustrations with "Fig." and Arabic numerals, beginning anew with each numbered plate in a continuous series (Plates XVIII to XXI); and one that simply uses Arabic numerals without "Fig." (for a set of twelve illustrations that fit onto a single plate [Plate XVII]). As in the previous installments, some enumerated illustrations are multipart. These are also labelled variously: either as repeated letters with superscript strokes; or, for the *gagaku* section of illustrations, simply with small letters.

The jumbled order of plates containing the two sets of illustrations that are enumerated with upper- and lower-case letters, respectively, may be startling on a first look at our table. However, this out-of-order appearance belies an organization that in fact closely follows the order in which they are dealt with in Müller's text. In his essay Müller refers to the illustrations in first place by giving the number of the plate, then by locating the figure as enumerated on that particular plate; for all enumerated illustrations he supplies the designation "Fig.", regardless of how they are labelled on his plates (for example, Taf. XI, Fig. J, but Taf. XIX, Fig. 1).

The twelve illustrations of Chinese musical instruments squeezed onto Plate XVII and numbered with Arabic numerals are those evidently sent in by Herr Stein to accompany his contribution; Müller accommodates the accompanying text for this extra list right at the end of the installment, following the section on ancient Chinese musical thought. Finally, there are two more conspicuous cases of squeezing-in: an illustration of the *shakubyōshi* clappers on Plate XII, Fig. y, and one of the *jaw harp*

common among the Ainu, fitted into a space on the penultimate plate of *gagaku* notations, Plate XX, Fig. 5.

A final note is in order for two figures, one labelled with an upper-case X (on Plate XV), the other with a lower-case b (on Plate XVI), and both encircled on our table. First to the encircled upper-case X. Now, the sequence of upper-case labels stops with letter "O" (Plate XI); that with lower-case letters exhausts the complete alphabet (ending with multipart "z" on Plate XVI). In the latter class, however, lower-case "x" (on Plate XII) contains a name of a bell, *hanshō*; since the figure given the upper case X (on Plate XV) contains a closely related larger bell, *tsurigane*, it seems Müller wished to record the relationship by using the same letter of the alphabet. (Upper-case and lower-case designations are muddled in the essay, however, when he refers to the *hanshō* on Plate XII.) Regarding the multipart figure "b" on Plate XVI, since Müller had exhausted the lower-case alphabet with "z" for one of the *taiko*-drums depicted on this plate, he takes this way out to label a second *taiko*-drum also depicted there.

Organization of Plates and Figures

Plate						
	Fig.1					
II	Fig.2	Fig.3				
III	Fig.4		Fig.34	Fig.35	Fig.36	[Fig.37]	Fig.38
IV	Fig.5	Fig.6	Fig.7	Fig.8	Fig.10a,b,c	
V	Fig.15	Fig.18	Fig.19	Fig.20		
VI	Fig.9	Fig.10	Fig.11	Fig.12	Fig.13	Fig.14	Fig.16	Fig.17
VII	Fig.21	Fig.22	Fig.23			
VIII	Fig.23	cont.	Fig.24	Fig.27		
IX	Fig.25	Fig.26		Fig.28	Fig.29	Fig.30	Fig.31	Fig.32	Fig.33
X	Fig.39	Fig.40	Fig.21 rectified			

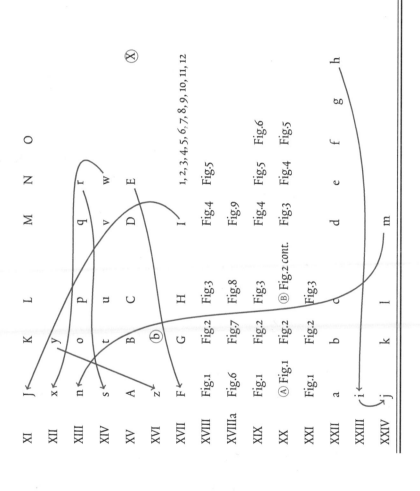

References to Plates and Figures in "Notes"

Index

CORNELL EAST ASIA SERIES